ECOLOGICAL
FEMINIST
PHILOSOPHIES

Dedicated to my students

ECOLOGICAL FEMINIST PHILOSOPHIES

Edited by Karen J. Warren

Indiana University Press

BLOOMINGTON & INDIANAPOLIS

The paper used in this publication meets the minimum requirements of
American National Standard for Information Sciences—Permanence of
Paper for Printed Library Materials, ANSI Z39.48-1984.

MANUFACTURED IN THE UNITED STATES OF AMERICA

Library of Congress Cataloging-in-Publication Data

Ecological feminist philosophies / edited by Karen J. Warren.
    p.   cm. — (A Hypatia book)
    Includes bibliographical references and index.
    ISBN 0-253-32966-3 (cl : alk. paper). — ISBN 0-253-21029-1 (pa : alk. paper)
    1. Ecofeminism. 2. Feminist theory. I. Warren, Karen, date. II. Series.
HQ1233.E29   1996
305.42'01—dc20   95-22518

1 2 3 4 5   01 00 99 98 97 96

Contents

Acknowledgments

I am indebted to many people and institutions for the publication of this anthology. Most importantly, Linda Lopez McAlister, the Board, and the staff of *Hypatia: A Journal of Feminist Philosophy* believed in the importance of proceeding with the first ever distinctively philosophical publication on ecological feminism when they approved and published the 1991 Special Issue of *Hypatia*. They have assisted me assiduously in the process of compiling this expanded version of that special issue. They deserve special commendation for supererogatory acts in the process of producing this book. It simply would not have come to fruition without the attention given to it by Linda Lopez McAlister and the editorial staff of *Hypatia*. I am deeply grateful to them all.

Both the original issue and the present anthology reflect the work and support of many people. These include Senior Editor Joan Catapano of Indiana University Press; many anonymous referees; students, faculty, and administrators at Macalester College; the administrative guidance of Peggy B. Stivers, Stephen Rembert, Barbara Wells-Howe, and Bonnie Plottner; my friends Jim Cheney, Adrienne Christiansen, Charme Davidson, Laura Christoff Doyle, Fran Dunne, Nisvan Erkal, Mic Hunter, Mark Jones, and Bruce Nordstrom; my mother, Marge Bails, and daughter, Cortney Warren. The unwavering support and understanding I received from each of you has nourished me throughout the editing process. To all of you I say, simply, thank you.

Ecological Feminist Philosophies:
An Overview of the Issues

KAREN J. WARREN

The past few decades have witnessed an enormous interest in the women's movement and the ecology (or environmental) movement.[1] Many feminists have argued that the goals of these two movements are mutually reinforcing and ultimately involve the development of worldviews and practices which are not based on models of domination. One of the first feminists to do so was Rosemary Radford Ruether who, in 1975, wrote in *New Woman/New Earth*:

> Women must see that there can be no liberation for them and no solution to the ecological crisis within a society whose fundamental model of relationships continues to be one of domination. They must unite the demands of the women's movement with those of the ecological movement to envision a radical reshaping of the basic socioeconomic relations and the underlying values of this [modern industrial] society. (204)

Subsequent feminist writings by animal rights activists and ecological and other environmental feminists have reinforced Ruether's basic point: There are important connections between feminism and environmentalism, an appreciation of which is essential for the success of the women's and ecological movements.

Just what are some of the connections between "feminism and the environment" that have attracted the attention of ecological feminist philosophers? How has recognition of these connections affected and informed the philosophical perspectives of feminism and environmental issues?

In this introduction I attempt to answer these questions by doing three things. First, I identify some of the connections between the domination of women and the domination of nature which have been suggested in the scholarly ecofeminist philosophical literature. Second, I identify a range of ecological ("eco") feminist philosophical positions which have emerged, particularly in the field of environmental ethics, in an attempt to provide a theoretical framework for understanding the connections between feminism and the environment. Third, I suggest what the philosophical significance of this emerging literature is, not only for feminism and environmental philosophy but for mainstream philosophy as well. While no attempt is made to provide an exhaustive account, hopefully this overview highlights some of the relevant issues and acquaints the newcomer with the nature and range of philosophical positions on "feminism and the environment," or ecological feminism.

A CHARACTERIZATION OF ECOFEMINISM

Just as there is not one feminism, there is neither one ecofeminism nor one feminist philosophy. "Ecological feminism" is the name of a variety of different feminist perspectives on the nature of the connections between the domination of women (and other oppressed humans) and the domination of nature. "Ecological feminist philosophy" is the name of a diversity of philosophical approaches to the variety of different connections between feminism and the environment. These different perspectives reflect not only different feminist perspectives (e.g., liberal, traditional Marxist, radical, and socialist feminism); they also reflect different understandings of the nature, and solution to, pressing environmental problems (see Warren 1987). So, it is an open question of how many, which, and on what grounds any of the proposed ecological feminist philosophies are properly identified as ecofeminist positions. What one takes to be a genuine ecofeminist philosophical position will depend largely on how one conceptualizes *both* feminism and ecological feminism.

What all ecofeminist philosophers *do* hold in common, however, is the view that there are important connections between the domination of women (and other human subordinates) and the domination of nature *and* that a failure to recognize these connections results in inadequate feminisms, environmentalism, and environmental philosophy. What the nature of these alleged connections is and which, if any, are accurate descriptions of the nature and root sources of the twin dominations of women and nature is largely what ecofeminist philosophers debate.

SOME ALLEGED CONNECTIONS BETWEEN FEMINISM AND THE ENVIRONMENT

There are at least eight sorts of connections which ecological feminists have identified as important to understanding the connections between feminism and the environment. No attempt is made here to critically assess the claims made about these connections. Furthermore, these eight categories are not to be viewed as competing or mutually exclusive. Indeed, many of the important claims made about one kind of connection (e.g., conceptual and theoretical) often depend on insights gleaned from others (e.g., historical and empirical). The aim in this section is simply to present for consideration the various elements of the overall "feminism and the environment" picture.

1. *Historical and causal.* One sort of alleged connection between feminism and the environment discussed by ecological feminist philosophers is primarily historical. When historical data are used to generate theories concerning the sources of the twin dominations of women and nature, it is also causal. In fact, some feminists characterize ecofeminism in terms of just such historical and causal claims: "Ecofeminism is a recent development in feminist thought which argues that the current global environmental crisis is a predictable outcome of patriarchal culture (Salleh 1988, 138, n.1). What are some of these historical and causal claims?

Some ecofeminists (e.g., Spretnak 1990; Reisler 1988) trace the historical and causal connections to prototypical patterns of domination begun with the invasion of Indo-European societies by nomadic tribes from Eurasia about 4500 B.C. (Lahar 1991). Riane Eisler describes the time before these invasions as a "matrifocal, matrilineal, peaceful agrarian era." Others (e.g., Griffin 1978; Plumwood 1991; Ruether 1975) focus on the historical role played by rationalism and important conceptual dualisms (discussed at 2, below) in classical Greek philosophy. Still other feminists (e.g., Merchant 1980, 1989; Shiva 1988) focus on cultural and scientific changes that occurred during the scientific revolution and sanctioned the exploitation of nature, unchecked commercial and industrial expansion, and the subordination of women.

What prompts and explains these alleged historical and causal connections between the domination of women and the domination of nature? What *else* was in place to permit and sanction these twin dominations? To answer these questions, ecofeminist philosophers have turned to the conceptual props which keep the historical dominations of women and nature in place.

2. *Conceptual.* Many ecofeminists and ecological feminist philosophers (e.g., Cheney 1987; Gray 1981; Griffin 1978; Y. King 1981, 1983, 1989a; Merchant 1980, 1990; Plumwood 1986, 1991; Ruether 1975; Salleh 1984; Warren 1987, 1988, 1990 [reprinted in this volume]) have argued that, ultimately, historical and causal links between the dominations of women and of nature are located in conceptual structures of domination and in the way women and nature have been conceptualized, particularly in the western intellectual tradition. Four such conceptual links have been suggested.

One account locates the conceptual basis of the twin dominations of women and nature in *value dualisms*, i.e., disjunctive pairs in which the disjuncts are seen as oppositional (rather than as complementary) and exclusive (rather than as inclusive), and *value hierarchies*, i.e., perceptions of diversity organized by a spatial Up-Down metaphor which attribute higher value (status, prestige) to that which is higher ("Up") (see Gray 1981; Griffin 1978, 1989a; Y. King 1981, 1983, 1990; Ruether 1975; Zimmerman 1987). Frequently cited examples of these hierarchically organized value dualisms include reason/emotion, mind/ body, culture/nature, human/nature, and man/woman dichotomies. These theorists argue that whatever is (historically) associated with emotion, body, nature, and women is regarded as inferior to that which is (historically) associated with reason, mind, culture, human (i.e., male), and men. One role of feminism and environmental ethics, then, is to expose and dismantle these dualisms and to rethink and reconceive those mainstay philosophical notions (e.g., reason, rationality, knowledge, objectivity, the self as knower and moral agent) which rely on them.

A second, related account expands on the first by housing the value dualistic, value hierarchical thinking (described above) in larger, oppressive patriarchal conceptual frameworks—ones undergirding *all* social "isms of domination," e.g., racism, classism, heterosexism, sexism as well as "naturism," or the unjustified domination of nonhuman nature (see Warren 1987, 1988, 1990). A conceptual framework is a socially constructed set of basic beliefs, values, attitudes, and assumptions that shape and reflect how one views oneself and others. It is oppressive when it explains, justifies, and maintains relationships of domination and subordination. An oppressive conceptual framework is patriarchal when it explains, justifies, and maintains the subordination of women by men. Oppressive and patriarchal conceptual frameworks are characterized not only by value dualisms and value hierarchies, but also by "power-over" conceptions of power and relationships of domination (Warren 1991) and by a "logic of domination," i.e., a structure of argumentation which justifies subordination on the grounds that *superiority justifies subordination* (Warren 1987, 1990). On this view, it is oppressive and patriarchal conceptual frameworks (and the behaviors which they give rise to) which sanction, maintain, and perpetuate the twin dominations of women and nature. Revealing and overcoming oppressive and patriarchal conceptual frameworks as they are manifest in theories and practices regarding women and nature are important tasks of feminism, environmentalism, and environmental ethics.

A third account locates the conceptual basis in sex-gender differences, particularly in differentiated personality formation or consciousness (see Cheney 1987; Gray 1981; Caldecott and Leland 1983; Salleh 1984). The claim is that female bodily experiences (e.g., of reproduction and childrearing), not female biology *per se* situate women differently with respect to nature than men. This difference is revealed in a different consciousness in women than men; it is rooted conceptually in "paradigms that are uncritically oriented to the dominant western masculine forms of experiencing the world: the analytic, non-related, delightfully called 'objective' or 'scientific' approaches" (Salleh 1988, 130)— just the sort of value dualisms which are claimed (above) to separate and inferiorize what is historically female—gender identified. These socio-psychological factors provide a conceptual link insofar as they are embedded in different conceptualization structures and strategies (different "ways of knowing"), coping strategies, and ways of relating to nature for women and men. A goal of feminism and environmental ethics, then, is to develop gender-sensitive language, theory, and practices which do not further the exploitative experiences and habits of dissociated, male-gender identified culture toward women and nature.

A fourth account draws on some of the historical connections mentioned earlier (at 1). It locates the conceptual link between feminism and the environment in the metaphors and models of mechanistic science which began during both the Enlightenment and pre-Enlightenment period (see Merchant 1980; Easlea 1981). The claim is that prior to the seventeenth century, nature was conceived on an organic model as a benevolent female, a nurturing mother; after the scientific revolution, nature was conceived on a mechanistic model as a (mere) machine, inert, dead. On both models, nature was female. The claim is that the move from the organic to the mechanistic model conceptually permitted and ethically justified the exploitation of the (female) earth by removing the sorts of barriers to such treatment that the metaphor of nature as a living organism previously prevented. The challenge to feminists, environmentalists, and environmental ethicists, then, is to overcome metaphors and models which feminize nature *and* naturalize women to the mutual detriment of both nature and women.

3. *Empirical and experiential.* Many ecofeminists and ecological feminist philosophers have documented empirical evidence linking feminism and the environment. Some point to various health and risk factors caused by the presence of low-level radiation, pesticides, toxics, and other pollutants and borne disproportionately by women and children (see Caldecott and Leland 1983; Diamond 1990; Kheel 1989; Philipose 1989). Others provide data to show that First World development policies foster practices regarding food, forests, and water which directly contribute to the inability of women to provide adequately for themselves and their families (e.g., Mies 1986; Salleh 1990; Shiva 1988; Warren 1988, 1989). Feminist animal-rights scholars argue that factory farming, animal experimentation, hunting, and meateating are tied to patriarchal concepts and practices (Adams 1990, 1991; Collard with Contrucci 1988; Kheel 1985, 1987–88). Appeals to such empirical data are intended to document the very real, felt, lived connections between the dominations of women and nature and to motivate the need for feminist critical analysis of environmental concerns.

Some ecofeminists and ecofeminist philosophers cite experiential connections which honor and celebrate important cultural and spiritual ties of women and indigenous peoples to the earth (see Allen 1986, 1990; Bagby 1990; Doubiago 1990; LaChapelle 1978; *Woman of Power* 1988). Indeed, documenting such connections and making them integral to the project of "feminism and the environment" is often heralded as one of the most important contributions to the creation of liberating, life-affirming, and post-patriarchal worldviews and earth-based spirituality or theology (see Christ 1990; McDaniels 1989, 1990; Ruether 1989; Spretnak 1989a, 1990; Starhawk 1989, 1990). Appreciating these connections and understanding the "politics of women's spirituality" is viewed as an important aspect of feminism, environmentalism, and environmental ethics.

4. *Epistemological.* The various historical, conceptual, and empirical/experiential connections which have been claimed to link feminism and the environment (discussed at 1–3, above) have also motivated the need for different feminist environmental epistemologies. Typically these emerging epistemologies build on scholarship currently underway in feminist philosophy which challenges mainstream views of reason, rationality, knowledge, and the nature of the knower (see *APA Newsletter on Feminism and Philosophy* 1989; Jaggar and Bordo 1989; Code 1987; Garry and Pearsall 1989; Harding and Hintikka 1983). Douglas Buege, for instance, argues for a feminist environmental epistemology that builds on Lorraine Code's responsibilist epistemology (Buege 1991). As Val Plumwood suggests, if one mistakenly construes environmental philosophy as only or mainly concerned with ethics, one will neglect "a key aspect of the overall problem which is concerned with the definition of the human self as separate from nature, the connection between this and the instrumental view of nature, and broader *political* aspects of the critique of instrumentalism" (Plumwood 1991). A feminist environmental epistemology would address these political aspects of the human/nature dichotomy.

Other ecofeminists appeal to the Critical Theory of Horkheimer (1974), Adorno (1973, 1974), Balbus (1982), and the Frankfurt circle, claiming that "their epistemology and substantive analysis both point to a convergence of feminist and ecological concerns, anticipating the more recent arrival of ecofeminism" (Salleh 1988, 131). For these feminists, Critical Theory provides a critique of the "nature versus culture" and an epistemological structure for critiquing the relationship between the domination of women and the domination of nature (see Salleh 1988; Mills 1987, 1991).

5. *Symbolic.* Many ecofeminists (see, e.g., *Heresies #13*; Bell 1988; Murphy 1990; Salleh 1988) explore the symbolic association and devaluation of women and nature that appears in art, literature, religion, and theology. Drawing on feminist literature (e.g., the literature of Atwood 1985; Bagby 1990; Corrigan and Hoppe 1989, 1990; Doubiago 1990; Gearhart 1979; Kolodny 1975; LeGuin 1985, 1987, 1988; Oliver 1983; Piercy 1976; Rich 1986; Silko 1987; Zahava 1988), some argue that patriarchal conceptions of nature and women have justified "a two-pronged rape and domination of the earth and the women who live on it" (Murphy 1988, 87), often using this as background for developing an ecofeminist literary theory (Murphy 1991). Others explore the potential of (eco)feminism for creating alternative languages (e g., Daly 1978; Griffin 1978),

religious/spiritual symbols (e.g., "Goddess" symbols), hypotheses (e.g., the "Gaia hypothesis"), theologies (e.g., Christ 1990; Daly 1978; Gray 1988; Ruether 1989; Spretnak 1982, 1989a; Starhawk 1989, 1990), and societies (e.g., the feminist utopias suggested by Gearhart 1979 and Piercy 1976).

Other ecofeminists explore the symbolic connections between sexist and naturist language, i.e., language which inferiorizes women and nonhuman nature. This may involve raising questions about whether the sex-gendered language used to describe "Mother nature" is, in Ynestra King's words, "potentially liberating or simply a rationale for the continued subordination of women" (King 1981, 12; see also Griscom 1981; Ortner 1974; Roach 1991). It may involve establishing connections between the languages used to describe women, nature, and nuclear weaponry (see Adams 1990; Cohn 1989; Strange 1989). For instance, women are often described in animal terms (e.g., as cows, foxes, chicks, serpents, bitches, beavers, old bats, pussycats, cats, birdbrains, harebrains). Nature is often described in female and sexual terms: Nature is raped, mastered, conquered, controlled, mined. Her secrets are penetrated and her womb is put into the services of the "man of science." Virgin timber is felled, cut down. Fertile soil is tilled and land that lies fallow is "barren," useless. The claim is that language which so feminizes nature and naturalizes women describes, reflects, and perpetuates the domination and inferiorization of both by failing to see the extent to which the twin dominations of women and nature (including animals) are, in fact, culturally (and not merely figuratively) analogous (Adams 1990, 61). The development of feminist theory and praxis which does not perpetuate this language and the power-over systems of domination they reinforce is, therefore, a goal of feminist environmentalism.

6. *Ethical.* Much of the ecological feminists' philosophical literature on feminism and the environment has linked the two ethically. The claim is that the interconnections among the conceptualizations and treatment of women, animals, and (the rest of) nonhuman nature require a feminist ethical analysis and response. Minimally, the goal of feminist environmental ethics is to develop theories and practices concerning humans and the natural environment which are not male-biased and which provide a guide to action in the prefeminist present (see Warren 1990; Warren and Cheney 1991b). Since a discussion of ethical concerns is intimately tied with alleged theoretical connections between feminism and the environment, consider now the range of theoretical positions which have emerged.

7. *Theoretical.* The varieties of alleged connections between feminism and the environment (identified at 1–6, above) have generated different, sometimes competing, theoretical philosophical positions in all areas of feminist and environmental scholarship. Nowhere is this more evident that in the field of

environmental ethics. For reasons of space and audience, the discussion of "theoretical connections" is limited here to the field of environmental ethics.

In many respects, contemporary environmental ethics reflects the range of positions in contemporary normative philosophical ethics. The latter includes tradition consequentialist (e.g., ethical egoist, utilitarian) and nonconsequentialist or deontological (e.g., Kantian, rights-based, virtue-based) positions, as well as challenges to them by nontraditional (e.g., some feminist, existentialist, Marxist, Afrocentric) positions. Similarly with environmental ethics. There are consequentialist (e.g., eco-utilitarian, utilitarian-based animal liberation) and nonconsequentialist (e.g., human rights-based, rights-based animal liberation, land stewardship) positions that extend traditional ethical considerations to animals and the nonhuman environment. There also are nontraditional approaches (e.g., holistic Leopoldian land ethics, social ecology, deep ecology, ecological feminism). Ecofeminists and ecofeminist philosophers who address environmental issues can be found defending each of these sorts of positions.

By extension, there is not one ecofeminist philosophical ethic. Given the newness of ecofeminism as a theoretical position, the nature of ecofeminist ethics is still emerging. Among the most visible are feminist animal-rights positions (e.g., Adams 1988, 1991; Kheel 1985; Slicer 1991) and feminist environmental ethics based on an ethic of care (e.g., Curtin 1991; see also R. King 1991), an ethic of respect (e.g., Westra 1989), themes in social ecology (e.g., Y. King 1981, 1983, 1989, 1990), and themes in bioregionalism (e.g., Cheney 1989b; Plant 1990). They all recognize important connections between the indefensible treatment of women and of nature, and they involve a commitment to developing ethics which are not male-biased. It remains an open question, then, of how many, which, and on what grounds any of the various positions in environmental ethics which acknowledge such feminist concerns are ecofeminist philosophical positions.[2]

8. *Political (Praxis)*. Françoise d'Eaubonne introduced the term "ecofeminisme" in 1974 to bring attention to women's potential for bringing about an ecological revolution (1974, 213–52). Ecofeminist and other feminist concerns for women and the environment have always grown out of pressing political and practical concerns. These range from issues of health concerning women and environmental health to development and technology, the treatment of animals, peace, and antinuclear and antimilitarism activism (see Griffin 1989b; Harris and King 1990; Lahar 1991; Spretnak 1989b). The varieties of feminist theoretical perspectives on the environment are properly seen as an attempt to take seriously the grassroots activism and political concerns by developing analyses of domination which explain, clarify, and guide that praxis (see *The Ecofeminist Newsletter*; Harris and King 1989; Y. King 1981, 1983, 1989, 1990; Spretnak 1989b; Warren 1991).

PHILOSOPHICAL IMPORTANCE OF THE ECOFEMINIST LITERATURE

In the preceding I have identified eight sorts of connections alleged by ecofeminists and ecofeminist philosophers between feminism and the environment. I have indicated why and how, if indeed there are these connections, feminism, environmentalism, and environmental ethics will need to take them seriously. What are some of the implications of these connections for mainstream philosophy? I suggest a few here.

The conceptual links (given above at 2) suggest that philosophical conceptions of the self, knowledge and the "knower," reason and rationality, objectivity, and "nature versus culture"—mainstay philosophical notions in ethics, epistemology, metaphysics, philosophy of science, history of philosophy, political philosophy—will need to be reconceived. The value dualisms which seem to pervade the western philosophical tradition since the early Greeks (e.g., reason/emotion, mind/body, culture/nature, human/nature) and the historical sex-gendered association of women with emotion, body, and nature will need to be examined for male-gender bias.

The historical and empirical links (given at 1 and 3, above) suggest that social scientific data on women and the environment is relevant to the theoretical undertakings in many areas of philosophy. In ethics, for example, this data on women and nature raises issues of anthropocentric and androcentric bias. Can mainstream normative ethical theories generate an environmental ethic which is not male biased? In epistemology, data on the "indigenous technical knowledge" (see Warren 1988) of women who globally constitute the main agricultural production force (e.g., at least 80 percent of the farmers in Africa are women) raises issues about women's "epistemic privilege" about farming and forestry (see Warren 1988): If there is such privilege, does it generate the need for "feminist standpoint epistemologies," as some feminists have claimed (see Garry and Pearsall 1989; Harding 1986; Harding and Hintikka 1983; Jaggar and Bordo 1989)? In metaphysics, data of the cross-cultural variability of "women-nature connections" raise issues about the concept of nature and the nature/cultural dichotomy. Is "nature" a given, a cross-cultural constant that stands in contrast to socially evolving and created "culture," or is nature, like culture, a social construct? Even if there really are trees, rivers, and ecosystems, does the way nature is conceived and theorized about reflect historical, socioeconomic factors in much the same way that, according to many feminists, conceptions and theories about "humans" and "human nature" are constructed? In political philosophy, data about the inferior standards of living of women globally raise issues about political theories and theorizing. What roles do unequal distributions of power and privilege play in the maintenance of systems of domination over both women and nature? How do they affect the content and methodology of political theories and theorizing? In the history of philosophy, data on the historical inferiorization and associations of women and nature raise issues about the nature and substantive content of the philosophical theories advanced in any given time period: Do they inherit biases against women and nature which bear on the critical assessment of the theories themselves? In philosophy of science, particularly philosophy of biology, the data raise issues about the relationships between feminism and science, particularly ecology. As Carolyn Merchant asks, "Is there a set of assumptions basic to the science of ecology that also holds implications for the status of women? Is there an ecological ethic that is also a feminist ethic?" (Merchant 1985, 229). Are there important parallels between contemporary feminist environmental ethics and ecosystems ecology which suggest ways in which they are engaged in mutually supportive projects (see Y. King 1989; Warren and Cheney 1991)? These are the sort of questions raised by a philosophical look at the significance of issues concerning "feminism and the environment."

ESSAYS IN THIS VOLUME

Ecofeminist philosophy has certainly risen to the forefront of feminist and environmental concerns since the publication of the first journal issue devoted exclusively to ecofeminist philosophy: *Hypatia: A Journal of Feminist Philosophy,* Special Issue on Ecological Feminism (1991). This special issue was the first collection ever published of explicitly *philosophical* articles on ecological feminism. It broke new ground by inviting feminist philosophers to join ecofeminist scholars in the philosophical exploration of issues involving women and nonhuman nature (or "the environment"). Although the number of scholarly articles, anthologies, and books on ecological feminism has blossomed since then, this anthology, a revised and expanded version of that special issue, remains the first volume ever to offer distinctively feminist philosophical essays on ecofeminism.

The essays contained in this anthology vary both in perspectives and in subject matter. Some essays (e.g., Karen J. Warren's, Deane Curtin's, and Roger J. H. King's) address the nature of a distinctively ecofeminist ethic and the role of patriarchal conceptual frameworks (e.g., Warren) in perpetuating the twin dominations of women and nature. Some (e.g., Stephanie Lahar's and Chris Cuomo's) address the grassroots origins and nature of a thoughtful ecofeminist practice or *praxis*. Some (e.g., Val Plumwood's and Robert Sessions's articles) focus on the now infamous "ecofeminism—deep ecology debate" in environmental philosophy. Others (e.g., Deborah Slicer's, Carol J. Adams's, Patricia Jagentowicz Mills's, and Victoria Davion's essays) address concrete issues around deep ecological treatment of animal rights and the omission of ecofeminist analyses of the domination of animals, abortion, and nuclear deterrence, respectively. Still others (e.g., Catherine Roach's, Patrick D. Murphy's, and Carol H. Cantrell's essays) address issues of language and literary practice: Roach problematizes the environmental slogan "Love Your Mother"; Murphy uses the dialogics of Russian theorist Bakhtin to show the need for a mutually enhancing ecofeminist philosophy and literary theory; and Cantrell uses ecofeminist Susan Griffin's classic book *Woman and Nature: The Roaring Inside Her* (1978) to show the formative role of language in establishing analogies between women and nature. Finally, the essay by Karen J. Warren and Jim Cheney addresses ten ways in which ecofeminism and the science of ecology are or could be engaged in complementary, supportive projects.

As feminists, environmentalists, and philosophers continue to see that any analysis of what it is for humans to be ecological beings, what parameters constitute an appropriate human-nonhuman nature relationship, and the impact of the omission of gender as a category of analysis in contemporary discussions of environmental problems, a solid, critical ecological feminist philosophical scholarship will continue to be necessary. The articles in this anthology form an important and (as an outgrowth of the highly successful 1991 *Hypatia* volume) a historically unprecedented step in that direction.

CONCLUSION

The scholarship on the eight alleged sorts of connections between feminism and the environment addressed by ecofeminists generally and ecofeminist philosophers in particular illustrates the importance of ecofeminist concerns about how one conceives feminism, environmentalism, and environmental philosophy. If one takes seriously alleged ecofeminist philosophical connections between feminism and the environment, the nature and scope of bona fide concerns in mainstream philosophy will be affected significantly. Presumably, signs of taking these issues seriously would be to revise the courses we teach and to rethink our scholarship accordingly. As with any attempt to incorporate the scholarship on women and feminism into our curricula and scholarship, such revising projects can be quite challenging. With regard to feminism and the environment, they also may be vital—not only for women, animals, and planet Earth, but for the development of worldviews and practices which are ecologically responsible and socially just for us all.

The 1990s have often been dubbed "The Decade of the Environment." Certainly the Earth Summit held in Rio de Janeiro during June 1992 brought the countries of the world together to address such issues as biodiversity, global warming, acid rain, pollution, deforestation and desertification, species endangerment, preservation of wilderness, and energy consumption to international attention. Included among the various seminars and conferences—the Global Forum—that constituted satellite meetings to the Earth Summit was a special seminar, "Ecofeminism: Gender, Development, and the Environment," hosted by the University of Rio de Janeiro. This satellite seminar focused explicitly on ecological feminism: It made visible crucial and often overlooked environmental concerns—the eight sorts of concerns discussed in this introduction—that ecofeminists think are necessary to any adequate environmental policy, theory, or philosophy.

As a participant in this satellite "Ecofeminism" seminar, it was readily apparent to me what impact this "gender invisibility" (or the invisibility of what women do) has in the analysis and practices of global environmental concerns. By publishing this book, I hope to provide one sort of remedy to this "invisibility," viz., to make ecofeminist issues philosophically significant, and to make ecofeminist philosophy a vital player on the field of feminist and environmental concerns. If this anthology does that, it will successfully call attention in an expressly philosophical way to the importance of ecofeminist insights to all aspects of feminist, philosophical, and environmental scholarship and practice.

NOTES

1. Major portions of this introduction are taken from two of my previously published works (in APA Newsletter 1991, 108-16 and in Zimmerman 1993, 253-67).

2. Indeed, just what the similarities and differences are between ecological feminism and "deep ecology," "social ecology," and "animal rights" positions in environmental ethics is an issue which receives considerable scholarly attention, particularly in the leading journal in the field, *Environmental Ethics*. The so-called debate between ecofeminism and deep ecology (the position advocated by Bill Devall and George Sessions (1985), Arne Naess (1973, 1986), and Warwick Fox (1985, 1989), to name a few) has probably received the most attention. The "debate" between them will undoubtedly continue. In his preface to the Spring 1989 issue of *Environmental Ethics*, marking the beginning of the journal's second decade, editor Eugene C. Hargrove committed the journal to providing a forum for that debate:

> In the coming decade the journal can be expected to chart some new territory. Much attention is currently being given to deep ecology and ecofeminism and the various conflicts between the two, both as movements and as philosophies. Because deep ecologists and ecofeminists are as yet not even completely in agreement about what they are disagreeing about, this debate can be expected to be rather lengthy. (1989, 3)

REFERENCES

Adams, Carol J. 1990. *The sexual politics of meat: A feminist-vegetarian critical theory*. New York: Continuum.

———. 1991. Ecofeminism and the eating of animals. *Hypatia* 6(1): 125–45.

Adorno, Theodor W. 1973. *Negative dialectics*. Trans. E. B. Ashton. New York: Seabury Press.

———. 1974. *Minima moralia: Reflections from damaged life*. Trans. E. F. M. Jephcott. London: New Left Books.

Allen, Paula Gunn. 1986. *The sacred hoop: Recovering the feminine in American Indian tradition*. Boston: Beacon Press.

———. 1990. The woman I love is a planet; The planet I love is a tree. In *Reweaving the world: The emergence of ecofeminism*. See Diamond and Orenstein, 1990.

Atwood, Margaret. 1985. *The handmaid's tale*. New York: Fawcett Crest.

Bagby, Rachel L. 1990. Daughters of growing things. In *Reweaving the world: The emergence of ecofeminism*. See Diamond and Orenstein, 1990.

Balbus, Isaac. 1982. *Marxism and domination: A neo-hegelian, feminist, psychoanalytic theory of sexual, political, and technological liberation*. Princeton: Princeton University Press.

Bell, Barbara Currier. 1988. "Cable of blue fire": Glimpsing a group identity for mankind. *Studies in the Humanities* 15(2): 90–107.

Buege, Douglas. 1991. Epistemic responsibility to the natural: Toward a feminist epistemology for environmental philosophy. *American Philosophical Association Newsletter* 9(1): 73–78.

Caldecott, Leonie, and Stephanie Leland, eds. 1983. *Reclaim the earth*. London: The Women's Press.

Cheney, Jim. 1987. Eco-feminism and deep ecology. *Environmental Ethics* 9(2): 115–45.

———. 1989a. The neo-stoicism of radical environmentalism. *Environmental Ethics* 11(4): 293–326.

———. 1989b. Postmodern environmental ethics: Ethics as bioregional narrative. *Environmental Ethics* 11(2): 117–34.

Christ, Carol P. 1990. Rethinking theology and nature. In *Reweaving the world: The emergence of ecofeminism*. See Diamond and Orenstein, 1990.

Code, Lorraine. 1987. *Epistemic responsibility*. Hanover, NH: University Press of New England.

Cohn, Carol. 1989. Sex and death in the rational world of defense intellects. In *Exposing nuclear phallacies*. See Russell, 1989.

Collard, Andrée, with Joyce Contrucci. 1988. *Rape of the wild: Man's violence against animals and the earth*. Bloomington: Indiana University Press.

Corrigan, Theresa, and Stephanie T. Hoppe. 1989. *With a fly's eye, whale's wit, and woman's heart: Animals and women*. Pittsburgh: Cleis Press.

———. 1990. *And a deer's ear, eagle's song, and bear's graces: Relationships between animals and women*. Pittsburgh: Cleis, Press.

Daly, Mary. 1978. *Gyn/Ecology*. Boston: Beacon Press.

Devall, Bill and George Sessions. 1985. *Deep ecology: Living as if nature mattered*. Salt Lake City: Peregrine Smith Books.

Diamond, Irene. 1990. Babies, heroic experts, and a poisoned earth. In *Reweaving the world: The emergence of ecofeminism*. See Diamond and Orenstein, 1990.

Diamond, Irene, and Gloria Feman Orenstein, eds. 1990. *Reweaving the world: The emergence of ecofeminism*. San Francisco: Sierra Club Books.

Doubiago, Sharon. 1990. Mama Coyotte talks to the boys. In *Healing the wounds: The promise of ecofeminism*. See Plant, 1989.

Easlea, Brian. 1981. *Science and sexual oppression: Patriarchy's confrontation with women and nature*. London: Weidenfeld & Nicholson.

d'Eaubonne, Françoise. 1974. *Le Feminisme ou la Mort*. Paris: Pierre Horay.

The ecofeminist newsletter: A publication of the national women's studies association (NWSA) ecofeminist task force, ed. Noel Sturgeon. Middletown, CT: Center for the Humanities, Wesleyan University.

Eisler, Riane. 1988. *The chalice & the blade: Our history, our future*. San Francisco: Harper and Row.

———. 1990. The gaia tradition and the partnership future. In *Reweaving the world: The emergence of ecofeminism*. See Diamond and Orenstein, 1990.

Fox, Warwick. 1985. A postscript on deep ecology and intrinsic value. *The Trumpeter* 2: 20–23.

———. 1989. The deep ecology-ecofeminism debate and its parallels. *Environmental Ethics* 11(1): 5–25.

Garry, Ann, and Marilyn Pearsall, eds. 1989. *Women, knowledge, and reality*. Boston: Unwin Hyman.

Gearhart, Sally. 1979. *The wanderground: Stories of the hill women*. Boston: Alyson Publications.

Gray, Elizabeth Dodson. 1981. *Green paradise lost*. Wellesley, MA: Roundtable Press.

Gray, Elizabeth Dodson, ed. 1988. *Sacred dimensions of women's experience*. Wellesley, MA: Roundtable Press.

Griffin, Susan. 1978. *Women and nature: The roaring inside her*. San Francisco: Harper and Row.

———. 1989a. Split culture. In *Healing the wounds: The promise of ecofeminism*. See Plant, 1989.

———. 1989b. Ideologies of madness. In *Exposing nuclear phallacies*. See Russell, 1989.

Griscom, Joan L. 1981. On healing the nature/history split in feminist thought. *Heresies #13* 4: 4–9.

Gwaganad. 1989. Speaking for the earth: The Haida way. In *Reweaving the world: The emergence of ecofeminism*. See Diamond and Orenstein, 1990.

Harding, Sandra. 1986. *The science question in feminism*. Ithaca, NY: Cornell University Press.

Harding, Sandra, and Merrill Hintikka, eds. 1983. *Discovering reality: Feminist perspectives on epistemology, metaphysics, methodology, and the philosophy of science*. Dordrecht: Reidel Publishing Co.

Harris, Adrienne, and Ynestra King. 1990. *Rocking the ship of state: Toward a feminist peace politics*. Boulder, CO: Westview Press.

Horkheimer, Max. 1974. *Eclipse of reason*. New York: Seabury Press.

Jaggar, Alison M., and Susan R. Bordo, eds. 1989. *Gender/body/knowledge: Feminist reconstructions of being and knowing*. New Brunswick, NJ: Rutgers University Press.

Kheel, Marti. 1985. The liberation of nature: A circular affair. *Environmental Ethics* 7(2): 135–49.

———. 1987–1988. Animal liberation is a feminist issue. *The New Catalyst Quarterly* 10: 8–9.

———. 1989. From healing herbs to deadly drugs: Western medicine's war against the natural world. In *Healing the wounds: The promise of ecofeminism*. See Plant, 1989.

King, Roger J. H. 1991. Environmental ethics and the case of hunting. *Environmental Ethics* 13(1): 59-85.

King, Ynestra. 1981. Feminism and the revolt of nature. *Heresies #13* 4(1):12–16.

———. 1983. The eco-feminist imperative. In *Reclaim the earth*. See Caldecott and Leland, 1983.

———. The ecology of feminism and the feminism of ecology. In *Healing the wounds: The promise of ecofeminism*. See Plant, 1989.

———. 1990. Healing the wounds: Feminism, ecology, and the nature/culture dualism. In *Reweaving the world: The emergence of ecofeminism*. See Diamond and Orenstein, 1990.

Kolodny, Annette. 1975. *The lay of the land: Metaphor as experience and history in American life and letters*. Chapel Hill: University of North Carolina Press.

LaChapelle, Dolores. 1978. *Earth wisdom*. Silverton, CO: Way of the Mountain Learning Center and International College.

Lahar, Stephanie. 1991. Ecofeminist theory and grassroots politics. *Hypatia* 6(1): 28–45.

LeGuin, Ursula K. 1985. *Always coming home*. New York: Bantam Books.

———. 1987. *Buffalo gals and other animal presences*. Santa Barbara, CA: Capra Press.

———. 1988. *Wild oats and fireweed*. New York: Harper and Row.

———. 1989. Women/wilderness. In *Healing the wounds: The promise of ecofeminism*. See Plant, 1989.

McDaniel, Jay B. 1989. *Of god and pelicans: A theology of reverence for life*. Louisville, KY: Westminster/John Knox Press.

———. 1990. *Earth, sky, god, and mortals: Developing an ecological spirituality*. Mystic, CT: Twenty-Third Publications.

Merchant, Carolyn. 1980. *The death of nature: Women, ecology, and the scientific revolution*. San Francisco: Harper and Row.

———. 1985. Feminism and ecology. In *Deep ecology: Living as if nature mattered*. See Devall and Sessions, 1985.

————. 1989. *Ecological revolutions*. Chapel Hill and London: University of North Carolina Press.

————. 1990. Ecofeminism and feminist theory. In *Reweaving the world: The emergence of ecofeminism*. See Diamond and Orenstein, 1990.

Mies, Maria. 1986. *Patriarchy and accumulation on a world scale*. London: Zed Books Ltd.

Mills, Patricia Jagentowicz. 1987. *Woman, nature, and psyche*. New Haven: Yale University Press.

————. 1991. Feminism and ecology: On the domination of nature. *Hypatia* 6(1): 162–78.

Murphy, Patrick D. 1988. Introduction: Feminism, ecology, and the future of the humanities. *Studies in the Humanities* 15(2): 85–89.

————. 1991. Ground, pivot, motion: Ecofeminist theory, dialogics, and literary practice. *Hypatia* 6(1): 146–62.

Naess, Arne. 1973. The shallow and the deep, long-range ecology movement: A summary. *Inquiry* 16: 95–100.

————. 1986. The deep ecological movement: Some philosophical aspects. *Philosophical Inquiry* 8: 10–31.

Oliver, Mary. 1983. *American primitive*. Boston: Little Brown.

Ortner, Sherry B. 1974. Is female to male as nature is to culture? In *Woman, culture, and society*. Michelle Rosaldo and Louise Lamphere, eds. Stanford: Stanford University Press.

Philipose, Pamela. 1989. Women act: Women and environmental protection in India. In *Reweaving the world: The emergence of ecofeminism*. See Diamond and Orenstein, 1990.

Piercy, Marge. 1976. *Woman on the edge of time*. New York: Fawcett Crest.

Plant, Judith. 1990. Searching for common ground: Ecofeminism and bio-regionalism. In *Reweaving the world: The emergence of ecofeminism*. See Diamond and Orenstein, 1990.

Plant, Judith, ed. 1989. *Healing the wounds: The promise of ecofeminism*. Santa Cruz, CA: New Society Publishers.

Plumwood, Val. 1986. Ecofeminism: An overview and discussion of positions and arguments. *Australasian Journal of Philosophy* Supplement to Vol. 64:120–37.

————. 1991. Nature, self, and gender: Feminism, environmental philosophy, and the critique of rationalism. *Hypatia* 6(1): 3–27.

Rich, Adrienne. 1986. *Your native land, your life*. New York: Norton.

Roach, Catherine. 1991. Loving your mother: On the woman-nature relation. *Hypatia* 6(1): 46–59.

Ruether, Rosemary Radford. 1975. *New woman/new earth: Sexist ideologies and human liberation*. New York: The Seabury Press.

————. 1989. Toward an ecological-feminist theory of nature. In *Healing the wounds: The promise of ecofeminism*. See Plant, 1989.

Russell, Diana, ed. 1989. *Exposing nuclear phallacies*. New York: Pergamon Press.

Salleh, Ariel Kay. 1984. Deeper than deep ecology: The eco-feminist connection. *Environmental Ethics* 6(4): 339–45.

———. 1988. Epistemology and the metaphors of production: An eco-feminist reading of critical theory. *Studies in the Humanities* 5(2): 130–39.

———. 1990. Living with nature: Reciprocity or control? In *Ethics of environment and development*, ed. R. and J. Engel. Tucson: University of Arizona Press.

Shiva, Vandana. 1988. *Staying alive: Women, ecology, and development*. London: Zed Books.

Silko, Leslie Marmon. 1987. Landscape, history, and the Pueblo imagination. In *On nature: Nature, landscape, and natural history*, ed. Daniel Halpern. San Francisco: North Point.

Slicer, Deborah. 1991. Your daughter or your dog? A feminist assessment of animal research issues. *Hypatia* 6(1): 108–24.

Spretnak, Charlene. 1989a. Toward an ecofeminist spirituality. In *Healing the wounds: The promise of ecofeminism*. See Plant, 1989.

———. 1989b. Naming the cultural forces that push us toward war. In *Exposing nuclear phallacies*. See Russell, 1989.

———. 1990. Ecofeminism: Our roots and flowering. In *Reweaving the world: The emergence of ecofeminism*. See Diamond and Orenstein, 1990.

Spretnak, Charlene, ed. 1982. *The politics of women's spirituality*. Garden City, NY: Anchor Press.

Starhawk. 1989. Feminist, earth-based spirituality and ecofeminism. In *Healing the wounds: The promise of ecofeminism*. See Plant, 1989.

———. 1990. Power, authority, and mystery: Ecofeminism and earth-based spirituality. In *Reweaving the world: The emergence of ecofeminism*. See Diamond and Orenstein, 1990.

Strange, Penny. 1989. It'll make a man of you: A feminist view of the arms race. In *Exposing nuclear phallacies*. See Russell, 1989.

Warren, Karen J. 1987. Feminism and ecology: Making connections. *Environmental Ethics* 9(1): 3–20.

———. 1988. Toward an ecofeminist ethic. *Studies in the Humanities* 15(2): 140–56.

———. 1989. Water and streams: An ecofeminist perspective. *Imprint* (June): 5–7.

———. 1990. The power and the promise of ecological feminism. *Environmental Ethics* 12(2): 125–46. Reprinted in this volume.

———. 1991b. Introduction. *Hypatia* 6(1): 1–2.

———. 1991a. Toward a feminist peace politics. *Journal of Peace and Justice Studies* 3(1): 87–102.

Warren, Karen J., and Jim Cheney. 1991. Ecofeminism and ecosystem ecology. *Hypatia* 6(1): 179–97.

Westra, Laura. 1989. Ecology and animals: Is there a joint ethics of respect? *Environmental Ethics* 11(3):215–30.

Woman of power. 1988. Nature Issue. 9 (Spring).

Zahava, Irene. 1988. *Through other eyes: Animal stories by women.* Freedom, CA: The Crossing Press.

Zimmerman, Michael. 1987. Feminism, deep ecology, and environmental ethics. *Environmental Ethics* 9(1):21–44.

———. 1993. *Environmental philosophy: From animal rights to radical ecology.* Englewood Cliffs, NJ: Prentice Hall.

ECOLOGICAL
FEMINIST
PHILOSOPHIES

Ecofeminist Theory and Grassroots Politics

STEPHANIE LAHAR

Ecofeminism makes such big promises! The convergence of ecology and feminism into a new social theory and political movement challenges gender relations, social institutions, economic systems, sciences, and views of our place as humans in the biosphere. According to Charlene Spretnak, "Ecofeminists address the crucial issues of our time, from reproductive technology to Third World development, from toxic poisoning to the vision of a new politics and economics—and much more" (1988, 8). Ecofeminism is potentially a "global movement that is founded on common interests yet celebrates diversity and opposes all forms of domination and violence," writes Ynestra King (1989, 20). Underneath these encompassing visions, however, there are almost as many definitions of what ecofeminism is as there are theorists and activists.

Ecofeminism has gained national and international recognition in the last fifteen years as a progressive and critical social theory and as a grassroots activist movement. The newness of the movement, the breadth of issues it encompasses, and the diversity of people thinking and writing about ecofeminism have resulted in considerable confusion about what ecofeminism actually is, who ecofeminists are, and what they have to say about current issues ranging from women's health to development and biotechnology. In the most inclusive claims about who makes up the ecofeminist movement, homemakers organizing to eliminate toxic chemicals from their homes and neighborhoods, professors teaching and writing in universities, activists standing between trees and the bulldozers coming to fell them, and protestors making peace encampments at military bases are all ecofeminists, whether or not they identify themselves as such. In other formulations, only those who explicitly affiliate themselves with a particular theory are ecofeminists—but the theory varies according to who is describing it. Broadly, however, ecofeminist theory includes a systemic analysis of domination that specifically includes the oppression of women and environmental exploitation, and it advocates a synthesis of ecological and feminist principles as guiding lights for political organizing and the creation of ecological,

Hypatia vol. 6, no. 1 (Spring 1991) © by Stephanie Lahar

socially equitable life-styles. The question is, can ecofeminism speak to many different people in potentially overlapping but sometimes extremely disparate spheres of activity? Is ecofeminism even a single theory or movement?

In this essay I explore how ecofeminist theory and the political activism with which it originated in the middle to late 1970s and early 1980s are linked, highlighting several important debates and differences within ecofeminist thought. I then present parameters I believe are important to the future development of ecofeminism, working out an ontological and moral ground for ecofeminist theory. My aim is to contribute to the development of a coherent general framework through which diverse ideas and projects can be elaborated and energized. Finally, I show critical connections between ongoing theoretical development and political activism.

ECOFEMINISM'S ANALYSIS OF SOCIAL DYSFUNCTION

An ecofeminist analysis includes the human exploitation of the nonhuman environment in its list of interwoven forms of oppression such as sexism and heterosexism, racism and ethnocentrism. Specific theories differ as to the cause or causes of social and environmental domination and exploitation, but conceptual dichotomies are seen as key to maintaining such conditions. These include oppositional and value-laden categories of masculine and feminine, mind and body, public and private, and nature and society, which in turn rest on and uphold a basically Cartesian, atomistic worldview that has characterized Western thought. Accompanying this is a sense of psychological splitting, an existential isolation in which people tend to lose touch with their own value and internal coherence as well as that of human and nonhuman others through processes of objectification. In human extremities such as pornography or war, for example, individuals are ultimately stripped of any sense of humanity or subjectivity as they are reduced to a sexual object or a faceless enemy.

The mutual exclusion that thinking in conceptual dichotomies engenders makes us think that violence against women, militarism, and the destruction of ecosystems are issues that can be analyzed separately. Politically, we may feel that we have to make trade-offs between social and environmental initiatives, choosing, for example, child-care programs *or* pollution cleanups. Furthermore, the existential isolation that is sign and symptom of the social condition that ecofeminism sees and critiques weakens us as potential agents of social and political change.

The central theme of most versions of ecofeminism, therefore, is the interrelationship and integration of personal, social, and environmental issues and the development of multidirectional political agendas and action. Ecofeminism is transformative rather than reformist in orientation, in that ecofeminists seek to radically restructure social and political institutions. Women's liberation is contextualized in human liberation and a more ecological way of living on the earth.

Within this broad context, how have ecofeminists expressed their values through political activism? What is the theory or theories that have supported ecofeminist politics up to this point, and what parameters and directives will lend coherence and robustness to continued political development?

GRASSROOTS ACTIVISM

In the New England town of Brattleboro, Vermont, a handful of women and men from an ecofeminist affinity group gathered on Mother's Day in 1987. On a dewy hillside surrounded by woods and marsh, they looked over a prototypical scene: a developer from another state had cleared much of the land in an area that had rapidly been losing open space and valuable wetlands. Eighty-six condominiums were to be built, second and third homes far beyond the means of most area residents. A long strip had been bulldozed near the condos right through the marsh. A member of the group describes their action:

> Eight of us went out early in the morning, with plants and gardening tools, and began to plant the strip. A great colorful, wonderful garden emerged—it didn't feel as though we were working on it, it just happened. The people who lived neighboring the development started to come out, and they brought flowers to plant and seeds. We claimed the strip as a community garden.[1]

In the afternoon the developer arrived, and the group blocked his way until he agreed to talk with them about their concerns. Several hours later, the protesters gave him "permission" to plow under the community garden. A week later the neighbors, who had not previously organized, went to a selectmen's meeting to object to the developer's plan to close the road for a week to blast to lay pipes— and they won. The victory was small but important. The Mother's Day Garden, like many ecofeminist actions, accomplished several goals. It was a direct protest as well as an invitation to the developer to consider community and environmental impacts. It also empowered people who were not initially involved to take responsibility for the community and area in which they lived.

The largest identifiably ecofeminist actions that have taken place in the history of the movement were the Women's Pentagon Actions in November of 1980 and November of 1981, which were organized by participants in the "Women and Life on Earth: Ecofeminism in the 1980s" conference in Amherst, Massachusetts. In these nonviolent direct actions, women surrounded the Pentagon, issuing a Unity Statement that called for social, economic, and reproductive rights as well as an end to the arms race and the exploitation of resources, people, and the environment. In the 1980s ecofeminism became a presence and, in some cases, an organizing principle in decentralized movements on the American and international left. Initiatives that ecofeminism has both drawn from and contributed to include the peace movement, the direct action movement, and Green party politics.[2] Ecofeminism shares overlapping goals with these other loosely organized movements, including equitable and peaceful social relations, and sustainable and nonexploitative economic systems and life-styles. It also shares a spirit of resistance to institutionalized power structures and is committed to nonviolence and open processes of communication. As has been the case in other activist movements, ecofeminists have attempted to implement these ideals among each other and outwardly. They have encountered through debates and differences a struggle to find ground between two poles: on the one hand a prematurely unified theory and political praxis that obscures and suppresses differences, and on the other an indiscriminate pluralism that results in vague thinking, passivity, and political inertia.

THEORETICAL ORIGINS

Ecofeminism draws theoretical concepts from ecology, especially a principle of life's interdependence, and from feminism, especially a social analysis of the domination of women that is also linked with racism and classism. Disparate strands from these sources and others including feminist spirituality and issue-oriented activism do not make for an easy, definitive synthesis, and various theorists have weighted their analyses differently.

Well-known theorists such as Ynestra King and Starhawk trace different lineages for ecofeminist theory, often echoing their own intellectual and political journeys. King acknowledges a debt to Murray Bookchin's philosophy of social ecology as well as to a long study of social and political theory and to feminist social analyses. She advocates a "critical analysis of and opposition to the uniformity of technological, industrial culture—capitalist and socialist—[that] is crucial to feminism, ecology, and the struggle of indigenous peoples" (1989, 177). This is a rational and politically anarchist position. According to Noël Sturgeon, King "has prominently figured in the promulgation of ecofeminism as a position on the American left which is deeply rooted in the politics and practice of the direct action movement" (1989, 15). King differentiates her conception of ecofeminism from other liberatory political movements, however, which according to her "see themselves as outgrowths of the past—even possibly as a vindication or revenge for the past, rather than as preceding or anticipating the future." She frames ecofeminism as "the practice of hope," explaining that "to have hope . . . is to believe that [the] future can be created by intentional human beings who now take responsibility [for it]."[3]

Starhawk, on the other hand, finds a base for ecofeminism in a very different background of feminist spirituality, claiming that "ecofeminism is a movement with an implicit and sometimes explicit spiritual base." She outlines feminist, or earth-centered, spirituality as a source for a value system for ecofeminism. For example, "the second base concept of earth-centered spirituality is that of interconnection . . . [this] translates into compassion, our ability to feel and identify with others—human beings, natural cycles and processes, animals and plants" (1989, 178). Starhawk draws a political agenda from principles she has developed through a practice of an earth-based religion.

King and Starhawk exemplify different backgrounds in thought and experience among ecofeminists, especially as they urge, in King's case, a conceptual/rational transformation and, in Starhawk's, a spiritual/psychological one as the motivational core of social change. As a result of these different paths to a similar, often identical activist politics, there is some friction and some complementarity in tracing ecofeminism's heritage as well as its fundamental principles.

A point of departure for ecofeminist theory in its earliest formulations was analyzing a transcultural symbolic association and devaluation of women and nature. Ecofeminists were, and are, interested not only in confronting the fallacies of biologically determined gender roles but in delving into the deeper psychological and cultural/mythic base of a value-laden polarization between "primitive" nature and "civilized" society. The so-called domestic sphere of women's work and activities across many times and cultures includes caring for children, the elderly, and the sick and working close to the land. This has traditionally been regarded as less "civilized" and therefore lesser in value than the public sphere of men's work and activities. Sherry Ortner analyzed this deep attitudinal split in an article written from a structuralist perspective and often cited by ecofeminist theorists, "Is Female to Male as Nature Is to Culture?" (1974).

The dark side of the woman/nature association is especially vivid in the intersections of women's oppression and the exploitation of nature in many developing countries today. For example, all over the world Western "green revolution" agricultural methods have been imported into developing countries either through a misplaced altruism or, increasingly, under pressure as a short-term intensive method of cash-crop production to pay off Third World debts. Green-revolution methods include growing crops in monocultures using genetically engineered seed, chemical pesticides, deep plowing, and intensive irrigation, which permanently destroys indigenous soils. These have replaced traditional methods that have long sustained soil fertility, including mixed and rotational cropping that renews soil nutrients and repels pests, using appropriate plowing depths and irrigation methods for the local soils, and integrating practices of animal husbandry, forestry, and agriculture. Vandana Shiva has shown how in India, as in many parts of the world, women's impoverishment has increased and their status decreased relative to men as the environment has been degraded, exacerbating prior gender inequities. A direct correlation has been noted between regions that have adopted the most green-revolution technology and increased violence and discrimination against women. As one example, Shiva notes:

> The Kallars, a landless community in Tamil Nadu, have, over the last 10 to 15 years, started routinely dispensing with their girl children. The logic of dispensability is linked to the green revolution which, through commercialisation, introduces a differential wage labour, on the one hand (with men getting Rs. 13 a day and women getting Rs. 6) and, on the other, creates a demand for dowry which has driven the poverty-stricken community to female infanticide. (1988, 119)

Through explicit and measurable links between environmental degradation and violence against women, Shiva shows that "in the perspective of women engaged in survival struggles which are, simultaneously, struggles for the protection of nature, women and nature are intimately related, and their domination and liberation similarly linked" (1988, 47).

One of the primary debates in ecofeminist theory concerns the causes of domination and the exploitation of women, nature, and others, as well as where and when these should be located. Riane Eisler and Charlene Spretnak, for example, each argue that prototypical patterns of domination can be traced to the invasion of Indo-European societies by nomadic tribes from Eurasia about 4500 B.C. According to this analysis European society in the Neolithic period was free of modern forms of oppression and, significantly, was also "matrifocal, matrilineal, peaceful [and] agrarian" until "barbarian invaders from the barren fringes of the globe [left] in their wake destruction. . . . What characterizes these invaders is that they [brought] with them male dominance along with their angry gods of thunder and war" (Eisler 1990, 29).

Aside from the questionable interpretations of the archaeological evidence on which this argument is based, some ecofeminist and feminist theorists have regarded a theory of domination describing origins in a collectively misogynist, anti-natural male consciousness that suddenly "arrives" as politically naive and irrelevant to a modern analysis and deconstruction of the dynamics of oppression (Biehl 1989; Prentice 1988). Such a claim based in ancient history does not address the processes by which a "dominator" consciousness and social practices originally developed. Instead, alternative models have connected the exploitation of women and nature to cultural, scientific, and economic factors that are more historically accessible, on the premise that examining the convergence of these factors can lead to an understanding of how to deconstruct them. Carolyn Merchant (1980, 1989) and Vandana Shiva (1988) both do this by tracing the transformations of cultural practices and symbols from the Enlightenment to the present day. Shiva claims that "the reductionist world-view, the industrial revolution, and the capitalist economy were the philosophical, technological, and economic components of the same process" (1988, 23). She calls the practices by which this complex expands "maldevelopment."

One manifestation of the combination of developments and maldevelopments Shiva refers to is the commodification of both "natural resources" and people. When landscapes and ecosystems are regarded as commodities, then members of an ecosystem, including human beings, are treated as "isolated and extractable units" (Cronon 1983, 21). One face of the problem lies in the values and reinforcing structures of most social and economic systems, but it is also internalized in individuals. Even with a high degree of personal awareness and maturity, we are conditioned by collective perceptual filters to experience in predetermined ways the subjectivity/objectivity of other persons, beings, and things. This means that social projects must be both deeply personal and political to render transformative changes. Ecofeminism's context for social analysis is nature, since it contains and includes all humans and human creations as well as nonhuman existence.

Ecofeminism must continue to dissemble the multiple layers and strands of ideologies and practices that power a dysfunctional society and make it dangerous to individuals and to the totality of life. I believe that the search for some singular and original seed of domination in the distant past does not really help us with this. We should proceed, instead, to further develop models of the interlocking dynamics of oppression, so that when we are working for liberation in one area we are able to see links and contribute to opening up other areas as well.

PARAMETERS AND CAUTIONS FOR A PROGRESSIVE THEORY

Ecofeminist theory aspires to an integrated and intersubjective view of human life and society in/as part of nature. Ultimately, this is an encompassing natural philosophy that we should think of not as a blueprint to be developed by one or two utopian thinkers but as a cultural revolution. In the face of various claims about key concepts and themes for ecofeminism, can and should we try to establish a set of general principles? What purposes would this serve?

My assertion is that we need to define guiding parameters for our theory that can continually be refined but that provide recognizable directives and contexts for the development of ecofeminist analyses and social projects. These are important for many reasons, but among them is the historical demonstration that some philosophies lend themselves to contemplation and inaction—for example, the largely mental politic of postmodernist deconstruction in its academic and literary forms, or the inward mysticism of metaphysicians such as Heidegger, touted by ecological theorists such as Arne Naess who advise us to think like a mountain.[4] Other philosophies lend themselves to action, the expression of will, and political participation; for example, the political analyses of Emma Goldman, foremother of direct action as protest. Ecofeminist theory has in the past developed in close dialogue with political praxis. In ecofeminist dialogue in the past several years, however, particularly in debates about environmental ethics and the relation of ecofeminism to feminist spirituality, reference to political praxis has decreased relative to earlier discussions.[5]

Ecofeminism is highly critical of most current social and political institutions and thereby serves a deconstructive or dissembling function that supports political resistance. To fulfill this deconstructive potential, its criticisms must continue to be acted upon by the expression of resistance through direct action on life-threatening issues (militarism, violence against women, the nuclear industry, pollution and toxics, environmental destruction). Ecofeminism also aspires to a creative and reconstructive function in society, as King's "practice of hope." To fulfill a reconstructive potential, a social philosophy must extend a social critique and utopian vision into imperatives for action. This means that life-preserving values and policies must be promoted and carried out beyond circles of personal affinity and academic philosophy and brought into public arenas. Reconstructive projects that ecofeminist theory and activism have contributed to include, for example, community forums on social or environmental issues and those at intersections such as biotechnology; state legislation supporting the civil rights and safety of groups that historically have had little political power; the reallocation of private and public resources and funds to socially responsible uses; alternative housing and land-use arrangements; and local alternative economic systems.[6] Unlike the largely mental politics of postmodern, poststructuralist social critiques in the academy as well as some systems of environmental ethics, ecofeminism's popular and political base in grassroots organizing and direct action has fanned the will to personal and collective action from its inception.

Maintaining a balance of critical and creative directions is crucial to the continued political potency of ecofeminism. Can we afford not to have an action-oriented philosophy at a crisis point in social and natural history, when we are literally threatened on a global scale by annihilation by nuclear war or ecological destruction? Ecofeminism's promise is that it provides not only an orientation and worldview but also a basis for responsible action. In order for the movement to fulfill this promise, I believe that it is necessary to establish broad parameters that diverse ideas and actions can be referred to, and to maintain critical and vitalizing links between theory and praxis.

I offer the following four points of focus to help create and maintain a firm ground for social and ecological responsibility and political participation. These are that we (1) treat ecofeminism as a moral theory, (2) engage in the project of working out an integrated philosophy of humanity and nonhuman nature, (3) view this theory as a living process inseparable from the individuals and groups who think and practice it, and (4) maintain an active political and participatory emphasis that is both deconstructive (reactive to current injustices) and reconstructive (proactive in creating new forms of thinking and doing).

The first parameter I have outlined is that ecofeminism be treated as a moral theory—a prescriptive psychological and social model that includes an idea of future potential and how best to unfold it, not just an analysis of how things were in the past or are currently. Philosopher Amélie Rorty defines such a theory and what it should do:

> Besides characterizing the varieties of well-lived lives, and formulating general principles and ideals for regulating conduct, a moral theory should tell us something about how to get from where we are to where we might better be. While it needn't prescribe a decision procedure for determining every detail of every choice and action, it should, in a general way, be action-guiding: constructing a robust ethical theory requires an astute understanding of *psychology and of history*. (1988, 15; italics added)

Furthermore, a moral theory must emerge out of a felt sense of need and personal connection with the issues at hand, not just out of an abstract process of reasoning. Ethical systems based only in abstracted values fail to draw real commitments and can too easily be used as tools of manipulation and deception—for example, to rationalize military aggression on the basis of furthering democracy. Ecofeminism must be adequately grounded and contextualized to be a "robust" and action-guiding ethical theory. It should, therefore, have a foundational characterization of reality (an ontology) and escape some of the traps of classical philosophy that have helped to support conceptual splitting and dualisms. In particular, ecofeminism needs to avoid assumptions of either classical materialism or classical idealism, with connotations of inanimate substance set in opposition to a purely subjective, psychic, or spiritual quality. This means that we must develop concepts and personal sensibilities of self and world that move beyond conceptual dichotomies. Our paradigms and experiences of self and world must be monistic but differentiated to reflect their real basis in earthly life, accounting for both the integrity of individuals and collective realities and functions.

Basically, we are looking to develop a better alternative to a classically Western, atomistic, materialist worldview—without simply flipping to its polar opposite, a holistic, idealist one with a mirror-image set of problems. Ultimately, an atomistic view that reduces life to its smallest increments endangers our lives through a fascination with the manipulation of genes and nuclear power, ignoring the interlocking relations, functions, and activities of natural and social communities. And yet holism as a principle that gives superior explanatory power and/or value to a collective entity or community can also endanger our lives by undermining the integrity of individuals and their specific needs and interests. Women and other oppressed categories of people should be especially wary of paradigms that could be construed as advocating the sacrifice of individual needs to a "greater whole"—whether that be the family, society, or "Gaia," a planetary entity. The latter has made its appearance as an ideal in some ecofeminist writing after James Lovelock took the ancient Greek earth goddess's name to describe his scientific theory of the earth as a self-regulating organism, and this was taken up by various poets, philosophers, and ethicists as a paradigm for nature. I believe, along with Marti Kheel, who writes from the context of animal liberation, that ecofeminist theory must be especially careful in outlining its guiding principles to "address the importance of individual beings *as well as* the larger whole" (1990, 9).

The key to incorporating the integrity of individual and collective realities is an expanded concept of nature that we, as gendered human beings, can then find a place in. We must understand "natural" and "social" histories (as well as our personal lives) as processes of differentiation and incorporation that are expressions of nature rather than emerging *out of* nature. This way we neither annihilate ourselves in nature (reducing ourselves to a small and therefore expendable part) nor sever ourselves from the nonhuman environment and from those aspects of ourselves unmediated by social processes.

At the core of the expanded concept of nature that I advocate is the rejection of a subject/object split at its root—the opposition of human consciousness and a mechanical nature—and the adoption, instead, of an ontology of nature as *fundamentally material and subjective*. This acknowledges different types of subjectivity in natural phenomena that include (but are not limited to) human life and mental processes. In these terms human consciousness is a specialized form of subjectivity but in no way exclusive or original. Imbuing nature with both materiality and subjectivity provides a substantial basis for commonality as well as differences between human beings and nonhuman life, without the mystification of a discontinuous conceptual leap from nature to human existence.

In a realm of human possibilities that exists continuously with, and as an aspect of, nature, we can proceed to explore gender, race, and other categories of human difference as particulars rather than as oppositional qualities. They are specific elaborations of the human species, complex constructs of biological givens and subjective mediations. In actuality, biological sex or genetic heritage is only a small part of what we experience as gender or race. As Donna Haraway reminds us, "race and gender are the world-changing products of specific, but very large and durable histories" (1989, 8). An expanded concept of nature affects our thinking and experience of human diversity in terms such as gender and race in two important ways: first, it prevents our collapsing them into purely biological/materialist explanations, thereby dismissing our own subjective creation and participation in those differences; second, it renders nonsensical the total detachment that characterizes extreme processes of objectification by providing us with an irrefutable basis for mutual identification with others, in a shared natural heritage and physical/subjective existence.

The purpose of working out an integrated philosophy of humanity and nature is not only to challenge dualisms to reflect more clearly our lived experience in theory but also to describe relations among women, men, society, and nonhuman nature in a way that is conducive to a high quality of life and antithetical to oppression and exploitation. There are a few potential pitfalls we need to be cognizant of as we develop a synthesis that relates an expanded sensibility of nature and specific social agendas. In outlining parameters for ecofeminism that are aimed at transforming personal sensibilities as well as deconstructing conceptual splits, it is important to acknowledge and integrate rational, emotional, visceral, imaginative, and intuitive modes of experience and expression. It is also critical, however, to distinguish ontological and phenomenological descriptions and emphasize a necessary discrimination between symbolic and literal existence.

In popular ecofeminist literature one commonly comes across feminized earth and nature images, but there is a troubling absence of critical discussion about them. To relate to the earth as a mother—an entreaty from bumper stickers as well as scholarly essays—is an analogy that is imaginatively inspiring. But "Mother Earth" and the pronouns "she" and "her" in philosophical/theoretical discourse (as in "her forests, rivers, and different creatures have intrinsic value" [Diamond and Orenstein 1990, xi] tend to reify precisely the unexamined woman/nature associations ecofeminism has challenged since its beginnings. Additionally, the psychological effect of understanding the earth as a fundamentally feminine parent is to reduce our sense of the vast and varied subjectivities of the planet and all its life to our projections of human consciousness and to blur the diversified forms of the natural world with our associations to human bodies, or even the particular human body of our own mother. When Paula Gunn Allen calls to "the planet, our mother, Grandmother Earth," and to us to attend to "her" as she "is giving birth" (1990, 52-54), the anthropomorphization diminishes more than expands our awareness, evoking good and bad psychological associations with parenting that we have received and given rather than a sense of wonder that comes from stretching our consciousness to relate to something much bigger than human existence.

Another potential pitfall, which is related to the confusion of symbolic and concrete realities, is for ecofeminists to promote unintentionally an essentialist view of gender differences. This confirms a fear of many outside of ecofeminism that it is a new version of biological determinism that privileges women's relationship to nonhuman nature. This happens, for example, in Brian Swimme's essay, which appears in the most recently published anthology of ecofeminist writing:

> My proposal is that we learn to interpret the data provided by the fragmented scientific mind with the holistic poetic vision alive in ecofeminism. What is this holistic vision? . . . I would simply point to the perspective, awareness and consciousness found most clearly in *primal peoples and women generally.* (1990, 17; italics added)

Marti Kheel and others have noted that conceptual and ethical frameworks marked by care, compassion, and person-to-person accountability can help model the type of thinking and decisionmaking that can help reconstruct human relations to nature, and perhaps this is what Swimme means to suggest (Kheel 1985). Feminist theorists have made phenomenological studies of predominately female traits that include an ethical/moral orientation—an "ethic of care"—and alternative epistemologies, or "women's ways of knowing" (Gilligan 1982; Belenky et al. 1986). These are useful as historically specific descriptions. There is a danger, however, for ecofeminism to reify unwittingly an "ethic of care" or "women's ways of knowing" as universal and biologically determined qualities (and thereby imply that women are limited to these) by dropping them into ecofeminist theory without the historical and cultural contexts in which they developed.

For ecofeminism to fulfill its promise as an emancipatory theory, we must be especially careful in accounting for traits that for complex historical reasons have become gender associated in our culture, even though these may at present describe collective norms. This means that we must be cognizant of what we omit from our theories as well as what we include. Our admission of a specific physical, cultural, and temporal position can give our ideas life and credibility while empowering others to articulate their own unique contribution. This helps us understand a body of ideas such as ecofeminism as embodied ideas—not an abstractable theory but a process inseparable from the persons who think, struggle with, carry, and live it in specific times and places.

SUSTAINING POLITICAL MOMENTUM

The struggle to develop an organic and discriminating view of nature and society, which also includes an understanding of gender and other human differences, is the futuristic edge of ecofeminist theory. But if ecofeminist theory is to remain accountable and connected to the people who have developed it in the past and who carry it now, imperatives for change must also be translatable into political action at the grassroots level. Clearly there are global issues that ecofeminism can and has already helped us analyze and organize around. But situations also rise up in our personal lives and in our communities each day that demand our comprehension, assessment, and action. Amélie Rorty cautions us to test the viability of theory with actual political situations: "a moral theory that recommends political and psychological reforms must also pay attention to the ways in which its proposed redirections can effectively and successfully be brought about, given actual conditions" (1988, 15).

Grace Paley, one of the organizers of the "Women and Life on Earth: Ecofeminism in the 1980s" conference, formed an affinity group with women in her rural Vermont town in 1977. She describes the value of a core group in which members can share ideas and experiences but remain connected to the community as a whole:

> You do find people come from our affinity groups and are working in the towns very seriously, and with other people. It's not an inward group, it's a group that goes outward. There are women that I've worked with who are doing marvelous things— agricultural conservation, and town work on recycling and energy. [One woman] does extraordinary work in schools . . . [she] has girls talk to their grandmothers and collect oral histories.[7]

Paley and others from her group have also been part of demonstrations at the Seabrook, New Hampshire, nuclear power plant for almost twenty years, as part of a larger umbrella network of antinuclear activists in New England, the Clamshell Alliance. Like many of us, she has found her political and community work informed and generated by many different sources, including ecofeminism. So how do we reconcile different alliances? Are there particular benefits in linking diverse actions and projects with ecofeminism? Does this mean that ties to other movements or theories must be broken? Are there reasons not to link activist projects with ecofeminism?

Anne Cameron is among those who raise objections to using the term ecofeminism as a rallying point for diverse activist initiatives. Her argument is that

> suddenly, "feminism" is being avoided as a term . . . the term "ecofeminism" suggests that the old "feminism" was not at all concerned with ecology, could not have cared less about the environment, had no analysis of industrial exploitation, and ignored the need for peace.
>
> The term "ecofeminism" is an insult to the women who put themselves on the line, risked public disapproval, risked even violence, and jail. It is an insult to the women who made rape openly and publicly unacceptable, it is an insult to the women who encouraged us . . . to stop sexual abuse of women and children, and the horror of incest. (1989, 64)

Cameron's argument is important in reminding us that ecofeminism is not an ahistorical revelatory vision that will save the world, negating the hard work and thinking that preceded and continues to inform it. I do not believe, however, that her criticism of ecofeminism is fair, nor is it an accurate reading of the intentions of those who originated the term—most of whom, like Ynestra King, have a long history of feminist activism and have in no way discarded the term feminist. Regarding oneself, a particular viewpoint, or an action as ecofeminist does not need to precipitate an identity crisis in the sense of having to give up other affiliations. Sometimes it renames and reworks social activism and feminist projects that already have a history but may not have distinguished or emphasized the social and ecological interrelations that ecofeminism reminds us of and holds us accountable to. There are a multiplicity of feminisms, for example, with widely differing analyses of sources of oppression as well as who or what is oppressed, the degree of change that is needed, and how it should be accomplished. Some of these are frankly incompatible with ecofeminism's principles; some are complementary. Theoretically and/or politically incompatible orientations include separatist cultural feminisms that do not perceive any basis for commonality with some other people, and some brands of liberal feminism that accept the status quo of most existing social institutions, promoting only women's movement within them. The hallmark of many socialist feminist orientations, on the other hand, is the interdependence of institutional oppressions such as capitalism, racism, and patriarchy. Ecofeminism shares this as part of its analysis but also challenges the limitations of a purely "social" frame of reference.

Donna Haraway notes that inside and outside the boundaries of feminist inquiry, some theoretical/political positions argue for "the historical superiority of particular structured standpoints for knowing the social world, and possibly the 'natural' world as well" (1989, 6). She gives the example of Marxism, which sees forces of economic production and reproduction as primary factors determining both social and human-environmental relations; I would add for comparison versions of radical feminism, which see human gender relations as central. In my definition of ecofeminism's parameters, nature is present as a context but there is no privileged axis of analysis that is equivalent to economic production or gender relations—rather, there is a focus on relations among multiple factors that compose a particular phenomenon rather than on one primary factor that others derive from or are secondary to. This is not to say that ecofeminism necessarily has a better or truer perspective on what is really at play in complex issues, but that the absence of a preconceived bias for a primary cause or factor enables a flexible analysis that is potentially more responsive to direct experience. It also provides for a wider array of confrontational or reconstructive responses. For example, an ecofeminist perspective on biotechnologies (reproductive technologies, genetic engineering) may bring social/historical contexts such as the gendered politics of science or environmental contexts such as the complex and fragile nature of biologic communities to bear on political activism aimed at making or changing public policies. But it is the mutual and cumulative effects of social/political/environmental processes that ecofeminism takes as a special responsibility to notice, describe, and respond to. These are often more serious or urgent than the effects of an isolated process or processes.

CONCLUSION

Ecofeminism is a growing theoretical and political movement. In its short history it has been characterized by considerable diversity among its participants as well as in some of its premises and assumptions. In general, ecofeminism brings strands of several philosophical orientations together in an incisive synthesis, including ecological principles of diversity and interdependence in human and nonhuman communities, and a particular feminist analysis of power relations and interlocking dominations. It also develops a utopian vision of human society integrated with the natural world. I have argued that ecofeminism can best be developed in the future by defining several parameters or points of focus that would serve as references for diverse ideas and claims. These would lend coherence to ecofeminist analyses while helping to avoid some pitfalls of theoretical contradiction and to maintain accountability between theory and political practice. One of the points of focus I suggest is the crucial philosophical project of continuing to develop an expanded concept of nature that can serve as a ground and context for social analyses and can also serve to connect us with our own embodiment and natural heritage. This needs to be worked out very carefully, with special attention to deconstructing cultural dualisms that have supported the association and concurrent devaluation of women, nonhuman nature, and other significant categories of people and things.

Ecofeminism's political goals include the deconstruction of oppressive social, economic, and political systems and the reconstruction of more viable social and political forms. No version of ecofeminist theory dictates exactly what people should do in the face of situations they encounter in personal and public life, nor is it a single political platform. The relation of ecofeminist theory to political activism is ideally informative and generative and not one of either prescribing or "owning" particular actions. Ecofeminist theory advocates a combined politics of resistance and creative projects, but the specific enactment of these is a result of dialogue between the individuals involved and the actual situation or issue. Ecofeminism contributes an overall framework and conceptual links to the political understanding of the interplay between social and environmental issues, and routes to political empowerment through understanding the effects of one's actions extended through multiple human and nonhuman communities.

Ecofeminism faces a challenge in maintaining, and to a certain degree, recovering a politically potent activist emphasis. Ecofeminism's critical frameworks and utopian visions are exciting and energizing—in one sense, it is a focus term for philosophies that integrate human society and nature and aim for an entirely new intellectual/perceptual/sensate experience of self and world. It is in no way ahistorical, however, as it is developed and lived by people with different backgrounds and asssumptions about the nature of gender roles, social arrangements, and human/environmental relations. Ecofeminism does make big promises. Their fulfillment depends on theorists and activists who can embody the broad and integrated sensibilities of self and world that ecofeminism helps develop and advocate and who can find the power and the energy to act on those sensibilities to make real social and political changes.

NOTES

I would like to thank Ariel Salleh, Karin Aguilar-San Juan, and other members of the South End Press collective, Karen J. Warren, and anonymous reviewers for their comments on earlier versions of this essay.

1. From a conversation with Sue Swain, who was one of the organizers and participants in the Mother's Day Garden.

2. For specific treatments of ecofeminism's relation to the peace movement see King (1986), to the direct action movement see Sturgeon (1989), and to Green Party politics see Tokar (1987, 39, 85, 137) and Spretnak (1988).

3. From a plenary discussion at the "Culture, Nature and Theory: Ecofeminist Perspectives" conference at USC-Los Angeles, March 1987.

4. See Naess (1985), who is credited with introducing the term deep ecology. Murray Bookchin (1988) has critiqued deep ecology's strange reverence for Martin Heidegger, whose mystical philosophy and ideological connection to Hitler's Nazi party give rise to profound questions about the suitability of his ideas as a basis for social revision and reconstruction.

5. In the three anthologies of ecofeminist essays that have been published (Caldecott and Leland 1983; Plant 1989; Diamond and Orenstein 1990) there is a progressive trend away from activist issues, which almost completely constitute the first anthology (in essays like "Black Ghetto Ecology" and "Greening the Desert: Women of Kenya Reclaim Land"), toward a greater proportion of philosophical discussions of ecofeminism's relation to environmental ethics and feminist spirituality in the last (in essays like "The Origins of God in the Blood of the Lamb" and "Deep Ecology and Ecofeminism: The Emerging Dialogue"). To what degree this trend is beneficial in rounding out and developing a more sophisticated theoretical base for ecofeminism and to what degree it may indicate a diminishment of political involvement and power or an unexamined change in who is defining ecofeminism are extremely important questions for ecofeminists to take up.

6. An example of one project that functions in several of the ways I have listed is Julia Russell's Eco-Home in Los Angeles, a demonstration home and community network that implements and distributes information on solar technology, water-conserving organic gardens, recycling, and composting; in addition it sponsors a community bartering system and revolving loan fund. In my home

state of Vermont ecofeminists have organized forums on reproductive technologies and environmental conservation through the Burlington Women's Council,
and ecofeminists were among those who lobbied against state legislation legaliz-
ing surrogate mother contracts and for a bill that recognizes and prosecutes "hate
crimes" against minority groups, gays, and lesbians.

7. From a 1988 conversation with Grace Paley.

REFERENCES

Allen, Paula Gunn. 1990. The woman I love is a planet, the planet I love is a tree.
In *Reweaving the world*. See Diamond and Orenstein 1990.
Belenky, Mary, Blythe Clinchy, Nancy Goldberger, and Jill Tarule. 1986.
Women's ways of knowing. New York: Basic Books.
Biehl, Janet. 1989. Goddess mythology in ecological politics. *New Politics* 2: 84-105.
Bookchin, Murray. 1988. Social ecology versus deep ecology. *Socialist Review* 3: 9-29.
Caldecott, Leonie, and Stephanie Leland, eds. 1983. *Reclaim the earth: Women
speak out for life on earth*. London: The Women's Press.
Cameron, Anne. 1989. First Mother and the rainbow children. In *Healing the
wounds*. See Plant 1989.
Cronon, William. 1983. *Changes in the land: Indians, colonists, and the ecology of
New England*. New York: Hill and Wang.
Diamond, Irene, and Gloria Feman Orenstein, eds. 1990. *Reweaving the world:
The emergence of ecofeminism*. San Francisco: Sierra Club Books.
Eisler, Riane. 1987. *The chalice and the blade*. San Francisco: Harper and Row.
Gilligan, Carol. 1982. *In a different voice*. Cambridge: Harvard University Press.
Haraway, Donna. 1989. *Primate visions: Gender, race and nature in the world of
modern science*. New York: Routledge.
Kheel, Marti. 1985. The liberation of nature: A circular affair. *Environmental
Ethics* 7: 135-49.
———. 1990. Animal liberation and environmental ethics: Can ecofeminism
bridge the gap? Paper presented at the 1990 National Women's Studies
Association conference.
King, Ynestra. 1986. In the interest of peace: Feminism, women and politics.
Unpublished paper.
———. 1989. Healing the wounds: Feminism, ecology, and nature/culture
dualism. In *Gender/body/knowledge: Feminist reconstructions of being and knowing*. Alison Jaggar and Susan Bordo, eds. New Brunswick and London: Rutgers
University Press.
Merchant, Carolyn. 1980. *The death of nature: Women, ecology and the scientific
revolution*. San Francisco: Harper and Row.
———. 1989. *Ecological revolutions*. Chapel Hill and London: University of
North Carolina Press.

Naess, Arne. 1985. Identification as a source of deep ecological attitudes. In *Deep ecology*. Michael Tobias, ed. San Diego: Avant Books.

Ortner, Sherry. 1974. Is female to male as nature is to culture? In *Woman, culture and society*. Michelle Rosaldo and Louise Lamphere, eds. Stanford, CA: Stanford University Press.

Plant, Judith. 1989. *Healing the wounds: The promise of ecofeminism*. Philadelphia: New Society Publishers.

Prentice, Susan. 1988. Taking sides: what's wrong with eco-feminism? *Women and Environments* (Spring): 9-10.

Rorty, Amélie. 1988. *Mind in action*. Boston: Beacon Press.

Shiva, Vandana. 1988. *Staying alive: women, ecology and development*. London: Zed.

Spretnak, Charlene. 1988. Ecofeminism: our roots and flowering. *Woman of Power* 9: 6-10.

Starhawk. 1989. Feminist, earth-based spirituality and ecofeminism. In *Healing the wounds*. See Plant 1989.

Sturgeon, Noël. 1989. What does the politics of poststructuralist feminism look like? Ecofeminism, positional feminism and radical feminism revisited. Paper presented at the 1989 National Women's Studies Association Conference.

Swimme, Brian. 1990. How to heal a lobotomy. In *Reweaving the world*. See Diamond and Orenstein 1990.

Tokar, Brian. 1987. *The green alternative*. San Pedro, CA: R. and E. Miles.

The Power and the Promise
of Ecological Feminism

KAREN J. WARREN

Introduction

Ecological feminism (ecofeminism) has begun to receive a fair amount of attention lately as an alternative feminism and environmental ethic.[1] Since Françoise d'Eaubonne introduced the term *ecofeminisme* in 1974 to bring attention to women's potential for bringing about an ecological revolution,[2] the term has been used in a variety of ways. As I use the term in this paper, ecological feminism is the position that there are important connections—historical, experiential, symbolic, theoretical—between the domination of women and the domination of nature, an understanding of which is crucial to both feminism and environmental ethics. I argue that the promise and power of ecological feminism is that *it provides a distinctive framework both for reconceiving feminism and for developing an environmental ethic which takes seriously connections between the domination of women and the domination of nature*. I do so by discussing the nature of a feminist ethic and the ways in which ecofeminism provides a feminist and environmental ethic. I conclude that any feminist theory *and* any environmental ethic which fails to take seriously the twin and interconnected dominations of women and nature is at best incomplete and at worst simply inadequate.

Feminism, Ecological Feminism, and Conceptual Frameworks

Whatever else it is, feminism is at least the movement to end sexist oppression. It involves the elimination of any and all factors that contribute to the continued and systematic domination or subordination of women. While feminists disagree about the nature of and solutions to the subordination of women, all feminists agree that sexist oppression exists, is wrong, and must be abolished.

A "feminist issue" is any issue that contributes in some way to understanding the oppression of women. Equal rights, comparable pay for comparable work, and food production are feminist issues wherever and whenever an understanding of them contributes to an understanding of the continued exploitation or subjugation of women. Carrying water and searching for firewood are feminist issues wherever and whenever women's primary responsibility for these tasks contributes to their lack of full participation in decision making, income producing, or high status positions engaged in by men. What counts as a feminist issue, then, depends largely on context, particularly the historical and material conditions of women's lives.

Environmental degradation and exploitation are feminist issues because an understanding of them contributes to an understanding of the oppression of women. In India, for example, both deforestation and reforestation through the introduction of a monoculture species tree (e.g., eucalyptus) intended for commercial production are feminist issues because the loss of indigenous forests and multiple species of trees has drastically affected rural Indian women's ability to maintain a subsistence household. Indigenous forests provide a variety of trees for food, fuel, fodder, household utensils, dyes, medicines, and income-generating uses, while monoculture-species forests do not.[3] Although I do not argue for this claim here, a look at the global impact of environmental degradation on women's lives suggests important respects in which environmental degradation is a feminist issue.

Feminist philosophers claim that some of the most important feminist issues are *conceptual* ones: these issues concern how one conceptualizes such mainstay philosophical notions as reason and rationality, ethics, and what it is to be human. Ecofeminists extend this feminist philosophical concern to nature. They argue that, ultimately, some of the most important connections between the domination of women and the domination of nature are conceptual. To see this, consider the nature of conceptual frameworks.

A *conceptual framework* is a set of *basic* beliefs, values, attitudes, and assumptions which shape and reflect how one views oneself and one's world. It is a socially constructed lens through which we perceive ourselves and others. It is affected by such factors as gender, race, class, age, affectional orientation, nationality, and religious background.

Some conceptual frameworks are oppressive. An *oppressive conceptual framework* is one that explains, justifies, and maintains relationships of domination and subordination. When an oppressive conceptual framework is *patriarchal*, it explains, justifies, and maintains the subordination of women by men.

I have argued elsewhere that there are three significant features of oppressive conceptual frameworks: (1) value-hierarchical thinking, i.e., "up-down" thinking which places higher value, status, or prestige on what is "up" rather than on what is "down": (2) value dualisms, i.e., disjunctive pairs in which the disjuncts are seen as oppositional (rather than as complementary) and exclusive (rather than as inclusive), and which place higher value (status, prestige) on one disjunct rather than the other (e.g., dualisms which give higher value or status to that which has historically been identified as "mind," "reason," and "male" than to that which has historically been identified as "body," "emotion," and "female"): and (3) logic of domination, i.e., a structure of argumentation which leads to a justification of subordination.[4]

The third feature of oppressive conceptual frameworks is the most significant. A logic of domination is not *just* a logical structure. It also involves a substantive value system, since an ethical premise is needed to permit or sanction the "just" subordination of that which is subordinate. This justification typically is given on grounds of some alleged characteristic (e.g., rationality) which the dominant (e.g., men) have and the subordinate (e.g., women) lack.

Contrary to what many feminists and ecofeminists have said or suggested, there may be nothing *inherently* problematic about "hierarchical thinking" or even "value-hierarchical thinking" in contexts other than contexts of oppression. Hierarchical thinking is important in daily living for classifying data, comparing information, and organizing material. Taxonomies (e.g., plant taxonomies) and biological nomenclature seem to require *some* form of "hierarchical thinking." Even "value-hierarchical thinking" may be quite acceptable in certain contexts. (The same may be said of "value dualisms" in non-oppressive contexts.) For example, suppose it is true that what is unique about humans is our conscious capacity to radically reshape our social environments (or "societies"), as Murray Bookchin suggests.[5] Then one could truthfully say that humans are better equipped to radically reshape their environments than are rocks or plants- a "value-hierarchical" way of speaking.

The problem is not simply *that* value-hierarchical thinking and value dualisms are used, but *the way* in which each has been used *in oppressive conceptual frameworks* to establish inferiority and to justify subordination.[6] It is the logic of domination, *coupled with* value-hierarchical thinking and value dualisms, which "justifies" subordination. What is explanatorily basic, then, about the nature of oppressive conceptual frameworks is the logic of domination.

For ecofeminism, that a logic of domination is explanatorily basic is important for at least three reasons. First, without a logic of domination, a description of similarities and differences would be just that-a description of similarities and differences. Consider the claim "Humans are different from plants and rocks in that humans can (and plants and rocks cannot) consciously and radically reshape the communities in which they live: humans are similar to plants and rocks in that they are both members of an ecological community." Even if humans are "better" than plants and rocks with respect to the conscious ability of humans to radically transform communities, one does not *thereby* get any *morally* relevant distinction between humans and nonhumans, or an argument for the domination of plants and rocks by humans. To get *those* conclusions one needs to add at least two powerful assumptions, viz., (A2) and (A4) in argument A below:

(A1) Humans do, and plants and rocks do not, have the capacity to consciously and radically chance the community in which they live.

(A2) Whatever has the capacity to consciously and radically change the community in which it lives is morally superior to whatever lacks this capacity.

(A3) Thus, humans are morally superior to plants and rocks.

(A4) For any X and Y, if X is morally superior to Y, then X is morally justified in subordinating Y.

(A5) Thus, humans are morally justified in subordinating plants and rocks.

Without the two assumptions that *humans are morally superior* to (at least some) nonhumans, (A2), and that *superiority justifies subordination*, (A4), all one has is some difference between humans and some nonhumans. This is true *even if* that difference is given in terms of superiority. Thus, it is the logic of denomination, (A4), which is the bottom line in ecofeminist discussions of oppression.

Second, ecofeminists argue that, at least in Western societies, the oppressive conceptual framework which sanctions the twin dominations of women and nature is a patriarchal one characterized by all three features of an oppressive conceptual framework. Many ecofeminists claim that, historically, within at least the dominant Western culture, a patriarchal conceptual framework has sanctioned the following argument B:

(B1) Women are identified with nature and the realm of the physical; men are identified with the "human" and the realm of the mental.

(B2) Whatever is identified with nature and the realm of the physical is inferior to ("below") whatever is identified with the "human" and the realm of the mental: or, conversely, the latter is superior to ("above") the former.

(B3) Thus, women are inferior to ("below") men; or, conversely, men are superior to ("above") women.

(B4) For any X and Y, if X is superior to Y, then X is justified in subordinating Y.

(B5) Thus, men are justified in subordinating women.

If sound, argument B establishes *patriarchy*, i.e., the conclusion given at (B5) that the systematic domination of women by men is justified. But according to ecofeminists, (B5) is justified by just those three features of an oppressive conceptual framework identified earlier: value-hierarchical thinking, the as-sumption at (B2): value dualisms, the assumed dualism of the mental and the physical at (B1) and the assumed inferiority of the physical vis-à-vis the mental at (B2); and a logic of domination, the assumption at (B4), the same as the previous premise (A4). Hence, according to ecofeminists, insofar as an oppressive patriarchal conceptual framework has functioned historically (within at least dominant Western culture) to sanction the twin dominations of women and nature (argument B), both argument B and the patriarchal conceptual framework, from whence it comes, ought to be rejected.

Of course, the preceeding does not identify which premises of B are false. What is the status of premises (B1) and (B2)? Most, if not all, feminists claim that (B1), and many ecofeminists claim that (B2), have been assumed or asserted within the dominant Western philosophical and intellectual tradition.[7] As such, these feminists assert, as a matter of historical fact, that the dominant Western philosophical tradition has assumed the truth of (B1) and (B2). Ecofeminists, however, either deny (B2) or do not affirm (B2). Furthermore, because some ecofeminists are anxious to deny any ahistorical identification of women with nature, some ecofeminists deny (B1) when (B1) is used to support anything other than a strictly historical claim about what has been asserted or assumed to be true within patriarchal culture—e.g., when (B1) is used to assert that women properly are identified with the realm of nature and the physical.[8] Thus, from an ecofeminist perspective, (B1) and (B2) are properly viewed as problematic though historically sanctioned claims: they are problematic precisely because of the way they have functioned historically in a patriarchal conceptual framework and culture to sanction the dominations of women and nature.

What *all* ecofeminists agree about, then, is the way in which *the logic of domination* has functioned historically within patriarchy to sustain and justify the twin dominations of women and nature.[9] Since *all* feminists (and not just ecofeminists) oppose patriarchy, the conclusion given at (B5), all feminists (including ecofeminists) must oppose at least the logic of domination, premise (B4), on which argument B rests—whatever the truth-value status of (B1) and (B2) *outside of* a patriarchal context.

That *all* feminists must oppose the logic of domination shows the breadth and depth of the ecofeminist critique of B: it is a critique not only of the three assumptions on which this argument for the domination of women and nature rests, viz., the assumptions at (B1), (B2), and (B4); it is also a critique of patriarchal conceptual frameworks generally, i.e., of those oppressive conceptual frameworks which put men "up" and women "down," allege some way in which women are morally inferior to men, and use that alleged difference to justify the subordination of women by men. Therefore, ecofeminism is necessary to *any* feminist critique of patriarchy, and, hence, necessary to feminism (a point I discuss again later).

Third, ecofeminism clarifies why the logic of domination, and any conceptual framework which gives rise to it, must be abolished in order both to make possible a meaningful notion of difference which does not breed domination and to prevent feminism from becoming a "support" movement based primarily on shared experiences. In contemporary society, there is no one "woman's voice," no *woman* (or *human*) *simpliciter*: every woman (or human) is a woman (or human) of some race, class, age, affectional orientation, marital status, regional or national background, and so forth. Because there are no "monolithic experiences" that all women share, feminism must be a "solidarity movement" based on shared beliefs and interests rather than a "unity in sameness" movement based on shared experiences and shared victimization.[10] In the words of Maria Lugones, "Unity—not to be confused with solidarity—is understood as conceptually tied to domination."[11]

Ecofeminists insist that the sort of logic of domination used to justify the domination of humans by gender, racial or ethnic, or class status is also used to justify the domination of nature. Because eliminating a logic of domination is part of a feminist critique—whether a critique of patriarchy, white supremacist culture, or imperialism—ecofeminists insist that *naturism* is properly viewed as an integral part of any feminist solidarity movement to end sexist oppression and the logic of domination which conceptually grounds it.

ECOFEMINISM RECONCEIVES FEMINISM

The discussion so far has focused on some of the oppressive conceptual features of patriarchy. As I use the phrase, the "logic of traditional feminism" refers to the location of the conceptual roots of sexist oppression, at least in Western societies, in an oppressive patriarchal conceptual framework characterized by a logic of domination. Insofar as other systems of oppression (e.g., racism, classism, ageism, heterosexism) are also conceptually maintained by a logic of domination, appeal to the logic of traditional feminism ultimately locates the basic conceptual interconnections among *all* systems of oppression in the logic of domination. It thereby explains at a *conceptual* level why the eradication of sexist oppression requires the eradication of the other forms of oppression.[12] It is by clarifying this conceptual connection between systems of oppression that a movement to end sexist oppression-traditionally the special turf of feminist theory and practice-leads to a reconceiving of feminism as *a movement to end all forms of oppression*.

Suppose one agrees that the logic of traditional feminism requires the expansion of feminism to include other social systems of domination (e.g., racism and classism). What warrants the inclusion of nature in these "social systems of domination"? Why must the logic of traditional feminism include the abolition of "naturism" (i.e., the domination or oppression of nonhuman nature) among the "isms" feminism must confront? The conceptual justification for expanding feminism to include ecofeminism is twofold. One basis has already been suggested: by showing that the conceptual connections between the dual dominations of women and nature are located in an oppressive and, at least in Western societies, patriarchal conceptual framework characterized by a logic of domination, ecofeminism explains how and why feminism, conceived as a movement to end sexist oppression, must be expanded and reconceived as also a movement to end "naturism." This is made explicit by the following argument C:

(C1) Feminism is a movement to end sexism.
(C2) But sexism is conceptually linked with naturism (through an oppressive conceptual framework characterized by a logic of domination).
(C3) Thus, feminism is (also) a movement to end naturism.

Because, ultimately, these connections between sexism and naturism are conceptual—embedded in an oppressive conceptual framework—the logic of traditional feminism leads to the embracement of ecological feminism.[13]

The other justification for reconceiving feminism to include ecofeminism has to do with the concepts of gender and nature. Just as conceptions of gender are socially constructed, so are conceptions of nature. Of course, the claim that women and nature are social constructions does not require anyone to deny that there are actual humans and actual trees, rivers, and plants. It simply implies that *how* women and nature are conceived is a matter of historical and social reality. These conceptions vary cross-culturally and by historical time period. As a result, any discussion of the "oppression or domination of nature" involves reference to historically specific forms of social domination of nonhuman nature by humans, just as discussion of the "domination of women" refers to historically specific forms of social domination of women by men. Although I do not argue for it here, an ecofeminist defense of the historical connections between the dominations of women and of nature, claims (B1) and (B2) in argument B, involves showing that within patriarchy the feminization of nature and the naturalization of women have been crucial to the historically successful subordinations of both.[14]

If ecofeminism promises to reconceive traditional feminism in ways which include naturism as a legitimate feminist issue, does ecofeminism also promise to reconceive environmental ethics in ways which are feminist? I think so. This is the subject of the remainder of the paper.

CLIMBING FROM ECOFEMINISM TO ENVIRONMENTAL ETHICS

Many feminists and some environmental ethicists have begun to explore the use of first-person narrative as a way of raising philosophically germane issues in ethics often lost or underplayed in mainstream philosophical ethics. Why is this so? What is it about narrative which makes it a significant resource for theory and practice in feminism and environmental ethics? Even if appeal to first-person narrative is a helpful literary device for describing ineffable experience or a legitimate social science methodology for documenting personal and social history, how is first-person narrative a valuable vehicle of argumentation for ethical decision making and theory building? One fruitful way to begin answering these questions is to ask them of a particular first-person narrative.

Consider the following first-person narrative about rock climbing:

> For my very first rock climbing experience, I chose a somewhat private spot, away from other climbers and on-lookers. After studying "the chimney," I focused all my energy on making it to the top. I climbed with intense determination, using whatever strength and skills I had to accomplish this challenging feat. By midway I was exhausted and anxious. I couldn't see what to do next—where to put my hands or feet. Growing increasingly more weary as I clung somewhat desperately to the rock, I made a move. It didn't work. I fell. There I was, dangling midair above the rocky ground below, frightened but terribly relieved that the belay rope had held me. I knew I was safe. I took a look up at the climb that remained. I was determined to make it to the top. With renewed confidence and concentration, I finished the climb to the top.
>
> On my second day of climbing, I rappelled down about 200 feet from the top of the Palisades at Lake Superior to just a few feet above the water level. I could see no one—not my belayer, not the other climbers, no one. I unhooked slowly from the rappel rope and took a deep cleansing breath. I looked all around me—really looked—and listened. I heard a cacophony of voices—birds, trickles of water on the rock before me, waves lapping against the rocks below. I closed my eyes and began to feel the rock with my hands—the cracks and crannies, the raised lichen and mosses, the almost imperceptible nubs that might provide a resting place for my fingers and toes when I began to climb. At that moment I was bathed in serenity. I began to talk to the rock in an almost inaudible, child-like way, as if the rock were my friend. I felt an overwhelming sense of gratitude for what it offered me—a chance to know myself and the rock differently, to appreciate unforeseen miracles like the tiny flowers growing in the even tinier cracks in the rock's surface, and to come to know a sense of *being in relationship* with the natural environment. It felt as if the rock and I were silent conversational partners in a longstanding friendship. I realized then that I had come to care about this cliff which was so different from me, so unmovable and invincible, independent and seemingly indifferent to my presence. I wanted to be with the rock as I climbed. Gone was the determination to conquer the rock, to forcefully impose my will on it; I wanted simply to work respectfully with the rock as I climbed. And as I climbed, that is

what I felt. I felt myself *caring* for this rock and feeling thankful that climbing provided the opportunity for me to know it and myself in this new way.

There are at least four reasons why use of such a first-person narrative is important to feminism and environmental ethics. First, such a narrative gives voice to a felt sensitivity often lacking in traditional analytical ethical discourse, viz., a sensitivity to conceiving of oneself as fundamentally "in relationship with" others, including the nonhuman environment. It is a modality which *takes relationships themselves seriously*. It thereby stands in contrast to a strictly reductionist modality that takes relationships seriously only or primarily because of the nature of the *relators* or parties to those relationships (e.g., relators conceived as moral agents, right holders, interest carriers, or sentient beings). In the rock-climbing narrative above, it is the climber's relationship with the rock she climbs which takes on special significance—which is itself a locus of value—in addition to whatever moral status or moral considerability she or the rock or any other parties to the relationship may also have.[15]

Second, such a first-person narrative gives expression to a variety of ethical attitudes and behaviors often overlooked or underplayed in mainstream Western ethics, e.g., the difference in attitudes and behaviors toward a rock when one is "making it to the top" and when one thinks of oneself as "friends with" or "caring about" the rock one climbs.[16] These different attitudes and behaviors suggest an ethically germane contrast between two different types of relationship humans or climbers may have toward a rock: an imposed conqueror-type relationship, and an emergent caring-type relationship. This contrast grows out of, and is faithful to, felt, lived experience.

The difference between conquering and caring attitudes and behaviors in relation to the natural environment provides a third reason why the use of first-person narrative is important to feminism and environmental ethics: it provides a way of conceiving of ethics and ethical meaning as *emerging out of* particular situations moral agents find themselves in, rather than as being *imposed on* those situations (e.g., as a derivation or instantiation of some pre-determined abstract principle or rule). This emergent feature of narrative centralizes the importance of *voice*. When a multiplicity of cross-cultural *voices* are centralized, narrative is able to give expression to a range of attitudes, values, beliefs, and behaviors which may be overlooked or silenced by imposed ethical meaning and theory. As a reflection of and on felt, lived experiences, the use of narrative in ethics provides a stance from which ethical discourse can be held accountable to the historical, material, and social realities in which moral subjects find themselves.

Lastly, and for our purposes perhaps most importantly, the use of narrative has argumentative significance. Jim Cheney calls attention to this feature of narrative when he claims, "To contextualize ethical deliberation is, in some sense, to provide a narrative or story, from which the solution to the ethical dilemma emerges as the fitting conclusion."[17] Narrative has argumentative force by suggesting *what counts* as an appropriate conclusion to an ethical situation. One ethical conclusion suggested by the climbing narrative is that what counts as a proper ethical attitude toward mountains and rocks is an attitude of respect and care (whatever that turns out to be or involve), not one of domination and conquest.

In an essay entitled "In and Out of Harm's Way: Arrogance and Love," feminist philosopher Marilyn Frye distinguishes between "arrogant" and "loving" perception as one way of getting at this difference in the ethical attitudes of care and conquest.[18] Frye writes:

> The loving eye is a contrary of the arrogant eye.
>
> The loving eye knows the independence of the other. It is the eye of a seer who knows that nature is indifferent. It is the eye of one who knows that to know the seen, one must consult something other than one's own will and interests and fears and imagination. One must look at the thing. One must look and listen and check and question.
>
> The loving eye is one that pays a certain sort of attention. This attention can require a discipline but *not* a self-denial. The discipline is one of self-knowledge, knowledge of the scope and boundary of the self. . . . In particular, it is a matter of being able to tell one's own interests from those of others and of knowing where one's self leaves off and another begins. . . .
>
> The loving eye does not make the object of perception into something edible, does not try to assimilate it, does not reduce it to the size of the seer's desire, fear and imagination, and hence does not have to simplify. It knows the complexity of the other as something which will forever present new things to be known. The science of the loving eye would favor The Complexity Theory of Truth [in contrast to The Simplicity Theory of Truth] and presuppose The Endless Interestingness of the Universe.[19]

According to Frye, the loving eye is not an invasive, coercive eye which annexes others to itself, but one which "knows the complexity of the other as something which will forever present new things to be known."

When one climbs a rock as a conqueror, one climbs with an arrogant eye. When one climbs with a loving eye, one constantly "must look and listen and check and question." One recognizes the rock as something very different, something perhaps totally indifferent to one's own presence, and finds in that difference joyous occasion for celebration. One knows "the boundary of the self," where the self— the "I," the climber—leaves off and the rock begins. There is no fusion of two into one, but a complement of two entities *acknowledged* as separate, different, independent, yet *in relationship;* they are in relationship *if only* because the loving eye is perceiving it, responding to it, noticing it, attending to it.

An ecofeminist perspective about both women and nature involves this shift in attitude from "arrogant perception" to "loving perception" of the nonhuman world. Arrogant perception of nonhumans by humans presupposes and maintains *sameness* in such a way that it expands the moral community to those beings who are thought to resemble (be like, similar to, or the same as) humans in some morally significant way. Any environmental movement or ethic based on arrogant perception builds a moral hierarchy of beings and assumes some common denominator of moral considerability in virtue of which like beings deserve similar treatment or moral consideration and unlike beings do not. Such environmental ethics are, or generate, a "unity in sameness." In contrast, "loving perception" presupposes and maintains *difference*—a distinction between the self and other, between human and at least some nonhumans—in such a way that perception of the other as other is an expression of love for one who/which is recognized at the outset as independent, dissimilar, different. As Maria Lugones says, in loving perception, "Love is seen not as fusion and erasure of difference but as incompatible with them."[20] "Unity in sameness" alone is an *erasure of difference.*

"Loving perception" of the nonhuman natural world is an attempt to understand what it means *for humans* to care about the nonhuman world, a world *acknowledged* as being independent, different, perhaps even indifferent to humans. Humans *are* different from rocks in important ways, even if they are also both members of some ecological community. A moral community based on loving perception of oneself *in relationship with* a rock, or with the natural environment as a whole, is one which acknowledges and respects difference, whatever "sameness" also exists.[21] The limits of loving perception are determined only by the limits of one's (e.g., a person's, a community's) ability to respond lovingly (or with appropriate care, trust, or friendship)—whether it is to other humans or to the nonhuman world and elements of it.[22]

If what I have said so far is correct, then there are very different ways to climb a mountain and *how* one climbs it and *how* one narrates the experience of climbing it matter ethically. If one climbs with "arrogant perception," with an attitude of "conquer and control," one keeps intact the very sorts of thinking that characterize a logic of domination and an oppressive conceptual framework. Since the oppressive conceptual framework which sanctions the domination of nature is a patriarchal one, one also thereby keeps intact, even if unwittingly, a patriarchal conceptual framework. Because the dismantling of patriarchal conceptual frameworks is a feminist issue, *how* one climbs a mountain and *how* one narrates—or tells the story—about the experience of climbing also are *feminist issues.* In this way, ecofeminism makes visible why, at a conceptual level, environmental ethics is a feminist issue. I turn now to a consideration of ecofeminism as a distinctively feminist and environmental ethic.

Ecofeminism as a Feminist and Environmental Ethic

A feminist ethic involves a twofold commitment to critique male bias in ethics wherever it occurs, and to develop ethics which are not male-biased. Sometimes this involves articulation of values (e.g., values of care, appropriate trust, kinship, friendship) often lost or underplayed in mainstream ethics.[23] Sometimes it involves engaging in theory building by pioneering in new directions or by revamping old theories in gender sensitive ways. What makes the critiques of old theories or conceptualizations of new ones "feminist" is that they emerge out of sex-gender analyses and reflect whatever those analyses reveal about gendered experience and gendered social reality.

As I conceive feminist ethics in the pre-feminist present, it rejects attempts to conceive of ethical theory in terms of necessary and sufficient conditions, because it assumes that there is no essence (in the sense of some transhistorical, universal, absolute abstraction) of feminist ethics. While attempts to formulate joint necessary and sufficient conditions of a feminist ethic are unfruitful, nonetheless, there are some necessary conditions, what I prefer to call "boundary conditions," of a feminist ethic. These boundary conditions clarify some of the minimal conditions of a feminist ethic without suggesting that feminist ethics has some ahistorical essence. They are like the boundaries of a quilt or collage. They delimit the territory of the piece without dictating what the interior, the design, the actual pattern of the piece looks like. Because the actual design of the quilt emerges from the multiplicity of voices of women in a cross-cultural context, the design will change over time. It is not something static.

What are some of the boundary conditions of a feminist ethic? First, nothing can become part of a feminist ethic—can be part of the quilt—that promotes sexism, racism, classism, or any other "isms" of social domination. Of course, people may disagree about what counts as a sexist act, racist attitude, classist behavior. What counts as sexism, racism, or classism may vary cross-culturally. Still, because a feminist ethic aims at eliminating sexism and sexist bias, and (as I have already shown) sexism is intimately connected in conceptualization and in practice to racism, classism, and naturism, a feminist ethic must be anti-sexist, anti-racist, anti-classist, anti-naturist and opposed to any "ism" which presupposes or advances a logic of domination.

Second, a feminist ethic is a *contextualist* ethic. A contextualist ethic is one which sees ethical discourse and practice as emerging from the voices of people located in different historical circumstances. A contextualist ethic is properly viewed as a *collage* or *mosaic*, a *tapestry* of voices that emerges out of felt experiences. Like any collage or mosaic, the point is not to have *one picture* based on a unity of voices, but a *pattern* which emerges out of the very different voices of people located in different circumstances. When a contextualist ethic is *feminist*, it gives central place to the voices of women.

Third, since a feminist ethic gives central significance to the diversity of women's voices, a feminist ethic must be structurally pluralistic rather than unitary or reductionistic. It rejects the assumption that there is "one voice" in terms of which ethical values, beliefs, attitudes, and conduct can be assessed.

Fourth, a feminist ethic reconceives ethical theory as theory in process which will change over time. Like all theory, a feminist ethic is based on some generalizations.[24] Nevertheless, the generalizations associated with it are themselves a pattern of voices within which the different voices emerging out of concrete and alternative descriptions of ethical situations have meaning. The coherence of a feminist theory so conceived is given within a historical and conceptual context, i.e., within a set of historical, socioeconomic circumstances (including circumstances of race, class, age, and affectional orientation) and within a set of basic beliefs, values, attitudes, and assumptions about the world.

Fifth, because a feminist ethic is contextualist, structurally pluralistic, and "in-process," one way to evaluate the claims of a feminist ethic is in terms of their *inclusiveness*: those claims (voices, patterns of voices) are morally and epistemologically favored (preferred, better, less partial, less biased) which are more inclusive of the felt experiences and perspectives of oppressed persons. The condition of inclusiveness requires and ensures that the diverse voices of women (as oppressed persons) will be given legitimacy in ethical theory building. It thereby helps to minimize empirical bias, e.g., bias rising from faulty or false generalizations based on stereotyping, too small a sample size, or a skewed sample. It does so by ensuring that any generalizations which are made about ethics and ethical decision making include—indeed cohere with—the patterned voices of women.[25]

Sixth, a feminist ethic makes no attempt to provide an "objective" point of view, since it assumes that in contemporary culture there really is no such point of view. As such, it does not claim to be "unbiased" in the sense of "value-neutral" or "objective." However, it does assume that whatever bias it has as an ethic centralizing the voices of oppressed persons is a *better bias*—"better" because it is more inclusive and therefore less partial—than those which exclude those voices.[26]

Seventh, a feminist ethic provides a central place for values typically unnoticed, underplayed, or misrepresented in traditional ethics, e.g., values of care, love, friendship, and appropriate trust.[27] Again, it need not do this at the exclusion of considerations of rights, rules, or utility. There may be many contexts in which talk of rights or of utility is useful or appropriate. For instance, in contracts or property relationships, talk of rights may be useful and appropriate. In deciding what is cost-effective or advantageous to the most people, talk of utility may be useful and appropriate. In a feminist *qua* contextualist ethic, whether or not such talk is useful or appropriate depends on the context; *other values* (e.g., values of care, trust, friendship) are *not* viewed as reducible to or captured solely in terms of such talk.[28]

Eighth, a feminist ethic also involves a reconception of what it is to be human and what it is for humans to engage in ethical decision making, since it rejects as either meaningless or currently untenable any gender-free or gender-neutral description of humans, ethics, and ethical decision making. It thereby rejects what Alison Jaggar calls "abstract individualism," i.e., the position that it is possible to identify a human essence or human nature that exists independently of any particular historical context.[29] Humans and human moral conduct are properly understood essentially (and not merely accidentally) in terms of networks or webs of historical and concrete relationships.

All the props are now in place for seeing how ecofeminism provides the framework for a distinctively feminist and environmental ethic. It is a feminism that critiques male bias wherever it occurs in ethics (including environmental ethics) and aims at providing an ethic (including an environmental ethic) which is not male biased—and it does so in a way that satisfies the preliminary boundary conditions of a feminist ethic.

First, ecofeminist is quintessentially anti-naturist. Its anti-naturism consists in the rejection of any way of thinking about or acting toward nonhuman nature that reflects a logic, values, or attitude of domination. Its anti-naturist, anti-sexist, anti-racist, anti-classist (and so forth, for all other "isms" of social domination) stance forms the outer boundary of the quilt: nothing gets on the quilt which is naturist, sexist, racist, classist, and so forth.

Second, ecofeminism is a contextualist ethic. It involves a shift *from* a conception of ethics as primarily a matter of rights, rules, or principles predetermined and applied in specific cases to entities viewed as competitors in the contest of moral standing, *to* a conception of ethics as growing out of what Jim Cheney calls "defining relationships," i.e., relationships conceived in some sense as defining who one is.[30] As a contextualist ethic, it is not that rights, or rules, or principles are *not* relevant or important. Clearly they are in certain contexts and for certain purposes.[31] It is just that what *makes* them relevant or important is that those to whom they apply are entities *in relationship with* others.

Ecofeminism also involves an ethical shift *from* granting moral consideration to nonhumans *exclusively* on the grounds of some similarity they share with humans (e.g., rationality, interests, moral agency, sentiencey, right-holder status) to "a highly contextual account to see clearly what a human being is and what the nonhuman world might be, morally speaking, *for* human beings."[32] For an ecofeminist, *how* a moral agent is in relationship to another becomes of central significance, not simply *that* a moral agent is a moral agent or is bound by rights, duties, virtue, or utility to act in a certain way.

Third, ecofeminism is structurally pluralistic in that it presupposes and maintains difference—difference among humans as well as between humans and at least some elements of nonhuman nature. Thus, while ecofeminism denies the "nature/culture" split, it affirms that humans are both members of an ecological community (in some respects) and different from it (in other respects). Ecofeminism's attention to relationships and community is not, therefore, an erasure of difference but a respectful acknowledgment of it.

Fourth, ecofeminism reconceives theory as theory in process. It focuses on patterns of meaning which emerge, for instance, from the storytelling and first-person narratives of women (and others) who deplore the twin dominations of woman and nature. The use of narrative is one way to ensure that the content ot the ethic—the pattern of the quilt—may/will change over time, as the historical and material realities of women's lives change and as more is learned about women-nature connections and the destruction of the nonhuman world.[33]

Fifth, ecofeminism is inclusivist. It emerges from the voices of women who experience the harmful domination of nature and the way that domination is tied to their domination as women. It emerges from listening to the voices of indigenous peoples such as Native Americans who have been dislocated from their land and have witnessed the attendant undermining of such values as appropriate reciprocity, sharing, and kinship that characterize traditional Indian culture. It emerges from listening to voices of those who, like Nathan Hare, critique traditional approaches to envionmental ethics as white and bourgeois, and as failing to address issues of "black ecology" and the "ecology" of the inner city and urban spaces.[34] It also emerges out of the voices of Chipko women who see the destruction of "earth, soil, and water" as intimately connected with their own ability to survive economically.[35] With its emphasis on inclusivity and difference, ecofeminism provides a framework for recognizing that what counts as ecology and what counts as appropriate conduct toward both human and nonhuman environments is largely a matter of context.

Sixth, as a feminism, ecofeminism makes no attempt to provide an "objective" point of view. It is a social ecology. It recognizes the twin dominations of women and nature as social problems rooted both in very concrete, historical, socioeconomic circumstances and in oppressive patriarchal conceptual frameworks which maintain and sanction these circumstances.

Seventh, ecofeminism makes a central place for values of care, love, friendship, trust, and appropriate reciprocity—values that presuppose that our relationships to others are central to our understanding of who we are.[36] It thereby gives voice to the sensitivity that in climbing a mountain, one is doing something in relationship with an "other," an "other" whom one can come to care about and treat respectfully.

Lastly, an ecofeminist ethic involves a reconception of what it means to be human, and of what human ethical behavior consists. Ecofeminism denies abstract individualism. Humans are who we are in large part by virtue of the historical and social contexts and the relationships we are in, including our relationships with nonhuman nature. Relationships are not something extrinsic to who we are, not an "add on" feature of human nature; they play an essential role in shaping what it is to be human. Relationships of humans to the nonhuman environment are, in part, constitutive of what it is to be a human.

By making visible the interconnections among the dominations of women and nature, ecofeminism shows that both are feminist issues and that explicit acknowledgment of both is vital to any responsible environmental ethic. Feminism *must* embrace ecological feminism if it is to end the domination of women because the domination of women is tied conceptually and historically to the domination of nature.

A responsible environmental ethic also *must* embrace feminism. Otherwise, even the seemingly most revolutionary, liberational, and holistic ecological ethic will fail to take seriously the interconnected dominations of nature and women that are so much a part of the historical legacy and conceptual framework that sanctions the exploitation of nonhuman nature. Failure to make visible these interconnected, twin dominations results in an inaccurate account of how it is that nature has been and continues to be dominated and exploited and produces an environmental ethic that lacks the depth necessary to be truly *inclusive* of the realities of persons who at least in dominant Western culture have been intimately tied with that exploitation, viz., women. Whatever else can be said in favor of such holistic ethics, a failure to make visible ecofeminist insights into the common denominators of the twin oppressions of women and nature is to perpetuate, rather than overcome, the source of that oppression.

This last point deserves further attention. It may be objected that as long as the end result is "the same"—the development of an environmental ethic which does not emerge out of or reinforce an oppressive conceptual framework—it does not matter whether that ethic (or the ethic endorsed in getting there) is feminist or not. Hence, it simply is *not* the case that any adequate environmental ethic must be feminist. My argument, in contrast, has been that it *does* matter, and for three important reasons. First, there is the scholarly issue of accurately representing historical reality, and that, ecofeminists claim, requires acknowledging the historical feminization of nature and naturalization of women as part of the exploitation of nature. Second, I have shown that the conceptual connections between the domination of women and the domination of nature are located in an oppressive and, at least in Western societies, patriarchal conceptual framework characterized by a logic of domination. Thus, I have shown that failure to notice the nature of this connection leaves at best an incomplete, inaccurate, and partial account of what is required of a conceptually adequate environmental ethic. An ethic which *does not* acknowledge this is simply *not* the same as one that does, whatever else the similarities between them. Third, the claim that, in contemporary culture, one can have an adequate environmental ethic which is *not* feminist assumes that, in contemporary culture, the label *feminist* does not add anything crucial to the nature or description of environmental ethics. I have shown that at least in contemporary culture this is false, for the word *feminist* currently helps to clarify just *how* the domination of nature is conceptually linked to patriarchy and, hence, how the liberation of nature, is conceptually linked to the termination of patriarchy. Thus, because it has critical bite in contemporary culture, it serves as an important reminder that in contemporary sex-gendered, raced, classed, and naturist culture, an unlabeled position fuctions as a privileged and "unmarked" postition. That is, without the addition of the word *feminist*, one presents environmental ethics as if it has no bias, including male-gender bias, which is just what ecofeminists deny: failure to notice the connections between the twin oppressions of women and nature *is* male-gender bias.

One of the goals of feminism is the eradication of all oppressive sex-gender (and related race, class, age, affectional preference) categories and the creation of a world in which *difference does not breed domination*— say, the world of 4001. If in 4001 an "adequate environmental ethic" is a "feminist environmental ethic," the word *feminist* may then be redundant and unnecesary. However, this is *not* 4001, and in terms of the current historical and conceptual reality the dominations of nature and of women are intimately connected. Failure to notice or make visible that connection in 1990 perpetuates the mistaken (and privileged) view that "environmental ethics" is *not* a feminist issue, and that *feminist* adds nothing to environmental ethics.[37]

CONCLUSION

I have argued in this paper that ecofeminism provides a framework for a distinctively feminist and environmental ethic. Ecofeminism grows out of the felt and theorized-about connections between the domination of women and the domination of nature. As a contextualist ethic, ecofeminism refocuses environmental ethics on what nature might mean, morally speaking, *for* humans, and on how the relational attitudes of humans to others—humans as well as nonhumans—sculpt both what it is to be human and the nature and ground of human responsibilities to the nonhuman environment. Part of what this refocusing does is to take seriously the voices of women and other oppressed persons in the construction of that ethic.

A Sioux elder once told me a story about his son. He sent his seven-year-old son to live with the child's grandparents on a Sioux reservation so that he could "learn the Indian ways." Part of what the grandparents taught the son was how to hunt the four leggeds of the forest. As I heard the story, the boy was taught "to shoot your four-legged brother in his hind area, slowing it down but not killing it. Then, take the four legged's head in your hands, and look into his eyes. The eyes are where all the suffering is. Look into your brother's eyes and feel his pain. Then, take your knife and cut the four-legged under his chin, here, on his neck, so that he dies quickly. And as you do, ask your brother, the four-legged, for forgiveness for what you do. Offer also a prayer of thanks to your four-legged kin for offering his body to you just now, when you need food to eat and clothing to wear. And promise the four-legged that you will put yourself back into the earth when you die, to become nourishment for the earth, and for the sister flowers, and for the brother deer. It is appropriate that you should offer this blessing for the four-legged and, in due time, reciprocate in turn with your body in this way, as the four-legged gives life to you for your survival." As I reflect upon that story, I am struck by the power of the environmental ethic that grows out of and takes seriously narrative, context, and such values and relational attitudes as care, loving perception, and appropriate reciprocity, and doing what is appropriate in a given situation—however that notion of appropriateness eventually gets filled out. I am also struck by what one is able to see, once one begins to explore some of the historical and conceptual connections between the dominations of women and of nature. A *re-conceiving* and *re-visioning* of both feminism and environmental ethics, is, I think, the power and promise of ecofeminism.

NOTES

This essay first appeared in *Environmental Ethics* 12(2), 1990: 125–46. It is reprinted here with permission.

Earlier versions of this paper were presented at the American Philosophical Association Meeting in New York City, December 1987, and at the University of Massachusetts, April 1988. The author wishes to thank the following people for their helpful comments and support: Bob Ackerman, Kim Brown, Jim Cheney, Mahmoud El-Kati, Eric Katz, Michael Keenan, Ruthanne Kurth-Schai, Greta Gaard, Roxanne Gudeman, Alison Jaggar, H. Warren-Jones, Gareth Matthews, Michal McCall, Patrick D. Murphy, Bruce Nordstrom, Nancy Shea, Nancy Tuana, Bob Weinstock-Collins, Henry West, and the anonymous referees of *Environmental Ethics*.

1. Explicit ecological feminist literature includes works from a variety of scholarly perspectives and sources. Some of these works are Leonie Caldecott and Stephanie Leland, eds., *Reclaim the Earth: Women Speak Out for Life on Earth* (London: The Women's Press, 1983); Jim Cheney, "Eco-Feminism and Deep Ecology," *Environmental Ethics* 9 (1987): 115–45; Andrée Collard with Joyce Contrucci, *Rape of the Wild: Man's Violence against Animals and the Earth* (Bloomington: Indiana University Press, 1988); Katherine Davies, "Historical Associations: Women and the Natural World," *Women & Environments* 9, no. 2 (Spring 1987): 4–6; Sharon Doubiago, "Deeper than Deep Ecology: Men Must Become Feminists," in *The New Catalyst Quarterly*, no. 10 (Winter 1987/88): 10–11: Brian Easlea, *Science and Sexual Oppression: Patriarchy's Confrontation with Women and Nature* (London: Weidenfeld & Nicolson, 1981); Elizabeth Dodson Gray, *Green Paradise Lost* (Wellesley, Mass.: Roundtable Press, 1979); Susan Griffin, *Women and Nature: The Roaring inside Her* (San Francisco: Harper and Row, 1978); Joan L. Griscom, "On Healing the Nature/History Split in Feminist Thought," in *Heresies #13: Feminism and Ecology* 4, no. 1 (1981): 4–9; Ynestra King "The Ecology of Feminism and the Feminism of Ecology," in *Healing Our Wounds: The Power of Ecological Feminism*, ed. Judith Plant (Boston: New

Society Publishers, 1989), pp. 18–28; "The Eco-feminist Imperative," in *Reclaim the Earth*, ed. Caldecott and Leland (London: The Women's Press, 1983), pp. 12–16, "Feminism and the Revolt of Nature," in *Heresies #13: Feminism and Ecology* 4, no. 1 (1981): 12–16, and "What is Ecofeminism?" *The Nation*, 12 December 1987; Marti Kheel, "Animal Liberation Is a Feminist Issue," *The New Catalyst Quarterly*, no. 10 (Winter 1987/88): 8–9; Carolyn Merchant, *The Death of Nature: Women, Ecology and the Scientific Revolution* (San Francisco, Harper and Row, 1980); Patrick Murphy, ed., "Feminism, Ecology, and the Future of the Humanities," special issue of *Studies in the Humanities* 15, no. 2 (December 1988); Abby Peterson and Carolyn Merchant, " 'Peace with the Earth': Women and the Environmental Movement in Sweden," *Women's Studies International Forum* 9, no. 5–6 (1986): 465–79; Judith Plant, "Searching for Common Ground: Ecofeminism and Bioregionalism," in *The New Catalyst Quarterly*, no. 10 (Winter 1987/88): 6–7; Judith Plant, ed., *Healing Our Wounds: The Power of Ecological Feminism* (Boston: New Society Publishers, 1989); Val Plumwood, "Ecofeminism: An Overview and Discussion of Positions and Arguments," *Australasian Journal of Philosophy*, Supplement to vol. 64 (June 1986): 120–37; Rosemary Radford Ruether, *New Woman/New Earth: Sexist Ideologies & Human Liberation* (New York: Seabury Press, 1975); Kirkpatrick Sale, "Ecofeminism—A New Perspective," *The Nation* 26 September 1987: 302–305; Ariel Kay Salleh, "Deeper than Deep Ecology: The Eco-Feminist Connection," *Environmental Ethics* 6 (1984): 339–45, and "Epistemology and the Metaphors of Production: An Eco-Feminist Reading of Critical Theory," in *Studies in the Humanities* 15 (1988): 130–39; Vandana Shiva, *Staying Alive: Women, Ecology and Development* (London: Zed Books, 1988); Charlene Spretnak, "Ecofeminism: Our Roots and Flowering," *The Elmswood Newsletter*, Winter Solstice 1988; Karen J. Warren, "Feminism and Ecology: Making Connections," *Environmental Ethics* 9 (1987): 3–21; "Toward an Ecofeminist Ethic," *Studies in the Humanities* 15 (1988): 140–156; Miriam Wyman, "Explorations of Ecofeminism," *Women & Environments* (Spring 1987): 6–7; Iris Young, " 'Feminism and Ecology' and 'Women and Life on Earth: Eco-Feminism in the '80s'," *Environmental Ethics* 5 (1983): 173–80; Michael Zimmerman, "Feminism, Deep Ecology, and Environmental Ethics," *Environmental Ethics* 9 (1987): 21–44.

2. Françoise d'Eaubonne, *Le Feminisme ou la Mort* (Paris: Pierre Horay, 1974), pp. 213–52.

3. I discuss this in my paper "Toward an Ecofeminist Ethic."

4. The account offered here is a revision of the account given earlier in my paper "Feminism and Ecology: Making Connections." I have changed the account to be about "oppressive" rather than strictly "patriarchal" conceptual frameworks in order to leave open the possibility that there may be some patriarchal conceptual frameworks (e.g., in non-Western cultures) which are *not* properly characterized as based on value dualisms.

5. Murray Bookshin, "Social Ecology versus 'Deep Ecology'," in *Green Perspectives: Newsletter of the Green Program Project*, no. 4–5 (Summer 1987): 9.

6. It may be that in contemporary Western society, which is so thoroughly structured by categories of gender, race, class, age, and affectional orientation, there simply is no meaningful notion of "value-hierarchical thinking" which does not function in an oppressive context. For purposes of this paper, I leave that question open.

7. Many feminists who argue for the historical point that claims (B1) and (B2) have been asserted or assumed to be true within the dominant Western philosophical tradition do so by discussion of that tradition's conceptions of reason, rationality, and science. For a sampling of the sorts of claims made within that context, see "Reason, Rationality, and Gender," ed. Nancy Tuana and Karen J. Warren, a special issue of the American Philosophical Association's *Newsletter on Feminism and Philosophy* 88, no. 2 (March 1989): 17–71. Ecofeminists who claim that (B2) has been assumed to be true within the dominant Western philosophical tradition include: Gray, *Green Paradise Lost*; Griffin, *Woman and Nature: The Roaring inside Her*; Merchant, *The Death of Nature*; Ruether, *New Woman/New Earth*. For a discussion of some of these ecofeminist historical accounts, see Plumwood, "Ecofeminism." While I agree that the historical connections between the domination of women and the domination of nature is a crucial one, I do not argue for that claim here.

8. Ecofeminists who deny (B1) when (B1) is offered as anything other than a true, descriptive, historical claim about patriarchal culture often do so on grounds that an objectionable sort of biological determinism, or at least harmful female sex-gender stereotypes, underlie (B1). For a discussion of this "split" among those ecofeminists ("nature feminists") who assert and those ecofeminists ("social feminists") who deny (B1) as anything other than a true historical claim about how women are described in patriarchal culture, see Griscom, "On Healing the Nature/History Split."

9. I make no attempt here to defend the historically sanctioned truth of these premises.

10. See, e.g., bell hooks, *Feminist Theory: From Margin to Center* (Boston: South End Press, 1984), pp. 51–52.

11. Maria Lugones, "Playfulness, 'World-Travelling,' and Loving Perception," *Hypatia* 2, no. 2 (Summer 1987): 3.

12. At an *experiential* level, some women are "women of color," poor, old, lesbian, Jewish, and physically challenged. Thus, if feminism is going to liberate these women, it also needs to end the racism, classism, heterosexism, anti-Semitism, and discrimination against the handicapped that is constitutive of their oppression as black, or Latina, or poor, or older, or lesbian, or Jewish, or physically challenged women.

13. This same sort of reasoning shows that feminism is also a movement to end racism, classism, age-ism, heterosexism and other "isms," which are based in oppressive conceptual frameworks characterized by a logic of domination. However, there is an important caveat: ecofeminism is *not* compatible with all

feminisms and all environmentalisms. For a discussion of this point, see my article "Feminism and Ecology: Making Connections." What it *is* compatible with is the minimal condition characterization of feminism as a movement to end sexism that is accepted by all contemporary feminisms (liberal, traditional Marxist, radical, socialist, Blacks and non-Western).

14. See, e.g. Gray, *Green Paradise Lost*; Griffin, *Women and Nature*; Merchant, *The Death of Nature*; and Ruether, *New Woman/New Earth*.

15. Suppose, as I think is the case, that a necessary condition for the existence of a moral relationship is that at least one party to the relationship is a moral being (leaving open for our purposes what counts as a "moral being"). If this is so, then the Mona Lisa cannot properly be said to have or stand in a moral relationship with the wall on which she hangs, and a wolf cannot have or properly be said to have or stand in a moral relationship with a moose. Such a necessary-condition account leaves open the question whether *both* parties to the relationship must be moral beings. My point here is simply that however one resolves *that* question, recognition of the relationships themselves as a locus of value is a recognition of a source of value that is different from and not reducible to the values of the "moral beings" in those relationships.

16. It is interesting to note that the image of being friends with the Earth is one which cytogeneticist Barbara McClintock uses when she describes the importance of having "a feeling for the organism," "listening to the material [in this case the corn plant]," in one's work as a scientist. See Evelyn Fox Keller, "Women, Science, and Popular Mythology," in *Machina Ex Dea: Feminist Perspectives on Technology*, ed. Joan Rothschild (New York: Pergamon Press, 1983), and Evelyn Fox Keller, *A Feeling for the Organism: The Life and Work of Barbara McClintock* (San Francisco: W. H. Freeman, 1983).

17. Cheney, "Eco-Feminism and Deep Ecology," 144.

18. Marilyn Frye, "In and Out of Harm's Way: Arrogance and Love," *The Politics of Reality* (Trumansburg, New York: The Crossing Press, 1983), pp. 66–72.

19. Ibid., pp. 75–76.

20. Maria Lugones. "Playfulness," p. 3.

21. Cheney makes a similar point in "Eco-Feminism and Deep Ecology," p. 140.

22. Ibid., p. 138.

23. This account of a feminist ethic draws on my paper "Toward an Eco-feminist Ethic."

24. Marilyn Frye makes this point in her illuminating paper "The Possibility of Feminist Theory," read at the American Philosophical Association Central Division Meetings in Chicago, 29 April-1 May 1986. My discussion of feminist theory is inspired largely by that paper and by Kathryn Addelson's paper "Moral Revolution," in *Women and Values: Reading in Recent Feminist Philosophy*, ed. Marilyn Pearsall (Belmont, Calif.: Wadsworth Publishing Co., 1986), pp. 291–309.

25. Notice that the standard of inclusiveness does not exclude the voices of men. It is just that those voices must cohere with the voices of women.

26. For a more in-depth discussion of the notions of impartiality and bias, see my paper "Critical Thinking and Feminism," *Informal Logic* 10, no. 1 (Winter 1988): 31–44.

27. The burgeoning literature on these values is noteworthy. See, e.g., Carol Gilligan, *In a Different Voice: Psychological Theories and Women's Development* (Cambridge: Harvard University Press, 1982); *Mapping the Moral Domain: A Contribution of Women's Thinking to Psychological Theory and Education*, ed. Carol Gilligan, Janie Victoria Ward, and Jill McLean Taylor with Betty Bardige (Cambridge: Harvard University Press, 1988); Nel Noddings, *Caring: A Feminine Approach to Ethics and Moral Education* (Berkeley: University of California Press, 1984); Maria Lugones and Elizabeth V. Spelman, "Have We Got a Theory for You! Feminist Theory, Cultural Imperialism, and the Women's Voice," *Women's Studies International Forum* 6 (1983): 573–81; Maria Lugones, "Playfulness"; Annette C. Baier, "What Do Women Want in a Moral Theory?" *Nous* 19 (1985): 53–63.

28. Jim Cheney would claim that our fundamental relationships to one another as moral agents are not as moral agents to rights holders, and that whatever rights a person properly may be said to have are relationally defined rights, not rights possessed by atomistic individuals conceived as Robinson Crusoes who do not exist essentially in relation to others. On this view, even rights talk itself is properly conceived as growing out of a relational ethic, not vice versa.

29. Alison Jaggar, *Feminist Politics and Human Nature* (Totowa, N.J.: Rowman and Allanheld, 1980), pp. 42–44.

30. Henry West has pointed out that the expression "defining relations" is ambiguous. According to West, "the 'defining' as Cheney uses it is an adjective, not a principle—it is not that ethics defines relationships; it is that ethics grows out of conceiving of the relationships that one is in as defining what the individual is."

31. For example, in relationships involving contracts or promises, those relationships might be correctly described as that of moral agent to rights holders. In relationships involving mere property, those relationships might be correctly described as that of moral agent to objects having only instrumental value, "relationships of instrumentality." In comments on an earlier draft of this paper, West suggested that possessive individualism, for instance, might be recast in such a way that an individual is defined by his or her property relationships.

32. Cheney, "Eco-Feminism and Deep Ecology," p. 144.

33. One might object that such permission for change opens the door for environmental exploitation. This is not the case. An ecofeminist ethic is anti-naturist. Hence, the unjust domination and exploitation of nature is a "boundary condition" of the ethic; no such actions are sanctioned or justified on ecofeminist grounds. What it *does* leave open is some leeway about what counts as domina-

tion and exploitation. This, I think, is a strength of the ethic, not a weakness, since it acknowledges that *that* issue cannot be resolved in any practical way in the abstract, independent of a historical and social context.

34. Nathan Hare, "Black Ecology" in *Environmental Ethics*, ed. K. S. Shrader-Frechette (Pacific Grove, Calif.: Boxwood Press, 1981), pp. 229–36.

35. For an ecofeminist discussion of the Chipko movement, see my "Toward an Ecofeminist Ethic," and Shiva's *Staying Alive*.

36. See Cheney, "Eco-Feminism and Deep Ecology," p. 122.

37. I offer the same sort of reply to critics of ecofeminism such as Warwick Fox who suggest that for the sort of ecofeminism I defend, the word *feminist* does not add anything significant to environmental ethics and, consequently, that an ecofeminist like myself might as well call herself a deep ecologist. He asks: "Why doesn't she just call it [i.e., Warren's vision of a transformative feminism] deep ecology? Why specifically attach the label *feminist* to it . . . ?" (Warwick Fox, "The Deep Ecology—Ecofeminism and Its Parallels," *Environmental Ethics* 11, no. 1 [1989]: 14, n. 22). Whatever the important similarities between deep ecology and ecofeminism (or, specifically, my version of ecofeminism)—and, indeed, there are many—it is precisely my point here that the word *feminist* does add something significant to the conception of environmental ethics, and that any environmental ethic (including deep ecology) that fails to make explicit the different kinds of interconnections among the domination of nature and the domination of women will be, from a feminist (and ecofeminist) perspective such as mine, inadequate.

Toward Thoughtful
Ecofeminist Activism

CHRIS CUOMO

If ecofeminism is a theory, a movement, and/or a critique which aims to address the intersecting oppressions of women, nature, people of color, the poor, and others categorized as inferior by phallocratic systems, then what counts as ecofeminist activism? In other words, how might nontheoretical yet self-consciously ecofeminist practice address multiplicitous and shifting causes and aspects of oppression? How can we understand an activism that is dialectically related to theory and that has decentered targets and objectives? Ecofeminists need to explore these questions and move toward the creation of a significant, self-consciously ecofeminist activist movement if ecofeminism is to be instrumental in shaping significant social change.

A large amount of self-consciously ecofeminist work, that is, work labeled "ecofeminist" by the people doing it, is written work, and much of that is the kind of work that is generally categorized as "theoretical." Many ecofeminist writers are concerned with ethical questions and issues, although a growing number are exploring the possibilities of ecofeminist epistemologies and ontologies. In the following pages I will attempt to articulate how this kind of work can intersect with other kinds of political activity by looking closely at the relationship between ethical theory and applied ethics. Although I will be using concepts such as "theory," "practice," and "activism," I believe that these categories are not fixed, separate, distinct, or solid. I am tempted to avoid fixing these concepts by referring to them with phrases like "so-called theory" and "what feminists generally refer to as 'activism,' " but alongside my acknowledgment of the slipperiness of the space between the concepts "theory" and "practice," I want also to recognize the differences in the ways those words are actually used. In order to negotiate the ambiguous middle space, I will ground my uses of the concepts of theory and practice in definitions developed by John Dewey.

Webster's defines activism as "the doctrine or policy of taking positive, direct action to achieve an end, especially a political or social end," and direct action as "action directly at achieving an objective; esp., the use of strikes, demonstrations, civil disobedience, etc. in disputes or struggles for rights" (*Webster's New World Dictionary*, 1994). Activism is conscious, purposeful, political activity. Now, there is no reason to assume that holding a demonstration has any more *direct* impact on a situation than publishing an article does, though there are significant differences between these two forms of activity. Theoretical writing addresses its specific audience with words on paper; it aims to directly engage the intellect. As a practice, it can appear incredibly disembodied or can entail abstraction from the body. Even the author who writes forthrightly and explicitly from her bodily experience cannot be certain of the extent to which her audience will be consciously embodied, or accepting, of the writer's embodiment. Nonetheless, critical perspectives that consider the product of writing to be disembodied text created by the mind encourage a problematic, hard dualism which marks intellectual activity as separate from and superior to physical activity. Writing theory is an activity, a physical activity, though it is lived through the body in ways generally different from activities like painting or marching. Given this, it is not nonsensical to think of theory as a form of activism—as a practice.

The "other" kind of activism—the work that students refer to when they say, "I don't want to do theory; I'm interested in *activism*"—is unmistakably bodily. It directly puts one face up against another, it lays its body down on the street, it yells and claps and breaks things, it sits down and stands up, and it can be photographed and then seen on TV and in the newspaper. Yet this activity is not unintellectual. It can be conceptually grounded, transgressive, and influential, and its effectiveness often rests on the creativity of its language. Activism entails movement, and this movement can be theoretical and thoughtful, as well as physical.

Thus far, the relationship between ecofeminist theory and activism has been somewhat backward-looking: Ecofeminist theorists tend to cite various instances and forms of feminist and environmental activism and claim them as ecofeminist. Examples of activist movements claimed by ecofeminists include the Chipko movement in India, the global fight for women's reproductive freedom, the "woman-centered" peace and antinuclear movements, and the fight for animal rights. Although these movements have not often been self-consciously constructed as ecofeminist, theorists lay claim to them insofar as the movements explicitly or implicitly acknowledge and address, at the very least, ways in which sexism and misogyny are related to human maltreatment of the environment and its members (Lahar 1990).

The lack of a significant, easily identifiable ecofeminist activist movement in the United States makes me curious about the possibility of an ecofeminist activism that is not centered around creating, disseminating, or understanding the written word. If the term "ecofeminist" is not to serve merely as an umbrella term under which various forms and instances of activism are retroactively classified, what other kinds of ecofeminist activist practices are possible? I believe that ecofeminist activism is necessary and significant and that ecofeminists should be concerned with both claiming various activisms as ecofeminist and creating and motivating specifically, stridently, self-consciously ecofeminist activisms. An emphasis on the dialectical relationship between theory and practice can ground rich, politically strategic, thoughtful ecofeminist practice.

I. BETWEEN ETHICAL THEORY AND APPLIED ETHICS

In "Toward a Bread and Butter Pragmatism: The Significance of Practical Activity in the Philosophy of John Dewey," Lisa Heldke argues that Dewey offers a valuable analysis of the relationship between theory and practice, one which "impel(s) a radical rethinking of the way that philosophical attention has been distributed over human endeavors," and "reconnect(s) the practice of philosophy to ordinary concerns—the emotional, intellectual, and practical affairs of daily life" (Heldke 1994, 1–2). Despite the fact that much of Dewey's work is based on the premise that philosophy should start with practices, or "common experiences," Heldke believes he fails to adequately consider the philosophical significance of much common experience, especially of rudimentary, daily practices typically identified as the work of women, slaves, servants, and laborers (Heldke 1994, 3). Although Heldke is critical of Dewey's own theoretical practice, she and other feminist philosophers have shown the usefulness of Dewey's critique of the hierarchical dichotomy between theory and practice, and his assertions that theory making is actually a form of practice (1993, Bickford, Kaufman-Osborn, Nelson, Rooney, Seigfried). In light of Dewey's articulations of the relatedness of theory and practice, Heldke characterizes theoretical work as a form of "thoughtful practice" (Heldke 1994, 9). I find this concept useful for describing the kind ecofeminist theory I recommend below, and I also believe it opens up possibilities for understanding the thoughtfulness of practice that is not formally theoretical.

The dualistic understanding of theory and practice against which Dewey argues, and which is still assumed in some feminist and other political circles, rests on presuppositions similar to those behind some philosophers' characterizations of the differences between ethical theory and applied ethics. Those philosophers think of environmental ethics and feminist ethics as examples of applied ethics: In environmental ethics we apply ethical theory to environmental problems (e.g., is it ethical to cause pain to nonhuman animals?), and in feminist ethics we apply ethical theory to feminist issues (e.g., is it fair to pay women less than men for the same work?). But to conceive of the field of applied ethics in this manner is to misunderstand the relationship between ethical theory and ethical decision making. Further, to characterize feminist, environmental and, hence, ecofeminist ethics this way is to misrepresent much of that work. In fact, as philosophical work in these fields often locates itself in spaces where abstraction and material practice intersect and inform each other, many "practical" feminist and environmental considerations have resulted in dramatic conceptual shifts.

Philosophers tend to refer to ethical theory and applied ethics as though they are significantly separate spheres. Such separation rests partially on the assumption that ethical theory gives us abstract truths about what is right and wrong or good and bad, and those truths are applied to real ethical dilemmas in the field of applied ethics. Certainly it is no secret that ethical theory has traditionally been constructed abstractly. The work of Kant, Mill, and Rawls evinces the belief that the best way to explore notions of what is right, good, or just is to consider concepts in the abstract, guided by questions such as: To what do the words generally refer? How are they used? What might the most pure interpretation of the concepts resemble? The abstraction, universality, and presumed objectivity of such ethical theory render it closer to empirical science and, hence, more philosophically sophisticated than applied ethics, in which philosophers consider the details of material contingencies and the difficulties of actual ethical practices.

Abstract ethical queries are not without merit. They have at times helped to reorient intellectuals, and even larger sectors of societies, toward certain values and away from others. They have helped to clarify thinking about particular examples of ethical decision making (especially about the ways philosophers conceptualize ethical dilemmas); about the realm of ethical thought; and about the relationships among ethics, law, religion, and other social and political systems. They have also sometimes provided helpful frameworks through which to ask whether social values and conceptions of right behavior and good character are justified, consistent, or attainable.

But ethical theory *in and of itself* does not actually help people live better lives. First of all, ethical theory is not necessary for ethical life. In fact, most people who could be said to live "good" lives have had absolutely no exposure to ethical theory. Second, I would assert that those students, philosophers, and other interested parties who are exposed to formal ethical theory do not accept a theory based on its abstract elegance and then, subsequently, apply it in appropriate moments of ethical uncertainty. Rather, we begin with our experiences—our practical expertise in "applied ethics"—and we evaluate and recreate ethical theory from there. Sometimes the theory, or aspects of it, rings true. Often, finding it inadequate to address our real ethical problems, we discover places where the theory must be modified. Sometimes we abandon theories altogether because they have absolutely no relevance to ethical practice. In other instances we find theories wholly irrelevant to real problem solving, yet we continue to discuss them because of their historical significance or beautiful logic.

One might ask whether ethical theory, or the work of those who consider themselves to be experts in the field of ethics, *should* do anything but critically analyze ethical concepts. Isn't the work of philosophy to clarify concepts, analyze assumptions, and identify implications? But even the history of traditional, male, Western ethical theory counters such assertions. Many ethical theorists, including Socrates, Hume, Bentham, and Mill, are said to have been motivated not merely by a love of pure wisdom, but also by a desire to discover how to live good lives and a wish to motivate, inspire, and educate others. The history of ethics is the story of both descriptive and prescriptive ventures, however subtle, indirect, and faulty those prescriptions may be. Its directives have generally been attempts to answer questions about how individual and social agents might live better lives and make good decisions. With the current social and environmental crises that face nearly all inhabitants of the planet, ethical thinkers are increasingly engaged by questions about how to best solve practical, material problems and what we can learn about goodness, right and wrong, relationships, and responsibility as we struggle to negotiate these problems. It is in the dialogue between ethical theory, or abstract ethical principles and values, and real-life ethical decision making, or practice, that we can learn about how to make better ethical and political decisions. Dewey's formulation of the relationship between theory and practice is helpful to ecofeminists insofar as it helps us conceptualize a dialectic in which written theoretical work and other practical work are seen as politically and philosophically necessary.

The central claim here is not merely about the practical relevance of theory. As Dewey writes in *The Quest for Certainty*, "Theory separated from concrete doing and making is empty and futile" (Dewey 1929, 281).[1] As Dewey's claim about the relationship between theory and practice suggests, ethical theory enables us to live better lives only when it informs and is informed by the decisions real people make in their lives—about how to interact with each other, how to act as members of groups, how to live respectfully even when conflict seems inevitable. Ecofeminist ethical theory, which is born out of the difficulty of solving real, complex, ethical problems, as well as out of frustration with the inadequacies of traditional ethical theories, must maintain its connection to real ethical dilemmas and those who must solve them while grappling with the abstract concepts and questions that inevitably arise from such problem solving.

Both environmental and feminist ethics illustrate the importance of the dialogue between ethical theory and applied ethics because both feminist and ecological perspectives have found traditional ethical theory severely lacking. Most traditional ethical theory gives us no way to adequately discuss and evaluate issues of gender and cross-species interaction because it does not even recognize the particular ethical relevance of women and nonhuman nature. Feminist philosophers were the first to discuss the extent to which traditional male ethical theorists devalue women as a group and to notice that the writings of those theorists provide very little guidance concerning the kinds of ethical problems typically faced by women. Attempts to create ethics that are more relevant to women, to include women's heretofore ignored voices in ethical theory, and to respond to other feminist critiques of traditional ethics have led to a veritable revolution in ethics. Likewise, Aldo Leopold (1970) recognized that traditional Western ethical systems are inadequate when the problems at hand include nonhuman entities and that to acknowledge the inherent moral value of natural entities is to expand the range of ethical thought. He, too, wrote of moral revolution.

Feminist and environmental ethics also press us to question the very nature and relevance of ethical inquiry. Though ecofeminist theory is not a simple hybrid of feminist and environmental philosophies, I argue elsewhere that a helpful ecofeminist ethic incorporates the important insights, analyses, and innovations of both feminist and environmental ethics.[2] These analyses include highlighting the faults of traditional ethical thought, but also, more importantly, identifying the tremendous ethical and metaethical questions about who makes ethical decisions, where values and principles originate, and to whom or what they refer—questions appreciable most dramatically when we are ethical actors, not theorists.

II. AMONG THEORIES AND ACTIVISMS

Arguably the best way for ecofeminist ethics to maintain a position that transcends a dualistic understanding of theoretical and applied ethics, or theory and practice, is by strengthening its ties to various forms of ecofeminist activism and explicitly mapping out potential activist agendas and strategies. Stephanie Lahar argues that close links between theory and political activism are necessary for ecofeminism's vitality. She recommends the following examples:

> [Ecofeminism's] criticisms must continue to be acted upon by the expression of resistance through direct action on life-threatening issues (militarism, violence against women, the nuclear industry, pollutions and toxins, environmental destruction). . . . To fulfill a reconstructive potential, a social philosophy must extend a social critique and utopian vision into imperatives for action . . . for example, community forums on social or environmental issues and those at intersections such as biotechnology; state legislation supporting the civil rights and safety of groups that historically have had little political power; the reallocation of private and public resources and funds to socially responsible uses; alternative housing and land-use arrangements, and local alternative economic systems. (Lahar 1991, 35)

Emphasizing the extent to which theory making is thoughtful practice also entails deconstructing the privileges associated with theorizing. Possessors of those privileges have a responsibility to open up dialogues among various kinds of ecofeminist practices, making explicit both the practical potentials of theory and the theoretical value of activism without exaggerating the importance of theoretical skills or talents. As Susan Bickford writes:

> The very idea of democratic participation rests on the claim that all people possess, or are capable of developing through engagement, the skills or knowledge necessary for political deliberation and decision making. The thoughtfulness of citizens (be they lawyers, food servers, computer programmers) is what is needed for engaging in political deliberation, strategizing, and action. The knowledge that a theorist has and the skills she possesses *as theorist* do not make her a better citizen; only practice does that. Neither does the theorist's knowledge give her a better sense of what the end of political deliberation should be. What the theorist (qua theorist) can hope to provide is a better understanding of the nature and extent of political problems, the nature of the context in which they arise, and possible long-range implications of different courses of action. (Bickford 1993, 112)

Of course, ecofeminist philosophers and theorists can participate in activist projects not only as "private citizens" and community members, but also as skilled arguers and analysts. Philosophical training is a useful tool in a movement that depends on deconstructive rhetoric, persuasion, fleshing out the implications of policies, and envisioning alternative paradigms. Ecofeminist theorists should use these skills in not only the creation of articles, books, and lectures, but also in helping to make the more hand-dirtying steps toward change.

If ecofeminist theory is to meet both feminist and pragmatist epistemological agendas, as theory that begins with and addresses experience, it must be informed by practice. The reversal of Dewey's emphasis on the practical relevance of theory requires that lectures, books, and articles articulate knowledge and data that come from participation in activist projects. Theorists interested in creating ecofeminist philosophies must allow a variety of forms of experience and insight to inform our theories. We may consider our theoretical projects as more collaborative efforts and include our practical knowledge in our accounts and analyses. An incorporation of our own activist narratives can continue to enrich ecofeminist ethical theory by emphasizing the ties between ethical decision making, abstract ethical concepts, and personal experience. Given that the problems ethical agents now face seem to transcend greatly those considered by our historical predecessors in both scope and urgency, it seems only right that the perspectives from which we come to address our problems are ambitious, broad-based, and bold.

III. Ecofeminist Activism

As is the case with most political movements, the possibilities for ecofeminist activism are nearly limitless. Individuals make personal choices in light of their ecofeminist politics and may consider their recycling, their vegetarianism, their work against sexual assault, their antiracist work, or their protests against toxic dumping to be part of their ecofeminist activism. Insofar as ecofeminism influences personal choice, it is a contributor to social, ecological change. But ecofeminists also organize together to identify and work against interlocking systems of oppression that are harmful to women, people of color, the poor, the environment, and animals. If ecofeminist analyses and agendas are to have a wide-scale effect on contemporary understandings of the mechanisms and causes of oppression, and the interrelatedness of various social and environmental issues, these agendas must be presented and pursued in ways that make these connections clear. If ecofeminism is to have a prominent place in contemporary global politics and to significantly affect social and political decisions, ecofeminist activism must be identifiable, powerful, and complex. Hence I am calling for a multifaceted, decentered, loud, empowering ecofeminist activist movement. Though I do not know, nor would I want to dictate, the profile of such a movement, I believe helpful historical and contemporary models of such movements exist. The recent activities of ACT-UP (AIDS Coalition To Unleash Power) and the Lesbian Avengers, two direct-action political groups based in the United States, offer interesting models of activist movements that explicitly address the existence of interlocking systems of oppression and which have been effective in educating, annoying, or recruiting target audiences (as appropriate).

Both ACT-UP and the Lesbian Avengers effectively locate themselves at the intersections among various forms of oppression. This is accomplished through self-representation as well as political posturing. For example, an ACT-UP poster proclaiming, "Kissing Doesn't Kill—Greed and Indifference Do," pictures three biracial kissing couples: one lesbian, one gay, and one heterosexual. As these images confront racism and homophobia, the slogan locates contemporary racism and homophobia in the United States in the context of corporate, capitalist greed and social and political attempts to keep lesbians, the poor, and gay men invisible. The text also names the fact that these interlocking forces and silences have resulted in death. It is impossible to characterize this widely disseminated piece of political art as about just one issue; the basic message is that racism, greed, and homophobia are intrinsically related in contemporary, capitalist America.

Likewise, the work of the Lesbian Avengers, though far less slick and widely disseminated than that of ACT-UP, evidences the complexity of their analysis of the causes of lesbian invisibility (including homophobia, misogyny, classism, housing and health issues, and patriarchal fear of the radical potential of lesbian existence). Theater, humor, deconstructions and transgressions of gender and sexuality, and methodologies that are decidedly "in your face" contribute to the effective destabilization of the notion of single-issue politics. Activist approaches grounded in multiplicity question not only their obvious targets, but also standard notions of activism and political movement. The Lesbian Avengers emphasize that they are a "direct-action, activist group . . . for women want to be involved in activism, work in community, be creative, do shit-work, take responsibility on a regular basis, have their minds blown, change their opinions and share organizing skills" (1993).

It is no simple task to organize multidimensional, political, direct-action groups or events. In fact, complex political analyses and agendas are more likely than single-issue campaigns to spark conflict and disagreement. The activist model put forth by the Lesbian Avengers is particularly interesting in this regard, because although their overarching priority is to directly confront lesbian invisibility, they feel their abstract goals are best met by prioritizing action.

In closing, I do not want to neglect the fact that ecofeminists would be wise to remember the many lessons about political strategizing and organizing learned through histories of feminist movements, including points of interest ranging from methods of conflict resolution and fund-raising to spray-painting and wheat-pasting techniques. Ultimately, it is feminist insight that motivates ecofeminism and which demands meaningful action. As Bickford sums up:

> For feminists, it is the relation to practice (to women's lives and our attempts to change the world) that gives theory meaning. . . theorists can self-consciously counter their role as "privileged interpreters of society" by critiquing the "power of experts". . . . Theorists do have access to diffuse social, and specific institutional, resources. . . . We have the responsibility to use those resources in the service of what we say we believe (to paraphrase Audre Lorde) and in collaboration with those with whom we both claim and are trying to create solidarity. (Bickford 1993, 113)

NOTES

I would like to thank Lisa Heldke, Peter Godfrey-Smith, Felicia Kruse, and Linda Lopez McAlister for their helpful comments and support, and Diana Moyer for research assistance.

1. However, Heldke implies that Dewey's work only sufficiently vindicated *theory* and *theorists*, allowing theorists the comfort of understanding ourselves as meaningful, worldly actors when we engage in practices that are often remarkably, and perhaps needlessly, solitary and isolating. Though Dewey provided a rationale for also vindicating practice, Heldke convincingly argues that his own

theorizing fails to address the importance of common practice and does not give serious attention to the theoretical significance and power of those practices not directly manifested as argument, articulation, and explanation—in accord with the scientific model (1994, 9–10).

2. I don't mean to imply that what ought to count as ethically "helpful" or "important" is ever obvious. In an earlier essay (Cuomo 1992), I argue that aspects of feminist and environmental ethics that are used by ecofeminists should be critically analyzed and contextualized. Several of the papers in this collection also aim to do the theoretical work of articulating justifications for claims that some aspect of feminist or environmental philosophy is ecofeminist.

REFERENCES

Bickford, Susan. 1993. Why we listen to lunatics: Antifoundational theories and feminist politics. *Hypatia* 8(2): 104–23.

Cuomo, Christine J. 1992. Unravelling the problems in ecofeminism. *Environmental Ethics* 15(4):351–63.

Dewey, John. 1929. *The quest for certainty.* New York: Minton, Balch and Company.

Heldke, Lisa. 1994. Toward a bread and butter pragmatism: The significance of practical activity in the philosophy of John Dewey. Unpublished paper.

Kaufman-Osborn, Timothy V. 1993. Teasing feminist sense from experience. *Hypatia* 8(2):124–44.

Lahar, Stephanie. 1990. Ecofeminist theory and grassroots politics. *Hypatia* 6(1):28–45.

Leopold, Aldo. 1970. *A Sand County almanac.* New York: Ballantine Books.

Lesbian Avengers. 1993. Organizing flier.

Nelson, Lynn Hankinson. 1993. A question of evidence. *Hypatia* 8(2):172–89.

Rooney, Phyllis. 1993. Feminist-pragmatist revisionings of reason, knowledge, and philosophy. *Hypatia* 8(2):15–37.

Seigfried, Charlene Haddock. 1993. Shared communities of interest: Feminism and pragmatism. *Hypatia* 8(2):1–14.

Webster's new world dictionary of the English language. 1994. New York: Prentice Hall.

For information on the Lesbian Avengers, contact: The Lesbian Avengers, c/o The Center, 208 West 13th Street, New York, New York 10011.

For information on the AIDS Coalition to Unleash Power, contact: ACT-UP NY, 135 West 29th Street 10th Floor, New York, New York 10001.

Loving Your Mother:
On the Woman-Nature Relation

CATHERINE ROACH

The environmental movement seems to have gathered such momentum these days that wherever one looks one finds posters, bumper-stickers, slogans, advertisements, and other eco-paraphernalia urging us to do this or that in the name of environmental soundness. In this essay I want to examine one such poster from an ecofeminist point of view. This poster (which I have also seen in T-shirt and bumper-sticker incarnations) consists of a picture and a short phrase. The picture is of the Earth as seen from outer space with the phrase "Love Your Mother" printed beside it. I see this poster as a particularly interesting example of the relation that has often been posited between woman and nature and I will use the poster as an occasion to examine this relation in some detail.

Two aspects of the woman-nature link, treated respectively in the first and second halves of this essay, are of particular interest to me. The first aspect, and the one under which I will give most consideration to the "Love Your Mother" poster, concerns the perception of nature as female and, more specifically, as maternal. We speak of "Mother Nature" and "Mother Earth." How does the image of Earth as mother function in our patriarchal world, and how is the environment affected by this association with the female and the maternal? I argue that engendering the Earth as female mother, given the meaning and function traditionally assigned to "mother" and "motherhood" in patriarchal culture, will not achieve the desired aim of making our behaviour more environmentally sound, but will instead help to maintain the mutually supportive, exploitative stances we take toward our mothers and toward our environment. This analysis brings out one of the fundamental points of ecofeminism: the way we think about and treat the environment is related to the way we think about and treat women.

The second aspect of the woman-nature link concerns the perception of women as being closer to nature than are men, who are themselves perceived as being closer to culture. How are women affected by this association with nature? In examining this second aspect, I look at the ecofeminist debate on the question

Hypatia vol. 6, no. 1 (Spring 1991) © by Catherine Roach

of whether women are "closer to nature" and its implications for the dualism between nature and culture. I argue against the usefulness of this question and against the idea that nature and culture are dualistic and opposing concepts. I suggest that this question and this idea are environmentally unsound and that they need to be biodegraded, or rendered less harmful to the environment.

*
* *

I will structure my consideration of the first aspect of the woman-nature link, the aspect of nature as female, around a closer examination of the "Love Your Mother" environmental poster. The "mother" referred to in the poster is clearly "Mother Nature," the earth, the planet, the environment, the biosphere, or nature, whichever term one wishes to use (although, as I will discuss later, I think one's choice of terms is significant). The Earth is metaphorically equated with our mother. In directing us to love our mother, environmentalists employing this slogan communicate two messages to us. The first message, conveyed through the use of the imperative "love," is the exhortation to care for and maintain the health of the Earth. The second message, conveyed through the use of the term "mother," is that we are all closely tied to the environment, that our very existence derives from and depends on a healthy environment, as our existence once depended on a mother or mother-figures almost always female.[1]

The question then arises: why, if this is what they want to say, do they not simply say it? Why do these environmentalists choose to pass through the metaphor of loving one's mother in order to express their message of environmental soundness? The text is deceptive to the extent that although it does not refer to our real-life mothers, it nevertheless does seek to take advantage of the fact that certain ideas about motherhood and about the connection between the Earth and motherhood are often assumed as part of the way motherhood functions. These generally assumed ideas lend the slogan its aura of aptness. Two of these ideas are that we all should and can love our real-life mothers and that we all can intuitively grasp how the Earth is, in a sense, our mother. By imaging Earth as mother, the poster plays on our love for our real-life mothers.

How well does the metaphor of "mother" apply to the Earth? How appropriate a metaphor is this? On first consideration, the Earth or nature does seem to fit reasonably enough into the metaphor of "mother." After all, it is from the environment that we draw our oxygen, food, water, and all of the raw materials out of which we fashion the endless items that make up the materiality of our culture. The Earth or the environment is certainly life-giving and life-sustaining, as were and are our mothers. And yet the Earth is not our mother. Sallie McFague discusses the "is" and "is not" function of metaphors (1987, 33-35). A metaphor should both shock us (the "is not") and evoke recognition (the "is"); a metaphor is not a definition but a likely account. While I do not deny that the Earth is like our mothers in certain ways, because mothering and motherhood function problematically in patriarchal culture, the metaphorical equation of Earth or nature with mother also becomes problematical and to a certain degree unhealthy, both for women and for the environment.[2] For pragmatic reasons then, because of the exigencies of our environmental situation, I stress the "is not" of the Earth as our mother.[3]

Since this stress rests on the problematical nature of the meaning and function of "mother" and "motherhood," and since the poster's text makes reference, through the "is" of its metaphor, to our actual mothers, we need to ask first how motherhood functions for us humans and how we understand our love for our mothers and our mothers' love for us. It strikes me that we do not unambiguously love our mothers. Mothers' housework and child-rearing are unpaid and seldom recognized or appreciated by society, except in condescending eulogies of the joys of motherhood or of the ideal mother and in platitudes about motherhood and apple pie. Mothers are too often abandoned and left to raise their children without a father. Dorothy Dinnerstein in *The Mermaid and The Minotaur* (1976) explains how the sexual arrangement of women providing almost all early childhood care results in mothers becoming the targets for deeply ambivalent feelings. To a baby the caretaker appears all-powerful and caring but also capricious and malevolent. The baby thus comes to love and desire but also to hate and fear the caretaker. Because the mother is usually this caretaker, she rarely is a "clean" parent like the father. According to Dinnerstein, then, mothers bear the burden of being too powerful and mysterious because we were too completely dependent on them. Loving one's mother is a difficult task and that love is often to some extent ambivalent. To change this, as Dinnerstein and others have argued, we need to have mothers and fathers share equally in the task of child-rearing in order that both might then bear the brunt of infants' ambivalent feelings toward the early parent or parents.

Along with this ambivalence, Dorothy Dinnerstein explains how our sexual arrangements for parenting result in a merging of the categories of "woman" and "nature." To the infant, mother appears as a "global, inchoate, all-embracing presence," as unbounded and amorphous, as the "monolithic representative of nature" (1976, 93, 95). Because of this all of us, men and women alike, have trouble perceiving mothers as autonomous subjects. As Jessica Benjamin points out, "the view of mother as object resounds throughout our culture" (1988, 77). Mothers and women remain for us closer to object than to subject, closer to nature than to culture. "We cannot believe," as Dinnerstein notes, "how accidental, unconscious, unconcerned—i.e., unmotherly—nature really is; and we cannot believe how vulnerable, conscious, autonomously wishful—i.e., human—the early mother really was" (1976, 108). Elizabeth Dodson Gray makes the same point about the objectification of women and the personification of the environment when she notes how "as adults we still have difficulty believing our surroundings really are impersonal or, on the other hand, that our mothers are really fully human persons" (1982, 105). Our parenting arrangements of women being responsible for almost all early child care ensure that we hold tight to the childhood belief that our first, magic parent was a semihuman force of nature and the idea that nature is our semihuman mother.

If it is difficult for us to love our mothers and to perceive them as fully human, equally problematic is the way we expect our mothers to love us. This point is especially significant for environmentalists using the "Love Your Mother" slogan, for we expect our mothers to love us in a way we can never expect the environment to love us. *There is no "Mother Nature" wanting to nurture and care for us, no "Mother Earth" who loves us.* As Elizabeth Dodson Gray (1989) insists, we must withdraw our weighty projections and try to see clearly the Earth as Earth and not as the mother or female we have imagined the Earth to be. Instead of leading us to greater environmental soundness, the strategy of picturing the Earth as our mother could have the exact opposite effect. Mother in patriarchal culture is she who provides all of our sustenance and who makes disappear all of our waste products, she who satisfies all of our wants and needs endlessly and without any cost to us. Mother is she who loves us and will take care of us no matter what (Gray 1982, 102-5). The last thing the environmental movement should do is encourage us to think of the environment in these terms. Our ecological breakdown has arisen, in part, precisely from our attitude that nature is a storehouse of riches which will never empty and which we may use at will for any purpose we desire, without incurring any debt or obligation of replacement.

Luce Irigaray makes this last point in her book *Sexes et parentés* (1987). She observes that we act in the environment as if there were no cost attached to our use of natural resources, as if they existed purely for our use, and as if they would never be depleted. Our behaviour can be explained in part, she suggests, by the fact that we assume the mother will, without charge and without limit, nourish and care for the child in particular and for the man and society in general. We expect the same from "Mother Earth" as we do from mother. In an environmental context, the "Love Your Mother" slogan keeps these expectations intact. I am reminded here of a quote by the scientist and science writer Richard Feynman: "Let's face it, nature is absurd so accept nature as she is" (1989, 6). If Feynman is correct, then nature is not only female but also inherently absurd. Feynman's choice of the word absurd is interesting, for its definition as "irrational and ridiculous" derives from an etymological meaning of "completely deaf." Do we feel that nature is deaf to our calls and unresponsive to our needs? Do we hear echoed in Feynman's statement the plaintive whine of children who feel ignored by their mothers? Given the way motherhood functions now, it currently is not possible for us to love unambiguously the Earth as our mother, and loving the Earth as our mother would not necessarily help us to be more environmentally sound. For the slogan to be effective in encouraging environmentally sound behaviour, mothering would first have to be different.

The picture chosen to accompany the slogan "Love Your Mother" is itself significant. The picture is of the Earth as seen from outer space. It shows the full circle of the Earth swirled in its atmosphere, set alone in empty space. Although, on the positive side, this image reveals the oneness, beauty, and finiteness of the planet, it also shows the Earth as a remote ball suspended in space in a way we never at firsthand see or experience the planet, unless we are participating in a . multimillion dollar space project. This image is of the Earth as separate and very distant from our viewpoint, as an isolated object without context. Choosing this image of the Earth for the "Love Your Mother" slogan emphasizes for me those negative aspects of patriarchal motherhood I have discussed: mother as idealized, the perfectly round globe-breast; mother as mysterious, shrouded in cloud; mother as ambivalent love-object, abandoned up in space.[4]

*
*   *

A second way we can look at the woman-nature link is to ask not just how nature is affected by its association with motherhood but how women are affected by their association with nature. The "Love Your Mother" slogan helps perpetuate the idea that women are closer to nature and, implicitly, that men are closer to culture. Here I use traditional Western definitions of culture as "that which is human or made by humans" and nature as "that which is not human nor made by humans."[5] Much work has been done in feminist and ecofeminist theory to document how women have traditionally been perceived as closer to nature and men as closer to culture and how women in patriarchal culture have suffered from these perceptions. Sherry Ortner, Colette Guillaumin, Dorothy Dinnerstein, Carolyn Merchant, Elizabeth Dodson Gray, Susan Griffin, and others have all contributed to our understanding of these points. The basic argument is that in patriarchal culture, when women are seen as closer to nature than men, women are inevitably seen as less fully human than men. Susan Griffin, for example, in her passionate and poetic book *Woman and Nature: The Roaring Inside Her* (1978) juxtaposes negative comments about women with those about nature in order to illustrate how the two are perceived to be on an equal and lowly plane quite outside the properly human (that is, the male). In a series of evocative chapters Griffin shows how this association, as it has functioned in patriarchal culture, has contributed to women's voicelessness and powerlessness by assigning woman the roles of passive and obedient reproducer and nurturer (in her chapter entitled "Cows"), obstinate and dull-witted drudge, bred for labor the breeders do not wish to do (in the "Mules" chapter), and well-trained and well-groomed gratifier of her master (in "The Show Horse" chapter).

One way to put this point about the woman-nature connection is to say that in patriarchal culture nature is overpersonified and women are underpersonified. Women are perceived to merge with nature, to be part of the nonhuman surround and only semihuman. Similarly, nature is perceived as female, as virgin resource to be exploited or raped, as sharing in woman's semihuman quality. Women are perceived "as a natural resource," Dinnerstein says, "as an asset to be owned and harnessed, harvested and mined, with no fellow-feeling for her depletion and no responsibility for her conservation or replenishment" (1976, 36-37). Even when women are exalted as purer than men, as less bestial, and as the "guardians of culture and morals," Ortner points out that these seeming "inversions" merely place women "above" instead of "below" culture and that women are still in both cases excluded from the realm of culture (1974, 86).

Although we do understand nature as our semihuman parent, we also, according to another pattern or motif, understand nature as an inert, lifeless machine. Carolyn Merchant helps explain the historical confluence of these two patterns of interpretation in her persuasive reassessment of the rise of science entitled *The Death of Nature: Women, Ecology, and the Scientific Revolution* (1980). Merchant documents how during the scientific revolution of the sixteenth and seventeenth centuries, a new ethic developed that sanctioned the greater control and domination of both nature and women and their treatment as resources. The prevailing image of nature changed in these two centuries from an organic model of the cosmos as living being to a mechanistic model of the cosmos as machine or inanimate, dead, physical system. Nature was no longer seen as "nurturing . . . sensitive, alive, and responsive to human action" but as a "disorderly and chaotic realm to be subdued and controlled" (Merchant 1980, 20-22, 127). As a result, Merchant notes, "the constraints against penetration associated with the earth-mother image were transformed into sanctions for denudation" (1980, 189). Most feminists and ecofeminists seem to agree on the implications of these assessments: as long as we perceive women as closer to nature within a model which perceives nature to be on the one hand mechanical, on the other hand semihuman, and in both cases legitimately exploitable, then we will see women as a resource, and both women and the environment will suffer.

Faced with the apparent disempowerment women have experienced from being identified with nature and with nature being identified as female, ecofeminists have begun to explore preferable alternatives to these identifications. How can we rethink or re-vision our understanding of nature and of the historical link between woman and nature in order for these understandings to be healthier, both for women and for the environment? In an ecofeminist analysis three courses of action seem possible, the choice among these three constituting a main point of debate in ecofeminist theory. First, we can agree that women are closer to nature but disagree that this association must be disempowering. We can instead promote this association as enriching, liberating, and as according both women and nature high value. This choice is often called the "nature feminist" position; one of its proponents is Ariel Kay Salleh. Second, we can stress that women are fully cultural beings and disagree that women are in any way closer to nature than men, rejecting this latter claim as false and as sexist biological reductionism. Proponents of this second choice include Sherry Ortner, Colette Guillaumin, and Nicole-Claude Mathieu.

Note that the choice between these two options is partly one of strategy. Can we reclaim our connection with nature by asserting that yes, women are closer to nature, closer than men because we have never lost the knowledge of our deep connection with all other life? Or is the more important task that of claiming our place in culture? Which strategy would most benefit women and most benefit the environment?

The third course of action, and the one that I will defend, rejects the nature-culture dichotomy of these first two options and seeks to minimize the strictness and antagonism of the male-female dichotomy, thereby opening the way for multiple possibilities of gender identity.[6] In the remainder of this section I will present my reservations about the first two options and then briefly present some basic points of the third.

Consider first the position of the nature feminists. I do not find very convincing either the biological or the social conditioning arguments they proffer for women's greater attunement to the environment. On the biological level, although men do not menstruate, bear children, or breast-feed, they do share all other human biological processes (eating, sleeping, eliminating wastes, getting sick, dying), and in addition, in their ejaculation of semen they have experience of a tangible stuff of the reproduction of life. Furthermore, there are many women who do not bear children and even more who do not breast-feed. If these biological processes attune women to nature, then are the women who do not experience these processes out of tune? Emily Erwin Culpepper (1987) makes this same point in the context of Goddess spirituality. She notes how an overemphasis on the Goddess as mother overemphasizes the place of mother-hood in women's lives, excludes women who are not mothers, and obscures the presence of lesbians, of single women, and of heterosexism.

In terms of the argument that women's conditioning—as opposed to their biology—renders them closer to nature, although this conditioning does in some ways provide women with a greater sense of connection to the environment, in patriarchal culture the cost of this sense of connection is that women do not to the same degree and with the same ease as men perceive themselves as capable, powerful individuals able to bring about change, to get angry, or to assert will. In other words, as Catherine Keller argues in From a Broken Web (1986), the sense of the "connective" self that women's conditioning helps develop slides all too easily into an unhealthy sense of the "soluble" self. Keller and Dinnerstein suggest how our traditional social and psychological conditioning could be changed so that instead of producing a (female) soluble sense of self and a (male) separative sense of self, we could raise both girls and boys to have a more connective sense of self.[7] Presumably at least some of the antagonism of the man-woman dichotomy would then fade, because although men and women would still be different from each other, they would be more similar than they are now, more connective, and, through their recognition of interconnection, more ecologically minded.

In addition to the problem of the unconvincing arguments proffered in support of the idea that women are closer to nature, there is a more fundamental problem with the first "nature feminist" approach and with the second "woman-as-cultural" approach described above: both take at face value the question "Are women closer to nature than men?" The first approach answers yes and the second no. The third approach, the one I mentioned earlier that I want to defend, proposes that neither answer is entirely correct because the question itself is conceptually flawed.[8] This question is, I believe, misleading on two fronts.

First, the question of which sex is closer to nature is misleading when reflected upon in light of environmental insights. In no way can anyone or anything be "closer to nature" than any other being or thing because, through the inextricable implication of all in an environmental web of interconnection, all is already and equally "natural," that is, part of nature, the environment, or the Earth.[9] None of us can be "farther away" from nature for there is nowhere we can go, nothing we can do to get away from this implication in the environment. All our actions and creations, even the most elaborate, sophisticated products of our culture, are not totally apart from "nature" or the environment that gave rise to them. Although the work of nature feminists is very important in reminding us that we are a part of the Earth, in helping us to celebrate our bodies, and in breaking down our overly strict divisions between the human and the nonhuman, it does not convince me that women are "closer to nature" than men. Similarly, although the work of those feminists who insist that women are just as cultural as men is invaluable in showing the damaging restrictions women suffer from being identified with nature, it does not convince me that women and men together are "closer to culture" and "further from nature."

The question of whether women are closer to nature is misleading in a second way. This question assumes the validity of the hierarchical dualisms that are instead problematized and denied in the third approach. The first, nature feminist approach often sets up the hierarchical dualism of women as relatively "good" (closer to nature) and men as relatively "bad" (farther from nature) (Griscom 1981, 8). A hierarchical dualism is equally set up by the second approach's insistence that women are just as "cultural" and distanced from nature as men. Culture is here set up over nature. Sherry Ortner, for example, talks of culture's "transcendence" over and "subsumption" of nature (1974, 73).

From the point of view of the third approach, the hierarchical dualism between "nature" and "culture" or between the nonhuman and the human is questioned; these terms are not understood as descriptive of mutually opposed and differently valued realities. The main problem with the first and second approaches is that they both maintain and perpetuate this environmentally unsound nature-culture dualism. This dualism is unsound because it encourages the belief that "culture" and humanity are quite apart from "nature" and that we humans may thus use and abuse the environment at will, without ourselves suffering from the damage we inflict. Any understanding of the world that posits an important or unbridgeable difference between the realm of the human and the nonhuman risks creating a gulf between the two in which the human, because of our inherent chauvinism or anthropocentrism, would inevitably be more highly valued than the nonhuman. From a pragmatic standpoint, in our time of ecological breakdown such an understanding must be rejected as environmentally unsound, for it does not sufficiently support the project of caring for the environment as the necessary and inescapable context of human life.

The third course of action, then, takes the ecofeminist project to be one of dismantling domination structures in the form of the dualistic "either/or" or the hierarchical "closer/further." This option could be called that of "biodegrading" these structures: breaking down the "nature versus culture" dichotomies of the first two approaches, as my dictionary defines biodegrade, into ecologically harmless products.[10] This approach shifts the viewpoint of the first two and seeks to melt down their rigidity by making their concepts of "nature" and "culture" less rigid or fixed and more "biodegradable" or environmentally sound.

*
*   *

In discussing this third option, I do not attempt here to present a fully formulated position on the question of the relation of woman and nature. With my discussion of environmental soundness and biodegradability I want merely to suggest that accepting the question "Are women closer to nature than men?" does not help us much in the project of protecting the soundness of the environment; the nature-culture dualism inherent in this question needs to be examined and broken down. What further questions, then, should be asked about the connection between woman and nature?

First, one must ask if there is any sense in which we could speak of "Mother Nature," of loving our mother, of women as closer to nature. What if, in a postpatriarchal world, motherhood functioned in a different, healthier way than it does now, if the equal child-rearing desired by feminists came about? Could we not then reclaim Earth as our mother? Perhaps at times we could understand the Earth as our mother and, at other times, in other situations, as our father or our parent or our sister (Griffin 1978, 219) or our child (Cleveland 1985). As women, similarly, at certain times, when we celebrate our bodies or the cycles of life in which we participate, we could see ourselves as clearly embedded in the environment and connected with other life forms (seeing ourselves "as closer to nature"), and at other times we could place greater emphasis on our unique role as observers and shapers of the environment, as "nature seeing nature . . . nature with a concept of nature . . . nature speaking of nature to nature"—seeing ourselves "as closer to culture" (Griffin 1978, 226).

A second, related question that must be addressed is that of the positive role of the "Mother Earth" image. Although I have in this paper sought to investigate the unhealthy aspects of this image, I would not deny that the image of Earth as mother is nonetheless compelling, important, and appropriate in certain circumstances. It is an image that makes much intuitive sense to feminists and nonfeminists alike. The Earth has functioned in non-Western cultures as a very powerful and ancient center for worship and for seeing the divine as female and, before the Western scientific revolution, as Carolyn Merchant explains, has been understood as our "active teacher and parent" instead of as "a mindless, submissive [female] body" (1980, 190). These positive images of Earth as mother need to be further explored.

A third question concerns the role or place of humans in an environment in which I claim the division between nature and culture to be overemphasized. Are humans, then, no different from any other species? If not different, then would not our skyscrapers and even our toxic waste dumps have just as much right to exist as a bird's nest or a beaver's dam? If all parts are equal members of a whole, what are our criteria for decision making and for promoting any one course of action over another? These questions have serious implications for understanding our human relations to and in the environment. I will only note here that to say that we are one species among many, interrelating and interconnected to all other species, is not to say that we are the same as all other species or that all species are the same. On the contrary, each species is unique. At this historical point, the significance of our uniqueness as humans seems to be that we have a large degree of control over the fate of many other species and of the planet as a whole. This particular ability gives us the responsibility for acting more carefully and less destructively, in order to ensure the continued and healthy existence of life on Earth, including our own.

One last question: if I am correct in suggesting that a present-day ecofeminist should not urge us to "Love our Mother," what then should she (or, as we perhaps head toward a postpatriarchal world, he) urge? I have recently seen another poster that offers an intriguing alternative. This poster, like the first, was encouraging environmentally sound behaviour and pictured our planet. It said of the Earth: "This is our neighborhood. Let's care for it." This metaphor of the neighbourhood, and similar ones of the Earth as our community and home, are often suggested by bioregionalists, who focus their planetary environmental concern in local regions.[11] More work could be done with alternative metaphors and symbols such as these, exploring whether they are presently more biodegradable and environmentally sound than the metaphor of Earth as mother.[12]

To summarize: In this essay I have explored the relation between woman and nature, focusing on the problem of engendering the Earth, the problem of the meaning and function of mother and motherhood in patriarchal culture, the problem of the perceived closeness of women to nature, and the problem of nature-culture dualism. In the first half of the essay I argued that the "Love Your Mother" slogan, especially when accompanied by the image of Earth from space, is problematic because of our tendency to relate to our mothers as ambivalent love-objects, expected to care for all our needs, and that for this reason, instead of achieving the desired result of encouraging us toward environmental sound-ness, this slogan has almost the opposite effect of helping to maintain exploit-ative patterns toward the earth and mother. In the essay's second half, after examining ecofeminist responses to the question of woman's closeness to nature, I argued that the question is conceptually flawed and that the nature-culture dualism on which it is predicated is in need of being biodegraded for the sake of environmental soundness.

I close my paper with a final question—a very large question—in order to show what I perceive as the ecofeminist project that has been the context for all my reflections: how can we think about and live the differences and commonali-ties of being female and male and the complexities of being self-conscious, prolific builders within the environment, in order that we may, on the one hand, be more just and more supportive of one another and, on the other (connected) hand, be more environmentally sound?

NOTES

This essay has undergone many changes. I would like to acknowledge that much of the value of the essay derives from the friendship and guidance of Naomi Goldenberg. I would also like to thank Patrice Brodeur, Charlotte Chin, Adam Chippindale, Elizabeth Dodson Gray, Sean Kelly, Ted Trost, Karen J. Warren, Sharon Welch, and the Ecology and Religion Cooperative of Harvard Divinity School, all of whom provided me with very helpful commentary and support. An earlier version of this paper was presented at the national meeting of the American Academy of Religion in Anaheim, California, in November 1989 under the title "Looking at Woman Looking at Nature: Feminist and Ecological Perspectives on Woman-Nature/Man-Culture." My work is supported by a fellowship from the Social Sciences and Humanities Research Council of Canada.

1. While it is not universally the case that the biological mother has respon-sibility for all of the care of her children, in cultures where extended families or neighbours share "mothering" tasks it is still almost always women who look after, or are expected to look after, children.

2. To paraphrase Sallie McFague by substituting "the Earth" for "God": "To speak of the Earth as mother is to invite us to consider some qualities associated with mothering as one partial but perhaps illuminating way of speaking of certain aspects of the Earth's relationship to us" (1987, 34). This section of my essay consists of a problematizing of the phrase "qualities associated with mothering."

3. I use pragmatic here in reference to the pragmatic philosophy of William James, which I find very useful as a basis for an ecological and liberational ethic. James counsels that we must judge ideas by the "fruits of their action," by their

pragmatic effects. We should try out different types of ideas and, then, as the criterion of whether they are "useful" or "fruitful," we should "listen to the cries of the wounded" which result from their implementation into action. The wounded will determine which ideas or ethics are "best," in the sense of which cause the least suffering. See James (1956 and 1978).

4. In connection with this image of "Mother Earth," the work of Jessica Benjamin (1988) is interesting for its analysis of the evolution of the infantile psyche. Her theorizing about our relation to the mother as object and to the "other" in general as object might help explain why this distant and objectified image of the Earth is chosen to accompany the slogan, instead of a more everyday and proximal image of the environment.

5. I form these definitions from a synthesis of my reading and in particular from Ortner (1974).

6. Although I do not here develop this theme of flexible and plural gender identity, it is present in the work of many contemporary, often psychoanalyti- cally inclined, feminists. See, for example, Benjamin (1988, 113), Chodorow in Keller (1986, 139), and Suleiman (1990, 139-40).

7. On the "connective," "soluble," and "separative" senses of self, as Catherine Keller uses these terms: The connective self—open to the world and realizing its relation to all other life—is the ideal sense of self, in that it is most supportive of sound behaviour to our fellow humans and to the environment, but it is not the sense of identity possessed by most women or men. We all first develop and have the potential to retain a connective sense of self; however, because of the patriarchal context in which we all live, this connectivity is overencouraged in women and suppressed in men. The result is that men tend to develop a separative sense of self and women a soluble sense of self, neither of which is healthy. Women's soluble sense of self is an underdevelopment or negation of the self, a sense of having no self of one's own and of existing primarily for others. Men's separative sense of self is an overdevelopment of self, with overly strict boundaries and objectification of the other.

8. See Griscom (1981) and Warren (1987), who make this point that the question "Are women closer to nature than men?" is conceptually flawed.

9. Among humans, some of us could be more conscious of our environmental embeddedness than others, but still this consciousness would not render us "closer to nature," only more aware that we are all part of nature (the environ- ment or the Earth). To claim that someone is closer to nature because of his or her location or life-style (e.g., a forest hermit) would be to claim, conversely, that others are closer to culture or to industrial society (e.g., a Wall Street investment banker). Such claims replicate a nature-culture dualism that my discussion sees as environmentally unsound and seeks to break down.

10. I thank Naomi Goldenberg for suggesting this use of the term biodegrade.

11. See, for example, the work of a feminist bioregionalist such as Judith Plant, who emphasizes place, community, and neighbourhood. Such bio-

regionalists seek a philosophical shift from universality to particularity and historicity, seeing such a shift as demanded by the exigencies of our environmental breakdown. My variant spellings of "neighbo(u)rhood" are necessitated by the fact that I am quoting from the text of an American poster, but am Canadian and write with British-Canadian spellings. If one takes seriously the emphasis on place and community in bioregionalism, my inconsistency will hopefully be understood and forgiven.

12. Linda Teal Willoughby expresses some important reservations about the ecofeminist project of constructing alternative symbols and metaphors for the traditional "Mother Nature." She draws on Jungian theory to point out that no symbol "can be inherently harmless or accomplish the task of dismantling hierarchical dualism without going through the process of withdrawing projections and breaking up identities" (1990, 197). The problem is not only, or not so much, in the symbol itself as in the misguided attempt to consciously create symbols without attending to unconscious projection and content. I think her point is well taken. Attempts to overthrow one symbol and elevate another will not be successful if they attend only to the level of consciousness; symbols like "Mother Nature" derive their power precisely from their roots in our largely unconscious infantile relation to the mother, as I discuss in the first half of this essay. See Willoughby (1990, ch. 14), "Ecofeminism Enriched by Jungian Theory."

REFERENCES

Benjamin, Jessica. 1988. *The bonds of love: Psychoanalysis, feminism, and the problem of domination*. New York: Pantheon Books.

Cleveland, Peggy. 1985. Mothering the earth or nurturing nature. Unpublished paper.

Culpepper, Emily Erwin. 1987. Contemporary Goddess theology: A sympathetic critique. *Shaping new vision: Gender and values in American culture*. Clarissa W. Atkinson, Constance H. Buchanan, and Margaret R. Miles, eds. Ann Arbor: UMI Research Press.

Dinnerstein, Dorothy. 1976. *The mermaid and the minotaur: Sexual arrangements and human malaise*. New York: Harper and Row.

Feynman, Richard. 1989. Quoted by Jerome Kagan. In A conversation with Jerome Kagan. *Harvard Gazette*. 22 September.

Gray, Elizabeth Dodson. 1982. *Patriarchy as a conceptual trap*. Wellesley, MA: Roundtable Press.

———. 1989. An ecofeminist critique of Christianity. Lecture delivered at Harvard Divinity School, Cambridge, Massachusetts. 29 November.

Griffin, Susan. 1978. *Woman and nature: The roaring inside her*. New York: Harper and Row.

Griscom, Joan L. 1981. On healing the nature/history split in feminist thought. *Heresies: Feminism and ecology* 13 (4): 4-9.

Guillaumin, Colette. 1978. Pratique du pouvoir et idée de Nature: (2) Le discours de la Nature. *Questions féministes* 3: 5-28.

Irigaray, Luce. 1987. *Sexes et parentés*. Paris: Editions de Minuit.

James, William. 1956. [1897 and 1898]. *The will to believe* and *Human immortality*. New York: Dover.

———. 1975. *Pragmatism* and *The meaning of truth*. Intro. by H. S. Thayer. Cambridge: Harvard University Press.

Keller, Catherine. 1986. *From a broken web: Separation, sexism, and self*. Boston: Beacon Press.

McFague, Sallie. 1987. *Models of God: Theology for an ecological, nuclear age*. Philadelphia: Fortress Press.

Mathieu, Nicole-Claude. 1973. Homme-culture et femme-nature? *Homme* 13: 101-13.

Merchant, Carolyn. 1980. *The death of nature: Women, ecology, and the scientific revolution*. San Francisco: Harper and Row.

Ortner, Sherry B. 1974. Is female to male as nature is to culture? *Woman, culture, and society*. Michelle Zimbalist Rosaldo and Louise Lamphere, eds. Stanford, CA: Stanford University Press.

Plant, Judith. 1989. Towards a new world: An introduction. The circle is gathering. *Healing the wounds: The promise of ecofeminism*. Judith Plant, ed. Toronto: Between the Lines.

Salleh, Ariel Kay. 1984. Deeper than deep ecology: The eco-feminist connection. *Environmental Ethics* 6: 339-45.

Suleiman, Susan Rubin. 1990. *Subversive intent: Gender, politics, and the avant-garde*. Cambridge: Harvard University Press.

Warren, Karen J. 1987. Feminism and ecology: Making connections. *Environmental Ethics* 9: 3-20.

Willoughby, Linda Teal. 1990. *Mother Earth: Ecofeminism from a Jungian perspective*. Ph.D. dissertation. Presented to the Iliff School of Theology and the University of Denver (Colorado Seminary). May.

Toward an Ecological Ethic of Care

DEANE CURTIN

I. INTRODUCTION

Suddenly the animal rights movement is gaining the attention of the popular press as it never has before. Its hold on the public's attention may be due to the fact that while its proposals are viewed as radical, it responds to what have become core intuitions in our culture about the basic project of moral theory: the establishment of human or natural rights. But as rights are expanded to new domains, particularly as this expansion has begun to interact with feminist conceptions of morality, the question arises whether the language of rights is the best conceptual tool for exploring distinctively feminist insights about ecological ethics.

Ecofeminism is the position that "there are important connections—historical, experiential, symbolic, theoretical—between the domination of women and the domination of nature" (Warren 1990, 126). It argues that the patriarchal conceptual framework that has maintained, perpetuated, and justified the oppression of women in Western culture has also, and in similar ways, maintained, perpetuated, and justified the oppression of nonhuman animals and the environment. This paper affirms that perspective but raises questions about the best way to express from an ecofeminist position the moral connection between human and nonhuman animals. Karen J. Warren has raised the issue of how to express ecofeminist moral insights in beginning to develop "ecofeminism as a feminist and environmental ethic" (Warren 1990, 138). She notes that a feminist ethic is pluralist and it may use rights language "in certain contexts and for certain purposes," but she says, and I agree, that ecofeminism "involves a *shift* from a conception of ethics as primarily a matter of rights, rules, or principles predetermined and applied in specific cases to entities viewed as competitors in the contest of moral standing" to an ethic that "makes a central place for values of care, love, friendship, trust, and appropriate reciprocity-values that presuppose that our relationships to others are central to our understanding of who we are" (Warren 1990, 141 and 143).

Hypatia vol. 6, no. 1 (Spring 1991) © by Deane Curtin

I think Warren raises the critical issue. If ecofeminism is going to make good on its claim that there are important conceptual connections between the domination of nature and the domination of women, and furthermore, that since there are these connections, an environmental ethic is incomplete if it does not in some important ways take into account feminist ethical perspectives, the rights model must be examined for whether it is conceptually the best way of expressing ecofeminist insights.

I believe that the language of rights is not the best way of expressing ecofeminist insights and that a better approach can be found in a politicized ethic of care. I shall consider the animal rights project and its conceptual limitations for feminists (and for ecofeminists in particular); I shall then briefly rehearse some of the feminist arguments concerning an alternative ethic of care; finally, I shall extend a politicized version of that ethic to an ecologically based feminist ethic for the treatment of animals. Here, I shall be particularly interested in the way feminism and ecology are connected through our relations to what we are willing to count as food.[1]

II. FEMINISM AND ANIMAL RIGHTS

Though some ecofeminists, such as Carol J. Adams and Marti Kheel, are committed to animal rights, I am not clear from reading their works precisely what they think the connection is between ecofeminism and a rights perspective. In *The Sexual Politics of Meat: A Feminist-Vegetarian Critical Theory* Adams says, "Not only is animal rights the theory and vegetarianism the practice, but feminism is the theory and vegetarianism is part of the practice" (Adams 1989, 167). Yet, despite Adams's repeated connection of animal rights with a feminist practice that includes moral vegetarianism, careful inspection of these references leaves me in doubt about which of two interpretations to give the text. She could mean, minimally, that animal rights activists and feminist activists should see themselves as allies working to resist connected forms of oppression. On this reading, Adams would be working to establish a *practical* connection between feminism and the animal rights movement as a political strategy of coalition building. However, Adams's text is also consistent with the stronger interpretation, that ecofeminist moral practice is best elucidated *conceptually* by reference to the philosophical tradition of rights and obligations. The claim made by this latter interpretation is what I question.

A similar lack of specificity concerning whether ecofeminist goals are practical or conceptual can be found in Marti Kheel's work. As founder of Feminists for Animal Rights, she has worked to put ecofeminist thought into practice. But conceptually, it seems to me, her work is not best understood as emerging from the rights tradition. In "The Liberation of Nature: A Circular Affair," for example, Kheel criticizes Tom Regan, the best-known advocate of the philosophical view that animals have rights. Her criticisms are distinctively feminist for reasons I shall elucidate below.[2] The question arises, then, whether the feminist insights she brings to ecological ethics are best expressed as issues of animal rights.

My concern in addressing the conceptual issue is exclusively with two quite different views that have gone under the label of rights-based ethics. I make no claim within the context of this paper that these two alternatives exhaust the possibilities for rights-based ethics. My more limited point is to choose the two approaches that have played the most central role in the animal rights literature and argue that they cannot be understood as expressing distinctively feminist insights. The first, which has not proven very sympathetic to the interests of animals, I call the "exchange-value alternative." The second, which has been regarded as more promising, I call the "cross-species identity alternative."

A version of the exchange-value alternative has been defended by Alan White. A right, he says, "is something which can be said to be exercised, earned, enjoyed, or given, which can be claimed, demanded, asserted, insisted on, secured, waived, or surrendered. . . . A right is related to and contrasted with a duty, an obligation, a privilege, a power, a liability" (White 1989, 120). To be capable of having a right, he argues, is to be a subject capable of being spoken about in "the full language of rights." It follows, according to White, that only persons can have rights because only persons can be spoken about in the full language of rights. Infants, the unborn, the comatose are still persons, or potential persons, so "they are logically possible subjects of rights to whom the full language of rights can significantly, however falsely, be used" (White 1989, 120). By contrast, White contends, nonhuman animals cannot exercise a right, nor can they recognize a correlative obligation (White 1989, 121).

Jan Narveson has put the case against extending rights to animals bluntly. He insists that we recognize the rights of other beings only in contexts where we stand to gain from such recognition in the long run, and we observe rights relationships only with those who are capable of entering into and keeping an agreement. "Humans," he says, "have nothing generally to gain by voluntarily refraining from (for instance) killing animals or 'treating them as mere means' " (Narveson 1989, 193), nor are animals capable of making and sustaining agreements.

If we judge whether rights should be extended to new conceptual domains on the basis of considerations suggested by Narveson, nonhuman animals are left out of the picture. Animals, in this view, are to be used according to the self-interest of human beings. If there are any moral strictures on the treatment of animals, they are based on whether certain practices offend the moral sensibilities of those who do possess rights. Nonhuman animals possess no rights themselves.

The second approach to rights depends not on exchange value but on the cross-species identity of some rights-making characteristic. James Rachels's procedure depends on selecting clear cases in which humans can be said to have rights. He then asks whether there are relevant differences between humans and other animals that would justify refusing to ascribe the right possessed by the human to the nonhuman. If no difference is found, the right is said to be possessed by all animals that are identical in that respect, not just humans.

In some cases, Rachels finds that there are relevant differences. A right to exercise freedom of religion cannot be extended to other animals; the right to liberty can be. He asserts, "The central sense of Freedom is that in which a being is free when he or she is able to do as he or she pleases without being subject to external constraints on his or her actions" (Rachels 1989, 125). This definition of liberty based on doing whatever one wishes without external constraints applies across species. The caged tiger in the zoo is not free; the tiger in the "wild" is.

In a similar vein, Tom Regan has argued that "inherent value . . . belongs equally to those who are the experiencing subjects of a life" (Regan 1989, 112). He emphasizes that this is a theory about the inherent value of "individuals" and that "reason—not sentiment, not emotion—reason compels us to recognize the equal inherent value of these animals and, with this, their equal right to be treated with respect" (Regan 1989, 113).

Both of these approaches to animal ethics (particularly the cross-species identity approach since that has been regarded as the more likely alternative) make a number of assumptions that can be challenged if one's goal is to provide an ecofeminist ethic. My intention is not so much to make these arguments here as to rehearse positions that have been argued for elsewhere as a means of placing the present discussion in context.

First, it can be argued that views such as Rachels's and Regan's are too narrow to express feminist insights[3] because they allow us to recognize only those rights-making characteristics that nonhuman animals have in virtue of being in some way *identical* to humans. Rachels has granted, for example, that by his procedure of establishing animal rights on the basis of whether nonhuman animals are like humans, we are theoretically denied access to rights that other animals may possess uniquely (Rachels 1989, 124). (In fact, I am not sure what one could do to elucidate what this claim *means* given that we cannot, in principle, know what the criteria for such rights would be.) Rachels's procedure recognizes only identity of interests, not diversity. Similarly, Regan's criterion for possession of inherent value picks out a common denominator in virtue of which humans and nonhumans are identical. But many of the interests an ecological ethic may have rest precisely on the differences between humans and other animals.

The assumption that moral status depends on identity of interests has been challenged by some feminists.[4] A feminist ethic tends to be pluralistic in its intention to recognize heterogeneous moral interests. It sees the attempt to reduce moral claims to identity of interests as one strand in a moral fabric that has tended to exclude women's voices. If ecofeminism is to make the claim that there are important conceptual connections between ecology and feminism, it should question whether a feminist ecological ethic is best expressed through the extension of rights to nonhuman animals on the basis of their partial identity to human beings.

The second concern about the conceptual compatibility of ecofeminism with the rights approach is that the rights approach to treatment of animals is formalistic. It is committed to the idea that equal treatment based on a criterion of cross-species identity is the central concept of morality where this is defined as treatment that is neutral with respect to context. It recommends a decision procedure by which those beings that have rights can be separated from those that do not. Its aspirations are universalistic. Feminist approaches to ethics, however, tend to be not only pluralistic but contextual.[5] They tend to be based on actual interests in the narrative context of lived experiences.[6]

Third, the rights approach is inherently adversarial. As Joel Feinberg has said, "To have a right is to have a claim *to* something *against* someone" (Feinberg 1980, 139). Though conflict certainly may arise in contexts of a feminist understanding of morality, it does not begin from a theoretical assumption of conflict. Rather, a feminist understanding is more likely to be based in a pluralistic context that is dialogical and seeks mutual accommodation of interests (see Benhabib 1987, section 4).

Fourth, connected to a dialogical understanding of ethics, feminist moral thought tends to reconceptualize personhood as relational rather than autonomous (see Ferguson 1989 and Lugones 1987). Whereas the rights approach requires a concept of personhood that is individualistic enough to defend the sphere in which the moral agent is autonomous, feminist approaches to ethics tend to see moral inquiry as an ongoing process through which persons are defined contextually and relationally.

Fifth, whereas the rights approach has tended to argue that ethical judgments are objective and rational and do not depend on affective aspects of experience, this has been questioned by feminist critics partly on the grounds that the conception of the purely rational is a myth, and partly on the grounds that this myth has tended to marginalize the experiences of women by portraying them as personal rather than moral (Jaggar 1989, 139-43). Following the work of Carol Gilligan, many feminists suggest that an ethic of care is better able to express the connection between reason and feeling found in women's moral discourse.

Finally, as a result of the emphasis on the rational in traditional moral theory, feminist insights concerning the body as moral agent have been missed. But as some feminist philosophers have argued (see Bordo 1989), the identification of woman with body has been one pretext on which women's lives have been marginalized.

These six considerations suggest, then, that the rights approach as applied to the treatment of animals is not a very promising route for establishing a feminist ecological ethic. There may be contexts in which it would be helpful for feminists to present the case for moral treatment of animals in terms of rights.

However, I would argue that there is nothing distinctively feminist about this approach. If one accepts that there is a deep ideological connection between the oppression of nature and the oppression of women in Western culture, one must look to a distinctively feminist understanding of oppression.

I do not regard these six points as criticisms of Adams and Kheel. It fact, it would not be difficult to find passages in their works that implicitly or explicitly support what I have said here. Rather, my goal is to encourage a distinction between practical and conceptual alliances and to suggest that Adams's and Kheel's works are better understood conceptually in terms of an ethic of care.

III. A Politicized Ethic of Caring For

A source for much of the feminist literature on women's psychological and moral development is Carol Gilligan's *In a Different Voice*.[7] Whereas the rights approach tends to emphasize identity of moral interests, formalistic decision procedures, an adversarial understanding of moral discourse, personhood as autonomous, and a valorization of the nonbodily, Gilligan's research indicates that women's moral experiences are better understood in terms of recognition of a plurality of moral interests, contextual decision making, nonadversarial accommodation of diverse interests, personhood as relational, and the body as moral agent. Furthermore, an ethic of care has an intuitive appeal from the standpoint of ecological ethics. Whether or not nonhuman animals have rights, we certainly can and do care for them. This includes cases where we regularly experience care in return, as in a relationship to a pet, as well as cases where there is no reciprocity, as in the case of working to preserve natural habitats. It even seems possible to say we can care for nonsentient beings. Karen J. Warren has written about two attitudes one can bring to mountain climbing. One seeks to dominate and conquer the mountain; the other seeks to "climb respectfully with the rock." One can care for the rock partly *because* it is "independent and seemingly indifferent to my presence" (Warren 1990, 135).

While an ethic of care does have an intuitive appeal, without further development into a political dimension Gilligan's research may be turned against feminist and ecofeminist objectives. First, if not politicized, an ethic of care can be used to privatize the moral interests of women. In contrast to the rights model, which seeks to cordon off "my" territory over which I have control, the caring-for model may often suggest that the interests of others should, in certain contexts, come before one's own, and that knowing what to do in a particular situation requires empathetic projection into another's life. Putting the other in front of oneself can easily be abused. The wife who selflessly cares for her husband who cares only about himself is only too well known.

In a society that oppresses women, it does no good to suggest that women should go on selflessly providing care if social structures make it all too easy to abuse that care. The injunction to care must be understood as part of a radical political agenda that allows for development of contexts in which caring for can be nonabusive. It claims that the relational sense of self, the willingness to empathetically enter into the world of others and care for them, can be expanded and developed as part of a political agenda so that it may include those outside the already established circle of caring for. Its goal is not just to make a "private" ethic public but to help undercut the public/private distinction.

Second, an ethic of care that is not politicized can be *localized in scope*, thereby blunting its political impact. Caring for resists the claim that morality depends on a criterion of universalizability, and insists that it depends on special, contextual relationships. This might be taken to mean that we should care for the homeless only if our daughter or son happens to be homeless. Or, it might mean that persons in dominant countries should feel no need to care for persons in dominated countries. Or, it might mean that we should care only for those of the same species.

As part of a feminist political agenda, however, caring for can remain contextualized while being expanded on the basis of feminist political insights. To take a political example, one of the sources of the oppression of women in countries like India is that deforestation has a disproportionate effect on women whose responsibilities usually include food preparation. A common sight in these countries is village women walking farther every year in search of safe water and fuel for food preparation. In such contexts, the destruction of the environment *is* a source of women's oppression.[8] The point here is not that there is a single cause of women's oppression or even that in countries like India women's oppression is always ecologically based. Clearly, there are problems like the euphemistically termed "kitchen accident" in which women are burned to death by husbands who are disappointed with the dowry. I am arguing that in the mosaic of problems that constitute women's oppression in a particular context, no complete account can be given that does not make reference to the connection between women and the environment. Caring for women in such a context includes caring for their environment. A distinctively feminist understanding of community development in countries like India may, then, provide a common context of related (though not identical!) interests that would connect women in the United States with women and the environment in India.

A distinction can be drawn between caring *about* and caring *for* that helps clarify how caring can be expanded as part of a political agenda. Caring about is a generalized form of care that may have specifiable recipients, but it occurs in a context where direct relatedness to specific others is missing. For example, feminist perspectives may lead one to a sense of connection between oneself and the plight of women in oppressed countries. But if one has not experienced the condition of women in India, for example, and more than that, if one has not experienced the particular conditions of women in a specific village in a specific region of India, caring remains a generalized caring about. As an element in a feminist political agenda, such caring about may lead to the kinds of actions that bring one into the kind of deep relatedness that can be described as caring for: caring for particular persons in the context of their histories.

Similar comments may be made about classic environmental issues. By reading about the controversy surrounding logging of old-growth forests, one might come to care about them. But caring for is marked by an understanding of and appreciation for a particular context in which one participates. One may, for example, come to understand the issue partly in terms of particular trees one has become accustomed to looking for on a favorite hike, trees that one would miss given changes in logging regulations. With these political and ecological considerations in mind, I conclude that an ethic of care can be expanded as part of a feminist political agenda without losing its distinctive contextual character. It can resist privatization and localization, retaining the contextualized character that is distinctive of caring for.

A third possible problem with a politicized ethic of care is the contention, argued for notably by Nel Noddings, that caring for can only be elucidated conceptually through the idea of reciprocity. If this is correct, it would be difficult to extend a politicized version of caring for to contexts of community development or to nonhuman animals where reciprocity is either inappropriate or impossible. Noddings argues that "the caring relation . . . requires . . . a form of *responsiveness* or *reciprocity* on the part of the cared-for" to be a complete act of caring for (Noddings 1984, 150). Though she notes some cases where this may occur with nonhuman animals, she doubts in general whether our relations with animals do reach such a stage of completion in reciprocity. She doubts, therefore, whether we can really be said to care for nonhuman animals.

I find Noddings's requirement of reciprocity unconvincing. Reciprocity is important in certain contexts of caring for—those Noddings takes as her principal examples, such as caring education—because in those contexts we are looking for a response which indicates that caring has had the desired effect. But I regard these as special cases that become dangerous to feminist moral interests if generalized. Many of the contexts of caring for that an ecofeminist might be especially interested in are precisely those in which reciprocity cannot be expected. It seems quite possible that a feminist political consciousness may lead one to care for women in a Dalit village in India, and to work to relieve the oppressive consequences for their lives resulting from the destruction of the environment. But it would be dangerous to suggest that such caring for requires reciprocity. Is it really caring for if something is expected in return? What would be appropriate in return? We ought to distinguish the *contextualization* of caring for (the requirement that all caring for has a determinant recipient) from the *localization* of caring for, which resists the expansion of caring for to the oppressed who are geographically remote from us, or to nonhuman nature. A distinctive mark of caring for is that in some contexts it is expressed "selflessly."

In summary, ecofeminist philosophy seeks not only to understand the condition of women but also to use that understanding to liberate women and nature from the structures of oppression. In achieving a new sense of relatedness of the kind that feminist and ecofeminist political philosophy can provide, one is enabled to enter into caring for relationships that were not available earlier. One may come to see, for example, that the white, middle-class American woman's typical situation is connected with—though not identical to—the condition of women in oppressed countries. Caring for can also be generated by coming to see that one's life (unknowingly) has been a cause of the oppression of others. The caring-for model does not require that those recipients of our care must be "equal" to us. Neither does it assume they are not equal. It is based on developing the capacity to care, not the criterion of equality. The resultant caring for may lead to a new sense of empowerment based on cultivating the willingness to act to empower ourselves and others.

IV. Contextual Moral Vegetarianism[9]

In this section I provide an example of a distinctively ecofeminist moral concern: our relations to what we are willing to count as food. Vegetarianism has been defended as a moral obligation that results from rights that nonhuman animals have in virtue of being sentient beings (Regan 1983, 330-53). However, a distinctively ecofeminist defense of moral vegetarianism is better expressed as a core concept in an ecofeminist ethic of care. One clear way of distinguishing the two approaches is that whereas the rights approach is not inherently contextual[10] (it is the response to the rights of all sentient beings), the caring-for approach responds to particular contexts and histories. It recognizes that the reasons for moral vegetarianism may differ by locale, by gender, as well as by class.

Moral vegetarianism is a fruitful issue for ecofeminists to explore in developing an ecological ethics because in judging the adequacy of an ethic by reference to its understanding of food one draws attention to precisely those aspects of daily experience that have often been regarded as "beneath" the interest of philosophy. Plato's remark in the *Gorgias* is typical of the dismissive attitude philosophers have usually had toward food. Pastry cooking, he says, is like rhetoric: both are mere "knacks" or "routines" designed to appeal to our bodily instincts rather than our intellects (Plato 1961, 245).

Plato's dismissive remark also points to something that feminists need to take very seriously, namely, that a distinctively feminist ethic, as Susan Bordo and others argue, should include the body as moral agent. Here too the experiences of women in patriarchal cultures are especially valuable because women, more than men, experience the effects of culturally sanctioned oppressive attitudes toward the appropriate shape of the body. Susan Bordo has argued that anorexia nervosa is a "psychopathology" made possible by Cartesian attitudes toward the body at a popular level. Anorexics typically feel alienation from their bodies and the hunger "it" feels. Bordo quotes one woman as saying she ate because "my stomach wanted it"; another dreamed of being "without a body." Anorexics want to achieve "absolute purity, hyperintellectuality and transcendence of the flesh" (Bordo 1988, 94 and 95; also see Chernin 1981). These attitudes toward the body have served to distort the deep sense in which human beings are embodied creatures; they have therefore further distorted our being as animals. To be a person, as distinct from an "animal," is to be disembodied.

This dynamic is vividly exposed by Carol Adams in *The Sexual Politics of Meat* (Adams 1989, part 1). There are important connections through food between the oppression of women and the oppression of nonhuman animals. Typical of the wealth of evidence she presents are the following: the connection of women and animals through pornographic representations of women as "meat" ready to be carved up, for example in "snuff" films; the fact that language masks our true relationship with animals, making them "absent referents" by giving meat words positive connotations ("That's a meaty question"; "Where's the beef?") while disparaging nonflesh foods ("Don't watch so much TV! You'll turn into a vegetable"); men, athletes and soldiers in particular, are associated with red meat and activity ("To have muscle you need to eat muscle"), whereas women are associated with vegetables and passivity ("ladies' luncheons" typically offer dainty sandwiches with no red meat).

As a "contextual moral vegetarian," I cannot refer to an absolute moral rule that prohibits meat eating under all circumstances. There may be some contexts in which another response is appropriate. Though I am committed to moral vegetarianism, I cannot say that I would never kill an animal for food. Would I not kill an animal to provide food for my son if he were starving? Would I not generally prefer the death of a bear to the death of a loved one? I am sure I would. The point of a contextualist ethic is that one need not treat all interests equally as if one had no relationship to any of the parties.

Beyond personal contextual relations, geographical contexts may sometimes be relevant. The Ihalmiut, for example, whose frigid domain makes the growing of food impossible, do not have the option of vegetarian cuisine. The economy of their food practices, however, and their tradition of "thanking" the deer for giving its life are reflective of a serious, focused, compassionate attitude toward the "gift" of a meal.

In some cultures violence against nonhuman life is ritualized in such a way that one is present to the reality of one's food. The Japanese have a Shinto ceremony that pays respect to the insects that are killed during rice planting. Tibetans, who as Buddhists have not generally been drawn to vegetarianism, nevertheless give their own bodies back to the animals in an ultimate act of thanks by having their corpses hacked into pieces as food for the birds.[11] Cultures such as these have ways of expressing spiritually the idea "we are what we eat," even if they are not vegetarian.

If there is any context, on the other hand, in which moral vegetarianism is completely compelling as an expression of an ecological ethic of care, it is for economically well-off persons in technologically advanced countries. First, these are persons who have a choice of what food they want to eat; they have a choice of what they will count as food. Morality and ontology are closely connected here. It is one thing to inflict pain on animals when geography offers no other choice. But in the case of killing animals for human consumption where there is a choice, this practice inflicts pain that is completely unnecessary and avoidable. The injunction to care, considered as an issue of moral and political develop- ment, should be understood to include the injunction to eliminate needless suffering wherever possible, and particularly the suffering of those whose suffer- ing is conceptually connected to one's own. It should be understood as an injunction that includes the imperative to rethink what it means to be a person connected with the imperative to rethink the status of nonhuman animals. An ecofeminist perspective emphasizes that one's body is oneself, and that by inflicting violence needlessly, one's bodily self becomes a context for violence. One becomes violent by taking part in violent food practices. The ontological implication of a feminist ethic of care is that nonhuman animals should no longer count as food.

Second, most of the meat and dairy products in these countries do not come from mom-and-pop farms with little red barns. Factory farms are responsible for most of the 6 billion animals killed for food every year in the United States (Adams 1989, 6). It is curious that steroids are considered dangerous for athletes, but animals that have been genetically engineered and chemically induced to grow faster and come to market sooner are considered to be an entirely different issue. One would have to be hardened to know the conditions factory-farm animals live in and not feel disgust concerning their treatment.[12]

Third, much of the effect of the eating practices of persons in industrialized countries is felt in oppressed countries. Land owned by the wealthy that was once used to grow inexpensive crops for local people has been converted to the production of expensive products (beef) for export. Increased trade of food products with these countries is consistently the cause of increased starvation. In cultures where food preparation is primarily understood as women's work, starvation is primarily a women's issue. Food expresses who we are politically just as much as bodily. One need not be aware of the fact that one's food practices oppress others in order to be an oppressor.

From a woman's perspective, in particular, it makes sense to ask whether one should become a vegan, a vegetarian who, in addition to refraining from meat and fish, also refrains from eating eggs and dairy products. Since the consumption of eggs and milk have in common that they exploit the reproductive capacities of the female, vegetarianism is not a gender neutral issue.[13] To *choose one's diet* in a patriarchal culture is one way of politicizing an ethic of care. It marks a daily, bodily commitment to resist ideological pressures to conform to patriarchal standards, and to establishing contexts in which caring for can be nonabusive.

Just as there are gender-specific reasons for women's commitment to vegetari- anism, for men in a patriarchal society moral vegetarianism can mark the decision to stand in solidarity with women. It also indicates a determination to resist ideological pressures to become a "real man." Real people do not need to eat "real food," as the American Beef Council would have us believe.

V. CONCLUSION

An ethic of care provides a very important beginning for an ecofeminist ethic, but it runs the risk of having its own aims turned against it unless it is regarded as part of a distinctively feminist political agenda that consciously attempts to expand the circle of caring for. Ecofeminism is in a position to accomplish this expansion by insisting that the oppression of women, the oppression of the environment, and the oppressive treatment of nonhuman animals are deeply linked. As a kind of feminism it can emphasize that personhood is embodied, and that through the food which becomes our bodies, we are engaged in food practices that reflect who we are. Ecofeminism is also in a position to offer a politicized ethic that promises liberation from the forms of oppression that link women and the environment.

NOTES

I wish to express my appreciation to Lisa Heldke for many fruitful conversations, particularly on the topics addressed in section IV. Karen J. Warren and two anonymous readers for *Hypatia* provided comments that substantially improved this paper.

1. In attempting to work out a conception of morality that is consistent with ecofeminism, I am conscious of speaking as a man about the experiences of women. I do not intend to speak *for* women, but as a man who believes men as well as women can learn from the testimony of women's experiences. I believe, for example, that men can learn something important about what it means to be a person by listening to women speak about anorexia nervosa. This is not meant to deny that there are important gender differences in the ways women and men experience food.

2. For example, she doubts the claim that moral prescriptions must be universalizable and that they must issue from reason alone. Ethics for her must include a dimension of care (see Kheel 1985).

3. Feminist insights into ethics are those that can be seen as arising from and expressing the conditions of women's moral lives. While there is a broad range of views that have been advanced by feminist ethicists, there are also patterns of agreement. In what follows I am suggesting that these patterns of agreement are sufficiently well developed to call into question the conceptual link between ecofeminist ethics and the language of rights.

4. See Marilyn Frye (1983, 66-72), for the distinction between arrogant and loving perception; María Lugones (1987) on the distinction between unity,

which erases difference, and solidarity, which recognizes difference; and Seyla Benhabib (1987, 91) who describes the rights approach as "monological" in its inability to recognize the moral "other."

5. Iris Marion Young connects deontological theories with what Adorno called the "logic of identity," which "eliminate[s] otherness" by denying "the irreducible specificity of situations and the difference among moral subjects" (Young 1987, 61).

6. Not all feminists would agree that a feminist ethics should be inherently contextual. Susan Moller Okin has argued recently that the rights perspective can include both the requirement of universalizability and empathetic concern for others. She proposes that the rights approach can be contextualized; thus she doubts whether there is a "different voice" in morality. I question whether she has succeeded in showing this, however, since her suggestion that the rights perspective requires us "to think from the point of view of everybody, of every 'concrete other' whom one might turn out to be" still entails "*equal* concern for others" (Okin 1990, 32 and 34; italics added). This is still not fully compatible with the care perspective, which allows that a particular context of caring may include caring that is *un*equal. Even if contextualized, a rule-based ethic still proceeds by finding cross-situational identity. There is a difference between contextualizing a rule-governed theory, and a "theory" that is inherently context-ualized. I therefore tend to side with those who argue that there is a distinctively feminist ethic of care that cannot be reduced to the justice perspective.

In fact, I would be sympathetic to a position that is even more pluralistic than the alternatives of rights or care. Charles Taylor (1982, 133) argues that there are moral perspectives based on personal integrity, perfection, and liberation. These may not be reducible either to rights or care. I would suggest that an ecofeminist ethics of care is most appropriately developed in dialogue with what Taylor calls the liberation orientation rather than the rights orientation. I intend to do this by arguing in the next section that the care perspective needs to be politicized.

7. See Kittay and Meyers (1987) and Sunstein (1990) for useful collections of papers illustrating the influence of Gilligan's research. Owen Flanagan and Kathryn Jackson (1990) give a helpful overview of the large body of literature on this subject. They point out several changes that might be helpful to Gilligan's theory. For example, whereas she depicts the alternative between a rights perspective and a care perspective in terms of a gestalt shift, Flanagan and Jackson argue that this does not accurately represent the shift that occurs between the two perspectives. A gestalt shift, such as the duck-rabbit, only allows the image to be seen as either a duck or a rabbit. But research suggests that most people can see a particular moral situation from the perspective of either rights or care but that one of these perspectives is regarded as more important, and the distinction in importance tends to be gender based, women emphasizing care, men emphasizing rights (38-40). This suggests the two perspectives are

psychologically, not inherently, mutually exclusive, although one may find contexts in which the perspectives do conflict.

8. An excellent source is Vandana Shiva's *Staying Alive*. See particularly her account of the Chipko movement (1988, 67-77) which began when women in the Himalayan foothills literally hugged trees that were sacred to them to spare them from deforestation. The movement has grown into a full-scale human development project.

9. By this term, I intend to indicate a distinction between vegetarianism based on considerations of health and vegetarianism based on moral considerations.

10. Regan calls the animal's right not to be killed a prima facie right that may be overridden. Nevertheless, his theory is not *inherently* contextualized.

11. This practice is also ecologically sound since it saves the enormous expense of firewood for cremation.

12. See John Robbins (1987). It should be noted that in response to such knowledge some reflective nonvegetarians commit to eating range-grown chickens but not those grown in factory farms.

13. I owe this point to a conversation with Colman McCarthy.

REFERENCES

Adams, Carol J. 1989. *The sexual politics of meat: A feminist-vegetarian critical theory*. New York: Continuum Publishing.

Benhabib, Seyla. 1987. The generalized and the concrete other: The Kohlberg-Gilligan controversy and feminist theory. In *Feminism as critique: On the politics of gender*. Seyla Benhabib and Drucilla Cornell, eds. Minneapolis: University of Minnesota Press.

Bordo, Susan R. 1988. Anorexia nervosa as the psychopathology of popular culture. In *Feminism and Foucault: Reflections on resistance*. ed. Irene Diamond and Lee Quinby. Boston: Northeastern University Press. Reprinted from *The Philosophical Forum* 17, 2 (Winter 1985-86).

——. 1989. The body and the reproduction of femininity: A feminist appropriation of Foucault. In *Gender/body/knowledge: Feminist reconstructions of being and knowing*. Alison M. Jaggar and Susan R. Bordo, eds. New Brunswick, NJ: Rutgers University Press.

Chernin, Kim. 1981. *The obsession: Reflections on the tyranny of slenderness*. New York: Harper and Row.

Feinberg, Joel. 1980. The rights of animals and unborn generations. In *Responsibilities to other generations*. Ernest Partridge, ed. Buffalo: Prometheus Books.

Ferguson, Ann. 1989. A feminist aspect theory of the self. In *Women, knowledge, and reality: Explorations in feminist philosophy*. Ann Garry and Marilyn Pearsall, eds. Winchester, MA: Unwin Hyman. Reprinted from *Science, morality, and feminist theory*. Marsha Hanen and Kai Nielsen, eds. *Canadian Journal of Philosophy*, supplementary volume 13 (1988): 339-56.

Flanagan, Owen, and Kathryn Jackson. 1990. Justice, care, and gender: the Kohlberg-Gilligan debate revisited. In *Feminism and Political Theory*. See Sunstein 1990.

Frye, Marilyn. 1983. *The politics of reality: Essays in feminist theory*. Trumansburg, NY: The Crossing Press.

Gilligan, Carol. 1982. *In a different voice: Psychological theory and women's development*. Cambridge: Harvard University Press.

Heldke, Lisa. 1988. Recipes for theory making. *Hypatia* 3(2): 15-30.

Jaggar, Alison. 1989. Love and knowledge: Emotion in feminist epistemology. In *Gender/body/knowledge: Feminist reconstructions of being and knowing*. Alison M. Jaggar and Susan R. Bordo, eds. New Brunswick, NJ: Rutgers University Press.

Kheel, Marti. 1985. The liberation of nature: A circular affair. *Environmental Ethics* 7: 141-49.

Kittay, Eva Feder, and Diana T. Meyers, 1987. *Women and moral theory*. Totowa, NJ: Rowman and Littlefield.

Lugones, María. 1987. Playfulness, "world"-travelling, and loving perception. *Hypatia* 2(2): 3-19.

Narveson, Jan. 1989. A defense of meat eating. In *Animal rights and human obligations*. 2nd ed. Tom Regan and Peter Singer, eds. Englewood Cliffs, NJ: Prentice-Hall. Originally published as Animal rights revisited. In *Ethics and animals*. H. Miller and W. Williams, eds. Clifton, NJ: Humana Press, 1983.

Noddings, Nel. 1984. *Caring: A feminine approach to ethics and moral education*. Berkeley: University of California Press.

Okin, Susan Moller. 1990. Reason and feeling in thinking about justice. In *Feminism and political theory*. See Sunstein, ed. 1990. Reprinted from *Ethics* 99 (January 1989).

Plato. 1961. Gorgias. In *Plato: The collected dialogues*. Edith Hamilton and Huntington Cairns, eds. Princeton, NJ: Princeton University Press.

Rachels, James. 1989. Why animals have a right to liberty. In *Animal rights and human obligations*. 2nd ed. Tom Regan and Peter Singer, eds. Englewood Cliffs, NJ: Prentice-Hall. Published originally in the first edition (1976).

Regan, Tom. 1983. *The case for animal rights*. Berkeley: University of California Press.

———. 1989. The case for animal rights. In *Animal rights and human obligations*. 2nd ed. Tom Regan and Peter Singer, eds. Englewood Cliffs, NJ: Prentice-Hall.

Robbins, John. 1987. *Diet for a new America*. Walpole, NH: Stillpoint Publishing.

Shiva, Vandana. 1988. *Staying alive: Women, ecology and development*. London: Zed Books.

Sunstein, Cass R. 1990. *Feminism and political theory*. Chicago: University of Chicago Press.

Taylor, Charles. 1982. The diversity of goods. In *Utilitarianism and beyond*. Amartya Sen and Bernard Williams, eds. Cambridge: Harvard University Press.

Warren, Karen J. 1990. The power and the promise of ecofeminism. *Environmental Ethics* 12 (2): 125-46.

White, Alan. 1989. Why animals cannot have rights. In *Animal rights and human obligations*. 2nd ed. Tom Regan and Peter Singer, eds. Englewood Cliffs, NJ: Prentice Hall. As excerpted from Alan White. 1984. *Rights*. Oxford: Oxford University Press.

Young, Iris Marion. 1987. Impartiality and the civic public: Some implications of feminist critiques of moral and political theory. In *Feminism as critique: On the politics of gender*. Seyla Benhabib and Drucilla Cornell, eds. Minneapolis: University of Minnesota Press.

Caring about Nature:
Feminist Ethics and the Environment

ROGER J. H. KING

I.

Environmental ethics proposes to help reconstruct our moral relationship to the nonhuman world by locating and criticizing the flaws in moral perception and thought that underlie current harmful practices. In recent years, feminists have argued that this reconstructive project requires acknowledgment of the connections between the domination of nature and the domination of women. According to ecofeminism, the failures of moral perception and thought that can be found in human relations to nature are symptomatic of similar failures to be found in the relations between women and men.

Marti Kheel claims that much of the discussion of environmental ethics has failed to make "the open admission that we cannot even begin to talk about the issue of ethics unless we admit that we care (or feel something). And it is here that the emphasis of many feminists on personal experience and emotion has much to offer in the way of reformulating our traditional notion of ethics" (Kheel 1985, 144). In this paper I shall examine both the motivation for developing an ecofeminist ethics of care and some of the problems present in ecofeminist uses of this vocabulary.

Ecofeminists have assumed that a feminist environmental ethics can draw straightforwardly on the language of some version of an ethics of care.[1] Some ecofeminists follow an essentialist strategy and argue that women are closer to nature than are men. By virtue of their closer relationship to nature, it is claimed that women are more likely than men to care about nature and are better prepared to do so than men. The vocabulary of an ethics of care is seen from this perspective to emerge as the essential voice of women's lived experience and sense of self as embedded in relationship.

In contrast, some ecofeminists follow a conceptualist strategy. They claim that an ecofeminist environmental ethics must redress the conceptual opposition that patriarchal culture sets up between men and culture on the one hand

Hypatia vol. 6, no. 1 (Spring 1991) © by Roger J. H. King

and women and nature on the other. These dualisms underlie a parallel that exists between the oppression of women and the domination of nature in a patriarchal society. Although a conceptualist environmental ethics does not claim that the vocabulary of care represents the essential moral voice of women, this vocabulary does offer conceptual resources that have been ignored by much of contemporary environmental ethics (Warren 1990, 138-45).

Both strands of ecofeminism, essentialist and conceptualist, presuppose that environmental ethics will benefit from creating theoretical space for human relations to nature, personal lived experience, and the vocabulary of caring, nurturing, and maintaining connection. While I agree with this assessment, I shall argue that we must become clearer about what it means to care about nature. I do not think that these points are adequately thematized in current ecofeminist writing. The purpose of this essay is to demonstrate the need for further reflection on the meaning of a care perspective in environmental ethics.

II.

Ecofeminists have expressed dissatisfaction with the dominant approaches within environmental ethics on the grounds that they reflect a typically male set of experiences of the world and replicate aspects of patriarchal thinking. In order to explain why ecofeminist ethics emphasizes the vocabulary of care, we should examine its criticisms of some alternative possibilities. Two positions have been primary targets of ecofeminist criticism: the "moral extensionism" of animal rights theorists and the biocentric holism of deep ecology.

Proponents of animal liberation, such as Peter Singer (1975, 1985) and Tom Regan (1982), have argued that the moral community is not identical with the human species. According to Singer, all sentient beings, those capable of feeling either pleasure or pain, are members of the moral community and possess rights to moral consideration. It follows that even though some human beings—such as the fetus at an early stage of development—do not possess rights to moral consideration, some animals do. According to Singer, therefore, failure to take the moral standing of animals into equal consideration with that of humans is "speciesism," a form of unjustifiable prejudice.

Regan agrees with Singer that the moral community is not defined by membership in the human species. However, he employs the criterion of consciousness, and in particular of consciousness of oneself as a continuing subject, to demarcate the line between those who do possess rights and those who do not. While Singer is a consequentialist, Regan's approach is deontological and thus he disallows the legitimacy of balancing costs and benefits when deliberating about how to treat those affected by human actions.

These approaches share two features that are problematic for ecofeminists. First, they rely on abstract distinctions formulated in universal principles that necessarily impose a value hierarchy separating those who do and those who do not count morally. Second, their conception of the moral community is defined through an emphasis on identity and sameness rather than on uniqueness and difference.

Singer's and Regan's positions are abstract in the sense that they articulate their criteria of moral worth without reference to the concrete ways in which particular individuals are related. Human beings and animals are presupposed to be separate and isolated individual beings whose moral traits can and should be identified prior to any consideration of the ways in which they interact with others. This abstraction from concrete context facilitates the formulation of universal principles, but in the process we lose touch with the particularities of individual situations. Generalized criteria of moral worth abstract from the complexity of the actual traits and relations that constitute an individual. As a result, we learn to perceive the individual, whether human or nonhuman, primarily in the light of the traits that have been abstracted. One of the problems with this is, as Margaret Urban Walker notes, that reliance on general criteria of moral worth

> presses me to view you, for instance, as a holder of a certain right, or a promisee . . . or a focus of some specifiable set of obligatory responses. I am pressed to structure my response or appeal to you in terms which I can think of as applying repeatedly to any number of other cases. (Walker 1989, 22)

Feminists and ecofeminists are among those who have noted that the abstractness and generality of deontological and consequentialist moral principles and their vocabulary of rights, duties, and obligations obscures "the importance of attending to the needs of those with whom we are in relation" (Lauritzen 1989, 32). They claim that such approaches contribute to a neglect of the metaphysical connectedness of human beings and facilitate an inattentiveness to the ways in which relationships themselves are sources of moral responsibility.

The importance for moral thought that feminists place on relationship is often marked by the image of the web. This image "symbolizes the interdependence that is thought to characterize human relations, according to feminist thought. We are, each of us, at every point in our lives, inextricably tied to others. We are always someone's daughter or sister, mother, son, brother or father; we are always members of a community" (Lauritzen 1989, 33-34). For ecofeminists, this community extends beyond the human species to our relations with other animals, trees and plants, places and ecosystems (Zimmerman 1987, 34).

According to many ecofeminists, then, arguments such as Singer's and Regan's are conceptually inadequate because their extension of moral standing is divorced from a consideration of the actual concrete relations to nonhuman nature in which human beings already exist. But in addition, such theories repeat the dualisms that many ecofeminists identify with patriarchal ways of thinking.[2] By setting up abstract criteria for community membership, Singer and Regan set sharp lines of demarcation between those who count morally and those who do not. Outside the sphere of sentience or self-consciousness, the rest of the world can only be the object of devalued, instrumental relations with those whose intrinsic value has been secured. Ecofeminists see dualistic thinking as intimately related to oppression and domination when it serves not simply to mark differences but to legitimate subordination.[3] In particular, when combined in the form of an abstract universalism, dualistic thinking sets up rigid conceptual frameworks that do not accurately describe the many different ways in which human beings relate morally both to one another and to the nonhuman world.

This particular failing of abstraction in ethics can be expressed by saying that Singer and Regan construct moral community on the basis of sameness rather than leaving space for a community of difference. They seek to decide what sort of beings can make up the moral domain by trying to determine which beings might plausibly have the same claim upon us as other human beings. The extension of the moral domain to include some animals is possible because some people are willing to allow that suffering in animals, for example, is as morally wrong as suffering in human beings.

The ecofeminist criticism of this approach is that it excludes many beings in nature from moral consideration because no plausible argument can be made that their misfortunes make a claim on moral agents that is equal to the claims made by the misfortunes of humans. The underlying assumption is that membership is determined by the "abstract universal," that is, by criteria that all moral patients share in common in abstraction from their particularities and differences. Carol Gould's criticism of essentialist definitions of human nature that rely on abstract universality applies to Singer's and Regan's definitions of the moral domain as well; in practice they lead to choosing "those properties as essentially and universally human [moral] which the philosophers themselves have earlier explicitly identified as male [human] properties, or which were associated with roles and functions in which males [humans] predominated" (Gould 1983, 429). In this way nature's difference, like women's, is excluded from consideration.

Taking difference seriously in environmental ethics means acknowledging that our moral commitments arise out of our engagement with both the social and the nonhuman contexts within which we live. It also requires us to acknowledge the heterogeneity of the moral domain, of the kinds of things with which we can be in relationship (Warren 1990, 134-35). The value we place on particular places or animals should not, according to this view, be relegated to a secondary or "sentimental" status as exceptions to the universal and impartial claims of morality. Rather, the nonhuman sphere may, in some cases, have greater claim on us than does the human sphere. Whether this is so will depend upon the particular ways in which the individual is related to the natural world. For ecofeminists, then, it might be said that an adequate environmental ethics presupposes that humans, animals, and land form elements of a "differential unity," a "concrete universal." In other words, it presupposes that despite their differences, humans, animals, and land form a moral community.

Some of the same objections that ecofeminists raise for deontological and consequentialist forms of environmental ethics apply also to the theorizing of the deep ecology movement.[4] Ecofeminists have been critical of this movement's analysis of the origins of human domination of nature. According to deep ecologists, the root cause lies in anthropocentric ways of thinking and acting that are intrinsically inimical to the well-being of the nonhuman community. Their solution is to promote ways of being that will recognize and respect the intrinsic, rather than merely instrumental, value of the environment and its denizens.

But ecofeminists reject both the analysis and the form of deep ecology's proposed solution. By focusing on anthropocentrism, deep ecologists ignore the role of androcentric thinking and acting central to an ecofeminist understanding of the environmental crisis. In this criticism, both essentialists and conceptualists are united. Moreover, the deep ecologists' proposal to replace anthropocentrism with a form of personal and community renewal that fuses the individual self with the larger Self of the whole biotic community is too abstract (Cheney 1987). In seeking to form a different kind of relationship with nature, deep ecologists seem to seek an erasure of the differences among the individual members of the natural community, a kind of identity of each in the life of the whole.

No matter how this program might be fleshed out, from the ecofeminist standpoint it remains simply the abstract negation of the original patriarchal dualism: a move from abstractly demarcated difference to abstract identity. What is needed is not the recovery of a sense of oneness but an understanding of the real difficulties in the way of fostering the growth of concrete, multifaceted, caring relations among individuals, societies, and the nonhuman beings and systems among whom they live. Fruitful inquiry in environmental ethics, therefore, emphasizes difference as much as continuity in the attempt to break through the species barrier.

The moral theory of ecofeminism is motivated, then, by a dissatisfaction with approaches that either impose abstract lines of demarcation or submerge them in a quest for unity. Starting with plurality and difference as our basic assumptions, environmental ethics need acknowledge no conceptual limits to the extension of the moral domain. Those limits that exist at any given time are purely historical, particular, and subject to change by the actions of concrete individuals. It is hoped that an ecofeminist environmental ethics may better promote this project than have other forms of environmental ethics.

III.

The care perspective in ecofeminist ethics offers an alternative to the approaches discussed in the previous section. But the imperative to care about nature presupposes that we understand both what "care" is and what we mean by "nature." If "nature" is not a single thing, then we must ask what "nature" ecofeminism cares about. And similarly, without a clear understanding of the concept of "care," it is difficult to determine the moral relevance for environmental ethics of the ecofeminist injunction to care about nature.

I have argued elsewhere that "nature" is a cultural construct (King, 1990). What we care for, in caring about nature, is internally linked to a process of interpretation whereby we come to understand nature to have a determinate character. The problem for an environmental ethics of care is not so much that human beings fail to care but that there is a plurality of "natures" and a plurality of forms of caring. Caring and our construction of nature as an object of care are starting points, therefore, of moral inquiry, not something given with which moral theory can come to terms uncritically.

In this section I consider the use of the care perspective by both the essentialist and conceptualist strands of ecofeminist thinking. I shall argue that the essentialist position reveals only a limited concern for nature, since its ultimate concern is for the well-being of human beings. The conceptualist position, on the other hand, while making room for the vocabulary of a care ethics, does not adequately clarify what it means to care about nature nor how this care benefits the natural world.

For the essentialists, the impetus for using the vocabulary of care in the context of environmental ethics comes from the appropriation of an ethics of care as the voice of women's experience both of morality and of the "givenness" of relationship. The assumption is that there is a similar or parallel voice that women express in the context of their relationships to nature.

Many feminists have come to recognize the limitations and qualifications that need to be appended to claims about women's nature and experience. Racial and class background, nationality and religious belief, language, sexual orientation, and individual personality all contribute to particularizing an individual woman's conception of her relatedness to others. The general metaphysical fact of relatedness is articulated culturally, just as gender is the cultural articulation of sex differences. But if a sense of relatedness is a cultural artifact pertaining to gender as it is constructed within a culture, then we should expect that other "constructive" forces will also figure in constituting the relationships to which any particular woman pays attention.

These limitations on the moral articulation of relatedness are relevant to an understanding of an environmental ethics of care. In the increasingly urban societies of Western Europe and North America, it might be argued that the relation to nature is no more "given" for women than it is for men. Both women and men are increasingly cut off from direct experiential relationships with natural, as opposed to artificial and urban, environments, and thus, although we are unavoidably in relation to the nonhuman world, we do not, many of us, experience that relation to nature as "given" in all its concreteness and complexity.

However, it might be objected that women do in fact have a special relation to nature that is closed to men, namely, the relation women have to their bodies and to reproduction. Women, as Salleh puts it, "flow with the system of nature" (Salleh 1984, 340). And the importance of this intimate connection to nature's life forces might be demonstrated by women's front line participation in the peace movement and in community actions to protest pollution in the work place or the home community.

This objection points to an interesting ambiguity in the ecofeminist concern for the environment. Indeed, it raises the crucial question of what exactly we are caring about in caring about nature. According to Salleh, "Woman's monthly fertility cycle, the tiring symbiosis of pregnancy, the wrench of childbirth and the pleasure of suckling an infant, these things already ground a woman's consciousness in the knowledge of being coterminous with Nature" (1984, 340). She criticizes deep ecology for overlooking "the point that if women's lived experience were recognized as meaningful and were given legitimation in our culture, it could provide an immediate 'living' social basis for the alternative consciousness which the deep ecologist is trying to formulate and introduce as an abstract ethical construct" (1984, 340).

But this quotation underscores the necessity of examining what exactly it is that ecofeminists care about when they care about nature. And how is this care determined by what they feel a connection with in "lived experience"? The connection with nature that Salleh draws upon is the connection to a woman's bodily nature or, more precisely, only to her reproductive nature. Awareness of this connection and the care for it that can emerge have a logic that can link a woman's relation to her reproductive nature to a relation to the environment more generally. Articulating this logic, many ecofeminists have focused on those aspects of environmental destruction that impinge directly or indirectly on women's reproductive nature, that is, on the consequences of the environmental crisis for individual and local community health and the conditions necessary for nurturing the life and growth of future generations of human beings.

What this suggests, however, is that the essentialist ecofeminist project is primarily anthropocentric, that is, oriented to the welfare of human beings. Ecofeminism, like feminism more generally conceived, is first and foremost a political movement against the forces of patriarchy that harm and oppress women. The ecological insight is that the oppression of women takes on an ecological dimension in contemporary industrial society through the augmented effects of environmental degradation on the well-being of women. But this ecological insight does not entail any turn toward nature in its own right. The anthropocentrism of the essentialists' environmental stance is evident in Lee Quinby's comment about "the significance of ecofeminism as resistance politics":

> Struggling against specific sites of power not only weakens the junctures of power's networks but also empowers those who do the struggling. Two recent books [Caldecott and Leland (1983) and Garland (1988)] show, for example, how contamination of women's wombs and breast milk leads to struggle against chemical dumping; how compromises to our immunity systems, which render our bodies vulnerable to a whole host of viruses that formerly we could withstand, lead to challenges against late-capitalist food industries and the practices of Western medicine; how logging practices in India lead to women there struggling against the multinational destruction of the culture . . . Such episodes of activism show how feminism's struggle for women's freedom and ecology's struggle for planetary well-being have come together in an alliance called ecofeminism. (Quinby 1990, 124)

In speaking of radical feminism's contribution to ecofeminism, Carolyn Merchant also points to the same kinds of concern. The link between women and biological reproduction leads ecofeminists to address the consequences of nuclear radiation, toxic wastes, household chemicals, pesticides, and herbicides for women's reproductive organs, for pregnant women, and for children. But as she also notes, "A politics grounded in women's culture, experience, and values can be seen as reactionary" (1990, 102).

The essentialist strand of ecofeminism paradoxically makes the strongest claims about the connection between women's lived experience and environmental care while at the same time replicating the dualisms of patriarchal thinking. Essentialist, or radical, ecofeminism reproduces the dualism between what counts morally and what does not. It sets up an essential opposition between male and female natures, and its logic reveals an equally dualistic perception of nature, dividing it into those aspects that impinge on women's well-being and those that do not.

The "lived experience" of women, to which the essentialist ecofeminist appeals in formulating her environmental ethics of care, is as parochial as the "lived experience" of men that ecofeminists find so unpalatable in deep ecology and in arguments for hunting (Kheel 1990).[5] There is nothing in the logic of the essentialists' environmental ethics that entails a care for the wilderness and its inhabitants, for example, that is not ultimately self-referential. It is this constant return to the welfare of human beings as the standard of moral evaluation that deep ecologists such as Warwick Fox criticize as *anthropocentric* (Fox 1989, 25).

The conceptualist strand of ecofeminism, on the other hand, is critical of the dualism and the essentialism of radical feminism. In this view, the vocabulary of care and relationship is suggestive of a perspective that avoids many of the conceptual difficulties of animal liberationist arguments and deep ecology. This strand of ecofeminist theory does not aim simply to articulate the voice of women's experience but proposes an alternative moral vocabulary to supplement, if not entirely replace, the language of current environmental ethics.

Nonetheless, the conceptualist, like the essentialist, draws on the vocabulary of an ethics of care to help articulate an ecofeminist environmental ethics. According to Karen J. Warren,

> Ecofeminism is a contextualist ethic. It involves a shift from a conception of ethics as primarily a matter of rights, rules, or principles pre-determined and applied in specific cases to entities viewed as competitors in the context of moral standing, to a conception of ethics as growing out of what Jim Cheney calls "defining relationships," i.e., relationships conceived in some sense as defining who one is. . . . Ecofeminism makes a central place for values of care, love, friendship, trust, and appropriate reciprocity—values that presuppose that our relationships to others are central to our understanding of who we are. (Warren 1990, 141, 143)

Warren sees first-person narrative as an important vehicle for an ecofeminist ethics that will give expression to this care perspective. In "The Power and the Promise of Ecological Feminism" (1990), Warren offers a short narrative of her experience as a beginning rock climber as an example of how an ecofeminist ethics might emerge from narration of the lived experience of a relationship with the nonhuman world:

> I closed my eyes and began to feel the rock with my hands. . . . At that moment I was bathed in serenity . . . I felt an overwhelming sense of gratitude for what [the rock] offered me—a chance to know myself and the rock differently . . . to come to know a sense of *being in relationship* with the natural environment. It felt as if the rock and I were silent conversational partners in a long-standing friendship. I realized then that I had come to care about this cliff which was so different from me . . . I felt myself *caring* for this rock. . . . (Warren 1990, 134-35)

We find in this passage the language of caring, relationship, friendship, conversation, and personal experience that is so central to the care perspective. Reflecting on this narrative, we see the climber's care directed toward an entity radically unlike her and note how this care is a product of the relationship itself, not of "the nature of the *relators* or parties to those relationships (e.g., relators conceived as moral agents, right holders, interest carriers, or sentient beings)" (Warren 1990, 135).

The conceptualist use of the vocabulary of care is an advance on that of the essentialist because it avoids the latter's anthropocentric orientation and the accompanying dualism. Nonetheless, there are two concerns that I think need to be raised even here. First, lived experience is selective in that it results from cultural, as well as personal, interpretation of experience. Many people lack any concrete awareness of the workings of the environment and do not care very deeply about the fate of nonhuman beings and systems. But if this is so, then any reliance on lived experience and personal narrative as a basis for constructing a moral perspective in environmental ethics presupposes some reconstruction or education of lived experience that is not intrinsic to that experience itself.

Warren notes that first-person narrative "provides a way of conceiving of ethics and ethical meaning as *emerging out of* particular situations moral agents find themselves in, rather than as being *imposed on* those situations . . . This emergent feature of narrative centralizes the importance of *voice*" (Warren 1990, 136). But whose voice should we be listening to: the resort developer's, the agribusiness entrepreneur's, the hunter's, the tourist's, the weekend athlete's? These voices are not all compatible with one another, nor are they all interested in the well-being of the natural world.

It might be argued that the importance of personal narrative is not simply that it gives voice to a moral relationship to nature, but that it may be a vehicle for expressing and producing a caring relationship to the environment. Narratives might give evidence of, and create, caring relationships while bypassing the abstract question of whether the partners in the relationship "deserve" their moral standing. But we must still ask which narratives express this caring relationship; which narratives should we listen to and respect? Our choice of narratives will be grounded in a prior moral understanding of human relationships with the natural world. Therefore, any particular narrative of lived experience can only become a basis for moral reflection and conduct as a part of a general interpretation and understanding of nature and its moral standing.[6] If this is so, then we cannot give uncritical credence to the view that normative force emerges from the personal narratives of lived experience. This points to the need to concretize and particularize the reference to lived experience in order to avoid yet another abstract ethics.

My second concern about the conceptualist position is that to see the importance of personal narrative in an ecofeminist ethics of care is not yet to know what it means to care about nature. Indeed, Warren's own narrative reveals some of the difficulties here. Care in her narrative appears to be a subjective feeling linked to her awareness of the sights and sounds around her and her feelings of serenity. She suddenly feels "as if the rock and I were silent conversational partners in a longstanding friendship." However, the narrative does not clarify in what sense the climber and the rock were either conversational partners or friends, since no voice is given to the rock in the narrative. The rock is personified as a partner and friend, yet it merely submits silently to being climbed upon, giving unilaterally what the climber wants. In this particular narrative, therefore, the concepts of "conversational partner" and "friendship," as well as their moral significance, remain unexplicated.

Warren's narrative does not clarify what care means or what its moral significance is. She contrasts a climber who cares about the rock with one who seeks to conquer it, yet for the rock, it is all the same thing; the rock does not care. Indeed, the fact that the climber cares for the rock appears to have no practical consequences for the rock itself. What, then, is gained by the metaphors of conversation, partnership, and friendship when these are taken out of their human context and when the only speaker and ultimate beneficiary is still the human climber?

I have indicated in this section how both the essentialist and conceptualist strands of ecofeminism make use of the vocabulary of an ethics of care. While the conceptualist strategy avoids the problems associated with essentialism, it is still open to the objection that it relies too heavily on "lived experience" and an indeterminate conception of caring. If an ethics of care is to have moral significance for ecofeminism, some account of care needs to be given that shows how nature itself benefits from human care. We need not argue that the object of care reciprocate or acknowledge the care we extend to it.[7] Nonetheless, if care has no practical implications for the welfare of the one who is cared for, then it would seem to be little more than a subjective sense of aesthetic appreciation, with no particular moral importance.

IV.

One of the virtues of approaching environmental ethics through the vocabulary of an ethics of care is that we come to see the difficulties in the way of establishing meaningful and moral relationships with nature. The language of care and relationship allows us to state the nature of our problem but not necessarily the solution. If people do not care about nature, do not see, feel, or understand it, then an ethics of care is faced with the difficult task of educating the moral imagination to perceive and interpret nature in such a way that nature is consciously a presence in human life, rather than the absence it has become.[8]

Aldo Leopold observes that "no important change in ethics was ever accomplished without an internal change in our intellectual emphasis, loyalties, affections, and convictions" (Leopold 1966, 246). In order to expand the boundaries of the moral community beyond the domain of beings who are like us, to include what Leopold refers to as "land," it is not enough to set down abstract moral principles stipulating what kinds of being count and what kinds do not. Rather, as Jim Cheney puts it, "nonhuman nature must [become] located in the *ethical* space of the *moral* community" (Cheney 1989, 139). Human beings must develop a relationship with the nonhuman world based on "love, respect, and admiration of the land" (Leopold 1966, 261).

But this relocation of nonhuman nature into the ethical space of the moral community will not come about simply through an injunction to care about nature, enter into relationship with it, listen to its voice, or be "engrossed" in it. Marti Kheel suggests that the separation between emotion and reason in our approach to nature might be overcome by trying to "experience directly the full impact of our moral decisions. If we *think*, for example, that there is nothing wrong with eating meat, we ought, perhaps, to visit a factory farm or slaughter house to see if we still *feel* the same way" (Kheel 1985, 145). But what if we do feel the same way? And what reason is there to suppose that many people will not, since people have been butchering animals for food in more public fashion for most of human history? We must conclude, I think, that attention to lived experience will not necessarily guide us in an environmentally responsible direction.

I have argued in this essay that ecofeminism's use of the vocabulary of an ethics of care makes an ambiguous and problematic contribution to environmental ethics. On the one hand, it provides an important alternative starting point for conceptualizing the problem that humans face in understanding the moral dimension of their relationships to the nonhuman. As it is deployed by the conceptualist strand of ecofeminism, an ethics of care avoids the abstraction of animal rights approaches and deep ecology. In rejecting an abstract approach, it focuses our attention on the particularities of concrete situations, beings, and relationships. Our emotional attachments to animals, forests, places, landscapes, and ecosystemic dependencies thereby become moral realities to be illuminated by philosophical discourse, not secret yearnings to be hidden and discarded.

On the other hand, however, the care perspective runs the risk of appearing morally reactionary in the environmental context because of the predominantly anthropocentric orientation of our culture's "lived experience." The construal of nature as an object of care is necessarily an ongoing cultural project, not one that can be finished once and for all. But in order for this project to progress, we must arrive at some better understanding of what it means to "care" about nature. This, I have argued, is a problem that neither essentialist nor conceptualist ecofeminism has yet solved.

It remains true, as ecofeminists claim, that overcoming the oppressiveness of the duality that separates the human from the nonhuman is one of the crucial tasks of environmental ethics. In spite of the difficulties I have outlined, the conceptualist strategy in ecofeminist ethics holds out the possibility that by refusing to draw arbitrary lines between human and nonhuman, a space can be held open in which the imagination may at least be educated to "loving perception" of the nonhuman world as a member of the moral community of difference and an object of care.

NOTES

I would like to acknowledge the support of the University of Maine's Women-in-the-Curriculum program, which provided a Faculty Summer Grant in 1988 for the early stages of my research into ecofeminism. I also thank the editor and anonymous *Hypatia* reviewers who made many useful suggestions for improving an earlier version of this paper.

1. For formulations of an ethics of care, see Gilligan (1982), Noddings (1984), and Ruddick (1980).

2. The importance of dualistic thinking for an explanation of both patriarchal thinking and the environmental crisis is expressed in a number of works. See, for example, King (1990), Merchant (1990), Ortner (1986), Plumwood (1986), and Warren (1987, 1990).

3. Warren (1990) argues that dualisms are not necessarily oppressive but become harmful within an oppressive conceptual scheme constituted by a "logic of domination." This logic ranks one side of the opposition as superior to the other and uses this superiority to justify exclusion and domination.

4. For accounts of the deep ecology movement, see Devall (1980), Devall and Sessions (1985), Fox (1986), and Naess (1984). For ecofeminist critiques of deep ecology, see Cheney (1987), Fox (1989), Kheel (1985, 1990), Plumwood (1986), Salleh (1984), and Zimmerman (1987, 1990).

5. For critiques of hunting from an ecofeminist perspective, see Collard (1989) and King (1991).

6. See King (1990).

7. This is the position taken by Noddings (1984).

8. One suggestive discussion of this problem can be found in Keith Basso's (1987) account of Apache moral narratives. These narratives link moral lessons to features of the natural landscape to create an indelible link between the perception of nature and the understanding of moral conduct.

REFERENCES

Basso, Keith. 1987. "Stalking with stories": Names, places, and moral narratives among the Western Apaches. In *On nature: nature, landscape, and natural history*, 95-116. Daniel Halpern, ed. San Francisco: North Point Press.

Caldecott, Léonie, and Stephanie Leland. 1983. *Reclaim the earth: Women speak out for life on earth*. London: The Women's Press.

Cheney, Jim. 1987. Ecofeminism and deep ecology. *Environmental Ethics* 9 (2): 115-45.
———. 1989. Postmodern environmental ethics: ethics as bioregional narrative. *Environmental Ethics* 11 (2): 117-34.

Collard, Andrée, with Joyce Contrucci. 1989. *Rape of the wild: Man's violence against animals and the earth*. Bloomington: Indiana University Press.

Devall, Bill. 1980. The deep ecology movement. *Natural Resources Journal* 20 (1980): 299-322.

Devall, Bill, and George Sessions. 1985. *Deep ecology: Living as if nature mattered.* Salt Lake City: Peregrine Smith Books.

Fox, Warwick. 1986. *Approaching deep ecology: A response to Richard Sylvan's critique of deep ecology.* University of Tasmania Environmental Studies Occasional Paper 20. University of Tasmania.

————. 1989. The deep ecology–ecofeminism debate and its parallels. *Environmental Ethics* 11 (1): 5-25.

Garland, Anne. 1988. *Women activists: Challenging the abuse of power.* New York: Feminist Press.

Gilligan, Carol. 1982. *In a different voice: Psychological theory and women's development.* Cambridge: Harvard University Press.

Gould, Carol. 1983. The woman question: Philosophy of liberation and the liberation of philosophy. In *Philosophy of woman: An anthology of classic and current concepts.* Mary Briody Mahowald, ed. Indianapolis: Hackett.

Kheel, Marti. 1985. The liberation of nature: A circular affair. *Environmental Ethics* 6 (Winter): 339-45.

————. 1990. Ecofeminism and deep ecology: Reflections on identity and difference. In *Reweaving the world: The emergence of ecofeminism.* Irene Diamond and Gloria Fenman Orenstein, eds. San Francisco: Sierra Club Books.

King, Roger J. H. 1991. Environmental ethics and the case of hunting. *Environmental Ethics* 13 (1): 59-85.

————. 1990. How to construe nature: Interpretation and environmental ethics. *Between the Species* 6 (3): 101-108.

King, Ynestra. 1990. Healing the wounds: Feminism, ecology, and the nature/culture dualism. In *Reweaving the world: The emergence of ecofeminism.* Irene Diamond and Gloria Fenman Orenstein, eds. San Francisco: Sierra Club Books.

Lauritzen, Paul. 1989. A feminist ethic and the new romanticism—mothering as a model of moral relations. *Hypatia* 4 (2): 29-44.

Leopold, Aldo. 1966. *A Sand County almanac: With essays on conservation from Round River.* New York: Ballantine Books.

Merchant, Carolyn. 1990. Ecofeminism and feminist theory. In *Reweaving the world: The emergence of ecofeminism.* Irene Diamond and Gloria Fenman Orenstein, eds. San Francisco: Sierra Club Books.

Naess, Arne. 1984. A defense of the deep ecology movement. *Environmental Ethics* 6 (Fall): 265-70.

Noddings, Nel. 1984. *Caring: A feminine approach to ethics and moral education.* Berkeley: University of California Press.

Ortner, Sherry. 1986. Is female to male as culture is to nature? In *Women and values: Readings in recent feminist theory.* Marilyn Pearsall, ed. Belmont, CA: Wadsworth.

Plumwood, Val. 1986. Ecofeminism: An overview and discussion of positions and arguments. *Australasian Journal of Philosophy* supplement to vol. 64 (June): 120-38.

———. 1988. Women, humanity, and nature. *Radical Philosophy* 48 (Spring): 16-24.

Quinby, Lee. 1990. Ecofeminism and the politics of resistance. In *Reweaving the world: The emergence of ecofeminism*. Irene Diamond and Gloria Fenman Orenstein, eds. San Francisco: Sierra Club Books.

Regan, Tom. 1982. *All that dwell therein: Animal rights and environmental ethics*. Berkeley: University of California Press.

Ruddick, Sara. 1980. Maternal thinking. *Feminist Studies* 6 (1): 342-67.

Salleh, Ariel Kay. 1984. Deeper than deep ecology: The eco-feminist connection. *Environmental Ethics* 6 (Winter): 339-45.

Singer, Peter. 1975. *Animal liberation: A new ethics for our treatment of animals*. New York: Random House.

Singer, Peter, ed. 1985. *In defense of animals*. Oxford: Basil Blackwell.

Walker, Margaret Urban. 1989. Moral understandings: Alternative "epistemology" for a feminist ethics. *Hypatia* 4 (2): 15-28.

Warren, Karen J. 1987. Feminism and ecology: Making connections. *Environmental Ethics* 9 (Spring): 3-20.

———. 1990. The power and the promise of ecological feminism. *Environmental Ethics* 12 (2): 125-46.

Zimmerman, Michael. 1987. Feminism, deep ecology, and environmental ethics. *Environmental Ethics* 9 (1): 21-44.

———. 1990. Deep ecology and ecofeminism: The emerging dialogue. In *Reweaving the World: The emergence of ecofeminism*. Irene Diamond and Gloria Fenman Orenstein, eds. San Francisco: Sierra Club Books.

Your Daughter or Your Dog?
A Feminist Assessment of the
Animal Research Issue

DEBORAH SLICER

John Stuart Mill said that "every great movement must experience three stages: ridicule, discussion, adoption."[1] What is popularly called the animal rights movement is a significant contemporary social movement. And while this movement continues to take its undeserved share of ridicule, it has, for the most part, advanced beyond that first stage and into the second, discussion. There is even some encouraging evidence that its recommendations are being adopted by a significant number of people who are becoming vegetarians; buying "cruelty-free" toiletries, household products and cosmetics; refusing to dissect pithed animals in biology classes or to practice surgery on dogs in medical school "dog labs"; and rethinking the status of fur.

In the academy, a busy decade or more of writing and debate has coincided with a decade of intense social activism. A vast amount of literature in this area has been written by utilitarian theorist Peter Singer, rights theorist Tom Regan, and those who are responding to them.

Singer's and Regan's arguments share a number of features, and I refer to those collectively as the Singer-Regan approach.[2] I begin by outlining this approach in section I. In section II, I draw from recent ecofeminist critiques of ecological ethics, especially of deep ecology, to explain how, similarly, the Singer-Regan approach neglects context and concrete individuals, how it overestimates the scope of principles and discounts our affective responses in moral life. In section III, I discuss the use of live animals in biomedical research. Researchers constantly tell us that we must choose between "us" (human beings) and "them" (animals), between our daughters and our dogs. They tell us it is either medical progress via the current, virtually unchecked rate and standards of animal sacrifice, or else a return to the Dark Ages. I think that both this characterization *and* the Singer-Regan characterization of the issue are dangerously misleading, for reasons I explain in that section. Throughout the paper, I try to make clear why animal rights issues, including the research one, are feminist issues, and I will make clearer the connections between some recent ecofeminist work and animal rights issues.[3]

Hypatia vol. 6, no. 1 (Spring 1991) © by Deborah Slicer

I want to say that I have the utmost respect for both Singer and Regan as committed and inspiring activists and as academicians who have worked very hard to give these issues credibility in a discipline disposed toward dismissing them either as nonissues or as "pop" philosophy. Even though our scholarship differs, what we ultimately hope to accomplish for the several billion animals who are destroyed on this planet each year by and for the sake of human beings is the same.

I.

Singer and Regan question traditional criteria that are offered as necessary and sufficient conditions for an entity's being owed moral consideration—moral personality, an ability to enjoy the "higher" pleasures—on the grounds that such criteria exclude certain human "marginal" cases, e.g., infants, the severely mentally disabled, the very senile, and the comatose. Their approach is to search for what R.G. Frey (1980) has called a "lowest common denominator," a capacity or characteristic that is common to both the "normal" and the problematic human cases. The criterion they settle on is the capacity to have "interests."

Singer and Regan give basically the same account of these interests. In *The Case for Animal Rights*, Regan argues that at least mammalian animals, one year old or older, have both "preference" and "welfare" interests, which can be either frustrated or enhanced. By "preference" interests, Regan means "those things that an individual is *interested* in, those things he likes, desires, wants or, in a word, prefers having, or, contrariwise, those things he dislikes, wants to avoid or, in a word, prefers not having" (Regan 1983, 87). By "welfare" interests, he means those things that are *in* an individual's interests, something that would benefit an individual (Regan 1983, 88). Of course an individual may or may not be interested in what is in that individual's interests.

Wishing to avoid the problem of so-called marginal cases, Regan says that individuals with preference interests have inherent value and that this value is marked by certain minimal rights, the most basic of which is the right to "treatment that is respectful of the kind of value they have, and all are owed this treatment equally; in particular, individuals who have inherent value are not to be treated as if they were mere 'receptacles' of valuable experiences" (Regan 1983, 277).[4] Singer says that sentient beings have interests, much like Regan's preference interests, in, at least, avoiding painful experiences and acquiring pleasurable ones. Possessing such interests entitles an individual to have those interests given due weight in a utilitarian calculation.

As many critics have noted, a great deal hinges on the lowest common denominator argument, an argument that appeals to the rationalist's penchant for parsimony and logical consistency. It insists that we choose an essential—that is, a necessary and sufficient—criterion of moral considerableness and that we apply it consistently to bring a vast array of both human and nonhumans equally into the moral fold. Failure to give animals the moral consideration they are due is "speciesist," a moral wrong similar to racism and sexism. To paraphrase Singer, speciesism is an irrational bias toward members of one's own species and against members of other species (Singer 1977, 7).

According to Singer, a utilitarian calculation of both the animal and human pleasures and sufferings that result from such practices as flesh eating, product testing, biomedical research and education, and recreational hunting will in the vast majority of cases weigh in favor of the animals. According to Regan, these various practices violate an animal's right to respectful treatment, that is, we do not treat them in ways consistent with the recognition of their equal possession of inherent value. Instead, we treat them as receptacles of intrinsic value (e.g., pleasure), lacking any value of their own.

II.

Singer's and Regan's arguments are recognizable offshoots of what some feminists, following Carol Gilligan's analysis (1982), call the "justice tradition" in moral and political philosophy.[5] Here, I will focus on how such theories misrepresent our moral relations with animals rather than with other human beings.

1. ESSENTIALISM

Singer and Regan, like their mentors the utilitarians and Kant, respectively, have an "essentialist" view of the moral worth of both human beings and animals. This means that they propose a single capacity—the possession of interests—for being owed moral consideration. It is clear that they believe this condition is a sufficient one for being owed such consideration. And while they do not say specifically that possessing such interests is *necessary*, Singer and Regan *treat* the possession of preference interests as a necessary condition. For example, the lowest common denominator argument, which is central to their respective attempts to bring animals into the moral fold equally with human beings, is sound only if possessing interests is treated as necessary. Both writers say that those who do not possess interests are, at best, problematic. And both Singer and Regan condone sacrificing those without interests for the sake of those who do possess them.[6]

Essentialism is objectionable for a number of reasons. First, it renders inessential and unimportant certain relationships—familial relationships or friendships, for example—that do seem essential and important to many of the rest of us (Francis and Norman 1978). Second, as some feminist writers have noted, essentialism strips an individual of his or her "specific history, identity, and affective-emotional constitution" (Walker 1989, 18). Specifically, animal rights theories reduce individuals to that atomistic bundle of interests that the justice tradition recognizes as the basis for moral considerableness. In effect, animals are represented as beings with the *kind of capacity* that human beings most fully possess and deem valuable for living a full *human* life.

Several ecofeminists, including Marti Kheel (1985), Jim Cheney (1987), and Karen J. Warren (1990), have noted something very much like essentialism, or at least a certain arrogance underlying essentialism, in the environmental ethics literature, especially among deep ecologists.[7] Both Kheel and Warren show how such arrogance leads to hierarchical and dualistic thinking. Jim Cheney agrees with Ariel Kay Salleh, who claims that, as Cheney puts it, attempts by deep ecologists "to overcome human (really masculine) alienation from nature fail in the end because they are unable to overcome a masculine sense of the self and the kinds of ethical theory that go along with this sense of self" (Cheney 1987, 121). I agree with Cheney, who points out that some deep ecologists fail to recognize and respect the integrity of the "other," of animals and nonsentient nature, when they describe their relationship to nature in terms of nature being a part of them, when they merely expand "the self to *include* that in relationship to which it feels alienated" (Cheney 1987, 121). Cheney describes this metaphorically as a "megalomaniacal pond sucking up all the water of the world and becoming itself an ocean" (Cheney 1987, 124).

In contrast to this "megalomaniacal" view, as Karen J. Warren discusses her first rock-climbing experiences she compares a potentially "arrogant" relationship with the rock—as invasive, as conqueror, as coercive—with a climber's "loving" relationship. She says of the latter:

> One recognizes the rock as something very different, something perhaps totally indifferent to one's own presence, and finds in that difference joyous occasion for celebration. One knows "the boundary of the self," where the self—the "I," the climber— leaves off and the rock begins. There is no fusion of two into one, but a complement of two entities *acknowledged* as separate, different, independent, yet *in relationship;* they are in relationship *if only* because the loving eye is perceiving it, responding to it, noticing it, attending to it. (Warren 1990, 137)

Singer and Regan extend the moral community to include animals on the basis of sameness. They do not acknowledge, much less celebrate, differences between humans and other animals. This sort of self-centric importance, this assimilation of the other into the sameness of self, the "fusion of two into one" and the "erasure of difference," as Warren puts it, is central to the concept of arrogance that Marilyn Frye (1983) and Iris Murdoch (1970) have previously articulated.

Warren's loving attention to the rock's difference, independence, indifference did not result in her antipathy or moral apathy with regard to the rock.

Instead, she says, "I felt an overwhelming sense of gratitude for what it offered me—a chance to know myself and the rock differently, to appreciate unforeseen miracles like the tiny flowers growing in the even tinier cracks in the rock's surface, and to come to know a sense of *being in relationship* with the natural environment. . . . I felt myself *caring* for this rock" (Warren 1990, 135).

There is no reason why animals' differences, independence, indifference cannot be grounds for caring, for relationships characterized by such ethically significant attitudes as respect, gratitude, compassion, fellow or sisterly feeling, and wonder. Such animal ethologists as Jane Goodall (1971) have practiced for decades what Warren (1990), who is indebted to Marilyn Frye (1983), calls "loving attention." Goodall and other women (some of them feminist) scientists have suggested that such an attitude and its practice are not only appropriate moral attitudes with regard to the subjects they are studying but an epistemologically fruitful one as well (e.g., see Keller 1983).

Both Warren and Kheel note how arrogant essentialism re-creates moral hierarchies and dualistic thinking in ways that "establish inferiority and subordination" (Warren 1990, 129).[8] Marti Kheel puts the point like this: "Ironically, although many of these writers feel that they are arguing against notions of hierarchy, the vast majority simply remove one set of hierarchies only to establish another. Thus, many writers on the subject of animal liberation may raise the status of animals to a level that warrants our moral concern only to exclude other parts of nature, such as plants and trees" (Kheel 1985, 139). And there is even a pecking order among those in the upper echelons (among those who possess interests) of the hierarchy. Singer and Regan say that in dire cases, when we must choose between animal and human life, the life of the human, because it has more valuable potential experiences, takes priority.[9]

Central to an ecofeminist analysis of patriarchy is the claim that such value hierarchies, which categorize women, animals, and nonsentient nature on the same devalued side of the dualism, serve to oppress women along with nature in a vast array of similar ways.[10] Unfortunately, like many of the deep and certainly the "shallow" ecologists, Singer's and Regan's analyses do not cut deeply enough into our culture's objectionable use of these dualistic hierarchies. In fact, their "liberation" theories only perpetuate such thinking.

2. CONTEXT AND PRINCIPLES

A second feature of the justice tradition that has received attention is the propensity among those working in that tradition to characterize moral situations generally and abstractly and at the expense of contextual detail. What is lost in this kind of characterization of moral life or of a moral dilemma are historical, social, economic, familial, and other details that seem crucial to an assessment of a situation, a decision, or a character. Singer and Regan give us such delimited descriptions, and these descriptions allow them to formulate general, prescriptive principles that are applicable to similarly and superficially described situations. The use of such principles is a third feature of the Singer-Regan approach that I discuss.

As noted in section I, for Singer and Regan the animal research issue and the vegetarian issue are described similarly as situations in which animals' interests, given the strict and impartial consideration they are due, override human interests in eating them or in using them as experimental subjects. And the reasons our desires are overridden—because animals' desires are stronger or their rights given priority by an adjudicatory principle of justice that we have all decided on—should be recognized as good reasons by anyone capable of following a logical inference.

At least since Gilligan, a central task of feminist moral criticism has been to assess the role, proper status, and nature of principles in moral life. Some ecofeminists have raised similar questions about principles in reviewing work by deep ecologists and in deciding whether there is a place for principles in their own theories.[11] It is often said that general principles are too legalistic and abstract to be helpful in resolving unique, highly context-laden, nongeneralizable situations and that a "principled morality" leaves no room for virtue and affection.[12] While these writers do not eschew the use of principles entirely, they do reject any morality that worships principles while neglecting such things as virtue or the affections. I agree with these writers, and I object to the way rights and utilitarian principles are often presented to us in classrooms, textbooks, and scholarly books and articles as our only "reasonable" options. This is objectionable because if these are our only options, then we must sometimes disregard what our imaginations or hearts or the simple facts are telling us, in order to articulate situations, some of them very uncooperative, in a way that fits these principles and their corresponding conceptual frameworks. Singer's and Regan's awkward attempts to articulate interspecies moral relations using these standard theories and conceptual frameworks exemplify this point.

What principles we articulate and ultimately choose to rely on are relevant to a very complex web of "beliefs, feelings, modes of expression, circumstances and more, arranged in characteristic ways and often spread out over time" (Walker 1989, 18). In an essay on bioregional narrative, Jim Cheney suggests that we "extend these notions of context and narrative outward so as to include not just the human community, but also the land, one's community in a larger sense." Moreover, "for a genuinely contextualist ethic to include the land . . . the land must *speak* to us; we must stand in *relation* to it; it must *define* us, and we it" (Cheney 1989, 128-29). I should think that this concept of "the land" would entail sentient nature. And because we not only are *defined by* but also *define* this relationship—not in terms of static and essentialist necessary and sufficient conditions but in contextually rich and evolving terms—we will have opportunities to evaluate and alter aspects of the relationship when certain features of it (our arrogance and our waste, for example) are brought forcefully to our attention, and we may well want to recommend some of these alternatives universally.

Recently, Karen J. Warren articulated eight "boundary conditions"—necessary conditions that "delimit the territory of a piece without dictating what the interior . . . looks like"—of any feminist ethic and of any ecofeminist ethic. One of those conditions states that a feminist ethic or an ecofeminist ethic cannot be naturist—that is, cannot condone the oppressive domination of sentient and nonsentient nature—or contribute to any other " '-ism' which presupposes and advances a logic of domination." Warren defines a "logic of domination" as "a structure of argumentation which leads to a justification of subordination" (Warren 1990, 128). This "logic" entails a value system that designates "subordinates" and their "inferior" characteristics or capacities. A second condition holds that any theory should be fluid, in process, changing over time, and emerging out of "concrete and alternative descriptions of ethical situations." A third requires that feminist ethics must give a place to "values typically unnoticed, underplayed, or misrepresented in traditional ethics" and will do so while recognizing a role for traditional values (Warren 1990, 139-40).

These boundary conditions are also relevant to any critique of the animal rights literature and to attempts to reconceptualize our moral relationships with and obligations to the animals with whom Singer and Regan are concerned. I have already discussed how Singer and Regan retain an unfortunate "logic of domination" in their respective theories. Their atemporal, abstract, and acontextual characterizations of issues, of the values at stake, and of appropriate resolutions grossly oversimplify some of these highly complex issues, including, as I show in section III, the research one. Such characterizations also oversimplify our actual and potential relationships with and responses to animals, depriving us of opportunities to respond to and make responsible choices about the enormous cost to other sentient life of such intimate and routine practices involving, e.g., what we eat, the bath soap and shampoo that we use, and the pills that we take for a headache or to prevent a pregnancy.

3. THE AFFECTIONS

Peter Singer says that he does not "love" animals, that he has "argued" his case, "appealing to reason rather than to emotion or sentiment . . . because reason is more universal and more compelling in its appeal" (Singer 1977, 255). Regan says that we should make "a concerted effort not to indulge our emotions or parade our sentiments. And that requires making a sustained commitment to rational inquiry" (Regan 1983, xii).

A fair number of critics, after and long before Carol Gilligan, have said that such faith in the rational and universal force of principles at the expense of our emotional responses is naive, based on an insensitivity to our actual moral psychology and a Western and perhaps masculinist contempt for our emotions, which are considered "womanish." Critics have shown how this rationalist ideal fails to account for what motivates us in many of our personal relations, where love, or friendship, or the affections, for example, often are, and should be, a (or the) predominant motive.[13] Singer and Regan follow the tradition that polarizes reason and the emotions and that privileges reason when the two conflict.

There is no pat formula for deciding when our affective responses have a place, or how much weight they should have, in resolving dilemmas affecting either personal or public relations. For the most part, deciding when and to what extent our affective responses are appropriate and helpful involves entering into a particular narrative. Probably there are situations, even involving personal relations, that call for the use of some maxim that is impartial and dispassioned. Apportioning family goods, services, or energy among rivaling children might be an example. And certainly we sometimes do and should be allowed to respond affectively to strangers. We feel what might be an empathetic sympathy and embarrassment when we witness, for example, someone else's public humiliation or a parent pleading on television for the return of a missing child.

Marti Kheel (1985) has said that the argument Singer and Regan make from "marginal cases" relies on an emotional appeal. The argument holds that we either revoke the moral standing of "defective" human beings or else grant standing to those animals that are intellectually and emotionally on par with these humans. Since we have some very strong feelings or intuitions about the humans the argument is persuasive: we are willing to accord moral status to animals rather than deny it to the humans.

What Kheel advocates, along with Mary Midgley, Sara Ruddick, and Robin Morgan, is what Morgan calls a "unified sensibility," or a recognition of the "fusion of feeling and thought" as characteristic of moral life (Kheel 1985, 144). Karen J. Warren (1990) is advocating something similar when she says that an ecofeminist ethic will emerge out of individuals' concrete relationships and experiences and will recognize a variety of affective responses along with formal and abstract principles, all in their appropriate contexts.

Kheel and Warren suggest that whenever possible we must "*experience* the full impact of our moral decisions," especially of those decisions that we make daily and so casually and that have such an enormous impact on the rest of sentient life (Kheel 1985, 145). This implies that those individuals who believe that flesh eating is morally permissible or even morally neutral should visit chickens who are confined along with three to six other chickens in a cage the size of a record album cover in a battery shed that holds up to 10,000 other chickens. They should see bobby calves tethered in veal sheds and cows on the killing floor and witness a sow's confinement in the "iron maiden."[14] Those who condone animal research and testing should request a tour of laboratories at the nearest research university. They should see the equipment—the surgical tables, restraining chairs, "rape racks," and "guillotines"—and experience the smells and the sounds.[15]

Will these individuals still think and feel the same about such practices? I am not saying that moral disagreement will disappear when we expand the range of experiences or responses that enrich our moral lives. But I do agree with those who emphasize the importance of direct experience for making responsible choices *and* for articulating desperately needed new moral visions, particularly in animal and environmental ethics.

III.

In this section I begin to give the research issue the kind of contextual attention that Singer and Regan fail to give it. This needs to be done before we can assess the role of abstract principles, including Singer's and Regan's principles, and of the affections in resolving the issue. In the course of recontextualizing the issue, I examine it holistically and explore several related ecofeminist themes.

I limit the focus of my discussion to the use of animals in biomedical research. I do *not* attempt to justify the use of animals in any such studies. In fact, I am sympathetic with Singer's and Regan's repugnance over using animals as research tools, even though I disagree with their arguments. What I have to say here has some special bearing on feminist critiques of androcentric science and on recent attempts to articulate "feminine" and especially feminist alternatives. If, as ecofeminists say, naturism is something that feminists should condemn and always avoid in their own work, then the use of 20 million research animals annually in this country deserves more attention in this feminist literature than it has received.[16]

The few ecofeminists who have written in any depth about animal research (Kheel 1985; Collard 1988; Adams 1990) insist that we examine the issues contextually and holistically. Only then can we make knowledgeable and responsible decisions, in the rich sense of weighing facts, theoretical knowledge, and our affections. In this spirit, then, we should consider the many well-documented studies that demonstrate: (1) how animals are grossly over-used and misused in research that is trivial, duplicative to the point of redundancy, badly designed, or that fails to use existing nonanimal alternatives or to develop them;[17] (2) how many researchers use species with more demanding psychosocial needs when those with less demanding needs will do; (3) how animals often do not serve as reliable models for human beings and how it can be very dangerous to extrapolate from results obtained from one species to another;[18] and (4) how federal and in-house regulations that are supposed to protect laboratory animals are grossly inadequate and how regulatory agencies are extremely lax in enforcing the few regulations that do exist.

In addition, as a variety of activists and ecofeminists have said, our society, including the medical establishment, needs to insist on such *proactive* measures as cleaning our air, water, soil, and the poisons from our grocery shelves if we are serious about our physical and psychological well-being. Americans see precious little of that from the National Institutes of Health, the world's largest funder of reactive animal research, or from the American Medical Association. And of course we are unlikely to see a preventative emphasis from these institutions, as feminists writing about science (e.g., Harding 1986), women's health care (e.g., Corea 1988), and technology (e.g., Merchant 1980; Collard 1988) have pointed out. As Collard puts it, these institutions use a strategy "typical of patriarchal control . . . whereby the integrity of matter (living and nonliving) is broken, artificially restored/recombined, and marketed in such a way (cure, improvement, etc.) as to elicit gratitude" (Collard 1988, 79). Animal research is a part of the strategy, and animals are among its subjects, along with women, whose natural lives have been "enhanced" by these "helping" institutions in everything from our pregnancies to our breast size.

These mostly methodological considerations certainly are not lost on Singer and Regan, but they are superfluous to what Regan calls the "moral heart of the matter" (Regan 1983, 384): the conflict between human and animal interests and our unjustified willingness to sacrifice the latter for the former. But for many thoughtful people the question of *whether* animals should be used in research is more pertinently one of when they should be used and *how* they will be treated, just as, to make some very imperfect comparisons, for many people the question of whether euthanasia is morally permissible is also a question of how and when it is performed, and for some, the question of "just" war is not so much a question of whether it is justifiable but of how and when. I am not claiming here that these three practices— euthanasia, "just" war, and animal research—are analogous; they are, in fact, significantly disanalogous. Instead, my point is that many people will consider any characterization of these issues that leaves out information about methodology and other contextual features to be decontextualized to the point of being misleading, even irrelevant.

How, exactly, do Singer and Regan themselves resolve this "moral heart of the matter"? In his chapter on research Regan advocates the total abolition of the use of animals in research, even granting, as he puts it, "that we face greater prima facie harm than laboratory animals presently endure if future harmful research on these animals is stopped, and even granting that the number of humans and other animals who stand to benefit from allowing this practice to continue exceeds the number of animals used in it" (Regan 1983, 389).

But in his discussion of biomedical research, Regan also makes a distinction between "exceptional" sacrifice and "routine" or "institutionalized" sacrifice of animal life. And he says that any judgments we make about the former (lifeboat cases, for example) are not transferable to the latter (the routine and prevalent use of animals in research, for example); but he does not condemn the former, nonroutine sacrifice. This is a suggestive but much underdeveloped point. If Regan is saying that the nonroutine use of some animals might be justified in desperate times in extreme situations, then we will most certainly have to muck around in the contextual particulars to sort these cases out. Most of all, we will want to know what constitutes "nonroutine" use, that is, how many animals may be used with what frequency and for what. And I expect that there will be no pat formula for deciding this, that we will have to sort this out on a case-by-case basis.

Singer resorts to an argument that appears frequently in the literature. I call it the onus argument. His version of it follows:

> So whenever an experimenter claims that his experiment is important enough to justify the use of an animal, we should ask him whether he would be prepared to use a retarded human at a similar mental level to the animal he is planning to use. (Singer 1977, 67)

Singer does not advocate using human beings as research subjects. He is making a point about consistency: an experimenter cannot consistently condone the use of an animal while condemning the use of a human being when each will suffer roughly the same. Singer is basically correct when he says that the research community bears the onus of justifying its use of animals, even when it is clear that some significant benefits could come of it. But there is also an onus on the rights community to justify their abolitionist stance, to justify not using animals, especially when we stand to lose some significant future benefits. Singer's response to that onus is to lead us into a utilitarian impasse. Arguing that there are no defensible grounds on which to base a choice does not make the problem go away. Oddly, Singer considers this impasse a kind of victory. I think that he has reached something more like a dead end, that this impasse is an indication that utilitarianism, at least in itself, is unable to resolve this problem. Utilitarianism might even be the problem; an impartial or misleading characterization of an issue can make it seem obdurate, unresolvable.

Recently, ecofeminist Ynestra King (1987) took to task a certain "Malthusian wing" of deep ecologists for their shallow analyses of the political and social causes of such environmental problems as global over-population and for the impracticality and bureaucratic heartlessness of their proposed solutions. I feel a similar frustration with the shallow utilitarian analysis of the research issue that leads to Singer's impasse, with the impracticality of the impasse itself as some sort of proposed resolution, and with Singer's and Regan's assumptions that our allegiance to principled demands will and should cut cleanly through any preexisting emotional or other bonds we might have to members of our own species, community, friends, family, or lovers who may suffer as a result of Singer's and Regan's recommendations.[19] My point is not to justify any and all of these bonds as automatic trumps against animals' sufferings. Rather than say that these bonds should count for nothing (as the animal rights literature suggests) or that they count for everything (as the research community suggests), I have been trying to show all along that there are numerous relevant issues that are neglected by both sides, including this one, and there may well be more than just two sides.

The following are among some of the more significant issues neglected by mainstream writers on animal research. I only gesture at them here and hope that they receive more attention in the future. First, can we justify sacrificing beings who are extremely vulnerable to the whims and powers of human beings? How do we justify sacrificing beings who are "innocent," that is, who are neither actually nor potentially culpable or even capable of any wrongdoing? We all seem to recognize some fairly stringent moral prohibitions against taking advantage of the innocent and the vulnerable, *even* in cases of self-defense, even in lifeboat cases. In fact, taking such advantage is often seen as especially malign. Do animals fall outside the scope of this prohibition completely, and if so, why? If not, why not? And if sometimes, then when and why?

Andrée Collard (1988) suggests that along with the self-serving appropriation of animals for the ostensive purpose of advancing human health, there is also a familiar attitude that "might makes right" with regard to the capture, breeding, genetic engineering, use and disposal of research animals. Every feminist knows that women have been and are affected by this form of arrogance in science, in the streets, in our own bedrooms and elsewhere. To condone such an attitude and practice in any context is to perpetuate it in all. Ynestra King puts this basic ecofeminist thesis forcefully when she says that "the hatred of women and the hatred of nature are intimately connected and mutually reinforcing" (King 1989, 18).

Furthermore, one popular nineteenth-century antivivisectionist argument, advanced by George Bernard Shaw, among others, held that the appropriation of unwilling and unwitting subjects for research that is painful and deadly erodes any aspirations or pretensions we might have about living in a "civilized" society, about possessing a "civilized" character. Ecofeminists have made similar points with regard to the arrogant and violent appropriation of nonhuman nature and women, particularly by American and Anglo-European cultures. Collard says that we live in a society "dominated by the 'ideology of cultural sadism,' " one in which "violent acts are neutralized by virtue of being so common. In the case of animal experimentation, these acts are admired (published and replicated) and the actors honored (tenured and funded)" (Collard 1988, 68). The same culture that at best is apathetic about and at worst valorizes the deaths of 20 million research animals in U.S. laboratories annually also allowed the country's 750,000 *reported* rapes during the 1980s, the murder of 50,000 women by their male partners, and the hospitalization of more women from beatings by their male partners than from auto accidents during that decade.[20] All this seems at least prima facie evidence that acts of violence against women have been similarly neutralized.

As a final consideration, we might also examine the affective schizophrenia of a country that spends more money than any other in the world on its "pets," while spending more than any other on animal research, much of it involving the use of cats and dogs, hamsters and bunnies. How and why do we circumscribe our collective and individual imaginations in this manner? Certainly whatever is going on here is complicated and beyond the scope of this paper. But our reasons for such seemingly arbitrary circumscription must include such obvious things as consumer convenience and the research and testing industry's secrecy about and, more recently, outright denial of the violence of so-called routine testing and research. Do we want to condone whatever sophisticated emotional bracketing is at work here? I should hope not. To do so is to give up any significant account of collective and individual moral responsibility regarding, as I have said before, the impact on the rest of sentient life of some of our most routine and intimate practices (e.g., what we eat) and consumer purchases (e.g., the dish soap we buy).

Surely we will not and probably cannot have the same affections or degrees of affection for the cat or dog in the laboratory that we have for the animals in our households, nor can we have the same feeling for a stranger's lost or abused child that we would have for our own child in a similar situation. These special ties *do* bind, and I am not recommending that we bracket them for the sake of blind impartiality, at least not always. While we cannot feel or care the *same* for every human being or animal, the feeling or caring that we do have for our immediate companions should extend some, via imagination and empathy, to our feeling for, our caring about, the plight of more extended others. And for those who have a rich enough moral imagination, this regard will cross species boundaries. Someone who has cared about a rock or a tree or a dog or a cat may well care about what happens to, and particularly about the destruction of, other rocks, trees, cats, and dogs. Such particular relationships can and should enhance one's capacity to empathize, "feel with," and act on behalf of others.

I am not saying that everyone who cares about laboratory animals will condemn experimentation. I am saying that we will at least cease to condone the practice so cavalierly. We will find that there are certain elements of moral tragedy in having to make some choices despite the daunting complexity of these situations, despite having few, if any, principles or precedents to guide us, despite having little or no assurance that we have chosen rightly. And regardless of how we choose, we may have to live with, as some have recently put it, irresolute, nagging "moral remainders."[21]

IV.

I am convinced that as feminist theorists and practitioners we must address the interconnecting dominations of women, animals, and nonsentient nature, as ecofeminists insist, along with other social dominations, in order to understand sufficiently and correct any one and all of them. Ecofeminist analyses include those facets of patriarchal domination that are often neglected by other feminists, by environmental ethicists, and by animal rights proponents. I realize that

I have made very few recommendations about when, if ever, we may use animals in research, although I have made my general antipathy toward such use clear. Nonetheless, and this may be obvious, I still feel some ambivalence over this issue, a gut sense that my antipathy is appropriate but that its grounds are not yet well enough articulated. I hope to inspire other feminist voices to help articulate these grounds and to do so in a way that avoids simplistic characterizations in terms of daughters and dogs.

NOTES

Many thanks to the *Hypatia* referees, to Tony Crunk, and to Karen J. Warren for their comments on an earlier version of this paper. I also gratefully acknowledge Cora Diamond's influence on my thinking about these issues.

1. Tom Regan (1983, 400) cites this passage from Mill.

2. Cora Diamond (1978) also uses the term "Singer-Regan approach." My characterization of the approach shares certain features with hers, but our characterizations are not the same.

3. I use the popular term "animal rights" to refer to political and philosophical debates over the moral status of mostly domestic, agricultural, and laboratory animals. I do not argue anywhere that animals have moral or legal rights.

4. Regan includes mammalian animals, one year and older, who are not psychologically impaired under the jurisdiction of this principle because, he says, we can be assured that these animals have preference interests. He also says that his is a "minimal" case, which means that he does not rule out the possibility of nonmammals and of mammals younger than one year having preference interests.

5. See especially Kittay and Meyers (1987).

6. For example, Singer (1979) says that we may eat "humanely" raised and slaughtered chickens and ducks because, he claims, they probably have no interests in their future; in fact, they probably have no notion of a "future" whatsoever, he says. Regan (1983), who wants to give ducks and chickens and other nonmammals, as well as mammals younger than one year, the "benefit of the doubt," does say that it is permissible to sacrifice fetal mammals and nonmammals in their early stages of development because they do not possess interests.

7. Deep ecologists eschew "shallow" ecologists' anthropocentric philosophies. A major tenet of the deep ecology movement is that, as Arne Naess puts it, "the well-being of nonhuman life on Earth has a value in itself. This value is independent of any instrumental usefulness for limited human purposes" (Naess 1984, 266; see also Naess 1973).

8. "The problem is not simply *that* value-hierarchical thinking and value dualisms are used, but *the way* each has been used in *oppressive conceptual*

frameworks to establish inferiority and to justify subordination" (Warren 1990, 128-29).

9. Both Singer (1977, 21-22) and Regan (1983, 324) make a distinction between the value of a "normal" human life and that of an animal, and each say the human life is the more valuable.

10. See Susan Griffin (1978) and Carol Adams (1990).

11. See Jim Cheney (1987, 1989) and Karen J. Warren (1990).

12. See especially Murdoch (1970), Gilligan (1982), Noddings (1984), Ruddick (1980).

13. See Gilligan (1982) and Noddings (1984).

14. The "iron maiden" is used to confine a sow's movements after she delivers her litter. This is manufacturers' and breeders' slang for this device.

15. A "rape rack" immobilizes primates as they are impregnated (Benney 1983).

16. The U.S. Department of Agriculture and researchers currently say that 20 million animals are used annually for research in the United States. This figure may well be low because institutions are not required to report the use of mice and rats (80% of the animals used in research), and farm animals. Animal rights groups put the annual figure at 40-60 million.

17. Standards in the Animal Welfare Act that are supposed to define and control "trivial" experimentation and minimize redundancy are enforced by an institution's Animal Care and Use Committee, an in-house committee which generally consists of researchers and individuals friendly to animal research. Decisions about the numbers and types of animals used in an experiment and about whether to withhold pain medication are also left to the discretion of this in-house committee. I highly recommend the studies by the United Action for Animals, 205 East 42nd Street, New York, NY 10017 on duplication and redundancy.

18. Thalidomide was tested on several nonhuman animal species before being given to human beings. Insulin deforms mice and rabbits. Penicillin is toxic to guinea pigs.

19. Mary Midgley (1983) has made a very similar point.

20. These figures are cited in "Hate Crimes Bill Excludes Women," in *off our backs* 20, no. 6 (June 1990).

21. " 'Moral remainders' refers to some genuine moral demands which, because their fulfillment conflicted with other genuine moral demands, are 'left over' in episodes of moral choice, and yet are not nullified" (Walker 1989, 21).

REFERENCES

Adams, Carol J. 1990. *The sexual politics of meat: A feminist vegetarian critical theory.* New York: Crossroads/Continuum.

Benney, Norma. 1983. All of one flesh: The rights of animals. In *Reclaim the earth: Women speak out for life on earth*. Léonie Caldecott and Stephanie Leland, eds. London: The Women's Press.

Cheney, Jim. 1987. Ecofeminism and deep ecology. *Environmental Ethics* 9 (2): 115-45.

———. 1989. Postmodern environmental ethics: Ethics as bioregional narrative. *Environmental Ethics* 11 (2): 117-34.

Collard, Andrée, with Joyce Contrucci. 1988. *Rape of the wild: Man's violence against animals and the earth*. Bloomington: Indiana University Press.

Corea, Gena. 1988. *The mother machine: Reproductive technologies from artificial insemination to artificial wombs*. London: The Women's Press.

Diamond, Cora. 1978. Eating meat and eating people. *Philosophy* 53: 465-79.

Francis, Leslie Pickering, and Richard Norman. 1978. Some animals are more equal than others. *Philosophy* 53: 507-27.

Frey, R. G. 1980. *Interests and rights*. Oxford: Clarendon Press.

Frye, Marilyn. 1983. Arrogance and love. In *The politics of reality*. Freedom, CA: The Crossing Press.

Gilligan, Carol. 1982. *In a different voice*. Cambridge: Harvard University Press.

Goodall, Jane. 1971. *In the shadow of man*. Boston: Houghton Mifflin.

Griffin, Susan. 1978. *Woman and nature: The roaring inside her*. New York: Harper and Row.

Harding, Sandra. 1986. *The science question in feminism*. Ithaca and London: Cornell University Press.

Keller, Evelyn Fox. 1983. *A feeling for the organism: The life and work of Barbara McClintock*. New York: W.H. Freeman.

Kheel, Marti. 1985. The liberation of nature: A circular affair. *Environmental Ethics* 7 (2): 135-49.

King, Ynestra. 1987. What is ecofeminism? *The Nation*, 12 December.

———. 1989. The ecology of feminism and the feminism of ecology. In *Healing the wounds: The promise of ecofeminism*. Judith Plant, ed. Santa Cruz: New Society Publishers.

Kittay, Eva Feder, and Diana T. Meyers, eds. 1987. *Introduction to women and moral theory*. Totowa, NJ: Rowman and Littlefield.

Merchant, Carolyn. 1980. *The death of nature: Women, ecology and the scientific revolution*. San Francisco: Harper and Row.

Midgley, Mary. 1983. *Animals and why they matter*. Athens: University of Georgia Press.

Murdoch, Iris. 1970. *The sovereignty of good*. London: Routledge and Kegan Paul.

Naess, Arne. 1973. The shallow and the deep, long-range ecology movement: A summary. *Inquiry* 16: 95-100.

———. 1984. A defense of the deep ecology movement. *Environmental Ethics* 6(3): 265-70.

Noddings, Nell. 1984. *Caring: A feminine approach to ethics and moral education.* Berkeley and Los Angeles: University of California Press.

Regan, Tom. 1983. *The case for animal rights.* Berkeley and Los Angeles: University of California Press.

Ruddick, Sara. 1980. Maternal thinking. *Feminist Studies* 6 (2): 342-67.

Singer, Peter. 1977. *Animal liberation.* New York: Avon Books.

———. 1979. *Practical ethics.* Cambridge: Cambridge University Press.

Walker, Margaret. 1989. Moral understandings: Alternative "epistemology" for a feminist ethics. *Hypatia* 4(2): 15-28.

Warren, Karen J. 1990. The power and the promise of ecological feminism. *Environmental Ethics* 12(1): 125-46.

Ecofeminism and the Eating of Animals[1]

CAROL J. ADAMS

> Jean: Would you feel raping a woman's all right if it was happening to her and not to you?
>
> Barbie: No, I'd feel like it was happening to me.
>
> Jean: Well, that's how some of us feel about animals.
>
> —1976 conversation about feminism and vegetarianism

Ecofeminism identifies a series of dualisms: culture/nature; male/female; self/other; rationality/emotion. Some include humans/animals in this series. According to ecofeminist theory, nature has been dominated by culture; female has been dominated by male; emotion has been dominated by rationality; animals . . .

Where are *animals* in ecofeminist theory and practice?[2]

SIX ECOFEMINIST OPTIONS

Animals are a part of nature. Ecofeminism posits that the domination of nature is linked to the domination of women and that both dominations must be eradicated. If animals are a part of nature, then why are they not intrinsically a part of ecofeminist analysis and their freedom from being instruments of humans an integral part of ecofeminist theory? Six answers suggest themselves. I discuss each in turn.

1. ECOFEMINISM EXPLICITLY CHALLENGES THE DOMINATION OF ANIMALS

A strong case can be made for the fact that ecofeminism confronts the issue of animals' suffering and incorporates it into a larger critique of the maltreatment

Hypatia vol. 6, no. 1 (Spring 1991) © by Carol J. Adams

of the natural world. Consider the "Nature" issue of *Woman of Power: A Magazine of Feminism, Spirituality, and Politics* (1988). In it we find articles on animal rights (Newkirk); guidelines for raising children as vegetarians (Moran); a feminist critique of the notion of animal "rights" that argues that the best way to help animals is by adopting broad ecofeminist values (Salamone); an interview with the coordinator of a grassroots animal rights organization (Albino); and Alice Walker's moving description of what it means for a human animal to perceive the beingness of a nonhuman animal.[3] In addition to these articles, a resource section lists companies to boycott because they test their products on animals, identifies cruelty-free products, and gives the addresses of organizations that are vegetarian, antivivisection, and multi-issue animal advocacy groups. This resource list implicitly announces that praxis is an important aspect of ecofeminism.

Or consider one of the earliest anthologies on ecofeminism and one of the latest. *Reclaim the Earth* (1983) contains essays that speak to some of the major forms of environmental degradation, such as women's health, chemical plants, the nuclear age and public health, black ghetto ecology, greening the cities, and the Chipko movement. The anthology also includes an essay on animal rights (Benney 1983). The more recent anthology, *Reweaving the World* (1990), contains an essay proposing that "ritual and religion themselves might have been brought to birth by the necessity of propitiation for the killing of animals" (Abbott 1990, 36), as well as Marti Kheel's essay that explores the way hunting uses animals as instruments of human (male) self-definition (Kheel 1990). This was followed in 1993 by an anthology that placed animals central to ecofeminist theory, Greta Gaard's *Ecofeminism: Women, Animals, Nature* (1993).

Still other signs of ecofeminism's commitment to animals—as beings who ought not to be used as instruments—can be found. Greta Gaard identifies vegetarianism as one of the qualities of ecofeminist praxis, along with antimilitarism, sustainable agriculture, holistic health practices, and maintaining diversity (Gaard 1989). Ecofeminists carried a banner at the 1990 March for the Animals in Washington, D. C. Ecofeminist caucuses within feminist organizations have begun to articulate the issue of animal liberation as an essential aspect of their program. The Ecofeminist Task Force of the National Women's Studies Association recommended at the 1990 NWSA meeting that the Coordinating Council adopt a policy that no animal products be served at any future conferences, citing ecological, health, and humane issues.

Such ecofeminist attention to praxis involving the well-being of animals ought not to be surprising. Ecofeminism's roots in this country can be traced to feminist-vegetarian communities. Charlene Spretnak identifies three ways the radical feminist communities of the mid-1970s came to ecofeminism: through study of political theory and history, through exposure to nature-based religion, especially Goddess religion, and from environmentalism (Spretnak 1990, 5–6). A good example of these communities is the Cambridge-Boston women's community. One of the initial ecofeminist texts—Françoise d'Eaubonne's 1974 book *Le féminisme ou la mort*—was introduced that year to scores of feminists who took Mary Daly's feminist ethics class at Boston College. That same year, Sheila Collins's *A Different Heaven and Earth* appeared and was discussed with interest in this community. Collins saw "racism, sexism, class exploitation, and ecological destruction" as "interlocking pillars upon which the structure of patriarchy rests" (Collins 1974, 161). In 1975, Rosemary Radford Ruether's *New Woman/New Earth* was also greeted with excitement. Ruether linked the ecological crisis with the status of women, arguing that the demands of the women's movement must be united with the ecological movement. The genesis of the two book-length ecofeminist texts that link women and animals can be traced to this community and its association with Daly during those years.[4]

Interviews with members of the Cambridge-Boston women's community reveal a prototypical ecofeminism that locates animals within its analysis.[5] As one feminist said: "Animals and the earth and women have all been objectified and treated in the same way." Another explained she was "beginning to bond with the earth as a sister and with animals as subjects not to be objectified."

At a conceptual level, this feminist-vegetarian connection can be seen as arising within an ecofeminist framework. To apprehend this, consider Karen J. Warren's (1987) four minimal conditions of ecofeminism. Appeal to them indicates a vegetarian application articulated by these activist ecofeminists in 1976 and still viable in the 1990s.

Ecofeminism argues that there is an important connection between the domination of women and the domination of nature. The women I interviewed perceived animals to be a part of that dominated nature and saw a similarity in the status of women and animals as subject to the authority or control of another, i.e., as subordinate:

> Look at the way women have been treated. We've been com-
> pletely controlled, raped, not given any credibility, not taken
> seriously. It's the same thing with animals. We've completely
> mutilated them, domesticated them. Their cycles, their entire
> beings are conformed to humans' needs. That's what men have
> done to women and the earth.

Since ecofeminism is distinguished by whether it arises from socialist feminism, radical feminism, or spiritual feminism, many of the ecofeminists of 1976 identified themselves within these classifications as they extended them to include animals. Socialist feminists linked meat eating with capitalist forms of production and the classist nature of meat consumption; spiritual feminists emphasized the association of goddess worship, a belief in a matriarchy, harmony with the environment, and gentleness toward animals; radical feminists associated women's oppression and animals' oppression; and some held the position of "nature feminists" who see women as naturally more sensitive to animals.

The second of Warren's conditions of ecofeminism is that we must understand the connections between the oppression of women and the oppression of nature. To do so we must critique "the sort of thinking which sanctions the oppression" (Warren 1987, 6), what Warren identifies as patriarchal thinking allegedly justified by a "logic of domination" according to which "superiority justifies subordination" (Warren 1987; 1990). The women I interviewed rejected a "logic of domination" that justifies killing animals: "A truly gynocentric way of being is being in harmony with the earth, and in harmony with your body, and obviously it doesn't include killing animals."

The testimonies of the women I interviewed offer an opportunity to develop a radical feminist epistemology by which the intuitive and experiential provide an important source of knowledge that serves to challenge the distortions of patriarchal ideology. Many women discussed trusting their body and learning from their body. They saw vegetarianism as "another extension of looking in and finding out who I really am and what I like." From this a process of identification with animals arose. Identification means that relationships with animals are redefined; they are no longer instruments, means to our ends, but beings who deserve to live and toward whom we act respectfully if not out of friendship.

> Feminists realize what it's like to be exploited. Women as sex objects, animals as food. Women turned into patriarchal mothers, cows turned to milk machines. It's the same thing. I think that innately women aren't cannibals. I don't eat flesh for the same reason that I don't eat steel. It's not in my consciousness anymore that it could be eaten. For the same reason that when I'm hungry I don't start chomping on my own hand.

Another described the process of identification this way:

> The objectifying of women, the metaphors of women as pieces of meat, here's this object to be exploited in a way. I resent that. I identify it with ways that especially beef and chickens also are really exploited. The way they stuff them and ruin their bodies all so that they can sell them on the capitalist market. That is disturbing to me in the same way that I feel that I am exploited.

From this process of identification with animals' experiences as instruments arises an ecofeminist argument on behalf of animals: it is not simply that we participate in a value hierarchy in which we place humans over animals and that we must now accede rights to animals, but that we have failed to understand what it means to be a "being"—the insight that propelled Alice Walker some years later to describe her recognition of a nonhuman animal's beingness (see note 3). Becoming a vegetarian after recognizing and identifying with the beingness of animals is a common occurrence described by this woman in 1976:

> When I thought that this was an animal who lived and walked and met the day, and had water come into his eyes, and could make attachments and had affections and had dislikes, it disgusted me to think of slaughtering that animal and cooking it and eating it.

As women described animals, they recognized them as ends in themselves rather than simply as means to others' ends.

The third ecofeminist claim Warren identifies is that feminist theory and practice must include an ecological perspective. Ecofeminism reflects a praxis-based ethics: one's actions reveal one's beliefs. If you believe women are subordinated you will work for our liberation; if you believe that nature, among other things, is dominated you will judge personal behavior according to its potential exploitation of nature. In this regard, Frances Moore Lappé's powerful book *Diet for a Small Planet* had had a profound effect on numerous feminists I interviewed because it provided an understanding of the environmental costs of eating animals. One stated: "When I was doing my paper on ecology and feminism, the idea of women as earth, that men have exploited the earth just like they've exploited women and by eating meat you are exploiting earth and to be a feminist means to not accept the ethics of exploitation." What she recognizes is that ecofeminists must address the fact that our meat-advocating culture has successfully separated the *consequences* of eating animals from the *experience* of eating animals.[6]

2. THE ENVIRONMENTAL CONSEQUENCES OF EATING ANIMALS

One of ecofeminism's attributes is its concern with the consequences of the domination of the earth. It recognizes that the patriarchal philosophy that links women and nature has measurable, negative effects that must be identified and addressed. When we consider the consequences of meat production—and the way by which each meat eater is implicated in these consequences—ecofeminism faces the necessity of taking sides: will it choose the ecocide and environmental disaster associated with eating animals or the environmental wisdom of vegetarianism?[7]

The relationship between meat eating and environmental disaster is measurable.[8] In fact, advocates for a vegetarian diet have created images that translate the environmental profligacy of meat production to the level of the individual consumer: the average amount of water required daily to feed a person following a vegan diet is 300 gallons; the average amount of water required daily to feed a person following an ovo-lacto-vegetarian diet is 1,200 gallons; but the average amount of water required daily to feed a person following the standard United States meat-based diet is 4,200 gallons. Half of all water consumed in the United States is used in the crops fed to livestock, "and increasingly that water is drawn from underground lakes, some of which are not significantly renewed by rainfall" (Lappé 1982, 10). More than 50 percent of water pollution can be linked to wastes from the livestock industry (including manure, eroded soil, and synthetic pesticides and fertilizers).

Besides depleting water supplies, meat production places demands on energy sources: the 500 calories of food energy from one pound of steak requires 20,000 calories of fossil fuel. Sixty percent of our imported oil requirements would be cut if the U. S. population switched to a vegetarian diet (Hur and Fields 1985b, 25).

Vegetarians also point to other aspects of livestock production that precipitate ecocide: cattle are responsible for 85 percent of topsoil erosion. Beef consumption accounts for about 5 to 10 percent of the human contribution to the greenhouse effect. Among the reasons that our water, soil, and air are damaged by meat production are the hidden aspects of raising animals for food. Before *we* can eat animals, *they* must eat and live and drink water (and even burp).[9] Producing the crops to feed animals taxes the natural world. Frances Moore Lappé reports that "*the value of raw material consumed to produce food from livestock is greater than the value of all oil, gas, and coal consumed in this country.* . . . One-third of the value of *all* raw materials consumed for all purposes in the United States is consumed in livestock foods" (Lappé 1982, 66). Eighty-seven percent of United States agricultural land is used for livestock production (including pasture, rangeland, and cropland).

Not only is the analysis of consequences an important aspect of ecofeminist thought, but for ecofeminists a failure to consider consequences results from the dualisms that characterize patriarchal culture: consumption is experienced separately from production, and production is valued over maintenance. By this I mean that as a result of the fetishization of commodities associated with capitalist production, we see consumption as an end in itself, and we do not consider what have been the means to that end: eating (a dead) chicken is disassociated from the experience of black women who as "lung gunners" must each hour scrape the insides of 5,000 chickens' cavities and pull out the recently slaughtered chickens' lungs.[10] Both women workers and the chickens themselves are means to the end of consumption, but because consumption has been disembodied, their oppressions as worker and consumable body are invisible. This disembodied production of a tangible product is viewed as a positive indication of the economy, but maintenance—those actions necessary to sustain the environment—is neither measured nor valued. Currently, maintenance of domestic space or environmental space is not calculated in economic terms— housework is not calculated in the Gross National Product in the United States, nor are the environmental resources we value (Waring 1988). We do not measure the negative environmental effects of raising animals to be our food, such as the costs to our topsoil and our groundwater. Maintenance of resources is sacrificed to "meat" production.

An ethic that links maintenance with production, that refuses to disembody the commodity produced from the costs of such production, would identify the loss of topsoil, water, and the demands on fossil fuels that meat production requires and factor the costs of maintaining these aspects of the natural world into the end product, the meat. It would not enforce a split between maintenance and production. The cheapness of a diet based on grain-fed terminal animals exists because it does not include the cost of depleting the environment. Not only does the cost of meat not include the loss of topsoil, the pollution of water, and other environmental effects, but price supports of the dairy and beef "industry" mean that the government actively prevents the price of eating animals from being reflected in the commodity of meat. My tax money subsidizes war, but it also subsidizes the eating of animals. For instance, the estimated costs of subsidizing the meat industry with water in California alone is $26 billion annually (Hur and Fields 1985a, 17). If water used by the meat industry were not subsidized by United States taxpayers, "hamburger" would cost $35 per pound and "beefsteak" would be $89.

The hidden costs to the environment of meat production and the subsidizing of this production by the government maintain the disembodiment of this production process. It also means that environmentally concerned individuals are implicated, even if unknowingly and unwittingly, in this process despite their own disavowals through vegetarianism. Individual tax monies perpetuate the cheapness of animals' bodies as a food source; consequently meat eaters are not required to confront the reality of meat production. Tax monies are used to develop growth hormones like "bovine somatotropin" to increase cows' milk production rather than to help people learn the benefits and tastes of soyfoods such as soymilk—products that are not ecologically destructive.

The problem of seeing maintenance as productive occurs on an individual level as well. Activism is judged productive; maintenance as in cooking, especially vegetarian cooking, is usually considered time-consuming. "We don't have time for it—it impedes our activism," protest many feminists in conversations. By not viewing maintenance as productive, the fact that the years of one's activist life may be cut short by reliance on dead animals for food is not addressed.[11] The order we place at a restaurant or the purchase of "meat" at the meat counter also sends the message that maintaining our environment is not important either. A cycle of destruction continues on both a personal and economic-political level for the same reason, the invisible costs of meat eating.

After conducting the most detailed diet survey in history—the Chinese Health Project—Dr. T. Colin Campbell concluded that we are basically a vegetarian species. High consumption of "meat" and dairy products is associated with the risk of chronic illnesses such as cancer, heart disease, diabetes, and other diseases. For women, eating animals and animals products appears to be especially dangerous. A diet high in animal fats lowers the age of menstruation—which increases the incidence of cancer of the breast and reproductive organs while also lowering the age of fertility (Brody 1990; "Leaps Forward" 1990; Mead 1990).

The moment when I realized that maintenance must be valued as productive was while I was cooking vegetarian food; thus I was doing what we generally consider to be maintenance. The problem is to escape from maintenance to produce these or any "productive" thoughts. Seeing maintenance as productive is the other side of recognizing the ethical importance of the consequences of our actions.

3. THE INVISIBLE ANIMAL MACHINES

A child's puzzle called "Barn" displays chickens wandering freely, cows looking out the barnyard door, and smiling pigs frolicking in mud. But this is not an accurate depiction of life down on the farm these days. The fissure between image and reality is perpetuated by agribusiness that does not conduct its farming practices in this homespun way. Laws are being passed in various states that prevent the filming of animals who are living in intensive farming situations. (This phrasing is itself representative of the problem of image and reality: "intensive farming situation" usually means imprisonment in windowless buildings.) As Peter Singer points out, television programs about animals focus on animals in the wild rather than animals in the "factory farms"; frequently the only information on these "animal machines" comes from paid advertising. "The average viewer must know more about the lives of cheetahs and sharks than he or she knows about the lives of chickens or veal calves" (Singer 1990, 216). The majority of animals dominated by humans no longer appear to be a part of nature; they are domesticated, terminal animals who are maintained in intensive farming situations until slaughtered and consumed. Perhaps as a result, some ecofeminists and most meat eaters simply do not see farm animals at all, and thus cannot see them as a part of nature.

It is instructive, then, to remind ourselves of the lives of individual animals. Consider the case of pigs. A breeding sow is viewed, according to one meat company manager, as "a valuable piece of machinery whose function is to pump out baby pigs like a sausage machine" (Coats 1989, 32). Indeed, she does: about 100 piglets, averaging "2 1/2 litters a year, and 10 litters in a lifetime" (Coats 1989, 34). Since about 80 million pigs are slaughtered in the United States yearly, this means that at least 3.5 million pig "mother machines" are pregnant twice during any given year. For at least ten months of each year, the pregnant and nursing sow will be restricted in movement, unable to walk around. Though pigs are extremely social beings, sows "are generally kept isolated in individual narrow pens in which they are unable to turn round" (Serpell 1986, 9). She is impregnated forcefully either by physical restraint and mounting by a boar, artificial insemination, being tethered to a "rape rack" for easy access; or through "the surgical transplant of embryos from 'supersows' to ordinary sows" (Coats 1989, 34).

The now-pregnant sow resides in a delivery crate about two feet by six feet (60 cm x 182 cm) (Coats 1989, 36). In this narrow steel cage, "she is able to stand up or lie down but is unable to do much else. Despite this, sows appear to make frustrated attempts at nest-building" (Serpell 1986, 7). Prostaglandin hormone, injected into the sows to induce labor, also "causes an intense increase in motivation to build a nest" (Fox 1984, 66). After delivering her piglets, "she is commonly strapped to the floor with a leather band, or held down in a lying position by steel bars, to keep her teats continuously exposed" (Coats 1989, 39). The newborn piglets are allowed to suckle from their incarcerated mother for anything from a few hours to several weeks:

> In the most intensive systems the piglets are generally isolated within hours of birth in small individual cages which are stacked, row upon row, in tiers. . . . At 7 to 14 days, the piglets are moved again to new quarters where they are housed in groups in slightly larger cages. (Serpell 1986, 8)

Often farmers clip the pigs' tails shortly after birth to avoid the widespread problem of tail-biting (Fraser 1987). It is probable that tail-biting results from both a monotonous diet and the pigs' natural tendencies to root and chew on objects in their environment. In essence, "the telos of a hog is the will to root," which is frustrated by their existence in confinement sheds (Comstock 1990, 5).

> Once onto solid food, the . . ."weaners" are grown on in small groups in pens until they reach slaughtering weight at around six to eight months of age. For ease of cleaning, the pens have concrete or slatted metal floors, and no bedding is provided. . . . Foot deformities and lameness are common in animals raised on hard floors without access to softer bedding areas. (Serpell 1986, 8-9)

Ninety percent of all pigs are now raised in indoor, near-dark, windowless confinement sheds (Mason and Singer 1980, 8), a stressful existence that includes being underfed (Lawrence et al. 1988) and living in a saunalike atmosphere of high humidity (meant to induce lethargy). Porcine stress syndrome—a form of sudden death likened to human heart attacks—and mycoplasmic pneumonia are common. Once they are the appropriate size and weight, pigs are herded into a crowded livestock truck and transported to the slaughterhouse, where they are killed.

This information on the life cycle of these pigs requires some sort of response from each of us, and the sort of response one has matters on several levels. I respond on an emotional level with horror at what each individual pig is subjected to and sympathize with each pig, whose extreme sociability is evidenced by these animals' increased popularity as pets (Elson 1990). On an intellectual level I marvel at the language of automation, factory farming, and high-tech production that provides the vehicle and license for one to fail to see these animals as living, feeling beings who experience frustration and terror in the face of their treatment. As a lactating mother, I empathize with the sow whose reproductive freedoms have been denied and whose nursing experience seems so wretched. As a consumer and a vegetarian, I visualize this information when I witness people buying or eating "ham," "bacon," or "sausage."

Intensive factory farming involves the denial of the beingness of six billion animals yearly. The impersonal names bestowed on them—such as food-producing unit, protein harvester, computerized unit in a factory environment, egg-producing machine, converting machine, biomachine, crop—proclaim that they have been removed from nature. But this is no reason for ecofeminism to fail to reclaim farm animals from this oppressive system. It merely explains one reason some ecofeminists fail to do so.

4. The Social Construction of Edible Bodies and Humans as Predators

Ecofeminism at times evidences a confusion about human nature. Are we predators or are we not? In an attempt to see ourselves as natural beings, some argue that humans are simply predators like some other animals. Vegetarianism is then seen to be unnatural while the carnivorism of other animals is made paradigmatic. Animal rights is criticized "for it does not understand that one species supporting or being supported by another is nature's way of sustaining life" (Ahlers 1990, 433). The deeper disanalogies with carnivorous animals remain unexamined because the notion of humans as predators is consonant with the idea that we need to eat meat. In fact, carnivorism is true for only about 20 percent of nonhuman animals. Can we really generalize from this experience and claim to know precisely what "nature's way" is, or can we extrapolate the role of humans according to this paradigm?

Some feminists have argued that the eating of animals is natural because we do not have the herbivore's double stomach or flat grinders and because chimpanzees eat meat and regard it as a treat (Kevles 1990). This argument from anatomy involves selective filtering. In fact, all primates are primarily herbivorous. Though some chimpanzees have been observed eating dead flesh—at the most, six times in a month—some never eat meat. Dead flesh constitutes less than 4 percent of chimpanzees' diet; many eat insects, and they do not eat dairy products (Barnard 1990). Does this sound like the diet of human beings?

Chimpanzees, like most carnivorous animals, are apparently far better suited to catching animals than are human beings. We are much slower than they. They have long-projecting canine teeth for tearing hide; all the hominids lost their long-projecting canines 3.5 million years ago, apparently to allow more crushing action consistent with a diet of fruits, leaves, nuts, shoots, and legumes. If we do manage to get a hold of prey animals we cannot rip into their skin. It is true that chimpanzees act as if meat were a treat. When humans lived as foragers and when oil was rare, the flesh of dead animals was a good source of calories. It may be that the "treat" aspect of meat has to do with an ability to recognize dense sources of calories. However, we no longer have a need for such dense sources of calories as animal fat, since our problem is not lack of fat but rather too much fat.

When the argument is made that eating animals is natural, the presumption is that we must continue consuming animals because this is what we require to survive, to survive in a way consonant with living unimpeded by artificial cultural constraints that deprive us of the experience of our real selves. The paradigm of carnivorous animals provides the reassurance that eating animals is natural. But how do we know what is natural when it comes to eating, both because of the social construction of reality and the fact that our history indicates a very mixed message about eating animals? Some did; the majority did not, at least to any great degree.

The argument about what is natural—that is, according to one meaning of it, not culturally constructed, not artificial, but something that returns us to our true selves—appears in a different context that always arouses feminists' suspicions. It is often argued that women's subordination to men is natural. This argument attempts to deny social reality by appealing to the "natural." The "natural" predator argument ignores social construction as well. Since we eat corpses in a way quite differently from any other animals—dismembered, not freshly killed, not raw, and with other foods present—what makes it natural?

Meat is a cultural construct made to seem natural and inevitable. By the time the argument from analogy with carnivorous animals is made, the individual making such an argument has probably consumed animals since before the time she or he could talk. Rationalizations for consuming animals were probably offered when this individual at age four or five was discomforted upon discovering that meat came from dead animals. The taste of dead flesh preceded the rationalizations, and offered a strong foundation for believing the rationalizations to be true. And baby boomers face the additional problem that as they grew up, meat and dairy products had been canonized as two of the four basic food groups. (This occurred in the 1950s and resulted from active lobbying by the dairy and beef industry. At the turn of the century there were twelve basic food groups.) Thus individuals have not only experienced the gratification of taste in eating animals but may truly believe what they have been told endlessly since childhood—that dead animals are necessary for human survival. The idea that meat eating is natural develops in this context. Ideology makes the artifact appear natural, predestined. In fact, the ideology itself disappears behind the facade that this is a "food" issue.

We interact with individual animals daily if we eat them. However, this statement and its implications are repositioned so that the animal disappears and it is said that we are interacting with a form of food that has been named "meat." In *The Sexual Politics of Meat*, I call this conceptual process in which the animal disappears the structure of the absent referent. Animals in name and body are made absent as animals for meat to exist. If animals are alive they cannot be meat. Thus a dead body replaces the live animal and animals become absent referents. Without animals there would be no meat eating, yet they are absent from the act of eating meat because they have been transformed into food.

Animals are made absent through language that renames dead bodies before consumers participate in eating them. The absent referent permits us to forget about the animal as an independent entity. The roast on the plate is disembodied from the pig who she or he once was. The absent referent also enables us to resist efforts to make animals present, perpetuating a means-end hierarchy.

The absent referent results from and reinforces ideological captivity: patriarchal ideology establishes the cultural set of human/animal, creates criteria that posit the species difference as important in considering who may be means and who may be ends, and then indoctrinates us into believing that we need to eat animals. Simultaneously, the structure of the absent referent keeps animals absent from our understanding of patriarchal ideology and makes us resistant to having animals made present. This means that we continue to interpret animals from the perspective of human needs and interests: we see them as usable and consumable. Much of feminist discourse participates in this structure when failing to make animals visible.

Ontology recapitulates ideology. In other words, ideology creates what appears to be ontological: if women are ontologized as sexual beings (or rapeable, as some feminists argue), animals are ontologized as carriers of meat. In ontologizing women and animals as objects, our language simultaneously eliminates the fact that someone else is acting as a subject/agent/perpetrator of violence. Sarah Hoagland demonstrates how this works: "John beat Mary" becomes "Mary was beaten by John," then "Mary was beaten," and finally, "women beaten," and thus "battered women" (Hoagland 1988, 17-18). Regarding violence against women and the creation of the term "battered women," Hoagland observes that "now something *men do to women* has become instead something that is a part of *women's nature*. And we lose consideration of John entirely."

The notion of the animal's body as edible occurs in a similar way and removes the agency of humans who buy dead animals to consume them: "Someone kills animals so that I can eat their corpses as meat" becomes "animals are killed to be eaten as meat," then "animals are meat," and finally "meat animals," thus "meat." Something we do to animals has become instead something that is a part of animals' nature, and we lose consideration of our role entirely. When ecofeminism acknowledges that animals are absent referents but that we are meant to be predators, it still perpetuates the ontologizing of animals as consumable bodies.

5. CAN HUNTING BE RECONCILED TO ECOFEMINIST ETHICS?

Ecofeminism has the potential of situating both animals and vegetarianism within its theory and practice. But should vegetarianism become an *essential* aspect of ecofeminism? Are some forms of hunting acceptable ecofeminist alternatives to intensive farming? To answer this question we need to recognize that many ecofeminists (e.g., Warren) see the necessity of refusing to absolutize, a position consistent with a resistance to authoritarianism and power-over. Thus we can find a refusal to categorically condemn all killing. Issues are situated within their specific environments. I will call this emphasis on the specific over the universal a "philosophy of contingency."

An ecofeminist method complements this ecofeminist philosophy of contingency—it is the method of contextualization. It may be entirely appropriate to refuse to say, "All killing is wrong" and point to human examples of instances when killing is acceptable, such as euthanasia, abortion (if abortion is seen as killing), and the struggles of colonized people to overthrow their oppressors. Similarly, it is argued that the way in which an animal is killed to be food affects whether the action of killing and the consumption of the dead animal are acceptable or not. Killing animals in a respectful act of appreciation for their sacrifice, this argument proposes, does not create animals as instrumentalities. Instead, it is argued, this method of killing animals is characterized by relationship and reflects reciprocity between humans and the hunted animals. Essentially, there are no absent referents. I will call this interpretation of the killing of animals the "relational hunt."

The issue of method provides a way to critique the argument for the relational hunt. But first let us acknowledge that the relational hunt's ideological premise involves ontologizing animals as edible. The method may be different—"I kill for myself an animal I wish to eat as meat"—but neither the violence of the act nor the end result, meat, is eliminated by this change in actors and method.[12] As I argue in the preceding section, the ontologizing of animals as edible bodies creates them as instruments of human beings; animals' lives are thus subordinated to the human's desire to eat them even though there is, in general, no need to be eating animals. Ecofeminists who wish to respect a philosophy of contingency yet resist the ontologizing of animals could choose the alternative position of saying, "Eating an animal after a successful hunt, like cannibalism in emergency situations, is sometimes necessary, but like cannibalism, is morally repugnant." This acknowledges that eating animal (including human) flesh may occur at rare times, but resists the ontologizing of (some) animals as edible.

Applying the method of contextualization to the ideal of the relational hunt reveals inconsistencies. Because ecofeminist theory is theory in process, I offer these critiques sympathetically. It is never pointed out that this is *not* how the majority of people are obtaining their food from dead animals. Though the ecofeminist ethic is a contextualizing one, the context describing how we relate to animals is not provided. Just as environmentalists mystify women's oppression when they fail to address it directly, so ecofeminists mystify humans' relations with animals when they fail to describe them precisely.

Ecofeminism has not relied on the notion of speciesism to critique current treatment of animals, though its condemnation of naturism, explicitly and implicitly, offers a broadly similar critique. The word *speciesism* has been contaminated in some ecofeminists' eyes by its close association with the movement that resists it, the animal rights movement, which they view as perpetuating patriarchal discourse regarding rights. Animal rights, though, does recognize the right of each individual animal to continue living and this is its virtue. An antinaturism position does not provide a similar recognition; as a result the individual animal killed in a hunt can be interpreted "to be in relationship." In other words, hunting is not seen as inconsistent with an anti-naturist position, though it would be judged so from an anti-speciesist position.

An antinaturist position emphasizes relationships, not individuals; the relational hunt is said to be a relationship of reciprocity. But reciprocity involves a mutual or cooperative interchange of favors or privileges. What does the animal who dies receive in this exchange?

The experience of sacrifice? How can the reciprocity of the relational hunt be verified since the other partner is both voiceless in terms of human speech and furthermore rendered voiceless through his or her death? Once the question of the willingness of the silent and silenced partner is raised, so too is the connection between the relational hunt and what I will call the "aggressive hunt." Ostensibly the relational hunt is different from the aggressive hunt, which is seen to aggrandize the hunter's sense of (male) self rather than valuing any relationship with the hunted animal. Yet we can find in discussions of the relational hunt and the aggressive hunt a common phenomenon: the eliding of responsibility or agency. Consider the aggressive hunters' bible, *Meditations on Hunting*. In this book, José Ortega y Gasset writes:

> To the sportsman the death of the game is not what interests him; that is not his purpose. What interests him is everything that he had to do to achieve that death—that is, the hunt. Therefore what was before only a means to an end is now an end in itself. Death is essential because without it there is no authentic hunting: the killing of the animal is the natural end of the hunt and that goal of hunting itself; *not* of the hunter. (1985, 96)

The erasure of the subject in this passage is fascinating. In the end the hunter is not really responsible for willing the animal's death, just as the stereotypic batterer is presumed to be unable, at some point, to stop battering; it is said that he loses all agency. In the construction of the aggressive hunt, we are told that the killing takes place not because the hunter wills it but because the hunt itself requires it. This is the batterer model. In the construction of the relational hunt, it is argued that at some point the animal willingly gives up his or her life so that the human being can be sustained. This is the rapist model. In each case the violence is mitigated. In the rapist model, as with uncriminalized marital rape, the presumption is that in entering into the relationship the woman has said one unequivocal yes; so too in the relational hunt it is presupposed that the animal espied by the hunter at some point also said a nonverbal but equally binding unequivocal yes. The relational hunt and the aggressive hunt simply provide alternative means for erasing agency and denying violation.

I have not as yet discussed the fact that the relational hunt is based on eco-feminists' understanding of some Native American hunting practices and beliefs. Andy Smith, a member of Women of All Red Nations, raised the concern that

> interest in Native American hunting to the exclusion of all other aspects of Native culture is another way of holding to images of Native Americans as savages. This is then further reflected in the misconception that Native people were all hunter types who lived in sparsely populated areas rather than advanced civiliza-tions that were mainly agricultural. This then contributes to the ideology that it was good that natives were "discovered" because otherwise they would still be living these spartan hunter lifestyles. Moreover, what is true for Native cultures is not transferable to mainstream American culture. Such people would better spend their time preserving Native rights than appropriating their culture. (Conversation, February 1994; see also Smith 1993)

But given that many indigenous cultures experienced their relationship with animals very differently than we do today, even nonhierarchically, why do environmentalists gravitate to illustrations from Native American cultures that were hunting rather than horticultural and predominantly vegetarian? Why not hold up as a counterexample to our ecocidal culture gatherer societies that demonstrate humans can live happily without animals' bodies as food? And why not work in solidarity with Native Americans rather than cannibalizing what is presumed to be their hunting model?

Furthermore, what method will allow us to accomplish the relational hunt on any large scale? Can we create as an ideal method one developed in a sparsely populated continent and impose it upon an urban population that has by and large eliminated the wilderness in which Native American cultures flourished? The wilderness no longer exists to allow for duplication. As Rosemary Ruether poses the question: "Since there could be no return to the unmanaged wilder-ness, in which humans compete with animals as one species among others, without an enormous reduction of the human population from its present 5.6 billion back to perhaps a million or so, one wonders what kind of mass destruction of humans is expected to accomplish this goal?" (Ruether 1990, 19).

The problem with the relational hunt is that it is a highly sentimentalized individual solution to a corporate problem: what are we to do about the eating of animals? We either see animals as edible bodies or we do not.[13]

6. Autonomy and Ecofeminist-Vegetarianism

As long as animals are culturally constructed as edible, the issue of vegetarianism will be seen as a conflict over autonomy (to determine on one's own what one will eat versus being told not to eat animals). The question, "Who decided that animals should be food?" remains unaddressed. Rather than being seen as agents of consciousness, raising legitimate issues, ecofeminist-vegetarians are seen as violating others' rights to their own pleasures. This may represent the true "daughter's seduction" in our culture—to believe that pleasure is apolitical and to perpetuate a personalized autonomy derived from dominance. The way autonomy works in this instance appears to be: "By choosing to eat meat, I acquire my 'I-ness.' If you say *I can't* eat meat then I lose my 'I-ness.'" Often the basic premise of the supposed gender-neutrality of autonomy is accepted, leaving both the notion of autonomy and the social construction of animals unexamined. As a result, animals remain absent referents.

The ecofeminist-vegetarian response to this idea of autonomy is: "Let's redefine our 'I-ness.' Does it require dominance of others? Who determined that meat is food? How do we constitute ourselves as 'I's' in this world?"

Giving conceptual place to the significance of individual animals restores the absent referent. This ecofeminist response derives not from a rights-based philosophy but from one arising from relationships that bring about identification and thus solidarity. We must see ourselves in relationship with animals. To eat animals is to make of them instruments; this proclaims dominance and power-over. The subordination of animals is not a given but a decision resulting from an ideology that participates in the very dualisms that ecofeminism seeks to eliminate. We achieve autonomy by acting independently of such an ideology.

Ecofeminism affirms that individuals can change, and in changing we reposition our relationship with the environment. This form of empowerment is precisely what is needed in approaching the issue of where animals stand in our lives. Many connections can be made between our food and our environment, our politics and our personal lives. Essentially, the existence of terminal animals is paradigmatic of, as well as contributing to the inevitability of, a terminal earth.

NOTES

1. Earlier versions of this paper were presented at two conferences: "Ecofeminism: The Woman/Earth Connection," April 1990, Douglass College (sponsored by the Rutgers School of Law-Newark and *Women's Rights Law*

Reporter), and "Women's Worlds: Realities and Choices, Fourth International Interdisciplinary Congress on Women," June 1990, Hunter College. Thanks to Karen J. Warren, Nancy Tuana, Melinda Vadas, Marti Kheel, Batya Bauman, Greta Gaard, Tom Regan, Neal Barnard, and Teal Willoughby for assistance in thinking and writing on this topic.

2. My starting point in this essay is not that of animal rights theory, which seeks to extend to animals moral considerations based on their interests, sentiency, and similarity with humans. My writing is *informed* by this argument, but my starting point here is that ecofeminists seek to end the pernicious logic of domination that has resulted in the interconnected subordination of women and nature. From this starting point, I recognize many other issues besides that of animals' subordination as problematic. In fact, my thesis arises because the ecofeminist analysis of nature requires a more vocal naming of animals as a part of that subordinated nature. Thus I am not patching animals onto an undisturbed notion of human rights, but am examining the place of animals in the fabric of ecofeminist ethics—a starting point that already presumes that the exploitation of nature entails more than the exploitation of animals.

My emphasis here is on *ideology*. An ideology that ontologizes what are called "terminal" animals as edible bodies precedes the issues associated with animal rights discourse and ecofeminist theory. My attempt is to expose this ideology, not through what ecofeminists and environmentalists see as the animal rights strategy of ethical extensionism from humans to some nonhumans, but by exploring the result of the human-animal dualism that has precipitated both the animal rights movement as well as the suspicions of it among those who favor a more biotic way of framing the problem of the oppression of nature. The problem is that each time the biotic environmentalist discourse is willing to sacrifice individual animals as edible bodies, it demonstrates the reason that arguments for rights and interests of individual animals have been so insistently raised and endorses an ideology that is a part of the logic of domination they ostensibly resist, while participating in the human-animal dualism.

3. Walker appears to mean by this concept that each animal possesses a unique individuality, sentiency, and completeness of self in one's self and not through others, and should exist as such for human beings, not as images or as food. Since the concept of personhood is extremely problematic from the perspective of feminist philosophy, I will not use that term though I think that in a general, less philosophically based discourse, this is what my sources mean when talking about "beingness."

4. My own *The Sexual Politics of Meat* began as a paper for Daly's class on feminist ethics (see Adams 1975). In her book *The Rape of the Wild*, Daly's close friend Andrée Collard applies Daly's feminist philosophy of biophilia to animals. As early as 1975 Collard was working on the intersection of the oppression of women and oppression of animals.

5. In 1976 I interviewed more than seventy vegetarians in the Boston-area women's community. These interviews are intended as testimony to the fact that ecofeminism's theoretical potential, as well as its history, is clearly on the side of animals. They also attest to the importance of first-person narrative in (eco)-feminist theory building (see Warren 1990). Among those interviewed were activists and writers such as Judy Norsigian and Wendy Sanford of the Boston Women's Health Book Collective, Lisa Leghorn, Kate Cloud, Karen Lindsey, Pat Hynes, Mary Sue Henifin, Kathy Maio, Susan Leigh Starr, and many others.

6. Warren's fourth point, that ecological movements must include a feminist perspective, is not as apparent in the 1976 interviews. The animal liberation movement traces its roots to Singer's 1975 text *Animal Liberation;* thus the feminist critique of this movement was not readily apparent in 1976 because the movement itself was in its gestational period. Subsequent feminist writings apply a feminist critique to the animal liberation movement while agreeing with the premise that the exploitation of animals must be challenged (Kheel, Collard, Corea, Donovan, Salamone). The politics of identification is a de facto critique of arguments on behalf of animals based on dominant philosophies, since it does not attempt to establish criteria for rights but speaks to responsibility and relationships. In *The Sexual Politics of Meat*, I use feminist literary criticism as an antidote to "rights" language. By choosing this as my methodology, I immedi-ately located my terrain as the study of women's lives, thoughts, experiences, and writings. This was consistent with my theory that once we place women's lives and experiences as central to our understanding of animal advocacy, we are starting from a radically different place. In *Neither Man nor Beast: Feminism and the Defense of Animals*, I draw upon feminist philosophies to further this theory.

7. Some environmentalists have argued that the complete conversion to vegetarianism will precipitate a population crisis and thus is less ecologically responsible than meat eating (Callicott 1989, 35). This assumes that we are all heterosexual and that women never will have reproductive freedom.

8. For environmental issues associated with meat production see Akers (1983), Pimental (1975, 1976), Hur and Field (1984, 1985), Krizmanic (1990a and 1990b).

9. A by-product of livestock production is methane, a greenhouse gas that can trap twenty to thirty times more solar heat than carbon dioxide. Largely because of their burps, "ruminant animals are the largest producers of methane, account-ing for 12 to 15 percent of emissions, according to the E.P.A." (O'Neill 1990, 4).

10. Ninety-five percent of all poultry workers are black women who face carpal tunnel syndrome and other disorders caused by repetitive motion and stress (Clift 1990; Lewis 1990, 175).

11. On this see Robbins (1987) and poet Audre Lorde's (1980) description of the relationship between breast cancer and high-fat diets.

12. While some might argue that the method of the relational hunt elimi-

nates the *violence* inherent in other forms of meat eating, I do not see how that term, as it is commonly used today, can be seen to be illegitimately applied in the context in which I use it here. I use *violent* in the sense of the *American Heritage Dictionary*'s definition: "caused by unexpected force or injury rather than by natural causes." Even if the animal acquiesces to her/his death, which I argue we simply do not know, this death is still not a result of natural causes but of external force that requires the use of implements and the intent of which is to cause mortal injury. This is violence, which kills by wounding a being who would otherwise continue to live.

13. One of the anonymous reviewers raised the issue that plants have life, too. The current reality is that the greatest exploitation of plant foods, the accompanying deployment of pesticides and chemical fertilizers, and the production of monoculture crops that neglect the needs of the soil are all related *not* to humans' need to eat plants but to creating foods for terminal animals to eat before they become flesh. The extensive exploitation of the plant kingdom arises because of the extensive exploitation of animals. Moreover, to equate the process of gathering with the process of killing is simply lying about violence and a distortion of women's past. Plant gathering has historically been women's activity; sustainable, organic agriculture, which relies on nature's capacity to renew itself, has been women's contribution. Indeed, the historic model of gathering by women indicates that plants are not necessarily dominated by being harvested and consumed.

It could be argued that the position that "plants have life too and so we can eat animals" is implicitly patriarchal. To draw lines where lines should not exist (i.e., by claiming that eating an animal is essentially different from eating a human being) does not mean that we cannot draw lines at all (i.e., distinguishing between eating a cow and eating a carrot). Questioning the appropriateness of drawing such lines is an example of Cartesian doubt. As Catharine MacKinnon argues, Cartesian doubt is a function of human male privilege. This privilege enables a standpoint that considers that everything is made out of ideas (MacKinnon 1987, 57–58). It collapses the epistemological and the ontological. It may be theoretically asked whether carrots are being exploited, but once we situate ourselves within the lived reality we know as this world, we must surely know or intuit that the eating of a horse, cow, pig, or chicken is different from the eating of a carrot. The apparent failure of environmentalists to stipulate this is a failure to participate in embodied knowledge; it reinforces the idea that we live by abstractions. Abstractions and the absence of embodied knowledge arise from the bias toward masculine reasoning that is as much a part of the logic of domination as the eating of animals. Those who disassociate corpses from the process of producing corpses and instead associate them with the plant world perpetuate a mind/body and rational/emotional dualism that ecofeminism seeks to eliminate.

REFERENCES

Abbott, Sally. 1990. The origins of God in the blood of the lamb. In *Reweaving the world*, 35-40. Irene Diamond and Gloria Feman Orenstein, eds. San Francisco: Sierra Club Books.

Adams, Carol. 1975. The oedible complex: Feminism and vegetarianism. In *The lesbian reader*. Gina Covina and Laurel Galana, eds. Oakland, CA: Amazon.

————. 1990. *The sexual politics of meat*. New York: Continuum.

————. 1994. *Neither man nor beast: Feminism and the defense of animals*. New York: Continuum.

Ahlers, Julia. 1990. Thinking like a mountain: Toward a sensible land ethic. *Christian Century* (April 25): 433-34.

Akers, Keith. 1983. *A vegetarian sourcebook*. New York: G. P. Putnam's Sons.

Albino, Donna. 1988. C.E.A.S.E: Building animal consciousness. An interview with Jane Lidsky. *Woman of Power*. 9: 64-66.

Barnard, Neal. 1990. The evolution of the human diet. In *The power of your plate*. Summertown, TN: Book Publishing Co.

Benney, Norma. 1983. All of one flesh: The rights of animals. In *Reclaim the earth*. Léonie Caldecott and Stephanie Leland, eds. London: The Women's Press.

Brody, Jane E. 1990. Huge study indicts fat and meat. *The New York Times*. May 8.

Callicott, J. Baird. 1989. *In defense of the land ethic*. Albany: State University of New York Press.

Clift, Elayne. 1990. Advocate battles for safety in mines and poultry plants. *New Directions for Women* (May/June): 3.

Coats, C. David. 1989. *Old MacDonald's factory farm*. New York: Continuum.

Collard, Andrée, with Joyce Contrucci. 1988. *Rape of the wild: Man's violence against animals and the earth*. London: The Women's Press.

Collins, Sheila. 1974. *A different heaven and earth*. Valley Forge: Judson Press.

Comstock, Gary. 1990. Pigs and piety: A theocentric perspective on food animals. Presented at the Duke Divinity School conference, "Good News for Animals?" October 3-4, 1990.

Corea, Genoveffa. 1984. Dominance and control: How our culture sees women, nature and animals. *The Animals' Agenda* (May-June): 37.

Davis, Karen. 1988. Farm animals and the feminine connection. *The Animals' Agenda* (January-February): 38-39.

Donovan, Josephine. 1990. Animal rights and feminist theory. *Signs* 15 (2): 350-75.

d'Eaubonne, Françoise. 1974. Feminism or death [Le féminisme ou la mort]. In *New French feminisms: An anthology*. Elaine Marks and Isabelle de Courtivron, eds. New York: Shocken Books, 1981.

Ecofeminist Task Force Recommendation-Item no. 7. 1990. Presented to the National Women's Studies Association national meeting, June, Akron, Ohio.

Elson, John. 1990. This little piggy ate roast beef: Domesticated porkers are becoming the latest pet craze. *Time* (January 22): 54.

Fox, Michael W. 1984. *Farm animals: Husbandry, behavior, and veterinary practice (viewpoints of a critic)*. Baltimore: University Park Press.

Fraser, David. 1987. Attraction to blood as a factor in tail-biting by pigs. *Applied Animal Behaviour Science* 17: 61-68.

Gaard, Greta. 1989. Feminists, animals, and the environment: The transformative potential of feminist theory. Paper presented at the annual convention of the National Women's Studies Association, Towson State University, June 14-18, Baltimore.

Gaard, Greta, ed. 1993. *Ecofeminism: Women, animals, nature*. Philadelphia: Temple University Press.

Goodyear, Carmen. 1977. Man kind? *Country Women* (December): 7-9.

Hoagland, Sarah Lucia. 1988. *Lesbian ethics: Toward new values*. Palo Alto: Institute for Lesbian Studies.

Hur, Robin. 1985. Six inches from starvation: How and why America's topsoil is disappearing. *Vegetarian Times* (March): 45-47.

Hur, Robin, and Dr. David Fields. 1984. Are high-fat diets killing our forests? *Vegetarian Times* (February): 22-24.

———. 1985a. America's appetite for meat is ruining our water. *Vegetarian Times* (January): 16-18.

———. 1985b. How meat robs America of its energy. *Vegetarian Times* (April): 24-27.

Kevles, Bettyann. 1990. Meat, morality and masculinity. *The Women's Review of Books* (May): 11-12.

Kheel, Marti. 1987. Befriending the beast. *Creation* (September-October): 11-12.

———. 1988. Animal liberation and environmental ethics: Can ecofeminism bridge the gap? Paper presented at the annual meeting of the Western Political Science Association, March 10-12, 1988.

———. 1990. Ecofeminism and deep ecology: Reflections on identity and difference. In *Reweaving the world*, 128-37. Irene Diamond and Gloria Feman Orenstein, eds. San Francisco: Sierra Club Books.

Krizmanic, Judy. 1990a. Is a burger worth it? *Vegetarian Times* 152(April): 20-21.

———. 1990b. Why cutting out meat can cool down the earth. *Vegetarian Times* 152(April): 18-19.

Lappé, Frances Moore. 1982. *Diet for a small planet: Tenth anniversary edition*. New York: Ballantine Books.

Lawrence, A. B., M. C. Appleby, and H. A. Macleod. 1988. Measuring hunger in the pig using operant conditioning: The effect of food restriction. *Animal Production* 47: 131-37.

Leaps forward: Postpatriarchal eating. 1990. *Ms.* (July-August): 59.

Lewis, Andrea. 1990. Looking at the total picture: A Conversation with health activist Beverly Smith. In *The black women's health book: Speaking for ourselves*.

Evelyn C. White, ed. Seattle: The Seal Press.

Lorde, Audre. 1980. *The cancer journals.* Argyle, NY: Spinsters, Ink.

MacKinnon, Catharine A. 1987. *Feminism unmodified: Discourses on life and law.* Cambridge: Harvard University Press.

Mason, Jim, and Peter Singer. 1980. *Animal factories.* New York: Crown Publishers.

Mead, Nathaniel. 1990. Special report: 6,500 Chinese can't be wrong. *Vegetarian Times* 158 (October): 15-17.

Moran, Victoria. 1988. Learning love at an early age: Teaching children compassion for animals. *Woman of Power* 9: 54-56.

Newkirk, Ingrid, with C. Burnett. 1988. Animal rights and the feminist connection. *Woman of Power* 9: 67-69.

O'Neill, Molly. 1990. The cow's role in life is called into question by a crowded planet. *New York Times* (May 6) Section 4: 1, 4.

Ortega y Gasset, José. 1985. *Meditations on hunting.* Howard B. Wescott, trans. New York: Charles Scribner's Sons.

Pimental, David. 1975. Energy and land constraints in food protein production. *Science* 190: 754-61.

———. 1976. Land degradation: Effects on food and energy resources. *Science* 194: 149-55.

Pimental, David, P. A. Oltenacu, M. C. Nesheim, John Krummel, M. S. Allen, and Sterling Chick. 1980. The potential for grass-fed livestock: Resource constraints. *Science* 207: 843-48.

Robbins, John. 1987. *Diet for a new America.* Walpole: Stillpoint.

Ruether, Rosemary. 1975. *New woman/new earth: Sexist ideologies and human liberation.* New York: Seabury Press.

———. 1990. Men, women and beasts: Relations to animals in Western culture. Presented at the Duke Divinity School conference, "Good News for Animals?" October 3, 1990.

Salamone, Connie. 1973. Feminist as rapist in the modern male hunter culture. *Majority Report* (October).

———. 1982. The prevalence of the natural law within women: Women and animal rights. In *Reweaving the web of life: Feminism and nonviolence.* Pam McAllister, ed. Philadelphia: New Society Publishers.

———. 1988. The knowing. *Woman of Power* 9: 53.

Serpell, James. 1986. *In the company of animals: A study of human-animal relationships.* Oxford: Basil Blackwell.

Shiva, Vandana. 1988. *Staying alive: Women, ecology and development.* London: Zed Books.

Singer, Peter. (1975) 1990. *Animal liberation.* 2d ed. New York: A New York Review Book.

Smith, Andy. 1993. For all those who were Indian in a former life. In *Ecofeminism and the sacred.* Carol J. Adams, ed. New York: Continuum.

Spretnak, Charlene. 1990. Ecofeminism: Our roots and flowering. In *Reweaving the world*. Irene Diamond and Gloria Feman Orenstein, eds. San Francisco: Sierra Club Books.

Walker, Alice. 1986. Am I Blue, Ms. July 30.

————. 1988a. Why did the Balinese chicken cross the road? *Woman of Power* 9: 50.

Waring, Marilyn. 1988. *If women counted: A new feminist economics*. San Francisco: Harper & Row.

Warren, Karen J. 1987. Feminism and ecology: Making connections. *Environmental Ethics* 9: 3-21.

————. 1990. The power and the promise of ecological feminism. *Environmental Ethics* 12: 125-46.

Deep Ecology versus Ecofeminism: Healthy Differences or Incompatible Philosophies?

ROBERT SESSIONS

INTRODUCTION

One measure of the strength and importance of the feminist movement is the extent to which philosophers from a broad spectrum—from conservatives to radicals or from historians of ancient philosophy to deconstructionists—now see the discussion of gender issues as an important part of their discipline. Using a parallel yardstick, the environmental movement has grown rapidly in strength and importance: the range of philosophers who address environmental issues is probably as broad as that discussing gender. Given this rapid and dramatic rise of philosophical concern for environmental issues, we should expect and welcome serious disagreements about both the underlying conceptual and historical reasons for human destruction of the environment and the proposed solutions.

In this essay I will focus on the debate between deep ecology and ecofeminism, two of the several philosophies that criticize and attempt to supplant the prevailing environmental philosophies. The controversy between deep ecology and ecofeminism has been going on for nearly a decade.[1] On the positive side, many thinkers from these two camps have helped each other understand better their own views and those they oppose, and they have deepened their own and our understanding of the difficult issues we face. In contrast, some of the exchanges have been rather rancorous: some deep ecologists have accused ecofeminism of shallowness, anthropocentrism, shortsightedness, and environmental naivete, while various ecofeminists have called their accusers sexist, shallow, ahistorical, stoical, and even fascist. In this essay I will attempt to show how and why deep ecology and ecofeminism are at odds, and I will examine whether and how these differences could be overcome. I will conclude with a discussion of the key issues and differences that I believe need further attention if the "versus" in the title of this essay is to be replaced by a more compatible relationship.

Hypatia vol. 6, no. 1 (Spring 1991) © by Robert Sessions

Deep Ecology

According to Arne Naess, who coined the "deep ecology" label and who is looked upon by most deep ecologists as a seminal thinker in this tradition, deep ecology has eight basic characteristics, the first four of which he claims are conceptually fundamental: "(1) The well-being and flourishing of human and non-human Life on Earth have value in themselves. These values are independent of the usefulness of the non-human world for human purposes. (2) Richness and diversity of life forms contribute to the realization of these values and are also values in themselves. (3) Humans have no right to reduce this richness and diversity except to satisfy vital needs. (4) The flourishing of human life and cultures is compatible with a substantial decrease of the human population. The flourishing of non-human life requires such a decrease" (Naess 1986, 14). Naess and the many deep ecologists who agree with him begin by asserting the fundamental equality and inherent value of all beings and then draw inferences for human action from their original anti-anthropomorphism.

Warwick Fox sums up deep ecology as wanting to encourage an egalitarian attitude that "within obvious kinds of practical limits, allows entities (including humans) *the freedom to unfold in their own way unhindered by the various forms of human domination*" (Fox 1989, 6). This central concern with "ecocentric egalitarianism" (Fox's label) leads deep ecologists to oppose, above all else, the historical Western propensity to place humans at the center of the moral universe (to be anthropocentric). Deep ecologists trace most environmental destruction to the anthropocentric attitude that says (1) nonhuman nature has no value in itself, (2) humans (and/or God, if theistic) create what value there is, and (3) humans have the right (some would say the *obligation*) to do as they please with and in the nonhuman world as long as they do not harm other humans' interests. Thus deep ecologists criticize the human centeredness of prevailing Western attitudes and ethics by claiming that there are no good reasons in general for valuing a member of a species or a whole species over another individual or species or over any given ecosystem. They are not against human flourishing, but deep ecologists believe that this flourishing can generally occur without the destructive domination of nonhuman nature by humans, and insofar as it can, it should.

Naess and other deep ecologists believe we need an ethic that is not a mere extension of existing humanist ethics. Animal liberationist Peter Singer, for example, argues that we can provide a theoretical basis for vegetarianism by extending utilitarianism to include all sentient beings. Deep ecologists criticize Singer and other "extensionists" for holding onto "an increasingly arbitrary perspective in an age when the ecological imagination can shift reference points within the system and imagine the world to some extent from the standpoint of the muskrat and its environment" (Naess 1973, 96). Extensions of human-centered ethics perpetuate an unjustifiable bias humans have toward their own. Thus, just as an ethic that begins with men as distinct from women is sexist, utilitarianism (the best of the humanistic lot in this regard) and other Western ethics are "speciesist." Deep ecology tries to begin with a foundation that does not arbitrarily set "man apart" (to borrow a phrase from Robinson Jeffers). Hans Jonas puts the difference between shallow and deep ecology this way: "Only an ethic which is grounded in the breadth of being, not merely in the singularity or oddness of man, can have significance in the scheme of things" (Jonas 1983, 284).

The critical side of deep ecology, then, is aimed at anthropocentric domination of nature. The alternatives to anthropocentrism it recommends vary, depending on the non-domination-of-nature tradition(s) to which particular deep ecologists turn.[2] We will look at some of these frameworks briefly at the end of this essay; for now three points are important. First, given the very general nature of the change in attitude deep ecologists desire—from anthropomorphism to egalitarianism—we find greater diversity in the prescriptions given by deep ecologists to solve the problems caused by anthropocentric philosophies and practices than in the diagnosis of the sources of the problems. Deep ecologists are more unified in their analyses of the problem than in their recommended solutions. Second, while no specific prescription necessarily follows from the diagnosis, a type of alternative is demanded—one that eliminates anthropocentric domination. Finally, while the alternatives offered by deep ecologists are fairly diverse, they tend to be characterized as proposing that we seek a higher unity in the diversity of the world: for example, Naess often turns to Buddhism for a higher Self that transcends the ego-self of the individual; Fox talks of the transpersonal; and Devall and Sessions look to the unity of Spinoza's philosophy (see note 2).

When we examine the disputes between deep ecology and ecofeminism, it is crucial to separate their critiques of anthropocentric and androcentric environmental frameworks from their positive alternatives, for disapproval of one or several (or even all?) of deep ecology's positive frameworks is not to dismiss that movement's analysis of the domination of nature. On the other side, a dismissal of antianthropocentrism is to reject deep ecology. I hope to show that ecofeminism at most modifies (in important ways) deep ecology's negative analysis, and that while the tendency of ecofeminist solutions is perhaps contrary to the standard interpretations of deep ecology's images of unity, they are not logically incompatible with the negative side of the deep ecological framework, and they may not be incompatible with certain versions of the positive side either.

ECOFEMINISM

Finding a spokesperson for ecofeminism is more difficult, and this difference from deep ecology is not insignificant. While both men and women are to be found within each of these varieties of environmental philosophy, most deep ecologists are men, while women make up the strong majority in ecofeminism (see note 1). Part of the ecofeminist critique of deep ecology is that the masculinist nature of deep ecology can be seen in its rather unified program as well as in its use of language and logical style. I will return to this issue briefly at the end of this essay; for now bear in mind that the diversity of thought *seems* much greater in ecofeminism than in deep ecology. As a starting point I will use Ynestra King and Karen J. Warren as examplars of ecofeminist thought: they have both written a number of influential articles on ecofeminism, and they both identify strongly with this movement, as illustrated by their ardent defenses of ecofeminism against feminist as well as deep ecologist critics.

Warren says that ecofeminism is based on the following general claims: "(1) There are important connections between the oppression of women and the oppression of nature. (2) Understanding the nature of these connections is necessary to any adequate understanding of the oppression of women and the oppression of nature. (3) Feminist theory and practice must include an ecological perspective. (4) Solutions to ecological problems must include a feminist perspective" (Warren 1987, 4-5). She further contends that what feminism today needs is to be "transformative," to move beyond the current debate over the four leading versions of feminism (liberal feminism, traditional Marxist feminism, radical feminism, and socialist feminism) "and make an ecofeminist perspective central to feminist theory and practice" (1987, 5). Ecofeminism contains both a critique of the dominant "patriarchal conceptual framework" and offers a feminist framework that is "grounded in familiar ecological principles." The former, according to Warren,

> is one which takes traditionally male-identified beliefs, values, attitudes, and assumptions as . . . the standard; it gives higher status or prestige to what has been traditionally identified as "male" than to what has been traditionally identified as "female". . . . A patriarchal conceptual framework is characterized by value-hierarchical thinking. . . . Such . . . thinking gives rise to a logic of domination . . . which serves to legitimate inequality when, in fact, prior to the metaphor of Up-Down one would have said only that there existed diversity. (1987, 6-7)

For Warren, the ecofeminist critique of patriarchy is grounded in ecological principles: "Everything is interconnected with everything else; all parts of an ecosystem have equal value; there is no free lunch; 'nature knows best'; healthy, balanced ecosystems must maintain diversity; there is unity in diversity" (1987, 7). Warren believes this critique must embrace feminism because otherwise "the ecological movement will fail to make the conceptual connections between the oppression of women and the oppression of nature (and to link these with other systems of oppression)" (1987, 8).

Warren sharpens this analysis in a recent article (1990) by showing the parallel structures between the domination of nature by humans and the domination of women by men. Her version of the logic of the domination of nature (anthropocentrism) has five steps:

> (A1) Humans do, and plants and rocks do not, have the capacity to consciously and radically change the community in which they live.

> (A2) Whatever has the capacity to consciously and radically change the community in which it lives is morally superior to whatever lacks this capacity.

> (A3) Thus, humans are morally superior to plants and rocks.

> (A4) For any X and Y, if X is morally superior to Y, then X is morally justified in subordinating Y.

> (A5) Thus, humans are morally justified in subordinating plants and rocks. (Warren 1990, 129)

Warren next shows how women can be (and have been) substituted for plants and rocks in this argument and how women are identified with nature and men with mind. Thus (A1) becomes (Bl): "Women are identified with nature and the realm of the physical; men are identified with the 'human' and the realm of the mental" (1990, 130). She goes on to argue that the second and fourth premises are unwarranted value assumptions and that without them the arguments for domination of nature *and* women fail. Warren contends that this ecofeminist analysis not only exposes and successfully criticizes the domination of nature but also shows that the same logic is used to dominate women. Therefore, she argues, feminism is (should be) ecological (against naturism), and those who oppose naturism are (should be) simultaneously against sexism.

King emphasizes a further dimension of ecofeminism by showing that ecofeminism is naturally closely aligned with the peace movement and other struggles to end domination of people as well as nature. In a classic essay (1981) she calls ecofeminism "cultural feminism," which rejects both the denial of the nature/woman link (rationalist feminism) and the belief that women are more "natural" than men (radical feminism). King claims that "both these positions are unwittingly complicit with the nature/culture dualism. Women's oppression is neither strictly historical nor strictly biological. It is both" (King 1981, 13). Moreover, King believes that

> gender is a meaningful part of a person's identity. . . . As women

we are naturalized culture in a culture defined against nature. If the nature/culture antagonism is the primary contradiction of our time, it is also what weds feminism and ecology and makes women the historic subject. Without an ecological perspective which asserts the interdependence of living things, feminism is disembodied. (1981, 15)

Ecofeminism's critique of predominant Western environmental attitudes is at least in part quite like that of deep ecology: the central fault is an attitude, logic, and practice of dominating nature. Deep ecology's anthropocentrism and Warren's naturism appear to be the same. The central difference between their negative analyses seems to be that while deep ecology focuses exclusively on human domination of nature, ecofeminism insists that a proper analysis must also emphasize the intimate logical and historical connections between the various forms of domination—the same logic and attitudes of superiority and practices of domination humans (men?) display in their relations toward the nonhuman dimensions of the world are found in men's relations to women and in imperialistic, racist, and classist structures and practices. Some ecofeminists claim that deep ecologists reveal their male chauvinism when they at most allude to the connections among these various forms of domination, and they emphasize the deeply masculinist nature of all these interconnected forms of domination by proposing that the central problem is androcentrism rather than anthropocentrism.[3]

THE CONFLICT BETWEEN DEEP ECOLOGY AND ECOFEMINISM

In this section I will address this central ecofeminist criticism of deep ecology that it is androcentric. I will also examine the counterclaims by some deep ecologists that ecofeminism is shallow—that it does not get to the heart of environmental issues because it focuses on the connections among the various forms of domination rather than on the domination of nature itself.

At the core of deep ecology is the call for a new (or the return to an old) sensibility. Modern humans have lost touch with nature and thus with their own natures—we no longer feel the rhythms of nature within ourselves, we have split ourselves from the world (dualism), and we live at a distance (alienation) from what is natural, leaving us fearful (insecure) and able to deal with the world only on our own terms (control). We have become insensitive to ourselves and others by losing our natural sensibilities. Deep ecologists thus look to premodern and/ or holistic traditions for suggestions about how to experience the world—to American Indians, Buddhism, Spinoza and others (see note 2), or to the science of ecology. [4] In short, their critique focuses on the bifurcation of humans and nature that has its sources far back especially in Western history and deep within many inherited philosophies, and the basic strategy deep ecologists recommend for ending the domination of nature is to somehow reverse this dualism, to join together what humans have split asunder.

As we have seen, ecofeminists agree that domination of nature is much the issue, and many of them would further agree that historically the dualism of humans and nature is a major part of the mental substructure undergirding that domination. But they would not agree that this is the whole story. Warren, for example, says that "deep ecology makes a big conceptual error in supposing that the way to reduce a bad dualism is to affirm the neglected or historically undervalued member of the pair! The bad dualism is the problem, not simply what got undervalued."[5] She raises a parallel challenge to radical feminism, which wants to frame "the feminist debate over ecology in terms of the question 'Are women closer to nature than men?' In order for the question to be meaningfully raised, one must presuppose the legitimacy of the nature-culture dualism" (Warren 1987, 15).

Ecofeminists such as Warren are concerned that nature has become a discon-nected abstraction (and in some cases an obsession) for deep ecologists, with the result that although they are devoted to "nature," they relate to nature in a way parallel to that of the dualists they oppose—nature is a lost part of one's self (or one's self is a lost part of nature) that needs to be rejoined. Jim Cheney puts it this way:

> In discussing naturalism, it is natural and to a large extent unavoidable to rely on the familiar terminology of philosophical tradition to explain it. Since a considerable amount of that terminology is the product of dualism, the question arises as to whether this language can be used effectively to convey the different perspective of naturalism. Although philosophy has always involved a great deal of innovation in new terminology, the defenders of ordinary language argue that philosophical meaning can be adequately expressed in everyday terms. But what if the ordinary view of the world which is embedded in ordinary language is what one wants to avoid and wants to correct? (Cheney 1987, 111)

Throughout his article Cheney tries to paint a different picture of how we might conceive of our relationships with humans and nonhumans alike. He turns for his inspiration to the rich material to be found in recent feminist literature about friendship, love, care, and gifting.[6] Cheney believes deep ecologists reveal their ties to the patriarchal traditions they are trying to overcome by the sources and images they use for "reversing" the bifurcation of culture and nature. Despite its sincere concerns, deep ecology remains androcentric, and androcentrism is the real culprit. Thus deep ecology does not, according to this ecofeminist criticism, transcend the perspective it criticizes.

While there are intimate ties between analysis and solution, let us begin sorting out this dispute by differentiating deep ecology's diagnosis from its prescriptions to see just where and how ecofeminists find deep ecology lacking. Warren's analysis of the logic of domination concentrates on the diagnosis, while Cheney's alternative to deep ecology's images of unity is concerned mainly with prescriptions. At first glance Warren's analysis seems to add to or extend the basic critical analysis of deep ecology. Warwick Fox quotes "one ecofeminist-cum-deep ecologist" who read Warren's 1987 article and wondered "why she doesn't just call it [Warren's transformative feminism] deep ecology?" (Fox 1989, 14). For what Warren does, says Fox, is to show that the logic of domination that deep ecology sees as the source of naturism has its parallels in sexism, racism, and classism. According to Fox, anthropomorphism is what deep ecologists call this logic and attitude ("ideology") in human/nature relationships (Fox 1989, 19). He further contends that deep ecologists encourage an attitude of egalitarianism "toward all entities in the ecosphere—including *humans*" (1989, 21). Moreover, deep ecologists "completely agree with ecofeminists that men have been far more implicated in the history of ecological destruction than women. However, deep ecologists also agree with similar charges derived from other social perspectives: for example, that capitalists, whites, and Westerners have been far more implicated in the history of ecological destruction than pre-capitalist peoples, blacks, and non-Westerners" (1989, 14). Human centeredness, not a particular group of humans, is the target of deep ecology; thus, Fox claims that contrary to Cheney and other ecofeminists, deep ecologists are not androcentric.

Is Fox correct in his contention that the crucial difference between deep ecology and ecofeminism is a matter of focus—that deep ecology has its eye on environmental relations while ecofeminism is more concerned with how the logic of domination is also played out on women? Not according to Warren. She believes that the gendered nature of the logic of domination is more than an accident of history. She believes that feminism should be ecological at its core because the domination of nature and the domination of women are parts of a whole, and she believes that any satisfactory environmental philosophy must be feminist for the same reasons. She gives three arguments for the latter claim: (1) for the sake of historical accuracy we must "acknowledge the feminization of nature and the naturalization of women as part of the exploitation of nature"; (2) the oppressive dual dominations of women and nature at least in the West are "located in [a] patriarchal conceptual framework," and to ignore this connection is to give, at best, "an incomplete, inaccurate, and partial account of what is required of a conceptually adequate environmental ethic"; and (3) at least in contemporary culture the word *feminist* helps to clarify how the domination and liberation of nature are conceptually linked to patriarchy and its demise. Warren adds that "without the addition of the word 'feminist,' one presents environmental ethics as if it has no bias, including male-gender bias, which is just what ecofeminists deny: failure to notice the connections between the twin oppressions of women and nature *is* male-gender bias" (Warren 1990, 144).

This exchange between Fox and Warren, who are in many ways quite close in their concerns and analyses, helps to pinpoint what seems to be a critical difference between ecofeminism and deep ecology with regard to their diagnoses of the philosophical sources of environmental destructiveness. Warren and Cheney talk about this difference by emphasizing that the logic of domination is accompanied by a set of values:

> The third feature of oppressive conceptual frameworks is the most significant. A logic of domination is not *just* a logical structure. It also involves a substantive value system, since an ethical premise is needed to permit or sanction the "just" subordination of that which is subordinate. (Warren 1990, 128)

According to this ecofeminist criticism, Fox, like Naess and other deep ecologists, emphasizes an abstract equality between humans and all other beings, while ecofeminism is against the logic of domination *and* the particular historical values that result in the domination of a particular set of entities.

Fox defends deep ecology against this line of criticism by arguing that anthropocentrism is the most "fundamental kind of legitimation" that has been used to justify domination, whether of nature, of women, or of particular groups of people or nonhumans (Fox 1989, 21-25). He believes that "these classes of social actors have not sought to legitimate their positions on the grounds that they are, for example, men, capitalists, white or Western per se, but on the grounds that they have most exemplified whatever it is that has been taken to constitute the *essence of humanness*. . . . [They] have . . . habitually assumed themselves to be somehow *more fully human* than others, such as women, the 'lower' classes, blacks, and non-Westerners" (1989, 22).

Fox further defends deep ecology as non-sexist by pointing out that ecofeminists can be guilty of overemphasizing the domination of women and its link to the domination of nature. Since the logic of human centeredness can be used to justify domination of anything or anyone deemed lacking the magic essence, why don't ecofeminists give equal weight to the domination of people of color, aboriginal people, or poor people? In Fox's view:

> There appears to be two reasons for this. First, to do so would detract from the priority that ecofeminists wish to give to their own concern with androcentrism. Second, and more significantly, these charges could also be applied with equal force to the ecofeminist focus on androcentrism itself. (Fox 1989, 14)

At the very least, this exchange and others like it in the literature serve to warn us to be careful to understand these philosophies before criticizing them;

but such debates also highlight that the process of exchange itself is formative of the positions. Given these caveats, what are we to make of the current exchange? Is deep ecology sexist? Is deep ecology's analysis fundamental? Is ecofeminism "simplistic on both empirical and logical grounds" (Fox 1989, 15)?

My answers to these questions will in certain ways support both contingents. First, I think that Warren's analysis of the logic of domination shows that at least one ecofeminist understands clearly that what Fox calls "human centeredness" is the problem: the logical strategy is to place some person(s) in domination over other persons or entities based on the in-group possessing a special quality exclusively or more fully than the others. Thus I do not see that Fox levels a telling criticism of ecofeminism by insisting that anthropocentrism is fundamental; ecofeminists don't disagree, as far as that logical point goes. Second, while it is important to understand the logic of domination, it is also important to understand how, where, and on what it has been used. To simply insist that the logic of anthropomorphism is the problem is like criticizing technology for extending human control over nature without looking at which technologies are used in which ways to do what for or to whom. Furthermore, just as uses of technologies can be good or bad, not all forms of domination are bad, and not all bad forms are equally bad. To ignore the particular uses of the logic of domination is to be guilty of ahistorical and possibly essentialist philosophizing. Thus it is no accident that the characteristics of ecofeminism given by Warren emphasize context and process. Third, the supposed sexism of deep ecology is no simple matter. Fox and others are quite emphatic that the scope of their ecocentric egalitarianism includes all humans as well as nonhumans. *In theory*, they are not androcentric or misogynistic. Is this a situation where, as Warren claims, not to be for us is to be against us? Fox does not think so—he sees nothing in the logic *or* values of deep ecologists that precludes them from being concerned about sexism. But that is not the same as being actively concerned about the actual victims of dominance, nor is it to be sensitive to the particular uses to which the logic of domination has been put. Deep ecologists perhaps do not deserve to be put into the same camp as those who practice the logic of domination on women, but they are guilty of complicity if they do not recognize the particular dominations of the day and work to alleviate them at least by revealing the common logic and values of sexism and naturism.

In summary, while I can see why a deep ecologist might wonder why Warren does not call herself a deep ecologist since she begins with the logic of domination, at least with regard to the negative analysis of naturism, I think one could as easily wonder why deep ecologists like Fox don't call themselves ecofeminists. For ecofeminism not only comprehends the problem of anthropocentrism, but adds the crucial dimension of history— the actual ways in which the logic of domination has been used against particular beings and systems. A central tenet of ecofeminist thought is the rejection of either/or thinking; thus a good ecofeminist would say that both anthropocentrism *and* androcentrism are the problem.

Fox contends that ecofeminists can be guilty of the same transgressions of which they accuse deep ecologists if ecofeminists assert that androcentrism is the problem and mean that men are by nature or in history the only ones who have used or can use the logic of domination. I believe Fox is correct about this, as does Warren: "matriarchy is not the solution to patriarchy any more than saving nature and letting humans die is the solution to the problem of environmental destruction."[7] As demonstrated by the foregoing quotations from Warren and King, however, ecofeminists take pains to distinguish themselves from radical feminists in denying the very strategy Fox accuses ecofeminists of being tempted to adopt. Furthermore, it is important to note that the culprit is patriarchy, not all men, and the evidence from historians and anthropologists alike indicates that male dominance is ubiquitous if not universal.

Another of Fox's charges is that ecofeminists need to avoid overemphasizing the oppression of women and ignoring the domination of people of color, poor people, and aboriginal peoples. I believe Fox is again correct in asserting that this exclusion could happen as ecofeminists attempt to link feminism with ecological concerns; but again, the evidence from even the few quotations above shows that this warning has been heeded. If anything, deep ecologists are less prone than ecofeminists to take seriously the connections between the domination of nature and other forms of domination.[8]

The most serious challenge deep ecologists raise to ecofeminist thought is that it is "shallow." Arne Naess says that a philosophy is deep when it has "ultimate premises" (the "deepest") from which a system of belief and action flow (Naess, 1986, 28). Fox contends that ecofeminists show their lack of "depth" when they criticize deep ecology for not seeing that the root cause of environmental destruction is androcentrism rather than anthropocentrism:

> Empirically [ecofeminism] is simplistic (and thus descriptively poor) because it fails to give due consideration to the multitude of interacting factors at work in any given situation. . . . Such thinking fails . . . to adopt an ecological perspective with respect to the workings of human society itself. Logically, such thinking is simplistic (and thus facile) because it implies that the solution to our ecological problems is close at hand—all we have to do is remove "the real root" of the problem—when it is actually perfectly possible to conceive of a society that is nonandrocentric, socioeconomically egalitarian, nonracist, and nonimperialistic with respect to other human societies, but whose members nevertheless remain aggressively anthropocentric in collectively agreeing to exploit their environment for their collective benefit in ways that nonanthropocentrists would find thoroughly objectionable. (Fox 1989, 15)

Fox seems to be asserting that the nature/woman connection is an historical accident that, if it had not been made by patriarchy, would leave ecofeminism indistinct from other feminist philosophies. The ecology-feminism link is accidental because it does not flow from the philosophical foundations of ecofeminism; instead, ecofeminists are concerned about ecology because history has linked women to nature. Is this criticism sound?

We have already seen that the ecofeminist critique of "shallow" environmental perspectives shares deep ecology's rejection of human centeredness *and* that it adds a crucial historical dimension. Thus if ecofeminism is shallow in its critique, deep ecology is as well. Furthermore, deep ecologists should be careful not to confuse abstractness with depth. For a critique to be historical and include details of the sort ecofeminism adds to the analysis of the logic of domination is not to destroy the purity of a conceptual discussion, it is to tie that discussion to the real world. The fact that particular women (or trees or aboriginal people) have suffered from an "application" of the logic of domination should be understood by deep ecologists as a reminder that only in Platonic realms of ideas are logics separable from historical realities, rather than as a lack in ecofeminist thinking.

Ecofeminism is, I believe, on solid ground against the deep ecologist's challenge that it is shallow, if we are speaking of ecofeminism's critique. What of the depth of various ecofeminist alternatives to naturist frameworks? And can deep ecology respond adequately to ecofeminist challenges to its "unity" solutions to the dualism deep ecology finds at the heart of anthropocentric environmental frameworks?

POSITIVE IMAGES OF ENVIRONMENTAL RELATIONS: UNITY OR SOLIDARITY? SOME PRELIMINARY POINTS

While space does not permit a thorough examination of the positive environmental philosophies proposed by deep ecology and ecofeminism, I believe the following points help clear the way for well-focused discussions of the crucial issues. The most serious challenge by ecofeminists to deep ecology's "unity" alternatives to anthropocentric environmental frameworks seems to be that these proposals remain trapped within the dualistic mode of thinking they reject—in seeking unity nature becomes an abstract and glorified "other" with which one becomes unified in some kind of self-transcending love. The major challenge deep ecology raises to ecofeminism's "solidarity" proposals is that they are shallow—they do not encompass the breadth of perspective necessary to transcend the anthropocentrism they should oppose. I hope to suggest how both of these criticisms mainly miss the mark, and that the real work to be done is in articulating and justifying environmentally egalitarian communities.

What ecofeminists like King and Warren seem to object to in the deep ecology unity proposals is the assumption that the best way to solve our environmental problems is to rejoin the poles of a faulty duality. For not only does this strategy accept this dualism as definitive of how we relate to the world, but in seeking this unity, differences—the crucial and manifold features of the world—become obliterated. Is this accurate—does the deep ecology quest to transcend dualism and its unhappy consequences logically entail or otherwise imply destruction (or at least ignoring) of difference?

Naess says that his environmental philosophy, Ecosophy T, has as its fundamental norm "Self-realization":

> But I do not want to give this expression any narrow, individualist sense. I want to give it an expanded meaning based on the distinction between Self and self conceived in certain Eastern traditions of "atman". . . . [My maxim is:] maximum (long range, universal) Self-realization.
>
> [This philosophy has three crucial implications:] first, a somewhat extreme appreciation of diversity . . . ; enthusiasm for "the mere" diversity of species or varieties within a genus of plants or animals. . . . Secondly, I have a somewhat extreme appreciation of what Kant calls beautiful actions in contrast to dutiful ones . . . maturity in humans can be measured along a scale from selfishness to Selfishness, that is, broadening and deepening the self, rather than measures of dutiful altruism. . . . Thirdly, I believe that many-sided, high level Self-realization is more easily reached through a "spartan" life-style than through the material standard of average citizens of industrial states. (Naess 1986, 28-9)

If we add to this Naess's statement quoted earlier that we must learn to use our "ecological imagination [to] shift reference points," I do not believe deep ecology is necessarily guilty of the charge some ecofeminists level against it. For throughout the literature of deep ecology there is not only affirmation of Naess's commitment to this "extreme appreciation of diversity" but also much discussion (and practical attempts to intervene on behalf) of actual and diverse entities and systems. Thus if unity means obliteration of diversity (or disrespect for diversity), then deep ecologists are thinking and acting inconsistently. More likely, I believe, is that deep ecologists do not, as discussed in the previous section, pay enough attention to the complexity and diversity of *human* ecology, and furthermore they need to communicate more clearly what they mean by things like "unity" and "Self-realization."

I am not saying that deep ecologists have not attempted to articulate their positive philosophies. My suggestion is more specific: they need to attend to the question of the compatibility of diversity and unity. Naess's idea of imaginative variation of perspective takes us partway toward this goal in that it indicates an understanding that unity is one among many possible standpoints we can (and should, deep ecologists argue) take. And just as ecofeminists warn us not to take *only* a holistic view lest we forget the diversity of the world, deep ecologists believe we (in the West especially) have forgotten the whole and the links between the parts. Bear in mind too that deep ecology is urging a shift in attitude (sensibility) as well as in paradigms. Thus, while we should not ignore the values of (and differences among) individuals, we should also train our imaginations insofar as we can to observe, evaluate, and experience from (as?) the whole. Finally, I believe Fox's emphasis on egalitarianism helps to clarify this issue for deep ecology. Equality does not mean identity and does not imply ignoring of differences. In fact, egalitarianism seems to be precisely what ecofeminists desire when they advocate difference but not distinction.

In the previous section I argued that ecofeminism's negative critique is no shallower than that of deep ecology. What of its positive proposals? Recall that "depth" is a kind of code word for being antianthropocentric and also for thinking ecologically. When ecofeminists talk about community, solidarity, and unity in diversity, are they measuring up to this yardstick? First, I believe it is important to avoid beating people up with a yardstick, especially (if I may mix my metaphors) with a vague one. Surely the "breadth of being" deep ecologists wish to be considered in any *deep* ecology can be discussed in terms of community as well as in terms of unity. If anything, the science of ecology uses the language of community much more than referring to unity or wholeness. Furthermore, many images of community can focus our attention on the interrelationships among the diverse elements of the whole better than can many images of the whole.

The real complaint of those accusing ecofeminism of shallowness seems to be a caution not to forget the nonhuman world and the complex and intimate human relationships with it when discussing sexism, racism, and other forms of domination. There are many perspectives, such as radical feminist or socialist frameworks, in which people end up slighting the domination of nature. While these examples point to a real danger, there is nothing in the logic or details of ecofeminism which would encourage such a lapse, and in fact many ecofeminists take pains to criticize socialist and radical feminism precisely for this oversight. Furthermore, ecofeminists such as Warren insist on the intimate connections between the domination of women, blacks, and others *with* the domination of nature.

The real challenge to ecofeminism, I believe, is to articulate notions of community that include, in a comprehensible way, nonhuman nature. Spotted owls and aquifers are not our literal relatives, at least not in precisely the same ways as other humans can be. How are we to comprehend our relationships with the elements and inhabitants of the nonhuman world such that they are equal but different? This is the task to which ecofeminists and deep ecologists alike should turn, and the spatial metaphor of depth is not a particularly helpful guide in this part of the project.

NOTES

I would like to thank Karen J. Warren and two anonymous *Hypatia* readers for their help with this essay.

1. It would be very difficult to list all of the relevant sources on either deep ecology or ecofeminism—happily, a great number of people are turning their attention to environmental ethics and philosophy. I have tried to select sources of special import to these two positions for inclusion in the references at the end of this paper. For discussions of the conflict between deep ecology and ecofeminism I call your attention especially to the following: the special issue of *Philosophical Inquiry* 8 on ecology and philosophy; Biehl (1987); Cheney (1987, 1989); Fox (1989); Kheel (1988); King (1981, 1983); Naess (1973, 1984, 1986); Salleh (1984); Tobias (1984); Warren (1987, 1990); and Zimmerman (1987). *Environmental Ethics* is the journal that most consistently runs articles on deep ecology and ecofeminism and their interactions.

2. Devall and Sessions (1985) look to Spinoza's philosophy as an alternative to the inherited frameworks of the domination of nature; Naess (1984, 1986) looks to Buddhism; Jonas (1983) borrows heavily from the science of ecology; LaChapelle (1978) draws on Heidegger, systems theory, and Taoism; Macy (1987) looks to Buddhism, evolutionary ecology, systems theory and transpersonal psychology; Matthews (1988) looks to Spinoza; and Walsh and Vaughan (1980) and Weber (1986) draw on systems ideas from modern science and on Eastern and Western spiritual traditions.

3. Besides Cheney, the following assert that androcentrism rather than anthropocentrism is the problem: Biehl (1987), Kheel (1988), Salleh (1984a) and Spretnak (1982).

4. Aldo Leopold is a forerunner of deep ecology, and his admonition to "think like a mountain" (Leopold 1949) has been an influential image in shaping the positive philosophies of many deep ecologists.

5. Quoted from a response by Karen J. Warren to a draft of this essay.

6. Cheney's article includes a discussion of Hyde's (1983) analysis of gifting, Raymond's (1986) discussion of friendship, and Gilligan's (1982) analysis of the differences between male and female styles of moral thinking. Warren (1990) discusses the importance of narrative and context in an attempt to show some crucial differences between feminist and masculinist ways of being moral.

7. Quoted from a response by Karen J. Warren to a draft of this essay. The reference in this quote to saving nature and letting humans die is to a now infamous interview with deep ecologist David Foreman wherein he advocates a callous process of human depopulation as a necessary step in saving the environment. Many deep ecologists as well as ecofeminists and others have criticized Foreman for his intemperate remarks. Fox (1989), for example, carefully disassociates deep ecology's philosophy from Foreman's statements.

8. King (1981, 1983) is especially strong on this point, as is Daly (1978).

REFERENCES

Biehl, Janet. 1987. It's deep, but is it broad? An ecofeminist looks at deep ecology. *Kick It Over* (Winter).

Callicott, J. Baird. 1980. Animal liberation: A triangular affair. *Environmental Ethics* 2: 321-30.

———. 1982. Traditional American Indian and Western European attitudes toward nature. *Environmental Ethics* 4: 292-318.

———. 1984. Non-anthropocentric value theory and environmental ethics. *American Philosophical Quarterly* 21 (October): 299-309.

———. 1987. The intrinsic value of nonhuman species. In *The preservation of species*. Bryan G. Norton, ed. Princeton: Princeton University Press.

Cheney, Jim. 1987. Ecofeminism and deep ecology. *Environmental Ethics* 9: 115-46.

———. 1989. The neo-stoicism of radical environmentalism. *Environmental Ethics* 11: 293-326.

Daly, Mary. 1978. *Gyn/ecology*. Boston: Beacon Press.

Devall, Bill. 1980. The deep ecology movement. *Natural Resources Journal* 20: 299-322.

———. 1982. John Muir as deep ecologist. *Environmental Review* 6: 63-86.

Devall, Bill, and George Sessions. 1984. The development of natural resources and the integrity of nature. *Environmental Ethics* 6: 293-322.

———. 1985. *Deep ecology: Living as if nature mattered*. Layton, UT: Gibbs M. Smith.

Ecology and philosophy. 1986. Special issue of *Philosophical Inquiry* 8 (Winter-Spring).

Feminism and ecology. 1981. Special issue of *Heresies: A Feminist Journal of Art and Politics* 4.

Fox, Warwick. 1984. Deep ecology: Toward a new philosophy for our time? *The Ecologist* 14: 194-204.

———. 1985. A postscript on deep ecology and intrinsic value. *The Trumpeter* 2: 20-23.

———. 1986. Approaching deep ecology: A response to Richard Sylvan's critique of deep ecology. University of Tasmania. Environmental Studies Occasional Paper 20.

———. 1989. The deep ecology-ecofeminism debate and its parallels. *Environmental Ethics* 11: 5-26.

Gilligan, Carol. 1982. *In a different voice*. Cambridge: Harvard University Press.

Griffin, Susan. 1978. *Woman and nature*. New York: Harper and Row.

Hyde, Lewis. 1983. *The gift: Imagination and the erotic life of property*. New York: Random House.

Jonas, Hans. 1983. *The phenomenon of life*. Chicago: University of Chicago Press.

Kheel, Marti. 1985. The liberation of nature: A circular affair. *Environmental Ethics* 7: 135-49.

————. 1988. Ecofeminism and deep ecology. *The Elmwood Newsletter* (Winter).

King, Ynestra. 1981. Feminism and the revolt of nature. *Heresies* 13: 12-16.

————. 1983. Toward an ecological feminism and a feminist ecology. *Harbinger: The Journal of Social Ecology* 1.

LaChapelle, Dolores. 1978. *Earth wisdom*. Los Angeles: Guild of Tutors Press.

Leopold, Aldo. 1949. *A sand county almanac*. New York: Oxford University Press.

Macy, Joanna. 1987. Deep ecology and the council of all beings. *Re-Vision* Winter/Spring: 53-57.

Marietta, Don E., Jr. 1984. Environmentalism, feminism and the future of American society. *The Humanist* 44: 15-30.

Matthews, Freya. 1988. Conservation and self-realization: A deep ecological perspective. *Environmental Ethics* 10: 347-55.

Merchant, Carolyn. 1980. *The death of nature: Women, ecology and the scientific revolution*. New York: Harper and Row.

Naess, Arne. 1973. The shallow and the deep, long-range ecological movements: A summary. *Inquiry* 16: 95-100.

————. 1983. A critique of anti-anthropocentric biocentrism. *Environmental Ethics* 5: 245-56.

————. 1984. A defense of the deep ecology movement. *Environmental Ethics* 6: 265-70.

————. 1986. The deep ecology movement: Some philosophical aspects. *Philosophical Inquiry* 8: 10-29.

Plant, Judith. 1989. *Healing our wounds: The power of ecological feminism*. Boston: New Society Publishers.

Raymond, Janice. 1986. *A passion for friends: Toward a philosophy of female affection*. Boston: Beacon Press.

Salleh, Ariel Kay. 1984a. Deeper than deep ecology: The ecofeminist connection. *Environmental Ethics* 6: 339-46.

————. 1984b. The growth of ecofeminism. *Chain Reaction* 36: 26-28.

Singer, Peter. 1975. *Animal liberation: A new ethics for our treatment of animals*. New York: The New York Review Press.

Skolimowski, Henryk. 1984. The dogma of anti-anthropocentrism and eco-philosophy. *Environmental Ethics* 6: 283-88.

Spretnak, Charlene, ed. 1982. *The politics of women's spirituality*. Garden City, NY: Anchor Press.

Tobias, Michael, ed. 1984. *Deep ecology*. San Diego: Avant Books.

Walsh, Roger N., and Frances Vaughan. 1980. *Beyond ego: Transpersonal dimensions in psychology*. Los Angeles: J.P. Tarcher.

Warren, Karen J. 1987. Feminism and ecology: Making connections. *Environmental Ethics* 9: 3-20.

————. 1990. The power and the promise of ecological feminism. *Environmental Ethics* 12: 125-46.

Weber, Renee. 1986. *Dialogues with scientists and sages: The search for unity.* London: Routledge and Kegan Paul.

Zimmerman, Michael. 1983. Toward a Heideggerian ethos for radical environmentalism. *Environmental Ethics* 5: 99-131.

———. 1987. Feminism, deep ecology, and environmental ethics. *Environmental Ethics* 9: 21-44.

Nature, Self, and Gender: Feminism, Environmental Philosophy, and the Critique of Rationalism

VAL PLUMWOOD

Environmental philosophy has recently been criticized on a number of counts by feminist philosophers. I want to develop further some of this critique and to suggest that much of the issue turns on the failure of environmental philosophy to engage properly with the rationalist tradition, which has been inimical to both women and nature. Damaging assumptions from this tradition have been employed in attempting to formulate a new environmental philosophy that often makes use of or embeds itself within rationalist philosophical frameworks that are not only biased from a gender perspective, but have claimed a negative role for nature as well.

In sections I through IV I argue that current mainstream brands of environmental philosophy, both those based in ethics and those based in deep ecology, suffer from this problem, that neither has an adequate historical analysis, and that both continue to rely implicitly upon rationalist-inspired accounts of the self that have been a large part of the problem. In sections V and VI I show how the critique of rationalism offers an understanding of a range of key broader issues that environmental philosophy has tended to neglect or treat in too narrow a way. Among these issues are those connected with concepts of the human self and with instrumentalism.

I. Rationalism and the Ethical Approach

The ethical approach aims to center a new view of nature in ethics, especially universalizing ethics or in some extension of human ethics. This approach has been criticized from a feminist perspective by a number of recent authors (especially Cheney 1987, 1989). I partly agree with and partly disagree with these criticisms; that is, I think that the emphasis on ethics as the central part (or even the whole) of the problem is misplaced, and that although ethics (and especially the ethics of non-instrumental value) has a role, the particular ethical approaches that have been adopted are problematic and unsuitable. I shall

Hypatia vol. 6, no. 1 (Spring 1991) © by Val Plumwood

illustrate this claim by a brief discussion of two recent books: Paul Taylor's *Respect for Nature* (1986) and Tom Regan's *The Case for Animal Rights* (1986). Both works are significant, and indeed impressive, contributions to their respective areas.

Paul Taylor's book is a detailed working out of an ethical position that rejects the standard and widespread Western treatment of nature as instrumental to human interests and instead takes living things, as teleological centers of life, to be worthy of respect in their own right. Taylor aims to defend a biocentric (life-centered) ethical theory in which a person's true human self includes his or her biological nature (Taylor 1986, 44), but he attempts to embed this within a Kantian ethical framework that makes strong use of the reason/emotion dichotomy. Thus we are assured that the attitude of respect is a moral one because it is universalizing and disinterested, "that is, each moral agent who sincerely has the attitude advocates its universal adoption by all other agents, regardless of whether they are so inclined and regardless of their fondness or lack of fondness for particular individuals" (41). The essential features of morality having been established as distance from emotion and "particular fondness," morality is then seen as the domain of reason and its touchstone, belief. Having carefully distinguished the "valuational, conative, practical and affective dimensions of the attitude of respect," Taylor goes on to pick out the essentially cognitive "valuational" aspect as central and basic to all the others: "It is *because* moral agents look at animals and plants in this way that they are disposed to pursue the aforementioned ends and purposes" (82) and, similarly, to have the relevant emotions and affective attitudes. The latter must be held at an appropriate distance and not allowed to get the upper hand at any point. Taylor claims that actions do not express moral respect unless they are done as a matter of moral principle conceived as ethically obligatory and pursued disinterestedly and not through inclination, solely or even primarily:

> If one seeks that end solely or primarily from inclination, the attitude being expressed is not moral respect but personal affection or love. . . . It is not that respect for nature *precludes* feelings of care and concern for living things. One may, as a matter of simple kindness, not want to harm them. But the fact that one is so motivated does not itself indicate the presence of a moral attitude of respect. Having the desire to preserve or protect the good of wild animals and plants for their sake is neither contrary to, nor evidence of, respect for nature. It is only if the person who has the desire understands that the actions fulfilling it would be obligatory even in the absence of the desire, that the person has genuine respect for nature. (85-86)

There is good reason to reject as self-indulgent the "kindness" approach that reduces respect and morality in the protection of animals to the satisfaction of the carer's own feelings. Respect for others involves treating them as worthy of consideration for their own sake and not just as an instrument for the carer's satisfaction, and there is a sense in which such "kindness" is not genuine care or respect for the other. But Taylor is doing much more than this—he is treating care, viewed as "inclination" or "desire," as *irrelevant* to morality. Respect for nature on this account becomes an essentially *cognitive* matter (that of a person believing something to have "inherent worth" and then acting from an understanding of ethical principles as universal).

The account draws on the familiar view of reason and emotion as sharply separated and opposed, and of "desire," caring, and love as merely "personal" and "particular" as opposed to the universality and impartiality of understanding and of "feminine" emotions as essentially unreliable, untrustworthy, and morally irrelevant, an inferior domain to be dominated by a superior, disinterested (and of course masculine) reason. This sort of rationalist account of the place of emotions has come in for a great deal of well-deserved criticism recently, both for its implicit gender bias and its philosophical inadequacy, especially its dualism and its construal of public reason as sharply differentiated from and controlling private emotion (see, for example, Benhabib 1987; Blum 1980; Gilligan 1982, 1987; Lloyd 1983a and 1983b).

A further major problem in its use in this context is the inconsistency of employing, in the service of constructing an allegedly biocentric ethical theory, a framework that has itself played such a major role in creating a dualistic account of the genuine human self as essentially rational and as sharply discontinuous from the merely emotional, the merely bodily, and the merely animal elements. For emotions and the private sphere with which they are associated have been treated as sharply differentiated and inferior as part of a pattern in which they are seen as linked to the sphere of nature, not the realm of reason.

And it is not only women but also the earth's wild living things that have been denied possession of a reason thus construed along masculine and oppositional lines and which contrasts not only with the "feminine" emotions but also with the physical and the animal. Much of the problem (both for women and nature) lies in rationalist or rationalist-derived conceptions of the self and of what is essential and valuable in the human makeup. It is in the name of such a reason that these other things—the feminine, the emotional, the merely bodily or the merely animal, and the natural world itself—have most often been denied their virtue and been accorded an inferior and merely instrumental position. Thomas Aquinas states this problematic position succinctly: "The intellectual nature is alone requisite for its own sake in the universe, and all others for its sake" (Thomas Aquinas 1976, 56). And it is precisely reason so construed that is usually taken to characterize the authentically human and to create the supposedly sharp separation, cleavage, or discontinuity between all humans and the nonhuman world, and the similar cleavage within the human self. The supremacy accorded an oppositionally construed reason is the key to the anthropo-centrism of the Western tradition. The Kantian-rationalist framework, then, is hardly the area in which to search for a solution. Its use, in a way that perpetuates the supremacy of reason and its opposition to contrast areas, in the service of constructing a supposedly biocentric ethic, is a matter for astonishment.

Ethical universalization and abstraction are both closely associated with accounts of the self in terms of rational egoism. Universalization is explicitly seen in both the Kantian and the Rawlsian framework as needed to hold in check natural self-interest; it is the moral complement to the account of the self as "disembodied and disembedded," as the autonomous self of liberal theory, the rational egoist of market theory, the falsely differentiated self of object-relations theory (Benhabib 1987; Poole 1984, 1985). In the same vein, the broadening of the scope of moral concern along with the according of rights to the natural world has been seen by influential environmental philosophers (Leopold 1949, 201-2) as the final step in a process of increasing moral abstraction and generali-zation, part of the move away from the merely particular—my self, my family, my tribe—the discarding of the merely personal and, by implication, the merely selfish. This is viewed as moral progress, increasingly civilized as it moves further away from primitive selfishness. Nature is the last area to be included in this march away from the unbridled natural egoism of the particular and its close ally, the emotional. Moral progress is marked by increasing adherence to moral rules and a movement away from the supposedly natural (in human nature). The completion of its empire is, paradoxically, the extension of its domain of adherence to abstract moral rules to nature itself.

On such a view, the particular and the emotional are seen as the enemy of the rational, as corrupting, capricious, and self-interested. And if the "moral emo-tions" are set aside as irrelevant or suspect, as merely subjective or personal, we can only base morality on the rules of abstract reason, on the justice and rights of the impersonal public sphere.

This view of morality as based on a concept of reason as oppositional to the personal, the particular, and the emotional has been assumed in the framework of much recent environmental ethics. But as a number of feminist critics of the masculine model of moral life and of moral abstraction have pointed out (Blum 1980, Nicholson 1983), this increasing abstraction is not necessarily an im-provement. The opposition between the care and concern for particular others and generalized moral concern is associated with a sharp division between public (masculine) and private (feminine) realms. Thus it is part of the set of dualistic contrasts in which the problem of the Western treatment of nature is rooted. And the opposition between care for particular others and general moral concern is a false one. There *can* be opposition between particularity and generality of concern, as when concern for particular others is accompanied by *exclusion* of others from care or chauvinistic attitudes toward them (Blum 1980, 80), but this does not automatically happen, and emphasis on oppositional cases obscures the frequent cases where they work together—and in which care for particular others is essential to a more generalized morality. Special relationships, which are treated by universalizing positions as at best morally irrelevant and at worst a positive hindrance to the moral life, are thus mistreated. For as Blum (1980, 78-83) stresses, special relationships form the basis for much of our moral life and concern, and it could hardly be otherwise. With nature, as with the human sphere, the capacity to care, to experience sympathy, understanding, and sensitivity to the situation and fate of particular others, and to take responsibility for others is an index of our moral being. Special relationship with, care for, or empathy with particular aspects of nature as experiences rather than with nature as abstraction are essential to provide a depth and type of concern that is not otherwise possible. Care and responsibility for particular animals, trees, and rivers that are known well, loved, and appropriately connected to the self are an important basis for acquiring a wider, more generalized concern. (As we shall see, this failure to deal adequately with particularity is a problem for deep ecology as well.)

Concern for nature, then, should not be viewed as the completion of a process of (masculine) universalization, moral abstraction, and disconnection, discarding the self, emotions, and special ties (all, of course, associated with the private sphere and femininity). Environmental ethics has for the most part placed itself uncritically in such a framework, although it is one that is extended with particular difficulty to the natural world. Perhaps the kindest thing that can be said about the framework of ethical universalization is that it is seriously incomplete and fails to capture the most important elements of respect, which are not reducible to or based on duty or obligation any more than the most important elements of friendship are, but which are rather an expression of a certain kind of selfhood and a certain kind of relation between self and other.

II. RATIONALISM, RIGHTS, AND ETHICS

An extension to nature of the standard concepts of morality is also the aim of Tom Regan's *The Case for Animal Rights* (1986). This is one of the most impressive, thorough, and solidly argued books in the area of animal ethics, with excellent chapters on topics such as animal intentionality (see also Benton 1993). But the key concept upon which this account of moral concern for animals is based is that of rights, which requires strong individual separation of rights-holders and is set in a framework of human community and legality. Its extension to the natural world raises a host of problems (Midgley 1983, 61-64). Even in the case of individual higher animals for which Regan uses this concept of rights, the approach is problematic. His concept of rights is based on Mill's notion that if a being has a right to something not only should he or she (or it) have that thing but others are obliged to intervene to secure it. The application of this concept of rights to individual wild living animals appears to give humans almost limitless obligations to intervene massively in all sorts of far reaching and conflicting ways in natural cycles to secure the rights of a bewildering variety of beings. In the case of the wolf and the sheep, an example discussed by Regan, it is unclear whether humans should intervene to protect the sheep's rights or avoid doing so in order not to violate the wolf's right to its natural food.

Regan attempts to meet this objection by claiming that since the wolf is not itself a moral agent (although it is a moral patient), it cannot violate the sheep's rights not to suffer a painful and violent death (Regan 1986, 285). But the defense is unconvincing, because even if we concede that the wolf is not a moral agent, it still does not follow that on a rights view we are not obliged to intervene. From the fact that the wolf is not a moral agent it only follows that it is not *responsible* for violating the sheep's rights, not that they are not violated or that others do not have an obligation (according to the rights view) to intervene. If the wolf were attacking a human baby, it would hardly do as a defense in that case to claim that one did not have a duty to intervene because the wolf was not a moral agent. But on Regan's view the baby and the sheep do have something like the same rights. So we do have a duty, it seems, (on the rights view) to intervene to protect the sheep—leaving us where with the wolf?

The concept of rights seems to produce absurd consequences and is impossible to apply in many contexts, for example, of predators in a natural ecosystem, as opposed to a particular human social context in which claimants are part of a reciprocal social community and conflict cases either few or settleable according to some agreed-on principles. All this seems to me to tell against the concept of rights as the correct one for the general task of dealing with animals in the natural environment (as opposed, of course, to domestic animals in a basically humanized environment).[1] Alternative ethical resources, such as virtue theory, need to be developed for such contexts (Plumwood 1993).

Rights seem to have acquired an exaggerated importance, and their status as unique ethical focus, as part of the prestige of the public sphere and the masculine, and the emphasis on separation and autonomy, on reason and abstraction. A more promising approach for an ethics of nature, and also one much more in line with the current directions in feminism, would be to remove rights from the center of the moral stage and pay more attention to some other, less dualistic, moral concepts such as respect, sympathy, care, concern, compassion, gratitude, friendship, and responsibility (Cook 1977, 118-19). These virtue-based concepts, because of their dualistic construal as feminine and their consignment to the private sphere as subjective and emotional, have been treated as peripheral and given far less importance than they deserve for several reasons. First, rationalism and the prestige of reason and the public sphere have influenced not only the concept of what morality is (as Taylor explicates it, for example, as essentially a rational and cognitive act of understanding that certain actions are ethically obligatory) but of what is *central* to it or what count as moral concepts. Second, concepts such as respect, care, concern, and so on are resistant to analysis along lines of a dualistic reason/emotion dichotomy, and their construal along these lines has involved confusion and distortion (Blum 1980). They *are* moral "feelings" but they involve reason, behavior and emotion in ways that do not seem separable. Rationalist-inspired ethical concepts are highly ethnocentric and cannot account adequately for the views of many indigenous peoples, and the attempted application of these rationalist concepts to their positions tends to lead to the view that they lack a real ethical framework (Plumwood 1990). These alternative concepts seem better able to apply to the views of such peoples, whose ethic of respect, care and responsibility for land is often based on special relationships with particular areas of land via links to kin (Neidjie 1985, 1989). Finally these concepts, which allow for particularity and mostly do not require reciprocity, are precisely the sorts of concepts feminist philosophers have argued should have a more significant place in ethics at the expense of abstract, malestream concepts from the public sphere such as rights and justice (Gilligan 1982, 1987; Benhabib 1987). The ethic of care and responsibility they have articulated seems to extend much less problematically to the nonhuman world than do the impersonal concepts which are currently seen as central, and it also seems capable of providing an excellent basis for the noninstrumental treatment of nature many environmental philosophers have now called for. Such an approach treats ethical relations as an expression of self-in-relationship (Gilligan 1987, 24) rather than as the discarding, containment, or generalization of a self viewed as self-interested and non-relational, as in the conventional ethics of universalization.[2] As I argue later, there are important connections between this relational account of the self and the rejection of instrumentalism.

It is not that we need to abandon ethics or dispense with the universalized ethical approach entirely, although we do need to reassess the centrality of ethics in environmental philosophy.[3] What is needed is not so much the abandonment of ethics as a different and richer understanding of it (and, as I argue later, a richer understanding of environmental philosophy generally than is provided by ethics), one that gives an important place to ethical concepts owning to emotionality and particularity and that abandons the exclusive focus on the universal and the abstract associated with the nonrelational self and the dualistic and oppositional accounts of the reason/emotion and universal/particular contrasts as given in rationalist accounts of ethics.

III. The Discontuity Problem

The problem is not just one of restriction in ethics but also of restriction to ethics. Most mainstream environmental philosophers continue to view environmental philosophy as mainly concerned with ethics. For example, instrumentalism is generally viewed by mainstream environmental philosophers as a problem in ethics, and its solution is seen as setting up some sort of theory of intrinsic value. This neglects a key aspect of the overall problem that is concerned with the definition of the human self as separate from nature, the connection between this and the instrumental view of nature, and broader *political* aspects of the critique of instrumentalism.

One key aspect of the Western view of nature, which the ethical stance neglects completely, is the view of nature as sharply discontinuous or onto-logically divided from the human sphere. This leads to a view of humans as apart from or "outside of" nature, usually as masters or external controllers of it. Attempts to reject this view often speak alternatively of humans as "part of nature" but rarely distinguish this position from the obvious claim that human fate is interconnected with that of the biosphere, that humans are subject to natural laws. But on the divided-self theory it is the essentially or authentically human part of the self, and in that sense the human realm proper, that is outside nature, not the human as a physical phenomenon. The view of humans as outside of and alien to nature seems to be especially strongly a Western one, although not confined to the West. There are many other cultures which do not hold it, which stress what connects us to nature as genuinely human virtues, which emphasize continuity and not dissimilarity.[4]

As ecofeminism points out, Western thought has given us a strong human/nature dualism that is part of the set of interrelated dualisms of mind/body, reason/nature, reason/emotion, masculine/feminine and has important inter-connected features with these other dualisms.[5] This dualism has been especially stressed in the rationalist tradition. In this dualism what is characteristically and authentically human is defined against or in opposition to what is taken to be natural, nature, or the physical or biological realm. This takes various forms. For example, the characterization of the genuinely, properly, characteristically, or authentically human, or of human virtue, in polarized terms to exclude what is taken to be characteristic of the natural is what John Rodman (1980) has called "the Differential Imperative" in which what is virtuous in the human is taken to be what maximizes distance from the merely natural. The maintenance of sharp dichotomy and polarization is achieved by the rejection and denial of what links humans to the animal. What is taken to be authentically and characteristically human, defining of the human, as well as the ideal for which humans should strive is *not* to be found in what is shared with the natural and animal (e.g., the body, sexuality, reproduction, emotionality, the senses, agency) but in what is thought to separate and distinguish them—especially reason and its offshoots. Hence humanity is defined not as part of nature (perhaps a special part) but as separate from and in opposition to it. Thus the relation of humans to nature is treated as an oppositional and value dualism.

The process closely parallels the formation of other dualisms, such as mascu-line/feminine, reason/emotion, and spirit/body criticized in feminist thought (see, for example, Ruether 1975, Griffin 1978, Griscom 1981, King 1981, Lloyd 1983, Jaggar 1983) but this parallel logic is not the only connection between human/nature dualism and masculine/feminine dualism. Moreover, this exclusion of the natural from the concept of the properly human is not the only dualism involved, because what is involved in the construction of this dualistic conception of the human is the rejection of those parts of the human character identified as feminine—also identified as less than fully human—giving the masculine conception of what it is to be human. Masculinity can be linked to this exclusionary and polarized conception of the human via the desire to exclude and distance from the feminine and the nonhuman. The features that are taken as characteristic of humankind and as where its special virtues lie are those such as rationality, freedom, and transcendence of nature (all traditionally viewed as masculine), which are viewed as not shared with nature. Humanity is defined oppositionally to both nature and the feminine.

The upshot is a deeply entrenched view of the genuine or ideal human self as not including features shared with nature, and as defined *against* or in *opposition to* the nonhuman realm, so that the human sphere and that of nature cannot significantly overlap. Nature is sharply divided off from the human, is alien and usually hostile and inferior. Furthermore, this kind of human self can only have certain kinds of accidental or contingent connections to the realm of nature. I shall call this the discontinuity problem or thesis and I argue later that it plays a key role with respect to other elements of the problem.

IV. Rationalism and Deep Ecology

Although the discontinuity problem is generally neglected by the ethical stance, a significant exception to its neglect within environmental philosophy seems to be found in deep ecology, which is also critical of the location of the problem within ethics.[6] Furthermore, deep ecology also seems initially to be more likely to be compatible with a feminist philosophical framework, emphasizing as it does connections with the self, connectedness, and merger. Nevertheless, there are severe tensions between deep ecology and a feminist perspective. Deep ecology has not satisfactorily identified the key elements in the traditional framework or observed their connections to rationalism. As a result, it fails to reject adequately rationalist assumptions and indeed often seems to provide its own versions of universalization, the discarding of particular connections, and rationalist accounts of self.

Deep ecology locates the key problem area in human-nature relations in the separation of humans and nature, and it provides a solution for this in terms of the "identification" of self with nature. "Identification" is usually left deliberately vague, and corresponding accounts of self are various and shifting and not always compatible.[7] There seem to be at least three different accounts of self involved—indistinguishability, expansion of self, and transcendence of self—and practitioners appear to feel free to move among them at will. As I shall show, all are unsatisfactory from both a feminist perpective and from that of obtaining a satisfactory environmental philosophy, and the appeal of deep ecology rests largely on the failure to distinguish them.

A. THE INDISTINGUISHABILITY ACCOUNT

The indistinguishability account rejects boundaries between self and nature. Humans are said to be just one strand in the biotic web, not the source and ground of all value and the discontinuity thesis is, it seems, firmly rejected. Warwick Fox describes the central intuition of deep ecology as follows: "We can make no firm ontological divide in the field of existence . . . there is no bifurcation in reality between the human and nonhuman realms. . . . to the extent that we perceive boundaries, we fall short of deep ecological consciousness" (Fox 1984, 7). But much more is involved here than the rejection of discontinuity, for deep ecology goes on to replace the human-in-environment image by a holistic or gestalt view that "dissolves not only the human-in-environment concept, but every compact-thing-in-milieu concept"—except when talking at a superficial level of communication (Fox 1984, 1). Deep ecology involves a cosmology of "unbroken wholeness which denies the classical idea of the analyzability of the world into separately and independently existing parts."[8] It is strongly attracted to a variety of mystical traditions and to the Perennial Philosophy, in which the self is merged with the other—"the other is none other than yourself." As John Seed puts it: "I am protecting the rain forest" develops into "I am part of the rain forest protecting myself. I am that part of the rain forest recently emerged into thinking" (Seed et al. 1988, 36).

There are severe problems with these claims, arising not so much from the orientation to the concept of self (which seems to me important and correct) or from the mystical character of the insights themselves as from the indistinguishability metaphysics which is proposed as their basis. It is not merely that the identification process of which deep ecologists speak seems to stand in need of much more clarification, but that it does the wrong thing. The problem, in the sort of account I have given, is the discontinuity between humans and nature that emerges as part of the overall set of Western dualisms. Deep ecology proposes to heal this division by a "unifying process," a metaphysics that insists that everything is really part of and indistinguishable from everything else. This is not only to employ overly powerful tools but ones that do the wrong job, for the origins of the particular opposition involved in the human/nature dualism remain unaddressed and unanalyzed. The real basis of the discontinuity lies in the concept of an authentic human being, in what is taken to be valuable in human character, society, and culture, as what is distinct from what is taken to be natural. The sources of and remedies for this remain unaddressed in deep ecology. Deep ecology has confused dualism and atomism and then mistakenly taken indistinguishability to follow from the rejection of atomism. The confusion is clear in Fox, who proceeds immediately from the ambiguous claim that there is no "bifurcation in reality between the human and nonhuman realms" (which could be taken as a rejection of human discontinuity from nature) to the conclusion that what is needed is that we embrace an indistinguishability metaphysics of unbroken wholeness in the whole of reality. But the problem must be addressed in terms of this specific dualism and its connections. Instead deep ecology proposes the obliteration of all distinction.

Thus deep ecology's solution to removing this discontinuity by obliterating *all* division is far too powerful. In its overgenerality it fails to provide a genuine basis for an environmental ethics of the kind sought, for the view of humans as metaphysically unified with the cosmic whole will be equally true whatever relation humans stand in with nature—the situation of exploitation of nature exemplifies such unity equally as well as a conserver situation, and the human self is just as indistinguishable from the bulldozer and Coca-Cola bottle as the rocks or the rain forest. What John Seed seems to have in mind here is that once one has realized that one is indistinguishable from the rain forest, its needs would become one's own. But there is nothing to guarantee this—one could equally well take one's own needs for its.

This points to a further problem with the indistinguishability thesis, that we need to recognize not only our human continuity with the natural world but also its distinctness and independence from us and the distinctness of the needs of things in nature from ours. The indistinguishability account does not allow for this, although it is a very important part of respect for nature and of conservation strategy.

The dangers of accounts of the self that involve self-merger appear in feminist contexts as well, where they are sometimes appealed to as the alternative to masculine-defined autonomy as disconnection from others. As Jean Grimshaw writes of the related thesis of the indistinctness of persons (the acceptance of the loss of self-boundaries as a feminine ideal): "It is important not merely because certain forms of symbiosis or 'connection' with others can lead to damaging failures of personal development, but because care for others, understanding of them, are only possible if one can adequately distinguish oneself *from* others. If I see myself as 'indistinct' from you, or you as not having your own being that is not merged with mine, then I cannot preserve a real sense of your well-being as opposed to mine. Care and understanding require the sort of distance that is needed in order not to see the other as a projection of self, or self as a continuation of the other" (Grimshaw 1986, 182-83).

These points seem to me to apply to caring for other species and for the natural world as much as they do to caring for our own species. But just as dualism is confused with atomism, so holistic self-merger is taken to be the only alternative to egoistic accounts of the self as without essential connection to others or to nature. Fortunately, this is a false choice;[9] as I argue below, nonholistic but relational accounts of the self, as developed in some feminist and social philosophy, enable a rejection of dualism, including human/nature dualism, without denying the independence or distinguishability of the other. To the extent that deep ecology is identified with the indistinguishability thesis, it does not provide an adequate basis for a philosophy of nature.

B. THE EXPANDED SELF

In fairness to deep ecology it should be noted that it tends to vacillate between mystical indistinguishability and the other accounts of self, between the holistic self and the expanded self. Vacillation occurs often by way of slipperiness as to what is meant by identification of self with the other, a key notion in deep ecology. This slipperiness reflects the confusion of dualism and atomism previously noted but also seems to reflect a desire to retain the mystical appeal of indistinguishability while avoiding its many difficulties. Where "identification" means not "identity" but something more like "empathy," identification with other beings can lead to an expanded self. According to Arne Naess, "The self is as comprehensive as the totality of our identifications. . . . Our Self is that with which we identify."[10] This larger self (or Self, to deep ecologists) is something for which we should strive "insofar as it is in our power to do so" (Fox 1986, 13-19), and according to Fox we should also strive to make it as large as possible. But this expanded self is not the result of a critique of egoism; rather, it is an enlargement and an extension of egoism.[11] It does not question the structures of possessive egoism and self-interest; rather, it tries to allow for a wider set of interests by an expansion of self. The motivation for the expansion of self is to allow for a wider set of concerns while continuing to allow the self to operate on the fuel of self-interest (or Self-interest). This is apparent from the claim that "in this light . . . ecological resistance is simply another name for self defense" (Fox 1986, 60). Fox quotes with approval John Livingstone's statement: "When I say that the fate of the sea turtle or the tiger or the gibbon is mine, I mean it. All that is in my universe is not merely mine; it is *me*. And I shall defend myself. I shall defend myself not only against overt aggression but also against gratuitous insult" (Fox 1986, 60).

Deep ecology does not question the structures of rational egoism and continues to subscribe to two of the main tenets of the egoist framework—that human nature is egoistic and that the alternative to egoism is self-sacrifice.[12] Given these assumptions about egoism, the obvious way to obtain some sort of human interest in defending nature is through the expanded Self operating in the interests of nature but also along the familiar lines of self-interest.[13] The expanded-self strategy might initially seem to be just another pretentious and obscure way of saying that humans empathize with nature. But the strategy of transfering the structures of egoism is highly problematic, for the widening of interest is obtained at the expense of failing to recognize unambiguously the distinctness and independence of the other.[14] Others are recognized morally only to the extent that they are incorporated into the self, and their difference denied

(Warren 1990). And the failure to critique egoism and the disembedded, nonrelational self means a failure to draw connections with other contemporary critiques.

C. THE TRANSCENDED OR TRANSPERSONAL SELF

To the extent that the expanded Self requires that we detach from the particular concerns of the self (a relinquishment that despite its natural difficulty we should struggle to attain), expansion of self to Self also tends to lead into the third position, the transcendence or overcoming of self. Thus Fox urges us to strive for *impartial* identification with *all* particulars, the cosmos, discarding our identifications with our own particular concerns, personal emotions, and attachments (Fox 1990,12). Fox presents here the deep ecology version of universalization, with the familiar emphasis on the personal and the particular as corrupting and self-interested—"the cause of possessiveness, war and ecological destruction" (1990, 12).

This treatment of particularity, the devaluation of an identity tied to particular parts of the natural world as opposed to an abstractly conceived whole, the cosmos, reflects the rationalistic preoccupation with the universal and its account of ethical life as oppositional to the particular. The analogy in human terms of impersonal love of the cosmos is the view of morality as based on universal principles or the impersonal and abstract "love of man." Thus Fox (1990, 12) reiterates (as if it were unproblematic) the view of particular attachments as ethically suspect and as oppositional to genuine, impartial "identification," which necessarily falls short with all particulars.

Because this "transpersonal" identification is so indiscriminate and intent on denying particular meanings, it cannot allow for the deep and highly particularistic attachment to place that has motivated both the passion of many modern conservationists and the love of many indigenous peoples for their land (which deep ecology inconsistently tries to treat as a model). This is based not on a vague, bloodless, and abstract cosmological concern but on the formation of identity, social and personal, in relation to particular areas of land, yielding ties often as special and powerful as those to kin, and which are equally expressed in very specific and local responsibilities of care.[15] This emerges clearly in the statements of many indigenous peoples, such as in the moving words of Cecilia Blacktooth explaining why her people would not surrender their land:

> You ask us to think what place we like next best to this place where we always lived. You see the graveyard there? There are our fathers and our grandfathers. You see that Eagle-nest mountain and that Rabbit-hole mountain? When God made them, He gave us this place. We have always been here. We do not care for any other place. . . . We have always lived here. We would rather die

here. Our fathers did. We cannot leave them. Our children were
born here—how can we go away? If you give us the best place in
the world, it is not so good as this. . . . This is our home. . . . We
cannot live anywhere else. We were born here and our fathers are
buried here. . . . We want this place and no other. . . . (McLuhan
1979, 28)

In inferiorizing such particular, emotional, and kinship-based attachments,
deep ecology gives us another variant on the superiority of reason and the
inferiority of its contrasts, failing to grasp yet again the role of reason and
incompletely critiquing its influence. To obtain a more adequate account than
that offered by mainstream ethics and deep ecology it seems that we must move
toward the sort of ethics feminist theory has suggested, which can allow for both
continuity and difference and for ties to nature which are expressive of the rich,
caring relationships of kinship and friendship rather than increasing abstraction
and detachment from relationship.[16]

V. The Problem in Terms of the Critique of Rationalism

I now show how the problem of the inferiorization of nature appears if it is
viewed from the perspective of the critique of rationalism and seen as part of the
general problem of revaluing and reintegrating what rationalist culture has split
apart, denied, and devalued. Such an account shifts the focus away from the
preoccupations of both mainstream ethical approaches and deep ecology, and
although it does retain an emphasis on the account of the self as central, it gives
a different account from that offered by deep ecology. In section VI I conclude by
arguing that one of the effects of this shift in focus is to make connections with
other critiques, especially feminism, central rather than peripheral or accidental,
as they are currently viewed by deep ecologists in particular.

First, what is missing from the accounts of both the ethical philosophers and
the deep ecologists is an understanding of the problem of discontinuity as created
by a dualism linked to a network of related dualisms. Here I believe a good deal
can be learned from the critique of dualism feminist philosophy has developed
and from the understanding of the mechanisms of dualism ecofeminists have
produced. A dualistically construed dichotomy typically polarizes difference and
minimizes shared characteristics, construes difference along lines of superiority/
inferiority, and views the inferior side as a means to the higher ends of the
superior side (the instrumental thesis). Because its nature is defined oppositionally, the task of the superior side, that in which it realizes itself and
expresses its true nature, is to separate from, dominate, and control the lower
side. This has happened both with the human/nature division and with other
related dualisms such as masculine/feminine, reason/body, and reason/emotion.
Challenging these dualisms involves not just a reevaluation of superiority/

inferiority and a higher status for the underside of the dualisms (in this case nature) but also a reexamination and reconceptualizing of the dualistically construed categories themselves. So in the case of the human/nature dualism it is not just a question of improving the status of nature, moral or otherwise, while everything else remains the same, but of reexamining and reconceptualizing the concept of the human, and also the concept of the contrasting class of nature. For the concept of the human, of what it is to be fully and authentically human, and of what is genuinely human in the set of characteristics typical humans possess, has been defined oppositionally, by *exclusion* of what is associated with the inferior natural sphere in very much the way that Lloyd (1983), for example, has shown in the case of the categories of masculine and feminine, and of reason and its contrasts. Humans have both biological and mental characteristics, but the mental rather than the biological have been taken to be characteristic of the human and to give what is "fully and authentically" human. The term "human" is, of course, not merely descriptive here but very much an evaluative term setting out an ideal: it is what is essential or worthwhile in the human that excludes the natural. It is not necessarily denied that humans have some material or animal component—rather, it is seen in this framework as alien or inessential to them, not part of their fully or truly human nature. The human essence is often seen as lying in maximizing control over the natural sphere (both within and without) and in qualities such as rationality, freedom, and transcendence of the material sphere. These qualities are also identified as masculine, and hence the *oppositional* model of the human coincides or converges with a masculine model, in which the characteristics attributed are those of the masculine ideal.

Part of a strategy for challenging this human/nature dualism, then, would involve recognition of these excluded qualities—split off, denied, or construed as alien, or comprehended as the sphere of supposedly *inferior* humans such as women and blacks—as equally and fully human. This would provide a basis for the recognition of *continuities* with the natural world. Thus reproductivity, sensuality, emotionality would be taken to be as fully and authentically human qualities as the capacity for abstract planning and calculation. This proceeds from the assumption that one basis for discontinuity and alienation from nature is alienation from those qualities which provide continuity with nature in ourselves.

This connection between the rationalist account of nature within and nature without has powerful repercussions. So part of what is involved is a challenge to the centrality and dominance of the rational in the account of the human self. Such a challenge would have far-reaching implications for what is valuable in human society and culture, and it connects with the challenge to the cultural legacy of rationalism made by other critiques of rationalism such as feminism, and by critiques of technocracy, bureaucracy, and instrumentalism.

What is involved here is a reconceptualization of the human side of the human/nature dualism, to free it from the legacy of rationalism. Also in need of reconceptualization is the underside of this dualism, the concept of nature, which is construed in polarized terms as bereft of qualities appropriated to the human side, as passive and lacking in agency and teleology, as pure materiality, pure body, or pure mechanism. So what is called for here is the development of alternative conceptions of human virtue and of alternatives to mechanistic ways of viewing the world, which are also part of the legacy of rationalism.

VI. INSTRUMENTALISM AND THE SELF

There are two parts to the restructuring of the human self in relation to nature—reconceptualizing the human and reconceptualizing the self, and especially its possibilities of relating to nature in other than instrumental ways. Here the critique of the egoistic self of liberal individualism by both feminist and social philosophers, as well as the critique of instrumental reason, offers a rich set of connections and insights on which to draw. In the case of both of these parts what is involved is the rejection of basically masculine models, that is, of humanity and of the self.

Instrumentalism has been identified as a major problem by the ethical approach in environmental philosophy but treated in a rather impoverished way, as simply the problem of establishing the inherent worth of nature.[17] Connection has not been made to the broader account that draws on the critique of instrumental reason. This broader account reveals both its links with the discontinuity problem and its connection with the account of the self. A closer look at this further critique gives an indication of how we might develop an account that enables us to stress continuity without drowning in a sea of indistinguishability.

We might notice first the strong connections between discontinuity (the polarization condition of dualism) and instrumentalism—the view that the excluded sphere is appropriately treated as a means to the ends of the higher sphere or group, that its value lies in its usefulness to the privileged group that is, in contrast, worthwhile or significant in itself. Second, it is important to maintain a strong distinction and maximize distance between the sphere of means and that of ends to avoid breaking down the sharp boundaries required by hierarchy. Third, it helps if the sphere treated instrumentally is seen as lacking ends of its own (as in views of nature and women as passive), for then others can be imposed upon it without problem. There are also major connections that come through the account of the self which accompanies both views.

The self that complements the instrumental treatment of the other is one that stresses sharply defined ego boundaries, distinctness, autonomy, and separation from others—that is defined *against* others, and lacks essential connections to them. This corresponds to the object/relations account of the masculine self associated with the work of Nancy Chodorow (1979, 1985) and also to the self-interested individual presupposed in market theory (Poole 1985, 1990).[18] This self uses both other humans and the world generally as a means to its egoistic satisfaction, which is assumed to be the satisfaction of interests in which others play no essential role. If we try to specify these interests they would make no essential reference to the welfare of others, except to the extent that these are useful to serve predetermined ends. Others as means are interchangeable if they produce equivalent satisfactions—anything which conduces to that end is as valuable, other things being equal, as anything else which equally conduces to that end. The interests of such an individual, that of the individual of market theory and of the masculine self as theorized by Chodorow, are defined as essentially independent of or disconnected from those of other people, and his or her transactions with the world at large consist of various attempts to get satisfaction for these predetermined private interests. Others are a "resource," and the interests of others connect with the interests of such autonomous selves only accidentally or contingently. They are not valued for themselves but for their effects in producing gratification. This kind of instrumental picture, so obviously a misdescription in the case of relations to other humans, is precisely still the normal Western model of what our relations to nature should be.

Now this kind of instrumental, disembedded account of the relation of self to others has been extensively criticized in the area of political theory from a variety of quarters, including feminist theory, in the critique of liberalism, and in environmental philosophy (Benhabib 1987; Benhabib and Cornell 1987; Benjamin 1985; Chodorow 1985; Gilligan 1982, 1987; Grimshaw 1986; Jaggar 1983; Miller 1978; Plumwood 1980; Poole 1984, 1985, 1990; Warren 1990). It has been objected that this account does not give an accurate picture of the human self—that humans are social and connected in a way such an account does not recognize. People do have interests that make *essential* and not merely accidental or contingent reference to those of others, for example, when a mother wishes for her child's recovery, the child's flourishing is an essential *part* of her flourishing, and similarly with close others and indeed for others more widely ("social others"). But, the objection continues, this gives a misleading picture of the world, one that omits or impoverishes a whole significant dimension of human experience, a dimension which provides important insight into gender difference, without which we cannot give an adequate picture of what it is to be human. Instead we must see human beings and their interests as *essentially* related and interdependent. As Karen J. Warren notes, "Relationships are not something extrinsic to who we are, not an 'add on' feature of human nature; they play an essential role in shaping what it is to be human" (Warren 1990, 143). That people's interests are relational does not imply a holistic view of them— that they are merged or indistinguishable. Although some of the mother's interests entail satisfaction of the child's interests, they are not identical or even necessarily similar. There is overlap, but the relation is one of intentional inclusion (her interest is *that* the child should thrive, that certain of the child's key interests are satisfied) rather than accidental overlap.

This view of self-in-relationship is, I think, a good candidate for the richer account of self deep ecologists have sought and for which they have mistaken holistic accounts. It is an account that avoids atomism but that enables a recognition of interdependence and relationship without falling into the problems of indistinguishability, that acknowledges both continuity and difference, and that breaks the culturally posed false dichotomy of egoism and altruism of interests;[19] it bypasses both masculine "separation" and traditional-feminine "merger" accounts of the self. It can also provide an appropriate foundation for an ethic of connectedness and caring for others, as argued by Gilligan (1982, 1987) and Miller (1978).

Thus it is unnecessary to adopt any of the stratagems of deep ecology—the indistinguishable self, the expanded self, or the transpersonal self—in order to provide an alternative to anthropocentrism or human self-interest. This can be better done through the relational account of self, which clearly recognizes the distinctness of nature but also our relationship and continuity with it. On this relational account, respect for the other results neither from the containment of self nor from a transcendence of self, but is an *expression* of self in relationship, not egoistic self as merged with the other but self as embedded in a network of essential relationships with distinct others.

The relational account of self can usefully be applied to the case of human relations with nature and to place. The standard Western view of the relation of the self to the nonhuman is that it is always *accidentally* related, and hence the nonhuman can be used as a means to the self-contained ends of human beings. Pieces of land are real estate, readily interchangeable as equivalent means to the end of human satisfaction; no place is more than "a stage along life's way, a launching pad for higher flights and wider orbits than your own" (Berman 1982, 327). But, of course, we do not all think this way, and instances of contrary behavior would no doubt be more common if their possibility were not denied and distorted by both theoretical and social construction. But other cultures have recognized such essential connection of self to country clearly enough, and many indigenous voices from the past and present speak of the grief and pain in loss of their land, to which they are as essentially connected as to any human other. When Aboriginal people, for example, speak of the land as part of them, "like brother and mother" (Neidjie 1985, 51; 1989, 4, 146), this is, I think, one of their meanings. If instrumentalism is impoverishing and distorting as an account of our relations to other human beings, it is equally so as a guiding principle in our relations to nature and to place.[20]

But to show that the self can be essentially related to nature is by no means to show that it normally would be, especially in modern Western culture. What is culturally viewed as alien and inferior, as not worthy of respect or respectful knowledge, is not something to which such essential connection can easily be made. Here the three parts of the problem—the conception of the human, the conception of the self, and the conception of nature—connect again. And normally such essential relation would involve particularity, through connection to and friendship for *particular* places, forests, animals, to which one is particularly strongly related or attached and toward which one has specific and meaningful, not merely abstract, responsibilities of care.

One of the effects of viewing the problem as arising especially in the context of rationalism is to provide a rich set of connections with other critiques; it makes the connection between the critique of anthropocentrism and various other critiques that also engage critically with rationalism, such as feminism and critical theory, much more important—indeed essential—to the understanding of each. The problem of the Western account of the human/nature relation is seen in the context of the other related sets of dualisms; they are linked through their definitions as the underside of the various contrasts of reason. Since much of the strength and persistence of these dualisms derives from their connections and their ability to mirror, confirm, and support one another, critiques of anthropocentrism that fail to take account of these connections have missed an essential and not merely additional feature.

Anthropocentrism and androcentrism in particular are linked by the rationalist conception of the human self as masculine and by the account of authentically human characteristics as centered around rationality and the exclusion of its contrasts (especially characteristics regarded as feminine, animal, or natural) as less human. This provides a different and richer account of the notion of anthropocentrism, now conceived by deep ecology (Fox 1990, 5) in terms of the notion of equality, which is both excessively narrow and difficult to articulate in any precise or convincing way in a context where needs are so different. The perception of the connection as at best accidental is a feature of some recent critiques of ecofeminism, for example the discussion of Fox (1990) and Eckersley (1989) on the relation of feminism and environmental philosophy. Fox misses entirely the main thrust of the ecofeminist account of environmental philosophy and the critique of deep ecology which results or which is advanced in the ecofeminist literature, which is that it has failed to observe the way in which anthropocentrism and androcentrism are linked.[21] It is a consequence of my arguments here that this critique needs broadening—deep ecology has failed to observe (and often even goes out of its way to deny) connections with a number of other critiques, not just feminism, for example, but also socialism, especially in the forms that mount a critique of rationalism and of modernity. The failure to observe such connections is the result of an inadequate historical analysis and understanding of the way in which the inferiorization of both women and nature is grounded in rationalism, and the connections of both to the inferiorizing of the body, hierarchical concepts of labor, and disembedded and individualist accounts of the self.

Instead of addressing the real concerns of ecofeminism in terms of connection, Fox takes ecofeminism as aiming to replace concern with anthropocentrism by concern with androcentrism.[22] This would have the effect of making ecofeminism a reductionist position which takes women's oppression as the basic form and attempts to reduce all other forms to it. This position is a straw woman;[23] the effect of ecofeminism is not to absorb or sacrifice the critique of anthropocentrism, but to deepen and enrich it.

NOTES

An earlier version of this paper was read at the Women in Philosophy Conference in Canberra, July 1989. The author would like to thank Jim Cheney and Karen J. Warren for comments on an earlier draft.

1. Regan, of course, as part of the animal rights movement, is mainly con-cerned not with wild animals but with domestic animals as they appear in the context and support of human society and culture, although he does not indicate any qualification in moral treatment. Nevertheless, there may be an important moral boundary here, for natural ecosystems cannot be organized along the lines of justice, fairness and rights, and it would be absurd to try to impose such a social order upon them via intervention in these systems. This does not mean, of course, that humans can do anything in such a situation, just that certain kinds of intervention are not in order. But these kinds of intervention may be in order in the case of human social systems and in the case of animals that have already been brought into these social systems through human intervention, and the concept of rights and of social responsibility may have far more application here. This would mean that the domestic/wild distinction would demarcate an impor-tant moral boundary in terms of duties of intervention, although neither Regan (1986) nor Taylor (1986) comes to grips with this problem. In the case of Taylor's "wild living things" rights seem less important than respect for independence and autonomy, and the prima facie obligation may be nonintervention.

2. If the Kantian universalizing perspective is based on self-containment, its major contemporary alternative, that of John Rawls, is based on a "definitional identity" in which the "other" can be considered to the extent that it is not recognized as truly different, as genuinely other (Benhabib 1987, 165).

3. Contra Cheney, who appears to advocate the abandonment of all general ethical concepts and the adoption of a "contextual" ethics based in pure particularity and emotionality. We do need both to reintegrate the personal and particular and reevaluate more positively its role, but overcoming moral dualism will not simply amount to an affirmation of the personal in the moral sphere. To embrace pure particularity and emotionality is implicitly to accept the dualistic construction of these as oppositional to a rationalist ethics and to attempt to reverse value. In general this reactive response is an inadequate way to deal with such dualisms. And rules themselves, as Grimshaw (1986, 209) points out, are not incompatible with recognition of special relationships and responsibility to particular others. Rules themselves are not the problem, and hence it is not

necessary to move to a ruleless ethics; rather it is rules that demand the discarding of the personal, the emotional, and the particular and which aim at self-containment.

4. For example, Bill Neidjie's words "This ground and this earth / like brother and mother" (Neidjie 1985, 46) may be interpreted as an affirmation of such kinship or continuity. (See also Neidjie 1985, 53, 61, 62, 77, 81, 82, 88.)

5. The logic of dualism and the masculinity of the concept of humanity are discussed in Plumwood (1986, 1988) and Warren (1987, 1989).

6. Nonetheless, deep ecology's approach to ethics is, like much else, doubtfully consistent, variable and shifting. Thus although Arne Naess (1974, 1984, 1988) calls for recognition of the intrinsic value of nature, he also tends to treat "the maxim of self-realization" as *substituting for* and obviating an ethical account of care and respect for nature (Naess 1988, 20, 86), placing the entire emphasis on phenomenology. In more recent work, however, the emphasis seems to have quietly shifted back again from holistic intuition to a broad and extremely vague "biocentric egalitarianism" which places the center once again in ethics and enjoins an ethic of maximum expansion of Self (Fox 1990).

7. Other critics of deep ecology, such as Sylvan (1985) and Cheney (1987), have also suggested that it shifts between different and incompatible versions. Ecofeminist critics of deep ecology have included Salleh (1984), Kheel (1985), Biehl (1987), and Warren (1990).

8. Arne Naess, quoted in Fox (1982, 3, 10).

9. This is argued in Plumwood (1980), where a relational account of self developed in the context of an anarchist theory is applied to relations with nature. Part of the problem lies in the terminology of "holism" itself, which is used in highly variable and ambiguous ways, sometimes carrying commitment to indistinguishability and sometimes meaning only "nonatomistic."

10. Arne Naess, quoted in Fox (1986, 54).

11. As noted by Cheney (1989, 293-325).

12. Thus John Seed says: "Naess wrote that when most people think about conservation, they think about sacrifice. This is a treacherous basis for conservation, because most people aren't capable of working for anything except their own self-interest. . . . Naess argued that we need to find ways to extend our identity into nature. Once that happens, being out in front of bulldozers or whatever becomes no more of a sacrifice than moving your foot if you notice that someone's just about to strike it with an axe" (Seed 1989).

13. This denial of the alterity of the other is also the route taken by J. Baird Callicott, who indeed asserts that "the principle of axiological complementarity posits an essential unity between self and world and establishes the problematic intrinsic value of nature in relation to the axiologically privileged value of self" (1985, 275). Given the impoverishment of Humean theory in the area of relations (and hence its inability to conceive a self-in-relationship whose connections to others are not merely contingent but essential), Callicott has

little alternative to this direction of development.

14. Grimshaw (1986, 182). See also the excellent discussion in Warren (1990, 136-38) of the importance of recognition and respect for the other's difference; Blum (1980, 75); and Benhabib (1987, 166).

15. This traditional model of land relationship is closely linked to that of bioregionalism, whose strategy is to engage people in greater knowledge and care for the local areas that have meaning for them and where they can most easily evolve a caring and responsible life-style. The feat of "impartial identification with all particulars" is, beyond the seeking of individual enlightenment, strategically empty. Because it cares "impartially" for everything, it can, in practice, care for nothing.

16. Thus some ecofeminists, such as Cheney (1987, 1989) and Warren (1990), have been led to the development of alternative accounts of ethics and ethical theory building and the development of distinctively ecofeminist ethics.

17. Although the emphasis of early work in this area (for example, Plumwood 1975) was mainly directed toward showing that a respectful, noninstrumental view of nature was logically viable since that was widely disputed, it is certainly well past time to move beyond that. Although there is now wider support for a respectful, noninstrumental position, it remains controversial; see, for example, Thompson (1990) and Plumwood (1991).

18. Poole (1984) has also shown how this kind of self is presupposed in the Kantian moral picture, where desire or inclination is essentially self-directed and is held in check by reason (acting in the interests of universality).

19. In the sense of altruism in which one's own interests are neglected in favor of another's, essentially relational interests are neither egoistic nor altruistic.

20. On rationalism and place see Edward Relph (1976, 1981).

21. Fox (1990, 12), in claiming gender neutrality for cosmologically based identification and treating issues of gender as irrelevant to the issue, ignores the historical scholarship linking conceptions of gender and conceptions of morality via the division between public and private spheres (for example, Lloyd [1984] and Nicholson [1983]). To the extent that the ecofeminist thesis is not an essentialist one linking *sex* to emotionality and particularity or to nature but one linking social and historical conceptions of *gender* to conceptions of morality and rationality, it is not refuted by examples of women who buy a universalizing view or who drive bulldozers, or by Mrs. Thatcher. Fox's argument here involves a sex/gender confusion. On the sex/gender distinction see Plumwood (1989, 2-11).

22. Thus Fox (1990) throughout his discussion, like Zimmerman (1987, 37), takes "the ecofeminist charge against deep ecology" to be that "androcentrism is 'the real root' of ecological destruction" (1990, 14), so that "there is no need to worry about any form of human domination other than androcentrism" (1990, 18). Warren (1990, 144) tellingly discusses Fox's claim that "feminist" is redundant as an addition to a deep ecological ethic.

23. This reductionist position has a few representatives in the literature

(perhaps Andrée Collard [1988] and Sally Miller Gearhart [1982]), but cannot be taken as representative of the main body of ecofeminist work. Fox, I believe, is right to resist such a reduction and to insist on the noneliminability of the form of oppression the critique of anthropocentrism is concerned with, but the conclusion that the critiques are unrelated does not follow. Critiques and the different kinds of oppression they correspond to can be distinguishable but, like individuals themselves, still related in essential and not merely accidental ways. The choice between merger (reductive elimination) and disconnection (isolation) of critiques is the same false dichotomy that inspires the false contrasts of holism and atomism, and of self as merged, lacking boundaries, versus self as isolated atom, lacking essential connection to others.

REFERENCES

Benhabib, Seyla. 1987. The generalised and the concrete other. In *Women and moral theory*, 154-77. E. Kittay and D. Meyers, eds. Totowa, N.J.: Rowman and Allenheld.

Benhabib, Seyla, and Drucilla Cornell, eds. 1987. *Feminism as critique*. Minneapolis: University of Minnesota Press; Cambridge: Polity Press.

Benjamin, Jessica. 1985. The bonds of love: Rational violence and erotic domination. In *The future of difference*. H. Eisenstein and A. Jardine, eds. New Brunswick: Rutgers University Press.

Benton, Ted. 1993. *Natural Relations*. London: Verso.

Berman, Marshall. 1982. *All that is solid melts into air: The experience of modernity*. New York: Simon & Schuster; London: Penguin.

Biehl, Janet. 1987. It's deep, but is it broad? An ecofeminist looks at deep ecology. *Kick It Over* special supplement (Winter).

Blum, Lawrence A. 1980. *Friendship, altruism and morality*. Boston and London: Routledge & Kegan Paul.

Callicott, J. Baird. 1985. Intrinsic value, quantum theory, and environmental ethics. *Environmental Ethics* 7: 261-62.

Cheney, Jim. 1987. Ecofeminism and deep ecology. *Environmental Ethics* 9: 115-145.

———. 1989. The neo-stoicism of radical environmentalism. *Environmental Ethics* 11: 293-325.

Chodorow, Nancy. 1979. *The reproduction of mothering*. Berkeley: University of California Press.

———. 1985. Gender, relation and difference in psychoanalytic perspective. In *The future of difference*, 3-19. H. Eisenstein and A. Jardine, eds. New Brunswick: Rutgers University Press.

Collard, Andrée. 1988. *Rape of the wild: Man's violence against animals and the earth*. Bloomington: Indiana University Press; London: The Woman's Press.

Cook, Francis. 1977. *Hua-Yen Buddhism: The jewel net of Indra.* University Park: Pennsylvania State University Press. 118-119.

Eckersley, Robyn. 1989. Divining evolution: The ecological ethics of Murray Bookchin. *Environmental Ethics* 11: 99-116.

Fox, Warwick. 1982. The intuition of deep ecology. Paper presented at Environment, Ethics and Ecology Conference, Canberra. Also published under the title Deep ecology: A new philosophy of our time? *The Ecologist* 14 (1984): 194-200.

―――. 1986. Approaching deep ecology: A response to Richard Sylvan's critique of deep ecology. Environmental Studies Occasional Paper 20. Hobart: University of Tasmania Centre for Environmental Studies.

―――. 1989. The deep ecology-ecofeminism debate and its parallels. *Environmental Ethics* 11 : 5-25.

―――. 1990. *Towards a transpersonal ecology: Developing new foundations for environmentalism.* Boston: Shambala.

Gearhart, Sally Miller. 1982. The Future—if there is one—is female. In *Reweaving the web of life*, 266-285. P. McAllister, ed. Philadelphia and Santa Cruz: New Society Publishers.

Gilligan, Carol. 1982. *In a different voice.* Cambridge: Harvard University Press.

―――. 1987. Moral orientation and moral development. In *Women and moral theory*, 19-33. E. Kittay and D. Meyers, eds. Totowa, N.J.: Rowman and Allenheld.

Griffin, Susan. 1978. *Woman and nature: The roaring inside her.* New York: Harper and Row.

Grimshaw, Jean. 1986. *Philosophy and feminist thinking.* Minneapolis: University of Minnesota Press. Also published as *Feminist philosophers.* Brighton: Wheatsheaf.

Griscom, Joan L. 1981. On healing the nature/history split in feminist thought. *Heresies* 4(1): 4-9.

Jaggar, Alison. 1983. *Feminist politics and human nature.* Totowa, N.J.: Rowman & Allenheld; Brighton: Harvester.

Kheel, Marti. 1985. The liberation of nature: A circular affair. *Environmental Ethics* 7: 135-49.

King, Ynestra. 1981. Feminism and revolt. *Heresies* 4(1): 12-16.

―――. 1989. The ecology of feminism and the feminism of ecology. In *Healing the wounds.* J. Plant, ed., Philadelphia and Santa Cruz: New Society Publishers.

Leopold, Aldo. 1949. *A sand county almanac.* Oxford and New York: Oxford University Press.

Lloyd, Genevieve. 1983a. Public reason and private passion. *Metaphilosophy* 14: 308-26.

―――. 1983b. Reason, gender and morality in the history of philosophy. *Social Research* 50(3): 490-513.

————. 1984. *The man of reason*. London: Methuen.

McLuhan T. C., ed. 1973. *Touch the earth*. London: Abacus.

Midgley, Mary. 1983. *Animals and why they matter*. Athens: University of Georgia Press; London: Penguin.

Miller, Jean Baker. 1976, 1978. *Toward a new psychology of women*. Boston: Beacon Press; London: Pelican.

Naess, Arne. 1973. The shallow and the deep, long-range ecology movement: A summary. *Inquiry* 16: 95-100.

————. 1986. Intrinsic value: Will the defenders of nature please rise. In *Conservation Biology*. M. Soule, ed. Sunderland, MA: Sinauer Associates.

————. 1988. *Ecology, community and lifestyle.* Cambridge: Cambridge University Press.

Neidjie, Bill. 1985. *Kakadu man*. With S. Davis and A. Fox. Canberra: Mybrood P/L.

Neidjie, Bill, and Keith Taylor, eds. 1989. *Story about feeling*. Wyndham: Magabala Books.

Nicholson, Linda J. 1983. Women, morality and history. *Social Research* 50(3): 514-36.

Plumwood, Val. 1975. Critical notice of Passmore's *Man's responsibility for nature*. *Australasian Journal of Philosophy* 53(2): 171-85.

————. 1980. Social theories, self-management and environmental problems. In *Environmental Philosophy*, 217-332. D. Mannison, M. McRobbie, and R. Routley eds. Canberra: ANU Department of Philosophy Monograph Series RSSS.

————. 1986. Ecofeminism: an overview and discussion of positions and arguments. In *Women and philosophy*, Supplement to vol. 64 *Australasian Journal of Philosophy* (June 1986): 120-38.

————. 1988, 1990. Women, humanity and nature. *Radical Philosophy* 48: 6-24. Reprinted in *Feminism, socialism and philosophy: a radical philosophy reader*. S. Sayers, ed. London: Routledge.

————. 1989. Do we need a sex/gender distinction? *Radical Philosophy* 51: 2-11.

————. 1990. Plato and the bush. *Meanjin* 49(3): 524-36.

————. 1991. Ethics and instrumentalism: A response to Janna Thompson. *Environmental Ethics* #13(2): 139–49.

————. 1993. *Feminism and the mastery of nature*. London: Routledge.

Poole, Ross. 1984. Reason, self-interest and "commercial society": The social content of Kantian morality. *Critical Philosophy* 1: 24-46.

————. 1985. Morality, masculinity and the market. *Radical Philosophy* 39: 16-23.

————. 1990. Modernity, rationality and "the masculine." In *Femininity/Masculinity and representation*. T. Threadgold and A. Cranny-Francis, eds. Sydney: George Allen and Unwin, 1990.

Regan, Tom. 1986. *The case for animal rights*. Berkeley: University of California Press.

Relph, Edward. 1976. *Place and placelessness*. London: Pion.

———. 1981. *Rational landscapes and humanistic geography*. London: Croom Helm.

Rodman, John. 1980. Paradigm change in political science. *American Behavioural Scientist* 24(1): 54-55.

Ruether, Rosemary Radford. 1975. *New woman/new earth*. Minneapolis: Seabury Press.

Salleh, Ariel. 1984. Deeper than deep ecology. *Environmental Ethics* 6: 339-45.

Seed, John. 1989. Interviewed by Pat Stone. *Mother Earth News* (May/June).

Seed, John, Joanna Macy, Pat Fleming, and Arne Naess. 1988. *Thinking like a mountain: Towards a council of all beings*. Philadelphia and Santa Cruz: New Society Publishers.

Sylvan, Richard. 1985. A critique of deep ecology. *Radical Philosophy* 40 and 41.

Taylor, Paul. 1986. *Respect for nature*. Princeton: Princeton University Press.

Thomas Aquinas. 1976. *Summa contra Gentiles*. Bk. 3, Pt. 2, chap. 62. Quoted in *Animal rights and human obligations*, 56. T. Regan and P. Singer, eds. Englewood Cliffs, N.J.: Prentice Hall.

Thompson, Janna. 1990. A refutation of environmental ethics. *Environmental Ethics* 12(2): 147-60.

Warren, Karen J. 1987. Feminism and ecology: Making connections. *Environmental Ethics* 9: 17-18.

———. 1990. The power and the promise of ecological feminism. *Environmental Ethics* 12(2): 121-46.

Zimmerman, Michael E. 1987. Feminism, deep ecology, and environmental ethics. *Environmental Ethics* 9(1): 21–44.

When Lives Become Logic Problems: Nuclear Deterrence, an Ecological Feminist Critique

VICTORIA DAVION

This essay examines some ecological feminist critiques of liberal conceptions of the self, in the light of three mainstream discussions concerning the ethics of nuclear deterrence. While ecological feminists disagree on many points, they agree that there are links between the domination of nature and the domination of women in Western patriarchal societies.[1] They maintain that an understanding of these links reveals that because these dominations are based on the same logic, which Karen J. Warren calls the logic of domination, the movements to end these dominations are conceptually linked (Warren 1990, 125–46). Thus, the fight to end the oppression of women in Western patriarchies and the fight to end the exploitation of nature in Western patriarchies will require some of the same conceptual battles, battles against the logic of domination.

Analysis of value dualisms plays a prominent role in ecological feminist critiques of Western patriarchal cultures. A value dualism is a disjunctive pair in which the disjuncts are seen as oppositional and exclusive, and which places higher value on one disjunct than the other. Ecological feminists argue that a reason/nature dualism underlies the conceptual framework of Western patriarchal cultures. This dualism is thought to form the basis for a series of related dualisms in which whatever is associated with reason is viewed as fundamentally different and superior to whatever is associated with nature.

By applying one version of the ecological feminist critique of dualisms to mainstream literature on nuclear deterrence, I hope to show that much of this literature makes use of a dualistic construction of self/other and is therefore problematic from an ecological feminist perspective. Also, I shall argue that, although these critiques are compelling, there may be some valid reasons for ecological feminists to assume a rational egoistic conception of the self in approaching nuclear deterrence policies at this time.

ECOLOGICAL FEMINISM

Karen J. Warren provides the following two arguments to show how a reason/ nature dualism underlies the justification of the instrumental use of nature by humans and the instrumental use of men by women in Western patriarchal societies.

> (A1) Humans do, and plants and rocks do not, have the capacity to consciously and radically change the community in which they live.

> (A2) Whatever has this capacity. . . is morally superior to whatever [doesn't have it].

> (A3) Thus, humans are morally superior to plants and rocks.

> (A4) For any X and Y, if X is morally superior to Y, then X is morally justified in subordinating Y.

> (A5) Thus, humans are morally justified in subordinating plants and rocks. (Warren 1990, 129)

And:

> (B1) Women are identified with nature and the realm of the physical; men are identified with "human" and the realm of the mental.

> (B2) Whatever is identified with nature and the realm of the physical is inferior to ("below") whatever is identified with the "human" and the realm of the mental. . . .

> (B3) Thus, women are inferior to men. . . .

> (B4) For any X and Y, if X is superior to Y, then X is justified in subordinating Y.

> (B5) Thus, men are justified in subordinating women. (Warren 1990, 130)

In each case, the association of something with the realm of reason places it above that which is associated with nature.

Examples of such dualized pairs involve not only reason/nature, masculine/

feminine, but also mental/manual, civilized/primitive, and human/nature. These pairs function to legitimate a number of oppressions, including sex, race, and class oppression, which can all be seen in terms of the central dualism underlying the system, that of reason/nature. According to Val Plumwood:

> The key exclusions and denials of dependency for dominant conceptions of reason in Western culture include not only the feminine and nature, but all those human orders treated as nature and subject to denied dependency. (Plumwood 1993, 42)

Thus:

> The set of interrelated and mutually reinforcing dualisms which permeate Western culture forms a fault line which runs through the entire conceptual system. . . . Each of them has crucial connections to other elements and has a common structure with other members of the set. They should be seen as forming a system, an interlocking structure. (Plumwood 1993, 42)

According to Plumwood, although philosophers have focused on different pairs of value dualisms (for example, Hegel and Rousseau focused on public/private, male/female, universal/particular; while Descartes focused on mind/body, subject/object, human/nature, and human/animal; and Marx focused on freedom/ necessity, culture/nature, civilized/primitive, mental/manual, and production/ reproduction), lurking behind each of these is the reason/nature dualism that forms the backdrop for the logic of domination (Plumwood 1993, 45).

It is crucial to an accurate understanding of the ecofeminist critique of value dualisms to realize that not all differences are dualisms and that deconstructing value dualisms does not mean denying all differences between dualized pairs. The problem with value dualisms lies in the construction of dualized pairs as absolutely different in morally relevant ways, which leads to the construction and justification of moral hierarchies.

THE CONSTRUCTION OF VALUE DUALISMS

The construction of dualized identities involves five features according to Plumwood. These are (1) backgrounding, (2) radical exclusion, (3) incorporation, (4) instrumentalism, and (5) homogenization. Each of these features functions to validate the relationship of denied dependency that is at the core of dualistic relationships (Plumwood 1993, 48–54).

Backgrounding involves an oppressor's attempt to use the oppressed, which creates a dependency on the oppressed, and to simultaneously deny that dependency. This is often achieved by denying the importance of the contribution of the oppressed by devaluing the forms of life associated with the oppressed group. A good example is the devaluation of the so-called private realm of the family or household, which has been traditionally associated with women. The contribution of the oppressed is backgrounded, devalued, not the focus of attention.

The relation of radical exclusion involves not merely recognizing some differences between dualized pairs, but seeing them as radically different. The number and importance of differences in maximized, shared characteristics, which cannot be denied, are viewed as inessential. Thus, any continuity between the pair is either denied or seen as unimportant. This helps in the construction of the idea of radically different and separate "natures" of oppressed and oppressor, thus justifying oppression and domination and making it appear natural or inevitable.

Incorporation involves constructing the identity of the devalued side of the dualized pair in terms of its lacking the morally relevant features associated with the other side. Since qualities that don't fit into the scheme are ignored, the other is assimilated or incorporated into the oppressor's sense of self and does not have to be dealt with as an independent entity, important in its own right.

This leads to the next feature, instrumentalism. Those groups seen as morally inferior are constructed as having no morally important independent interests; thus, they are seen as valuable only instrumentally, insofar as they can be of use in promoting the interests of the morally relevant groups. Finally, homogenization involves denying the differences between those on the underside of dualized pairs, thus, seeing all women, or all slaves, as basically the same, as merely other.

CONCEPTS OF THE SELF

According to Plumwood, at the core of the traditional liberal theory of self lies a self/other dualism that conceptualizes the self in terms of rational egoism. This conception justifies the self's instrumental use of nature, and of other human beings, as both natural and inevitable (Plumwood 1993, 152).

To use something purely instrumentally is to treat it entirely as a means to one's own ends, without treating its own ends as limiting how one may ethically use it. Justifications for treating something purely instrumentally can involve either denying that the thing has its own ends at all or constructing a moral hierarchy in which the other's ends are unimportant and thus need not be considered. Plumwood maintains that liberal thought conceives egoism as an unfortunate fact about human nature, and egoism or self-denying altruism are seen as the only two alternatives for human motivation, with egoism being rational and altruism being praiseworthy but irrational. However, as Plumwood points out:

> Assumptions about the egoism of "human nature" conceal an implicitly male as well as class model, for while self-denying

> altruism is viewed as supererogation for men, whose identity is
> formed via the public sphere where rationalism prevails, such
> altruism is traditionally enjoined for women, whose identity is
> formed via the private. (Plumwood 1993, 143)

This dualistic self exhibits radical exclusion, stressing sharply defined ego
boundaries, distinctness from others, and separation. In the tally of reasons for
and against actions, the ends of others appear only as means to its own ends, as
enlightened or rational self-interest. Such a self is not constrained empathically
or morally by the other's needs. The central problem for such a conception of the
self is ethics, for selves conceived of in this way seem incapable of truly ethical
behavior, if the ethical is something other than the merely prudential.

This model results in the homogenization of others, for they are encountered
as instruments, interchangeable to the extent that they can be used to satisfy the
agent's ends. Also, because the self attempts to use others in the world to satisfy
private interests, such a self encounters others and defines them entirely in
relation to the self's needs, and thus others are incorporated by this self. This
inevitable drive to use the other instrumentally requires hyperseparation of the
kingdom of means and the kingdom of ends. Means must be seen as radically
different kinds of things or subjects from ends. This creates what Plumwood
refers to as a kind of moral dualism between means and ends. However, the
problem remains just how to ensure that the egoistic self will not start to use
other moral agents as means as well. In fact, it is impossible to see how such an
agent can do otherwise. The instrumental use of humans is officially wrong
according to the liberal humanist version of the modern reason/nature story.
However, Plumwood and others argue that given the other dualisms that form
the Western conceptual framework, instrumentalism affects all those on the
lower rungs of the rational meritocracy. In the case of other humans it is officially
repudiated, while in the case of nature, it is accepted and explicit in the Western
model, in which it is presented as inevitable and natural.[2]

Plumwood maintains that the denial of dependency on social others is present
in the liberal account of the founding of the state:

> The denial of dependency on the social other presupposed in
> the market conception of rationality is present in the original
> liberal account of the individual and of society and the state. In
> the founding fiction of the contract, society is treated as an
> instrumental association driven by self-interest, whose purpose is
> each individual's security and the co-ordinating and making
> available of the infrastructure for the market, conceived as the
> means to the satisfaction of the myriad individual desires. The
> individual's "contract" with these others testifies to their exter-
> nality to his needs, to their mere usefulness, their inessentialness.

> For such a lone, self-sufficient wanderer in the woods, he who
> encounters the other only accidentally, and occasionally, the
> well-being of others is merely a contingent, mutual arrangement
> of convenience, not an essential part of his well-being. (Plum-
> wood 1993, 152)

SOME WORDS OF CAUTION

Before showing how an ecofeminist analysis of the self/other dualism gives insight into policies concerning nuclear deterrence, I must first caution readers about some aspects of the analysis of self offered above and its association with the liberal tradition. First, while I find Plumwood's depiction of the self of traditional liberalism compelling for some accounts, I am not sure that it works for all liberal accounts. Certainly, many liberal theorists have denied a psychology of the self that is purely egoistic. David Hume, for example, states:

> It is, therefore, a just political maxim *That every man must be
> supposed a knave:* Though at the same time, it appears somewhat
> strange that a maxim should be true in *Politics* which is false in
> *fact.* But to satisfy us on this head, we may consider that men are
> generally more honest in their private than in their public capac-
> ity, and will go greater lengths to serve a party, than when their
> private interest is alone concerned. Honour is a great check upon
> mankind: but where a considerable body of men act together, this
> check is, in a great measure, removed; since a man is sure to be
> approved of by his own party, for what promotes the common
> interest; and he soon learns to despise the clamours of adversaries.
> (Hume 1987, 42–43)

And John Rawls, another well-known proponent of liberalism, states specifically that although representatives in the original position reason so as to try to gain the most primary goods for the parties that each represents, this does not mean that he is committed to a motivational account of human beings based on psychological egoism. He states:

> Finally, as we have seen, the reasonable (with its idea of reciproc-
> ity) is not altruistic (the impartial acting solely for the interests of
> others) nor is it the concern for the self (and moved by its ends and
> affections alone) . . . this reasonable society is neither a society of
> saints nor a society of the self-centered. (Rawls 1993, 54)

One might argue that although Rawls says these things, his theory is in fact based on uncompromising psychological egoism. Nevertheless, one would have to argue for this. In the case of Hume, on the other hand, I think that it might be easier to apply Plumwood's account directly and without a lot of supporting arguments because one might say that regardless of whether Hume really believed psychological egoism to be true, he encouraged people to treat others as if it were true in the political arena, and this may be enough.

At any rate, my purpose here is not to argue whether ecological feminist criticisms such as Plumwood's necessarily apply to the liberal tradition as a whole. Rather, it is to show that at least one liberal account, that of Thomas Hobbes, certainly falls prey to this criticism, and that some contemporary discussions of nuclear deterrence make use of an account of motivation stemming from Hobbes and are thus subject to ecological feminist criticisms such as Plumwood's as well.

THE ETHICS OF NUCLEAR DETERRENCE: SOME BACKGROUND

Much of the philosophical literature on the morality of nuclear deterrence presupposes the following dilemma: The most effective way to gain a highly desired deterrent effect is to sincerely threaten to retaliate against the population centers of potentially aggressive nations. However, it is also assumed that the fact of a strike by potential aggressors does not make retaliation against population centers morally permissible, as direct intentional strikes against civilians have traditionally been prohibited under the principles of just-war theory.[3] This raises the question of whether it can be morally permissible, even obligatory, for a moral agent to form a sincere intention (needed for a sincere threat) to retaliate. For, in order to form such an intention, the agent must be actually willing to follow through, since this is what makes the threat sincere. However, if it is wrong to do something, it is also wrong to form the sincere intention to do it. One should not plan on doing wrong, much less be obligated to make a plan to do wrong.

In what follows I shall first show how Plumwood's ecological feminist critique applies to the Hobbesian account of self and other, which forms the basis for societal interaction. I shall then examine three contemporary discussions of nuclear deterrence, showing how each makes use of the Hobbesian model of self and is therefore subject to this ecological feminist critique.

Thomas Hobbes maintained that rationality requires individuals to attempt to exit the state of nature, which he characterized as a state of war of all against all, in situations where mutually advantageous cooperation is possible (Hobbes 1968, ch.14 and 15). As those familiar with the liberal tradition are aware, Hobbes believed that an all-powerful sovereign was needed in order to force people to keep agreements. Without such a guarantor, people cannot trust that others will cooperate, so they see no reason to cooperate themselves whenever they are tempted not to do so. Thus, a sovereign is needed to punish people who fail to cooperate in order to make trust in others rational (Hobbes 1968, ch.13).

Hobbes argued that in the international arena, without an international sovereign, each nation is in a state of nature with respect to every other nation. Because there is no international sovereign, there can be no morality in force between nations. Nations are in a state of war with respect to each other, and thus may do whatever is necessary to survive (Hobbes 1968, ch.13).

Plumwood's ecological feminist critique applies fairly straightforwardly to the Hobbesian account of rationality and motivation. The only rational motivation for entering into society is that the state of nature is a state of war. However, because people are rational egoists, they cannot be trusted to keep agreements to exit the state of nature unless they are motivated to do so in strongly egoistic terms. Thus, the construction of the state of nature as one of war and the account of the self in egoistic terms makes use of a strict self/other dualism in which the other is radically separated from the self and is of only instrumental value to the self. The self backgrounds and incorporates the other; the other's projects are seen as unimportant and the other is not encountered as independent and important in its own right. The self homogenizes particular others by seeing all of them as the same, as simply other. What is important for this analysis is that actual justifications for nuclear deterrence make use of the kind of self suggested by Hobbes and critiqued by Plumwood.

Christopher Morris attempts to modify the Hobbesian account of the social contract for the international arena (Morris 1985, 490). Morris argues that although it may be wrong intentionally to aim at innocents when a morality is in force, a contractarian approach can be used to argue that there may be times when there is no morality in force and, therefore, no moral constraints against killing innocents. Basically, Morris attempts to show that if one nation launches a nuclear attack upon another, this places both nations in a state of nature with respect to one another, a state in which there are no moral obligations at all. In such a state it would not be morally wrong to kill the citizens of the attacking country. Nothing would be morally wrong. Because it would not be morally wrong to retaliate under such circumstances, it is not wrong to threaten to retaliate should such circumstances occur (Morris 1985, 490–91).

Morris attempts to modify the Hobbesian account by replacing the sovereign with mutual threats of annihilation. He suggests that most nations today are in circumstances of justice with respect to each other in that (1) they are interdependent, (2) resources are scarce, and (3) mutually beneficial interaction is possible. It would therefore be rational for such nations to wish to exit a state of nature with respect to each other by seeking cooperative interaction. However, there can be no morality in force without some system of enforcement analogous to Hobbes's sovereign. This is needed to make cooperation rational and thus to create moral obligations. Morris argues that a system of enforcement weaker than an absolute sovereign (world government) can do the job. He maintains that mutual threats of retaliation can provide the needed system of enforcement. The punishment for failing to abide by moral rules can come from the carrying out of these threats. There is no need for a sovereign.

> In many relations between individuals, where police protection is unavailable, norms of cooperation are adequately enforced by the parties themselves. The threat to retaliate can, in many situations, provide the requisite enforcement mechanism. (Morris 1985, 490)

Hence, we may be able to understand the moral obligations among and between nations as guaranteed through the knowledge that if agreements are not kept, war will be the result.

Morris argues that in the event of any enemy attack, cooperative relations have in fact ended. Once such relations end, nations return to a state of nature with respect to one another. At that time, nothing that nations do to one another can be considered morally wrong; all morality is suspended. However, even in the state of nature, the fundamental law of nature requires people to seek peace if this is possible. Morris maintains that a massive attack not only ends cooperative relations, but ends the possibility of rational cooperation:

> In the event of an enemy nuclear attack (or a massive attack on NATO forces), not only have cooperative relations in fact ended, but cooperative relations are no longer possible on terms acceptable to rational agents. (Morris 1985, 491)

Morris insists that while cooperation would still be possible in the event of many conflicts, a nuclear attack ends this possibility. Thus it would no longer be obligatory to seek peace and therefore would be permissible to use all the advantages of war.

Because it would not be morally wrong (or right) to retaliate should deterrence fail, it is morally permissible to threaten to retaliate should deterrence fail, thus counter-value deterrence policies can be justified. Morris offers the following principle to show this:

> A sincere threat to do X in circumstances C is morally permissible only if doing X in C is not morally impermissible. (Morris 1985, 490)

Hence, once it is established that actual retaliation is permissible, by this principle it can also be established that intending to retaliate is permissible.

I find this account extremely disturbing from an ecological feminist perspective for several reasons. Obviously, on this account, the potential moral community is limited to those capable of contracting, which leaves out most, if not all, of nonhuman nature and leaves certain human beings with questionable status as well. However, my purpose here is to examine Morris's position through the lens of Plumwood's ecological feminist critique of the self/other dualism.

The self/other dualism implicit in Hobbes's account is expanded here so that the self becomes the nation attempting deterrence, and the other becomes the potential aggressor. Proceeding from Hobbes's model of egoism as rationality, the nation attempting deterrence views the relation between itself and the other nation in terms of hyperseparation, seeing strict boundaries between self and other. The only motivation for cooperation is self-interest; thus, the other is only of instrumental value. The values and goals of the civilians in the aggressing nation are backgrounded, as their projects and goals are not seen as important factors in the equation. Individual citizens are incorporated into the larger self of the aggressing nation, which is in turn incorporated into the self of the nation seeking deterrence. This picture also involves homogenization, seeing all the individual citizens of an aggressing nation as the same, simply as other, rather than as particular individuals.

Morris's threat principle is disturbing as well. First, it seems just plain false to say that if it is permissible to do something under certain circumstances, it is permissible to threaten to do that thing should those circumstances occur. It may be morally permissible to take a child to the doctor if he or she becomes ill, but impermissible to frighten the child into doing something with threats of a visit to the doctor. The threat itself has consequences that are different from the consequences of doing the action which is threatened. Of course, deterrence theorists realize this, for it is precisely one of these other consequences, namely deterrence, that is sought in deterrence policy. The threat, however, takes place from within a morality according to Morris. Thus, the question becomes whether it is morally permissible to view people purely instrumentally from within a morality. Making such a threat shows clearly that the other nation and its citizens are viewed in terms of a strict self/other dualism, in which they are seen as having purely instrumental value, along with everything else that goes with this. However, treating others in this way is the opposite of treating them morally. It is to treat them purely as a means.

I have argued that Morris's account fails to justify the threat of retaliation, for it requires treating other moral agents purely instrumentally. Morris tries to justify the sincere threat to retaliate by showing that actual retaliation would not be morally wrong. It would not be morally right either, for no morality would be in force, given the end of cooperative relations. However, whether right, wrong, or neutral, actually retaliating against civilians because of the actions engaged in by their governments requires extreme homogenization.

I now turn to the next account to be examined through the lens of Plumwood's ecological feminist critique, that of David Gauthier (Gauthier 1984, 474–96). Gauthier attempts to defend deterrence policies by arguing that actual deterrence is rational, even if it will produce a negative outcome. He considers a situation in which one nation attempts to deter another from launching a massive strike by sincerely threatening to retaliate against civilians should such a strike occur. He imagines that the original strike would be large enough to wipe out the nation seeking deterrence. The question then becomes, what reason could a nation that has already had a massive strike launched against it have for retaliating? The nation that attempted deterrence and fails appears to have no reasons for retaliating. It cannot hope to gain anything from such retaliation, because it is about to be annihilated anyway. Using a probability-based consequentialist account, Gauthier maintains that it is in fact rational for such a nation to retaliate. He argues that policy makers should not focus solely on the cost of failure, but must balance the probabilities of failure against the probabilities of success. Thus:

> The argument for the irrationality of deterrence looks only at the cost of deterrent failure. Because there are such costs, it rejects the policy. My argument on the other hand related the probability-weighted costs of deterrent failure to the probability-weighted benefits of deterrent success, in order to assess the rationality of forming the conditional, nonmaximizing intention which is the core of deterrence policy. I claim that if it is rational to form the conditional, deterrent intention, then should deterrence fail and the condition be realized, it is rational to act on it. (Gauthier 1984, 486)

The question of whether retaliation is rational must only be asked once. Thus, to say that the deterrence policy is itself rational is to imply that all facets of that policy are rational, including what it says to do in the case of deterrent failure.

If it is determined that expected utility is maximized by having a deterrence policy based upon a sincere threat to retaliate, then retaliation itself is also rational, because it cannot be rational to form an intention on which it is irrational to act. Thus, Gauthier mantains that although retaliation would bring nothing but unwanted consequences, it is rational for moral agents to retaliate:

> Her reason for sticking to her guns is not to teach others by example, not to improve her prospects for the future, or anything of the sort. Her reason is simply that the expected utility or payoff of her failed policy depended on her willingness to stick to her guns. (Gauthier 1984, 489)

This justification comes along with a definition of rationality and of the fully rational actor. According to Gauthier:

> The fully rational actor is not the one who assesses her actions from now but rather the one who subjects the largest, rather than

> the smallest, segments of her activity to primary rational scrutiny,
> proceeding from policies to performances, letting assessment of
> the latter be ruled by the assessment of the former. (Gauthier
> 1984, 488)

Hence, once one has settled on a policy it is irrational to change it according to the actual results of the policy.

Once again, this analysis of deterrence makes use of a severe self/other dualism. The central question involves how the nation seeking deterrence can get what it wants. If it fails to get what it wants, the aggressor nation, including all of its innocent citizens, count for nothing at all. For if the retaliating nation valued anything about the aggressing nation and its peoples, surely it wouldn't retaliate. It is clear that the only nation that matters in these calculations is the nation attempting retaliation. Otherwise it might have at least some reasons to spare the other nation from total destruction. Gauthier's rationality is the rationality of extreme psychological egoism; the other nation never mattered in itself, and so there would indeed be no hesitation in destroying it even when no good is expected to come from doing so. This nightmarish scenario is not the result of attempting rational calculations about what is to be done. Rather, it is the result of making those calculations from within the framework of an extreme self/other dualism in which only the self matters.

This is most evident in Gauthier's discussions of rationality. The most important concern for the agent on his analysis is sticking to the policy. This desire outweighs any concern for the many people the agent is about to destroy. While it may appear irrational to kill many innocent people when this will provide no positive benefit for the killer, on Gauthier's analysis, rationality involves sticking to one's plans no matter what. It is about the agent's keeping his or her word, which under the circumstances is an incredibly self-absorbed concern. Again, only the self matters here.

I now turn to the final view to be examined, that of Gregory Kavka (Kavka 1987). Kavka puts a different twist on the discussion by arguing that although the act of retaliating would be wrong in situations of the sort we are discussing, forming the sincere intention to retaliate is right, and even morally obligatory. This is because forming the intention might be utility-maximizing, while acting on it would not be. This in turn leads to the paradox that there can be situations in which goodness, knowledge, and rationality combine to prevent a moral agent from being able to do the right thing (forming the needed intention).

In such situations, in order for a rational, knowledgeable, and morally good agent to be able to do the right thing, he or she would have to engage in some sort of willful self-corruption. In Kavka's words:

> The defender may have to create an agent of this third sort (an
> altered self willing to apply the sanction), in order to deter the

offense. . . . Initiating such a process involves taking a rather odd, though not uncommon attitude toward oneself; viewing oneself as an object to be molded in certain respects by outside influences rather than by inner choices. This is, for example, the attitude of the lazy but ambitious student who enrolls in a fine college, hoping that some of the habits and values will rub off on him. (Kavka 1987, 27)

I have argued elsewhere that the idea that an action-guiding theory could recommend this is incoherent and even if it were coherent, it is unlikely that probability-based consequentialism would recommend it in cases involving nuclear deterrence. In the first case (incoherence), an action-guiding conse-quentialist theory cannot remain an action guide while recommending that one become a person who ceases to follow it. The mistake is in thinking that there are really two decisions to make, one regarding forming the intention, and the other regarding whether to follow through on the intention. However, in forming the intention one makes the decision to do it. This is what it means to form the intention. Thus, unless the theory can tell one to do wrong, it cannot coherently tell one to intend to do wrong (Davion 1992).

In the second case mentioned above (that it is unlikely that a probability-based consequentialism would recommend attempting self-corruption in such situations), I have argued that Kavka's conclusion can be reached only at the expense of pretending that deterrent success is the only issue to be considered. However, this is surely not the case. In becoming someone who would be willing to retaliate should deterrence fail, one becomes someone who either no longer understands, or fails to care about, the moral considerations that yield conclusive reasons that retaliation is wrong, something which Kavka wishes to maintain. Hence, if retaliation is wrong because of the rights of civilians, or because of the importance of environmental protection, or for whatever reason, the retaliator would have to be someone who did not know or did not understand these reasons. However, someone who failed to understand these things would be a dangerous person to have in charge of policies concerning nuclear weapons! What is to prevent such misunderstandings from resulting in a first strike? I think a probability-based consequentialism that looked at the big picture would not be in favor of taking the risk of self-corruption, even if action-guiding theories could coherently suggest it (Davion 1993). Thus, I have argued that Kavka's argument fails both on theoretical and on applied grounds.

Again, ecological feminism adds important insights as to what has gone wrong here. The problem for Kavka is how to change from a person who is not inclined to treat others purely instrumentally into someone who is willing to do this. One must become an agent who sees the world in terms of strict self/other separations, who is able to background the projects of individuals in another nation and either homogenize them into one other deserving of retaliation or see them as completely lacking in intrinsic value altogether, so that retaliation is either deserved or inconsequential from a moral standpoint.

Kavka's conclusion requires that we view the deterrence question in isolation from other pressing social questions. For, placing someone morally corrupt in a position of power may have other extremely undesirable consequences, something which Kavka does not consider. In fact, I believe that all three views discussed above suffer from this problem. Philosophers thinking about nuclear deterrence tend to set up a dualism consisting of nuclear deterrence/other social problems and focus exclusively on how to achieve deterrence. Thus, the importance of other social issues is backgrounded, incorporated into the issue of nuclear deterrence, homogenized as simply other issues to be dealt with after deterrence is gained, and instrumentalized in that whatever happens in other areas is justified as long as nuclear deterrence is achieved. Thus, philosophers thinking about nuclear deterrence seem to view it as a logic problem, in fact the supreme logic problem, separate from all else. Once issues of nuclear deterrence are contextualized, we can see that the policies discussed above require treating others and, in the case of Kavka, even treating oneself simply as a means. This is the opposite of what morality is supposed to be, making use of and expanding the self/other dualism critiqued by Plumwood in most disturbing ways.

WHERE DO WE GO FROM HERE?

You might expect that I would advocate ceasing all nuclear deterrence based on counter-value threats given what I have said thus far. However, I am going to argue for the surprising conclusion that taking the ecological feminist critique seriously does not necessarily imply the cessation of all such threats, for reasons which I shall now elaborate.

Ecological feminist critiques claim that dualistic thinking is part of the Western tradition, but such thinking is not inevitable. Thus, it is a central part of these critiques that people do think dualistically in many parts of their lives at the moment. If this were not so, such critiques would be irrelevant. Taking the critique seriously means facing these disturbing facts. We cannot simply wish dualistic thinking away. Thus, we are still faced with the problem of how to deal with people who think in this way.

The critiques themselves suggest some ways to move away from dualistic thinking. They require that we stop seeing dualistic pairs in terms of radical difference and start reassessing traits and values appearing on both sides of dualistic divides. This is a complex project, for we do not want to simply create reverse dualisms in which, for example, femininity is now valued over masculinity. Rather, we need to stop conceiving of traits as sharply divided in this way and begin recognizing the fluid boundaries between dualized concepts, and thus between dualized groups. For example, feminists such as Sara Ruddick and

Virginia Held have suggested that ways of treating and conceiving of others traditionally associated with the private sphere may provide models for more relational conceptions of the self (Ruddick 1989, Held 1987).

Ceasing to think dualistically in the international arena means not defining other nations as evil while defining ourselves as good, and not homogenizing individual peoples of other nations into simply The Other. If I am correct, however, this way of thinking is simply an expansion of the way those of us raised in Western cultures are encouraged to relate to others on more personal levels, though perhaps not on the most personal level. Perhaps then, if we can begin deconstructing dualisms on a more personal level, alternative ways of thinking will expand to incorporate the international arena.

As I stated earlier, I do not think that taking ecological feminist critiques seriously necessarily means ceasing all deterrent threats, because part of taking such critiques seriously means believing that at present many people do think dualistically. In fact, if Plumwood's critique is correct, European white men as a group may be socialized to think more dualistically than others, given that they are reared for success in the public realm. And, given that they form the majority of powerful political leaders, if left unchecked a nuclear strike of some sort seems to be a distinct possibility. I want to make clear that I am not saying that men are somehow biologically predisposed to aggression while women are not. Indeed, women can and often do think dualistically. The point is that the group of people most likely to be successful in a political climate where dualistic thinking is prevalent are most likely to be dualistic thinkers themselves. And, since such thinking could lead to nuclear aggression, we must therefore face this possibility. While actually retaliating against citizens homogenized as the other would be morally outrageous, bluffing may be the best alternative for those having to deal with European white men, given the horrible truth that nuclear weapons exist and that many people think in the ways described above. This may seem to be a surprising conclusion from an ecological feminist perspective. Yet I believe that it is consistent with the critiques discussed here, because it recognizes the fact that in reality many people and nations do think dualistically, a major component of these critiques.

Of course, the ultimate goal must be a transformation of the dualistic self/other framework that makes thoughts of nuclear aggression possible. I shall suggest two ways in which we might do this. The first, which ecological feminists have been encouraging for a number of reasons, is to expand moral conceptions to include nonhumans as ethical beings. Areas of nonhuman nature are not easily thought of as divisable into different nations, and this will, therefore, encourage us to think less in terms of national boundaries in decision making. The second is for citizens to engage in more grassroots international projects that do not involve political leaders at all, which may help foster a sense of connection between citizens of different nations.[4] Hopefully, fostering such connections will eventually make thoughts of nuclear aggression appear irrational.

NOTES

1. For clarification on some of the different ecological feminist positions, see Karen Warren, "Feminism and the Environment: An Overview of the Issues," *American Philosophical Association Newsletter on Feminism and Philosophy* (Fall 1991).

2. For an interesting discussion of this, see Griffin (1978).

3. For detailed discussions of just war theory, see Walzer (1977, 3–44) and Nagel (1979, 53–72). For an excellent collection on the ethics of nuclear deterrence, see Sterba (1985).

4. For a discussion concerning ecological feminism and grassroots activism see Lahar (1991, 24–45).

REFERENCES

Davion, Victoria. 1992. Action-guides and wrongful intentions. *Public Affairs Quarterly* 6(4):365–74.

———. 1993. The ethics of self-corruption. *Journal of Social Philosophy* 24 (3): 233–42.

Gauthier, David. 1984. Deterrence, maximization, and rationality. *Ethics* 94 (2): 474–96.

Griffin, Susan. 1978. *Woman and nature: The roaring inside her.* New York: Harper and Row.

Held, Viginia. 1987. Feminism and moral theory. In *Women and moral theory*, eds. Eva Feder Kittay and Diana T. Meyers. Totowa, NJ: Rowman and Littlefield.

Hobbes, Thomas. [1651] 1968. *Leviathan*, ed. C. B. Macpherson. New York: Penguin Books.

Hume, David. [1777] 1987. *Essays moral political and literary*, ed. Eugene F. Miller. Indianapolis: Library Classics.

Kavka, Gregory. 1987. *Moral paradoxes of nuclear deterrence.* New York and London: Cambridge University Press.

Lahar, Stephanie. 1991. Ecofeminist theory and grassroots politics. *Hypatia* 6(1):28–45.

Morris, Christopher. 1985. A contractarian defense of nuclear deterrence. *Ethics* 95(3):479–96.

Nagel, Thomas. 1979. War and massacre. In *Mortal question*. Cambridge: Cambridge University Press.

Plumwood, Val. 1993. *Feminism and the mastery of nature.* London: Routledge.

Rawls, John. 1993. *Political liberalism.* New York: Columbia University Press.

Sterba, James, ed. 1985. *The ethics of war and nuclear deterrence.* Belmont, CA: Wadsworth Publishing Company.

Walzer, Michael. 1977. *Just and unjust wars.* New York: Basic Books.

Warren, Karen J. 1990. The power and the promise of ecological feminism. *Environmental Ethics* 12(2):125–46.

Women and Language in Susan Griffin's *Woman and Nature: The Roaring Inside Her*

CAROL H. CANTRELL

> A definition of language is always, implicitly or explicitly, a definition of human beings in the world. —Raymond Williams, *Marxism and Literature* (1977)

Ecology as a concept and as a social movement asks us to question the assumptions and effects of human-centered thinking. This challenge is of great importance for feminists, for it asks us to evaluate our thinking about women in the light of our human responsibilities to the earth we inhabit, while at the same time providing us with an invaluable tool for disentangling the "human" from what is in fact "male human." Ecological thinking can help us see the provincialism of patriarchal thinking.

Ironically, however, much feminist thought has revolved around questions of language which seem to marginalize or even preclude a focus on relationships between gender and nature. Assumptions about what language is and does differ radically between liberal or humanist feminists concerned with "voice" and access to public language and, on the other hand, poststructuralist feminists exploring subject positions in language. Yet, despite their differences, they share a sense of their projects of inquiry as limited to or by a self-created human world, as well as a vivid awareness of the dangers inherent in linking women with nature.

Susan Griffin's *Woman and Nature: The Roaring Inside Her* (1978) provides a useful challenge to this sense of limits by refusing to separate the creation of woman in language from the creation of nature in language. Griffin's emphasis on the formative role of language in establishing analogies between women and nature sets this book apart from supposedly unmediated equations between them. Griffin begins by problematizing the multiple Western philosophical and theological traditions that make the link between woman and nature so powerful and so damaging, those that tell us that language is what makes us distinctively human, that the human capacity for language distinguishes us from other

Hypatia vol. 9, no. 3 (Summer 1994) © by Carol H. Cantrell animals (Rollin 1981, 22). Her insistence on thinking about language in relation to women and nature, and women in relation to nature and language, challenges both commonsense notions that language is contained within nature and poststructuralist intimations that nature is contained within language. In *Woman and Nature* language is shown to be as much a function of nature as nature is of language: neither of these terms, in Griffin's enactment of their relations, is exclusively inside or contained by the other. Instead, Griffin represents language as embedded within nature, and nature as formed by language.

The focus of this article is on what we as feminists can learn from Griffin's conception of the relationships between women, language, and nature, particularly at a moment when language has become an issue of importance to virtually all of us. My argument is that Griffin's ecofeminist conception of language is enabling: its grounding in the material world undercuts the binary oppositions usually associated with language; its incorporation of silence and emphasis on the listener fosters movement from silence to speech; and its emphasis on language as process supports and elucidates the feminist practice of recovering lost and obscure "voices." *Woman and Nature* implicitly challenges assumptions common to much feminist theory and practice that language belongs only to the powerful, and that it is inherently violent.[1]

That the use of language is in fact a central issue in *Woman and Nature* is evident in its challenges to conventions of genre. The book is hard to describe. Most of it looks like prose on the page but the thought is fragmented, metaphorical, and discontinuous; there are plenty of stories, but they too are often elliptical and metaphorical. Though references to real people and to nonliterary documents abound, *Woman and Nature* is not a documentary or an essay—it is far too discontinuous, and too allegorical, for either. *Woman and Nature* may usefully be seen as a major long poem in the American tradition of Pound's *Cantos* and Williams's *Paterson*, although unlike those earlier difficult works it is read widely by "common readers" (DuPlessis 1990, 17). Like the *Cantos* and *Paterson*, *Woman and Nature* is a "poem including history," to use Pound's phrase, one whose reach includes historical documents and events. *Woman and Nature* is at the same time a telling of a collective history and a complex work of art concerned with the "how" of its saying at least as much as the "what." Griffin draws our attention to language in the making, and to language as profoundly relational.

These contingent and relational qualities of language in *Woman and Nature* are of great importance for feminists, for just these qualities make it possible to connect the process of coming to speech, of naming, of having a voice—different metaphors used by feminists to describe the connection between attaining personhood and an individual's use of language—with the larger task of changing language. This connection is especially significant given the difficulty of the task as it is magnified by conceptions of language tacitly assumed by many feminists.

The relation of gender to language has caught the imagination of a wide

variety of feminist thinkers—from humanist to radical feminist to poststructuralist—within the last twenty years or so. Some, such as Mary Field Belenky
and the other authors of *Women's Ways of Knowing* (1987), focus on discovering
developmental states in women as they move from inarticulateness to speech.
Others, such as Sandra Harding (1986), L. J. Jordanova (1980), and Mannette
Klein (1989), have shown the extent to which accepted analytical categories
conceal symbolic meanings detrimental to women. Still others, such as Mary
Daly (1980), have tried to retrieve lost meanings of words as part of a larger
project of inventing a language for women. Some French feminists have shifted
the focus to the "feminine," expressed in "the moment of rupture and negativity"
(Kristeva 1974, 167), in "my body, shot through with streams of song" (Cixous
1976, 253), in "statements [which] are never identical to anything" (Irigaray
1977, 103)

What these very diverse projects have in common is an emphasis on woman
as (non)speaker and a concomitant emphasis on language as passkey to participation in the public or shared symbolic world, to personhood, to power. These
analyses of language and language use dramatize an all but insoluble dilemma:
achieving "personhood," however defined, would seem to wait on changing the
language, a difficult task exacerbated by conceptions of language which assume
profound disconnections between language and users of language. Whether
language is centered in writing or in the speaker, it is functionally a powerful
monologue unaffected by real or potential listeners. In any such conception of
language, the gaps between language and language users create a theoretical
gridlock that makes changing language virtually impossible to imagine.

From a feminist point of view, an obvious problem with any such conception
of language is the difficulty of effecting historical change. From an ecological
point of view, a major difficulty is that such conceptions of language reinscribe
the superiority of the human over the animal, the speaker over the speechless,
the articulate over the dumb. The first problem, the problem of women's relation
to men's language, leads to the impasse of trying to invent a woman's language
out of whole cloth or of seeking forms of expression in the margins of the
symbolic order.[2] The second problem, the acceptance of a categorical difference
between those within and without language, challenges us to question the use of
language to organize distinctions between superior and inferior beings.

For example, if speech or writing is the guarantee of personhood and of
rationality, do we want to say that our foremothers were lesser beings than those
of us who are now able to speak and write in a public arena? What about
consciousness that remains unspoken? We know it exists; Patricia Hill Collins,
for example, has written movingly of the utter distinction black women must
often maintain between what they think and what they say (Collins 1986, 23).
In general, are we ready to jettison the major portion of women's experience
because it belongs to prehistory, that is, to undocumented history? Are all
silences, including our foremothers' silences, to be understood as absence of

speech, and thus of personhood? Are feminists in danger of replicating the patriarchal silencing of women by insisting on the link between speech or writing and personhood? Questions such as these suggest that, at the very least, we need to think through the relationship between definitions of language and the perpetuation of hierarchy by assumptions about language.

Woman and Nature places women's silences in the context of a nature assumed to be mute, and in parallel with the peoples of the world who are seen as embedded in nature. "These words," she writes in the book's dedication, "are written for those of us whose language is *not heard*, whose words have been stolen or erased, those robbed of language, *who are called voiceless or mute*, even the earthworms, even the shellfish and the sponges" (Griffin 1978).[3] Human superiority, European superiority, male superiority are enforced by selective deafness and designated dumbness: listeners create speakers.

> The world is a force, not a presence. (Wallace Stevens, "Adagia," 1957)

> We say there is no end to any act. The rock thrown in the water is followed by waves of water, and these waves of water make waves in the air, and these waves travel outward infinitely, setting particles in motion, leading to other motion and motion upon motion endlessly. (Griffin, 1978)

Woman and Nature begins with a section doubly titled "Matter," the name both of the first book and its first section. "Matter" consists of a forty-page long compendium of quotations and paraphrases from Western philosophical and theological writings in roughly chronological order, all having to do with intertwined generalizations about the nature of matter and the nature of woman. "Matter/Matter" consists of more than forty pages full of assertions such as the following:

> It is decided that matter is passive and inert, and that all motion originates from outside matter. . . . That matter is only a potential for form or a potential for movement. . . . It is decided that the nature of woman is passive, that she is a vessel waiting to be filled. (Griffin 1978, 5)
> It is decided that matter cannot know matter. (Griffin 1978, 14)
> And it is observed that woman is less evolved than man. Men and women differ as much, it is observed, as plants and animals do. (Griffin 1978, 26)

The responses of a group of women listeners to this succession of pronouncements are indicated in italics. Though these interspersed comments are refreshing to the eye, they are sparse, and their tone seems passive, numbed, afraid:

> *And we seek dumbness. . . . We practice muteness.* (Griffin 1978, 20)

> *We are nature, we are told, without intelligence.* (Griffin 1978, 29)

> *We open our mouths. We try to speak. We try to remember.* (Griffin 1978, 44)

These statements register the consciousness of listeners who seem to respond like the inert "matter" they have been told they are, passively taking the form impressed on it.

Woman and Nature thus begins ominously with a silence filled with pronouncements. The blocks of quotations which make up most of this first section are set within a context of virtually silent women listeners hearing again and again that the real, the good, the rational are defined as different from them, no matter what else is said. Quotation is central to the workings of *Woman and Nature*, and in its early sections quoted language represents a central mechanism of domination: reality is defined by a discourse inaccessible to listeners but which dominates their daily lives.

The power of this discourse is stronger for the networks of association within it which draw the whole world into its systems of classification. These networks manifest themselves most obviously in analogy, also a strongly marked stylistic feature in *Woman and Nature*. Analogy serves as the organizing principle of large and small features of the text, from sections to sentences. The analogy between woman and nature is highlighted by the book's title and repeated in seemingly endless variations: woman is—just to give a few examples—a hurricane, a volcano, a show horse, a mule, a stand of timber to be harvested. As the text proceeds, it becomes more and more clear to the reader that the groups of linked analogies elaborated within the quoted materials consistently work together to exclude women and analogous others, like dark-skinned people, from full humanity. Quotation and analogy, the warp and the woof of *Woman and Nature*, represent language at its most monopolistic, composed as it is of networks of association which leave nothing named untouched.

Griffin thus represents the feminist view that language is profoundly hostile to the "others" it denigrates and silences. Yet *Woman and Nature* has as its central movement the gradual inhabiting of language by women, a movement difficult or impossible to imagine for others who share this analysis. The reason why, I believe, is incipient in Griffin's conception of the potential power of the listener, and by extension, her conception of language as constantly negotiable.

Listening, for example, even in the desperate world of "Matter/Matter" is potentially an active rather than a passive activity. Indeed, the actuality of listeners insistently draws attention to the social and historical context in which even the most theoretical language act is positioned. Heard or overheard in the context of women's lives, analogies linking women to matter carry the weight of their material consequences. Elaine Scarry reminds us that "the notion of 'consequence,' of 'mattering,' is nearly inseparable from the substantive fact of 'matter.' Or, phrased in the opposite direction, when 'matter' goes from being a noun to being an active verb—when we go from saying of something that 'it is matter' or 'it has matter' to saying 'it matters'—then substance has tilted forward into consequence" (Scarry 1988, xxii). The philosophical statements Griffin quotes "matter" in the context of the listening women in a way that they did not for those who utter them; no statement can be abstract or neutral when it is "tilted forward into consequence" so vividly. The mere presence of the listener, in other words, "matters" in the process of creating meaning.

Thus while "Matter/Matter" begins with language at its most oppressive, destructive, and monopolistic, even here there is room within the language to be more than *only* oppressive and within women to be more than *only* oppressed. This room exists in the gaps and incongruities between the listeners' actual lives and the language supposedly describing life, in the illumination of theory by its effects, in the potential for misunderstanding or mockery on the part of the listener, and in the need of the speaker for the listener. The potential for irony, even comedy, to say nothing of critical response, opens up for Griffin's reader, who experiences a twofold sense of the listener's relations to language, for as she imagines a group of women listening to these statements, she also listens to herself listening to all those voices all her life.

Such a listener's experience of language and the significance of her relationship to it have been aptly described in V. N. Vološinov's *Marxism and the Philosophy of Language* (1929).[4] Vološinov rejects the study of language as a study of systems separable from their communities of users. Instead, he insists on the necessity of conceiving language as constantly touching and being touched by the daily lives and activities of those who use it: language "matters," in both senses of the word. Vološinov conceives of language as being constantly renewed and reshaped by those who hear it:

> Every outer ideological sign, of whatever kind, is engulfed in and washed over by inner signs—by the consciousness. The outer sign originates from this sea of inner signs and continues to abide there, since its life is a process of renewal as something to be understood, experienced, and assimilated. (Vološinov 1929, 33)

> In each speech act, subjective experience perishes in the objective fact of the enunciated word-utterance, and the enunciated word is subjectified in the act of responsive understanding in order to generate, sooner or later, a counter statement. (Vološinov 1929, 40-41)

Thus language never belongs exclusively to the powerful; even control of the ideology designating dominant meanings of words cannot control the possibility of misunderstanding, ironic interpretation, misplaced emphasis, and the like. Moreover, no statement is final, for statement creates the conditions for counter-statement: "Each word . . . is a little arena for the clash and criss-crossing of differently oriented social accents" (Vološinov 1929, 41).

It follows then that language cannot be the exclusive property of any one of the groups who use it: "Class does not coincide with the sign community. . . . Thus various different classes will use one and the same language. . . . Sign becomes an arena of the class struggle" (Vološinov 1929, 23). If we extend these comments to gender, as Vološinov did not, Griffin's "Matter/Matter" clearly represents an arena in which the struggle over meaning takes place. Indeed, Vološinov is particularly interested in moments when one speaker uses the words of another, for he implies that they are relatively transparent instances of the potential for contested meaning when words move from one consciousness to another (115-20). Moreover, according to Vološinov, language carries within it multiple meanings obscured at any given moment by whatever ideology domi-nates at the time; language is, as he puts it, "multiaccentual" (23).

In Griffin's text, quoted words are transformed—given a different accent—simply by being quoted. Thus the significance of moments of mimicry and mockery in Griffin's text, when, for example, "(Out of the corner of his eye, he sees a gesture. The image rubs against the inside of his head. . . . She did not know what she was doing, to imitate his carriage, to lift her head in that manner, calmly. There is something that repels him in that gesture)" (Griffin 1978, 149). Mimicry and caricature represent extreme versions of the potential within any act of listening, the potential to hear things on the listener's terms. Since speech is a "bridge thrown between myself and another," it is indeed "a two-sided act" (Vološinov 1929, 86). Even muteness is part of this "two-sided act"; it is not a condition belonging to an individual but a function of a relationship.[5]

> The real communicative "products" which are usable signs are . . .
> living evidence of a continuing social process. (Williams, 1977)

> My story, no doubt, is me, but it is also, no doubt, older than me.
> Younger than me, older than the humanized. (Trinh, 1989)

One of the things Griffin's listener hears is the extent to which the same analogies that govern her life circumscribe the way her culture imagines "life" itself, as though life were something from which one could separate oneself.[6] And the way this culture imagines life is deeply intertwined with the way it imagines her. "Woman" is associated with life, but this association is also powerfully a dissociation, disconnecting "man" from nature and man from woman. Such dissociations, Griffin has noted, "create . . . the definition of nature and culture as opposed" (Macauley 1991, 123).

These dissociations have the most serious possible material consequences for women, men, nature, and culture. To give one example: "She yields. She conceives. Her lap is fertile. Out of her dark interior, life arises. What she does to his seed is a mystery to him. . . . Whatever she brings forth he calls his own. He has made her conceive. His land is a mother. . . . He is determined he will master her. He will make her produce at will" (Griffin 1978, 53). In the characteristic passage following, Griffin interweaves long lists of chemicals poured into the earth with lists of drugs given to women to make both produce more, and more reliably. When we read, "She says now that the edges of what she sees are blurred" and that "the first pain is gone or that she cannot remember it, or that she cannot remember why this began, or what she was like before, or if she will survive without what he gives her to take" (54), it is impossible to determine whether earth or woman speaks.

In *Woman and Nature* this confusion of identity shows not that women are essentially tied to nature (any more or any less than men are) but that the analogy linking women and nature, and dividing both from man, has material, historical consequences for all. The cultural creation of hierarchical relation-ships between (some) humans and nature is inseparable from the way we see nature, and governs what we do to both. These hierarchies shape not just perceptions but bodies and landscapes. A striking example of this process is embodied in the "Show Horse" (Griffin 1978, 76-82), whose muscles, like her mind—whether animal or woman—are developed to please the master. The analogies in ordinary language that "matter" order the human shaping of the physical world.

Yet Griffin implies that the processes set in motion through language can flow in another direction as well; many sections of *Woman and Nature* imply that bodily experience can become language. In Vološinov's terms, experience goes into language by becoming a sign: "*The organism and the outside world meet here in the sign*" (Vološinov 1929, 26). No experience or expression is in and of itself off limits from language: "*Anything and everything occurring within the organism can become the material of experience*, since everything can acquire semiotic signifi-cance" (Vološinov 1929, 29). Thus, what counts as "the material of experience," that is, as having semiotic significance, is constantly negotiable.

Griffin's story of the lion's roar (Griffin 1978, 187) is a crucial example of the relation between physiological response and sign. After being tested and prod-ded by the pedants, the lion lets out an incomprehensible roar, incomprehensible to the pedants, that is. For them the roaring is not a sign, not a "bridge thrown between myself and another" (Vološinov 1929, 86); instead, "The roaring must be inside her, they conclude" (Griffin 1978, 187). Less arrogant listeners would be able to hear the roar as a warning; such listeners would not conceive of the difference between themselves and another species as absolute.

This example suggests that enlarging our sense of "what counts" as significant is rightly central to feminist studies. The recovery of women's history recorded in lost or neglected documents and of work and thought deemed trivial because it was done by women is, Vološinov's work would suggest, one way of setting in motion fundamental changes in language use. Yet with the possible exception of the efforts of gynocriticism to locate lost and neglected women writers, recovery activities are not integral to feminist thinking about language.[7] And even gynocriticism is limited by its focus on the written. Just as Julia Kristeva argues that "it is in the aspiration toward artistic and, in particular, literary creation that woman's desire for affirmation now manifests itself" (Kristeva 1981, 49), gynocriticism focuses on those ancestors who are most like "us," who do not live in the prehistory of what amounts to the oral culture of those who do not write.[8]

Griffin challenges two assumptions here: that an unbridgeable gulf divides the present from the past, and that the act of writing marks women's entry into history. Much of *Woman and Nature* takes place in an arena both invisible and monumental in local and global history. This is the arena of work characteristically assigned to women—the labor of caring for the body, of making sure that others have enough to eat, of looking after the sick—and the skills and knowledge which these acts produce. Many passages, like the following, detail such labor:

> And if we find this grace through our labor, with our fingers finding the loose thread in the garment, our ears late at night hearing the cries no one else hears, catching the milk in the pot as it begins to boil . . . or the seeing of the barely seeable, the unnamed, the slight difference in the expression of the eyes, . . . the small possibility, barely audible, nodding, almost inarticulate, yet allowing articulation . . . this grace of the unspoken . . . and if we find this, we have something of our own. (Griffin 1978, 75)

Though Griffin here is "giving voice" to marginalized experience, her emphasis is not on the importance of writing and the permanence that the written record provides. Rather, many of her examples emphasize that knowledge does not depend on written records to be generated and transmitted.

Here her work has affinities with that of Trinh Minh-ha, whose description of storytelling in oral cultures challenges print-oriented conceptions of history and truth. Rather than possessing permanence and objectivity, the stories in an oral tradition are transformed continuously as they are incorporated in each retelling within individual speakers' experiences. Thus, as it is passed along this sort of tradition belongs to everyone and to no one. Told and re-told, its stories weave together listeners' stories with the stories that precede them, and join present understanding with past history and knowledge (Trinh 1989, 122, 125, passim). Such a process accommodates difference and change while it acknowledges the importance (but not the uniqueness) of the teller, as "objective" written history does not.

Griffin, like Trinh, implies that these contrasting approaches to history rest on contrasting approaches to knowing the world. A pair of episodes in which women look at a corpse dramatize the contrast between "objective truth," which separates the observer from what she sees, and what we might call "woven truth." In the first, "The Anatomy Lesson," a medical student who "associates her own body with the coldness of this one" is told that "she must learn to move about the human body without feeling" and learns that "no one wonders if there might have been a use for that feeling" (Griffin 1978, 114). In the second episode, "Matter Revisited," this feeling is useful as a guide to knowledge. "She," the third-person objective observer, has become "we," located within a social context. Here "our" feeling for the dead woman's body combined with the knowledge we bring to the scene yields a wealth of information—an implied narrative incorporating the dead woman's past with our present.[9] As we look at the dead woman's hands, her knees, her skin, her breasts, we read the story of her daily life:

> From the body of the old woman, we can tell you something of the life she lived. We know that she spent much of her life on her knees. (Fluid in the bursa in front of her kneecap.) . . . From the look of certain muscles in her back, her legs, we can tell you something of her childhood, of what she did not do. (Of the running, of the climbing, of the kicking, of the movements she did not make) . . . and we can tell you that despite each injury she survived. (Griffin 1978, 208-209)

This "Anatomy Lesson" is guided by empathy and grounded in the possibility of our reading traces of history inscribed in the material world (here, the body). In many other passages in Woman and Nature, the everyday details of different women's lives—especially of their laboring lives—become the stuff of a powerful story. For Griffin, the question is not whether women can come to express themselves but how we can come to discover and read women's stories. In particular, Griffin urges us to look at what women and their immediate environments have done to each other, to join with Alice Walker "In Search of Our Mothers' Gardens" (1983). Whatever we choose to do, it will inevitably be part of the ongoing story women tell about themselves.

Woman and Nature celebrates such possibilities within the flow and re-creation of language. Underlying this celebration is an overarching sense that human activities, including those involved in making language, are embedded within natural processes no less than they are within history. "Embeddedness," "flow" and "re-creation" are, of course, metaphors; as such, they expose the foundationalism harbored within the language-as-violence metaphor, suggesting as it does that human violence toward the world is a given—in the nature of things, in the "always already." Woman and Nature, in contrast, implies that violence toward nature and violence toward women are interrelated problems stemming from the use of language, not from the nature of language.

Griffin shows us that what we make in language is always in response to, in play with, our social and natural worlds—and that the social and natural worlds cannot be separated. When we do separate them, the knowledge we produce gives back to us a "reflection of the knower's own severance from the world" (Holler 1990, 9). Griffin chooses instead to follow what happens when language is seen as integral to the human relationship with nature.

> *We never invented ourselves, we admit. . . . And my grandmother's body is now part of the soil, she said. Only now, we name ourselves. . . . We know ourselves to be made from this earth. We know this earth is made from our bodies. For we see ourselves. And we are nature. We are nature seeing nature. . . . Nature speaking of nature to nature.* (Griffin 1978, 226)

Instead of emphasizing hierarchy and division, Griffin's conception of language emphasizes interdependence and renewal. Above all, it asks us to conceive of the human activity of making culture—including our efforts as feminists to re-think gender—as interactive with, rather than as essentially antagonistic to, life processes.

NOTES

1. For a lucid discussion of conceptions within recent critical theory of violence as inherent in symbolic systems, see Diggory (1991, 5-13).

2. For problems with "women's languages," see Yaeger (1988, 24-27). See also Hedley's discussion of the limitations of Daly's stipulated language in contrast to Rich's commitment to making "a common language" (Hedley 1992, 40-59).

For an analysis of Kristeva, Irigaray, and Cixous, see Nye (1988, esp. "A Woman's Language" 172-228). Nye argues that for each of these writers, "feminist thought about language, beg[an] with theory, reacted to theory, attempted to valorize within theory a place from which a woman might speak" (Nye 1988, 211). In a parallel criticism of conceptions of language divorced from the social world, Raymond Williams writes, "Thus the living speech of human beings in their specific social relations in the world was theoretically reduced to instances and examples of a system which lay beyond them" (Williams 1977, 27).

3. All italics in quoted passages occur in the cited texts unless indicated otherwise.

4. The authorship of works ascribed to Vološinov remains controversial, some scholars maintaining that they were actually written by M. M. Bakhtin. The evidence is inconclusive at best, and it seems prudent to follow the course advocated by Morson and Emerson: "barring the presentation of new evidence,

there is no convincing reason to credit Bakhtin with authorship of disputed texts" (Morson and Emerson 1989, 31).

5. Arguing for the usefulness of the Bakhtinian dialogical method for an ecofeminist literary criticism, Patrick D. Murphy shows how the "other" has "the potential, as does any entity, to become a 'speaking subject' " (Murphy 1991, 151). Elsewhere, Murphy uses dialogics to argue for the centrality of *Woman and Nature* in the emerging genre of "nature writing" (Murphy, forthcoming).

6. A suggestive parallel is provided by Vološinov's attack on Saussure for abstracting "langue" from the social and the historical; he argues that Saussure treats language as a "cadaver," on the model of the study of "dead" languages (Vološinov 1929, 57-63, 71, 73).

7. Benstock in "Beyond the Reaches of Feminist Criticism: A Letter from Paris" notes that "the gynocritical approach works best when it examines the links between women writers and their works in literary periods in which language itself was not under inspection, when language itself was not a crucial issues for writers" (1987, 22).

8. Elaine Showalter describes "gynocritics" as "historical in orientation; it looks at women's writing as it has actually occurred and tries to define its specific characteristics of language, genre, and literary influence, within a cultural network that includes variables of race, class, and nationality" (1987, 37).

9. Writing about the post-Newtonian position of the observer, Linda Holler argues that "the denial of being *in* the world is historically and ontologically tantamount to the denial of the being *of* the world. Thus, to re-enter the world is to bring it back to life, and objectivity becomes a matter of attending to the object's multiple disclosures rather than the subject's singular detachment. The world becomes a full partner in the epistemological dialogue" (1990, 5).

REFERENCES

Belenky, Mary, Blythe Clinchy, Nancy Goldberg, and Jill Tarule. 1986. *Women's ways of knowing.* New York: Basic Books.

Benstock, Shari, ed. 1987. *Feminist issues in literary scholarship.* Bloomington: Indiana University Press.

Cixous, Hélène. 1976. The laugh of the Medusa. In *New French feminisms.* See Elaine Marks and Isabelle Courtrivon, 1981.

Collins, Patricia Hill. 1986. Learning from the outsider within: The sociological significance of black feminist thought. *Social Problems* 33(6): 14-32.

Daly, Mary. 1978. *Gyn/ecology: The metaethics of radical feminism.* Boston: Beacon Press.

Diggory, Terence. 1991. *William Carlos Williams and the ethics of painting.* Princeton: Princeton University Press.

DuPlessis, Rachel Blau. 1990. *The pink guitar: Writing as feminist practice*. New York: Routledge.

Griffin, Susan. 1978. *Woman and nature: The roaring inside her*. New York: Harper.

Harding, Sandra. 1986. The instability of the analytical categories of feminist theory. *Signs* 11(4): 645-64.

Hedley, Jane. 1992. Surviving to speak new language: Mary Daly and Adrienne Rich. *Hypatia* 7(2): 40-62.

Holler, Linda. 1990. Thinking with the weight of the earth: Feminist contributions to an epistemology of concreteness. *Hypatia* 5(1): 1-23.

Irigaray, Luce. 1977. This sex which is not one. In *New French feminisms*. See Elaine Marks and Isabelle de Courtrivon 1981.

Jordanova, L. J. 1980. Natural facts: A historical perspective on science and sexuality. In *Nature, culture and gender,* ed. Carol McCormack and Marilyn Strathern. New York: Cambridge University Press.

Klein, Hilary Mannette. 1989. Marxism, psychoanalysis, and Mother Nature. *Feminist Studies* 15(2): 255-78.

Kristeva, Julia. 1974. Oscillation between power and denial. In *New French feminisms*. See Elaine Marks and Isabelle de Courtivron, 1981.

———. 1981. Woman's time. Trans. Alice Jardine and Harry Blake. In *Feminist theory: A critique of ideology*, ed. Nannerl O. Keohane, Michelle Z. Rosaldo, and Barbara C. Gelpi. Chicago: University of Chicago Press.

Macauley, David. 1991. On women, animals and nature: An interview with ecofeminist Susan Griffin. *American Philosophical Association Newsletter on Feminism and Philosophy* 90(3): 116-27.

Marks, Elaine, and Isabelle de Courtivron, eds. 1981. *New French feminisms*. New York: Schocken Books.

Morson, Gary Saul, and Caryl Emerson, eds. 1989. *Rethinking Bakhtin: Extensions and challenges*. Evanston: Northwestern University Press.

Murphy, Patrick D. 1991. Ground, pivot, motion: Ecofeminist theory, dialogics, and literary practice. *Hypatia* 6(1): 146-61.

———. 1994. Voicing another nature. In *A dialogue of voices: Feminist literary theory and Bakhtin*, ed. Karen Hohne and Helen Wussow. Minneapolis: University of Minnesota Press.

Nye, Andrea. 1988. *Feminist theory and the philosophies of man*. New York: Routledge.

Rollin, Bernard. 1981. *Animal rights and human morality*. Buffalo: Prometheus Books.

Scarry, Elaine, ed. 1988. *Literature and the body: Essays on populations and persons*. Baltimore: Johns Hopkins University Press.

Showalter, Elaine. 1987. Women's time, women's space: Writing the history of feminist criticism. In *Feminist issues in literary scholarship*, ed. Shari Benstock. Bloomington: Indiana University Press.

Stevens, Wallace. 1957. *Opus posthumous*. New York: Knopf.

Trinh T. Minh-ha. 1989. *Woman, native, other*. Bloomington: Indiana University
  Press.

Vološinov, V. N. 1929. *Marxism and the philosophy of language*. Trans. Ladislav
  Matejka and I. R. Titunik. Cambridge: Harvard University Press, rpt. 1986.

Walker, Alice. 1983. In search of our mothers' gardens: *Womanist prose*. San
  Diego: Harcourt Brace.

Williams, Raymond. 1977. *Marxism and literature*. Oxford: Oxford University
  Press.

Yaeger, Patricia. 1988. *Honey-mad women: Emancipatory strategies in women's
  writing*. New York: Columbia University Press.

Feminism and Ecology:
On the Domination of Nature

PATRICIA JAGENTOWICZ MILLS

INTRODUCTION

The most insightful political interventions of the 1960s were directed to the problems and possibilities of a post-industrial society. The social critiques done by the first generation of the Frankfurt School (Herbert Marcuse, Max Hork-heimer, Theodor W. Adorno) and the social ecology movement (developed primarily by Murray Bookchin) are two influential strains of radical social thought that contributed to and maintain the innovative politics of the sixties. In both these intellectual perspectives the major conflict is seen as that between industrial society and nature, rather than between classes within industrial society, with the focus on "domination" rather than "exploitation." These critiques, based on the domination of nature, go beyond the mere condemnation of the ecological crisis to reveal a connection between the domination of nonhuman nature, social domination, and psychological domination. They argue that as nature comes to be viewed as nothing more than the material for human domination, we develop an anthropocentric view in which we see ourselves as "the measure of all things." In this way we lose an awareness of the dialectical relation between nature and history, as we lose an awareness of ourselves as part of nature.[1] Nature becomes an external Other, merely the "stuff of domination," and we become blind to our true goals, those that will lead to self-realization and liberation. Both perspectives then point to that which is left out or denied by the domination of nature, as Otherness is extended to particular social groups. In this sense, the problem of the domination of nature is seen as theoretically central to women's liberation, Afro-American and Third World liberation, sexual liberation, native struggles, and the peace and ecology movements: all these movements are centrally formed by the repressive power of industrial society on what is perceived and formed by it as the external Other.

The New Left neo-Hegelianism of Isaac Balbus and the ecofeminism of Ynestra King each seek to use the concept of the domination of nature as a theoretical point

Hypatia vol. 6, no. 1 (Spring 1991) © by Patricia Jagentowicz Mills

of unification to clarify and unite contemporary political struggles. For both thinkers a form of Hegelian reconciliation is central to the realization of freedom insofar as this reconciliation is said to overcome the dualisms of mind and matter, nature and history, subject and object, self and Other.

In this paper I challenge the adequacy of their projects through a focus on what I term their "abstract pro-nature" stance. This stance entails a highly selective approach both to theory, by assuming that one can simply extract parts from several theoretical traditions and fuse them into a new whole, and to contemporary politics, by sidestepping the feminist issue of reproductive freedom as it relates to the issue of abortion. I will argue that the abstract pro-nature stance of Balbus and King develops a political program that views "Nature" as benign, cooperative, and sharing with humans a form of consciousness or subjectivity that is to be emulated; it leaves out of consideration its opposite or contradictory moment—the moment of nature "red in tooth and claw." I conclude that their abstract pro-nature stance ignores important elements of women's liberation by depoliticizing feminism, making it merely a handmaid of the ecology movement.[2]

Central to my argument is a consideration of the distortion and misappropriation by both Balbus and King of the work of Horkheimer and Adorno on the domination of nature. It is with the tradition of critical theory developed by Horkheimer and Adorno that the domination of nature emerges as *the* fundamental problem for a critique of society. With their work, Marx's critique of capitalist exploitation is renewed and extended in a critique of the domination of nature that attempts to uncover the psychic and social basis of the solidification of repressive society. Horkheimer and Adorno, however, do not romanticize nature or leave out of consideration the regressive moment of nature, "the revolt of nature" that characterized German fascism.

HEGEL RECONSIDERED: BALBUS AND THE FRANKFURT SCHOOL

In *Marxism and Domination: A Neo-Hegelian, Feminist, Psychoanalytic Theory of Sexual, Political, and Technological Liberation*, Isaac Balbus asserts that his project is to find a unifying principle for all the liberation movements in contemporary society. This principle is identified in terms of the domination of nature, which grounds the process of objectification in society. The domination of nature is shown to entail social and psychic consequences that result in ecological crises, patriarchal domination, and repressive political forms in both capitalist and socialist societies. Instrumental reason (what Balbus calls the "instrumental mode of symbolization") is revealed as the specific form of reason through which nature is mastered. As a rationality of *means*, instrumental reason eliminates the question of *ends*, and in doing so it distorts not only the ends but also the means or techniques it uses by exalting them to ends. The unconscious roots of this instrumental logic or mode of symbolization are said to develop within a specific form of childcare in which women are the primary nurturers of infants (Balbus 1982, 269-302).[3]

In his effort to theorize and generate new possibilites of critical consciousness Balbus points to the necessity for a transformation in childrearing practices. Since the mode of childrearing is seen to determine significantly our unconscious life, and thereby to establish the limits of our ability to transform society as adults, a nondominating stance toward nature and others is to be achieved through shared heterosexual parenting. Leaning heavily on the work of Dorothy Dinnerstein, Balbus claims that fathers as well as mothers must be involved in the care of infants if we are to eliminate the development of an unconscious process that entails the domination of the Other as woman, nature, or political adversary. Once both men and women share the responsibility for childcare, the mother will no longer be seen as all-powerful, and with the dissolution of the first powerful (M)Other the logic of domination will disappear (303-52).

While the project of Balbus's book may be crucial for those interested in radical social change, the theoretical analysis developed by him for this political task is extremely problematic. We are led through an intellectual maze that begins with the work of Hegel and Marx, proceeds through Balbus's conception of Western or neo-Marxism, Marxist feminism, Freudianism, neo-Freudianism, feminist Freudianism, and a sociohistoric account of childrearing patterns. The theoretical pastiche Balbus creates as he journeys through this maze moves from logic to genetic theory in an effort to discredit Marx's focus on the mode of production (which accepts the logic of the domination of nature) and thereby to discredit the working class as the revolutionary agent of social change. Balbus argues that repressive technology, the state, and patriarchy are relatively autonomous forms of domination that should not be seen as automatically determined by the mode of production. He claims that the childrearing practices by which ecologists, peace activists, and feminists have been raised have led them to create movements structured around the principles of participatory democracy, and these movements have thereby superseded the working class as the revolutionary subject of history (389-90).[4]

It is true, as Balbus shows, that the Hegelian problem of the relation between identity and difference is at the heart of the modern project to create a free and equal society. That is, within all liberation struggles of the 1990s there is now a search for a form of intersubjective recognition (a relation between self and Other) that allows for concrete differences but does not on that account render the relation unequal by dominating the Other. However, it is *not* true that we can, as Balbus suggests, simply extract parts out of Hegel's system in order to eliminate some while we "apply" others. In fact, the abstraction of parts from the whole is precisely what Balbus faults neo-Marxists and Marxist feminists for doing with Marx's theory (4-6). The problem with Balbus's approach to Hegel emerges most clearly in his failure to address the problem of the domination of nature *within* Hegel's theory.

Balbus's claim that we can keep Hegel's notion of Absolute Knowledge as a final moment of reconciliation but eliminate the teleological movement of *Geist* or World Spirit on which it depends is extremely questionable (284-91). For Hegel, Spirit or *Geist* (self-thinking thought or the self-knowledge of the universe) moves dialectically through progressive stages in such a way that Spirit externalizes or alienates itself, overcomes this alienation or externalization, returns to itself, and is, finally, complete self-knowledge. Each of the initial stages of the dialectical process is "abstract" or "partial" because it leaves out its essential opposite. In each stage a contradictory "moment" or negation emerges through Spirit's self-alienation or externalization; a profound struggle between the two moments then takes place, from which emerges a third moment of reconciliation that simultaneously maintains, negates, and transcends the earlier moments. This is the negation of the negation that becomes a "positive" moment. Hegel uses a single term to describe this complex process: the original "moments" are *aufgehoben* (Hegel 1979, 1-57).

Through Hegelian dialectical logic, thought is said to think the relation between two concepts in such a way that both concepts are maintained—one is not dissolved into the other—while at the same time a true unity or reconciliation is achieved in the third moment. Thus, dialectical logic is said to reveal the movement of life as a process that overcomes the conceptual dualism or mutual exclusivity of the concepts of the understanding (*Verstand*). At the stage of reason or *Vernunft*, a higher unity of concepts emerges, fusing concepts without canceling out their differences: reason can apprehend the concepts in an identity-in-difference. Hegelian logic, therefore, claims to overcome the dualisms of subject and object, mind and matter, nature and history, self and Other.

Hegel assumes a necessary connection between his system of philosophy, its dialectical movement, and the historical evolution of humanity. Consciousness or Spirit does not transcend historical experience. Rather, rationality is nourished by history such that there are correlations between stages of the dialectic of consciousness and historical transformation. For Hegel the goal of philosophy is to present systematically the structure and teleological movement of Spirit, which culminates in the universe's knowledge of itself. Nature is conceived as Spirit's opposite, but it is an opposite that is the necessary precondition for the realization of the dialectical movement of Spirit's self-development. However, as the philosophical thought of Hegel attempts to recognize and conquer the actual world, nature gradually passes over into Spirit as its higher truth.

Rather than offering a *new* relation to nature as Balbus claims, Adorno has shown that Hegelian identity theory—the theory that latent in contradictions is an ultimate unity or identity-in-difference of subject and object, mind and matter, universal and particular, history and nature—has always meant domination: of the subject over the object, mind over matter, universal over particular, history over nature. Adorno, therefore, rejects Hegelian identity theory and attempts to provide a dialectical theory that remains a "negative dialectic" such that there is no third or final "positive" moment of identity as domination; it is a theory of nonidentity in which the "reconciliation" of difference is not one of domination but freedom (Adorno 1973, 146-74).

For Adorno "the matters of true philosophical interest at this point in history are those in which Hegel . . . expressed his disinterest. They are the nonconceptual, the individual, the particular . . . what Hegel called 'lazy Existenz' " (1973, 8; amended translation). While Adorno argues that identity philosophy is animated by a hostility to the Other, which results in the domination of all that is *deemed* Other, and necessarily excludes certain forms of experience, some feminists have argued that woman as Other has been "feared, idealized, and negated": she has been defined as different from man, and as the ontological principle of difference itself, to be dominated and excluded (Butler 1985). Thus, a theory of nonidentity becomes a prerequisite for a theory of women's liberation. Adorno argues for such a theory in *Negative Dialectics*, claiming that the nonidentity of nature and history, subject and object, particular and universal, does not mean an absolute dualism but a dialectic whose "reconciliation" avoids the annihilation of the Other: "The reconciled condition would not be the philosophical imperialism of annexing the alien [the Other]. Instead, its happiness would lie in the fact that the alien, in the proximity it is granted, remains what is distant and different, beyond the heterogeneous and beyond that which is one's own" (Adorno 1973, 191).

Balbus argues that the elimination of the domination of nature is to be achieved by a transformation of consciousness, the creation of a "postobjectifying mode of symbolization," that transcends objectification. With this change in consciousness, nature will no longer be the dominated object, the "alien, recalcitrant other," but will be understood as "an end in itself" (Balbus 1982, 285). For Balbus this occurs by moving beyond the anthropomorphic stance in which humans see themselves as "the measure of all things" to "the more modest, ecologically sound assumption that nature cannot be outwitted and that, in fact, 'Nature knows best' " (365). The result is that "human interaction with nature once again becomes a meaningful experience" (285). Balbus's position *may* be useful for the ecology, peace, and anti-nuclear movements, but it creates profound problems for many feminists because "Nature" in its "wisdom" creates not only ecological balance but unwanted pregnancies. That is, without a more careful analysis of the dialectical relation between nature and history, the "natural" event of pregnancy emerges as an end in itself rather than as part of the human historical enterprise. And this creates the possibility for interpreting abortion as a form of the domination of nature.

The "meaningful experience" of the interaction between humans and nature in Balbus's work amounts to an elevation of nature "itself" and a vagueness about how the "natural" world is to be transformed through historical intervention. Balbus's abstract pro-nature stance leaves the politics of abortion in limbo at best and, at worst, undermines those feminist arguments about the necessity for reproductive freedom based on the transformation of nature for human ends.[5] This stance is also the basis for the conflict between native groups, who live by hunting wolves, seals, or bears, and urban-based groups, who oppose all killing of animals. And of course, "Nature" creates famine, flood, and disease as well as ecological balance.

Within much feminist theory and within Balbus's analysis, there has been a shift away from the politics of abortion (non-motherhood) to a concern with reclaiming motherhood. But the liberatory roots of the attempt to reclaim and reconstruct motherhood *began* with women who found themselves suffering from the alienation of enforced motherhood—women who found themselves pregnant when they did not want to be and were forced either to have an unwanted child or to risk death with an illegal abortion. The politics of reproduction cannot forget its origins: it cannot be reduced to a call for a reconciliation with nature achieved through a form of shared heterosexual parenting that does not confront the issue of abortion. Pregnancy, understood as part of the historical enterprise, challenges any facile formulation of a "reconciliation" of nature with history. Feminists must remain committed first and foremost to a woman's right to choose *not* to reproduce, the right to *not* mother, because the compulsory motherhood that results from seeing pregnancy as merely "natural" maintains the domination of women within a patriarchal society. In addition, feminists must affirm the right to choose the form of birth (midwife/hospital) and to choose between heterosexual shared parenting and woman-only motherhood.[6]

Balbus admits that feminism is the weak link in his argument for the unification of the feminist, ecology, and participatory democracy movements. However, he believes that this is because the prolonged pre-Oedipal identification between sons and mothers creates a radical male psyche able to support ecology and participatory democracy while still retaining an unconscious need to dominate women (393). Against this claim, I believe that the political insufficiencies of his work are rooted in the theoretical eclecticism of an abstract pro-nature stance that entails a dismissive rather than a critical approach to the work of Horkheimer and Adorno on the domination of nature. Whereas Balbus states that the work of Horkheimer and Adorno amounts to nothing more than a footnote to Hegel (283), I would argue that the problem of the domination of nature is most powerfully articulated by these two members of the Frankfurt School.[7] Unlike their colleague Marcuse, who remains committed to identity theory as a form of Hegelian reconciliation with nature, Horkheimer and Adorno challenge this position as they analyze the destructive tendencies of "the revolt of nature" and oppose any romantic idealization of nature.[8]

There are, however, several important theoretical positions that Horkheimer and Adorno share with Balbus: they reject labor as the necessary source of liberation; they are concerned with overcoming the domination of nature by reconstituting subjectivity and eliminating the psychic oppression that maintains self-domination (what Kate Millet calls "interior colonization" or the internalization of the characteristics of oppression); and they hold to a theory of the relative autonomy of the psyche, the family, and cultural and political spheres. But while Balbus, like Marcuse, wants to reclaim Hegel, the formulations of Horkheimer and Adorno show the necessity for departing from the Hegelian system. They offer a sustained critique of the notion of reconciliation in Hegel's philosophy, which, they argue, creates a closed and uncritical system that maintains the domination of all that is deemed Other.

Within their critique of the domination of nature Horkeimer and Adorno distinguish the rational mastery of nature from its irrational forms, and they contend that a new and qualitatively different relation between humanity and nature is possible. However, they also retain a tension between the liberatory and repressive aspects of nature. That is, while these theorists search for a new relation to nature in terms of the historical possibilities of nature, they also analyze the regressive moments of nature that led to the rise of fascism. For Horkheimer and Adorno, German fascism, with its cry for a return to "blood and soil," was a form of nature's revenge on history: the "revolt of nature" against domination was transformed under fascism into an expression of the return of repressed nature in distorted and savage form (Horkheimer and Adorno 1972, 185–86). They root emancipatory promise in the necessity to *remember* nature, not in nature "itself": "By virtue of this remembrance of nature in the subject, in whose fulfillment the unacknowledged truth of all culture lies hidden, enlightenment is universally opposed to domination" (1972, 40). Memory breaks the vicious circle of dominated consciousness and opens the vision of a free future. For Horkheimer and Adorno it is the memory of distortion and suffering resulting from the domination of nature that motivates critique.[9] The domination of nature distorts repressed instincts, and the fragments of this distorted nature, though they may give rise to the vision of utopia, cannot erase the suffering of historical and psychological experience.

Adorno declares: "The suppression of nature for human ends is a mere natural relationship, which is why the supremacy of nature-controlling reason and its principle is a delusion. . . . The subject's desperate self-exaltation is its reaction to the experience of its impotence, which prevents self-reflection" (1973, 179–80). The domination of nature is a consequence *of* nature insofar as it is the result of the lack of self-reflection. Given this analysis, Horkheimer declares that "the sole way of assisting nature is to unshackle its seeming opposite, independent thought" (1974, 127). From this perspective Balbus represents an abstract pro-nature position, a position that advocates a naive reconciliation of humanity with nature that does not take into account the danger, distortion, and compulsion of "nature itself."

The work of Murray Bookchin, which has been influenced by the Frankfurt School, understands the complexity of the relation between freedom and barbarism within nature. In *The Ecology of Freedom* Bookchin notes that "an ecological ethics is not patterned on a naive vision of the natural world—either as it exists today or as it might exist in a 'pacified' social future. The wolf has no business lying down with a lamb" (1982, 277). However, Bookchin has a deep disagreement with the Frankfurt School. Whereas Horkheimer and Adorno maintain a conceptual distinction between human self-consciousness and nature, Bookchin regards nature as already imbued with consciousness as subjectivity: "From the biochemical responses of a plant to its environment to the most willful actions of a scientist in the laboratory, a common bond of primal subjectivity inheres in the very organization of 'matter' itself. In this sense, the human mind has never been alone, even in the most inorganic of surroundings" (1982, 276). This avers that plants share with humans some form of consciousness although what that consciousness is, is not clear. Here the philosophical dispute between the Frankfurt School and Bookchin touches on the most fundamental issue raised by critiques of the domination of nature: the question of the relation between human self-consciousness and nature. The political philosophy of the Frankfurt School derives the distinction between human self-consciousness and nature from German idealism (Hegel) through Marxism. While Marcuse differs from Horkheimer and Adorno in terms of his commitment to some form of Hegelian reconciliation, all three argue from a dialectical formulation that entails a rejection of what they see as the one-sided or partial position of anarchism. Even if one grants a form of "natural consciousness" to the animal and nonhuman world, that does not clarify the difference between "natural consciousness" and human *self*-consciousness, nor does it reveal how "nature" is to be understood as an "end in itself." Bookchin's work, rooted in an anarchist perspective, argues for the necessity to step outside the tradition of Hegelian Marxism to focus on a new understanding of nature as "subjective" "in-itself."[10]

Ynestra King's Ecofeminism: Critical Theory Denied

Clearly, the critical theory of the Frankfurt School and Bookchin's work on nature reveal a fundamental incompatibility, yet in her early work, Ynestra King attempts to use both sources as if they were not only compatible but profoundly so. King's "analysis," like that of Balbus, is an eclectic pastiche that does not confront the contradictions that emerge in the attempt to combine disparate theoretical perspectives. Like Balbus, King attempts to link the ecology and feminist movements through a consideration of the problem of the domination of nature, and, like Balbus, she maintains an abstract pro-nature stance that calls for a reconciliation with nature that does not deal with the issue of abortion. But whereas Balbus explicitly attempts to rehabilitate Hegel, King takes a rhetorical stance that calls for, but refuses, the difficult conceptual analysis of a philosophy of nature required by her position. And while Balbus takes over 300 pages to make his argument, King does it in a few short articles, so that her theoretical insufficiencies are more excusable if not less problematic.

In one of the first ecofeminist articles, "The Ecology of Feminism and the Feminism of Ecology," King focuses on a critique of dualistic philosophies that have denigrated nature and women; at the same time, however, she wants not only to affirm but to strengthen the connection between nature and women, and infers that women speak *for* nature (1983, 17 and 19). She claims that although the association of woman with nature as Other has in the past been one of domination, it can now be consciously embraced by women in the present to overcome dualisms, the domination of nature, and the domination of women. King argues that the association of woman with nature gives women "a particular stake in ending the domination of nature" that has poisoned the earth, created ecological chaos, and put us at the edge of nuclear annihilation (1983, 16). King's ecofeminism not only retains but accentuates the personification of nature as female, which becomes the plea to "save our mother-earth." From this perspective, women are not only responsible for their own liberation but become uniquely responsible for all life. And here, of course, is where the ecofeminist position becomes treacherous for a feminist politics of reproductive freedom. If women are "responsible" for life and an abstract pro-nature stance is advocated which claims that "Nature itself knows best" or that "Nature must become an end in itself," then the issue of a woman's right to abortion on demand is at risk. While it may be that some ecofeminists have resolved this tension for themselves, it is remarkable that in this ground-breaking article King is silent on the issue of the feminist concern to control one's own body.

Simone de Beauvoir's analysis of woman's association with nature as Other in *The Second Sex* is reclaimed by King, who then resists the logic of de Beauvoir's argument. De Beauvoir argues that man sees woman as that which calls him back to his natural state and makes him remember his own mortality. Woman's reproductive power, her ability to create new life, is said to be rooted in the immanence of nature, which pulls man back to his body, back to the fragility of the human condition in which each new beginning, each new birth, necessarily ends in death. This is the source of the womb/tomb association. Since man wants to forget his mortality, to transcend the flesh, he learns to objectify and dominate nature and to dominate woman as the representative of nature.

While de Beauvoir is noted by King for revealing the problem of the association of woman with nature as Other, she is promptly chastised for maintaining a dualism that urges women to get *beyond* this association rather than to embrace it. It is true that de Beauvoir accepts a dualistic ontology and valorizes (male) transcendence, but it is important to remember that for de Beauvoir women are no more or less connected to nature than are men. When asked whether she thought women had a special mission in terms of pacifism and the peace movement, de Beauvoir replied that such a claim was "absurd!—because women should desire peace as human beings, not as women! That whole line is completely irrational. . . . And if [women are] being encouraged to be pacifists in the name of motherhood, that's just a ruse by men who are trying to lead women back to the womb. Besides, it's quite obvious that once they're in power, women are exactly like men."[11]

For King, pacifism, defined as "the organic praxis of nonoppositional opposition" (1989, 132), is central to ecofeminism. This pacifism seems to emerge from woman's association with nature, originating in her unique capacity to bear and rear children. Thus in King's early article, "masculinity," revealed in the aggressive domination of women by men, is seen as the source of all exploitation and domination. What is implied in this position is that women are "better" than men, can achieve solidarity in diversity more easily than men, and, through an alternative, morally superior life-style to man's, can act to purify the politics of the ecology movement that has not dealt with male domination.[12]

In her most recent work, "Healing the Wounds: Feminism, Ecology, and Nature/Culture Dualism," King argues against the position she seemed to fall into earlier as she attempts to distance herself from the ecofeminism of Mary Daly and Susan Griffin. Here, Daly is shown to advocate a simple reversion of old dualisms, rather than providing a way beyond them, in her reification of the female over the male (King 1989, 124). Griffin's work, which King locates "somewhere between theory and poetry," is said to overemphasize what women share as victims of patriarchal oppression and lends itself to romanticizing the connection between women and nature, claiming that women retain a "natural" moral goodness due to their separation from the depravity of male culture and history (1989, 124-25). By focusing on what is common to women both theorists, according to King, underestimate the problem of differences among women, problems of race, class, ethnicity, sexual orientation and religion.

While I agree with King's assessment of Daly and Griffin, I find that her "arguments" remain rhetorical and polemical, so that this later work is no more sophisticated in its analysis and no closer to the "precise political philosophy and program" that she calls for than is her earlier piece. King's programmatic plundering of theories (the critical theory of the Frankfurt School, Bookchin's anarchism, socialist feminism, radical cultural feminism), which is meant to bolster the political project of ecofeminism, remains rooted in an abstract pro-nature stance that continues to *call* for theory but rarely provides it. She tells us over and over again that we must have a "truly dialectical theory" and a "reconciliation with nature" in order to "get beyond dualism," but she refuses the difficult conceptual work that might get us there. King's concern is first and foremost one of political practice—theory is the handmaid of practice for her, as feminism is the handmaid of the ecology movement.

In her search for the dialectical praxis that is to point the way to freedom, King refers to the important political work done by the women's health movement in the West to rescue childbirth from "medical experts," thereby reclaiming women's power over our bodies and our lives. But even as she reclaims a focus on women's procreational power she again fails to delineate a politics of abortion, offering no principle for grounding the feminist struggle for reproductive freedom.[13] She also cites "the hugging movement" initiated by women in India who wrap themselves around trees to prevent the destruction of their forests. These two movements represent the "nonoppositional opposition" that is the foundation of King's ecofeminist politics.

When King does turn to theory, she offers a critique of what she sees as the three dominant forms of feminism (liberal feminism, radical feminism, and socialist feminism) in terms of the problem of the domination of nature. What she then puts forward as a "solution" is an ecofeminism that is said to be a dialectical "synthesis" of radical cultural feminism and socialist feminism.[14] According to King this synthesis offers a "standpoint theory"[15] that recognizes biological difference and recognizes women as unique historical agents who do the mediating work ("mothering, cooking, healing, farming, foraging") that bridges the relation between nature and culture (1989, 130).

While critical of radical cultural feminism for its biological determinism, King argues that it has at least recognized the importance of "natural" sexual difference for the social world (1989, 129). And although King is critical of socialist feminism for its Marxist inclination to maintain the domination of nature and the social construction of reality (to the detriment of the qualitative, imaginative, and spiritual aspects of human life), she sees it as offering a resistance to the erasure of the subject by postmodernism. Beginning from the gynocentrism of radical cultural feminism we are to move to a "greener" and more "spiritual" socialist feminism that recants the domination of nature. According to King, "Separately [socialist feminism and radical cultural feminism] perpetuate the dualism of 'mind' and 'nature.' Together they make possible a new ecological relationship between nature and culture, in which mind and nature, heart and reason, join forces to transform the internal and external systems of domination that threaten the existence of life on earth" (1989, 132).

Just how is this dialectical "synthesis" of socialist feminism and radical cultural feminism to take place? Is this merely another form of neo-Hegelianism that is being called for? It seems so, insofar as King calls for a dialectical reconciliation of opposites in a final moment of identity-in-difference. If King's ecofeminism is just another form of neo-Hegelianism, then the fact that Hegel's philosophy remains committed to the domination of nature and all that is deemed Other prevents the realization of her project. If this is not a form of neo-Hegelianism, then how are we to understand King's project in which we are to take only what King deems "good" from each form of feminism while leaving aside what is "bad"? Without a more profound analysis of the contradictions that emerge out of the confrontation between these two forms of feminism, the call for their synthesis remains conceptually incoherent. It returns us to the problem of extracting parts from the whole, which was shown to be treacherous in my earlier critique of Balbus.

If the domination of nature is central to Marxism, in that Marx views freedom as the movement out of "natural" necessity *through* the domination of nature, what is left of socialism without it? Adorno has argued that Marx's advocacy of the domination of nature is in contradiction to the principle of nonidentity that is fundamental to dialectical materialism (Adorno 1973, 244), but King offers no such theoretical argument. Instead, King's position recalls earlier feminist analyses that saw an androgynous "synthesis" as the solution to the division between men and women: that is, King's synthesis and the androgynous synthesis both assume that they are referring to "the kinds of opposites which, when combined, will yield a proper balance of moderation" resulting in the "good" of each being combined (Morgan 1982, 256). This assumption has been shown to be untenable in the androgyny debates and, by extension, can be seen to undermine King's position.

King calls for "a new dialectical way of thinking about our relationship to nature to realize the full meaning and potential of feminism, a social ecological feminism." For her "the domination of nature originates in society and therefore must be resolved in society" (1989, 131). Moreover,

> both feminism and ecology embody the revolt of nature against human domination. They demand that we rethink the relationship between humanity and the rest of nature, including our natural, embodied selves. In ecofeminism, nature is the central category of analysis. An analysis of the interrelated domination of nature—psyche, and sexuality, human oppression, and non-human nature—and the historic position of women in relation to those forms of domination is the starting point of ecofeminist theory. (1989, 132)

Given these statements, and the fact that King has cited Horkheimer and Adorno in her first essay (1983, 16-18), one might reasonably expect her to turn explicitly to the work of Horkheimer and Adorno. Curiously, King *denies* the work of the Frankfurt School even as she appropriates its conceptual framework. She writes: "All hitherto existing philosophies of liberation, with the possible exception of some forms of social anarchism, accept the anthropomorphic notion that humanity should dominate nature and that the increasing domination of nonhuman nature is a precondition for true human freedom" (1989, 117). Now this last statement is patently false. The critical theory of the Frankfurt School provides a sustained, dialectical critique of the domination of nature, which, I would argue, makes it the most advanced philosophy of liberation of our time.

Instead of developing a feminist critical theory based on the concept of the domination of nature in the work of Horkheimer and Adorno, King simultaneously denies and misuses their work. When she claims, for example, that "both feminism and ecology embody the revolt of nature against human domination," she "borrows" Horkheimer's analysis but wrongly suggests that the revolt of nature is necessarily progressive. For example, in the *Eclipse of Reason* Hork-heimer argues that the domination of nature calls forth psychic and social revolt, but, as he sees it, there is nothing *necessarily* progressive in this revolt which can be manipulated by existing institutional powers to justify and maintain their domination.[16] In *Minima Moralia* Adorno explicitly links this understanding of the revolt of nature to feminist issues. Woman's domination, according to Adorno, creates feminine characteristics that lead to an abnegative recon-ciliation with nature, a reconciliation that does not challenge domination but reinforces it.[17] The assumption of the necessary progressiveness of the revolt of nature, rather than a careful consideration of this concept, is part of King's abstract pro-nature stance that refuses to acknowledge, much less analyze, the way in which an image of nature as "all good" can become part of the process of domination.

CONCLUSION

What emerges out of Balbus's neo-Hegelian thought and King's ecofeminism is what I have called an abstract pro-nature stance. Correctly perceiving that the domination of nature is the underlying issue for the liberation movements of the 1990s, this position suggests the elevation of nature "itself" as the creator of values but does not offer a "concrete" or comprehensive understanding of the problem of the domination of nature in that it ignores the regressive moment of nature that Horkheimer and Adorno focus on in their analysis. While the abstract pro-nature position points to the difficult task of developing a coherent philosophy of nature it simultaneously avoids this task by embracing neo-Hegelianism. Balbus's position is rooted in an explicit neo-Hegelianism, while King's seems rooted in an implicit one. Both theorists call for a reconciliation with nature, but both adopt a facile notion of the reconciliation of difference that does not address the problem of the domination of nature *within* Hegel's philosophy. And neither one considers the question of an abnegative or regres-sive reconciliation with nature that Horkheimer and Adorno discuss.

Both Balbus and King assume that an eclectic pastiche of theories can "somehow" provide us with a model of liberation that will realize a harmonious reconciliation with nature. In both cases feminism serves merely to purify the ecological movement (by removing male domination from its ranks) while the focus on nature in the ecology movement depoliticizes feminism. The purifica-tion of political life and the reconciliation with nature are achieved, for Balbus, through the transformation of parenting meant to defuse the power of the first (M)Other and through a coalition of various liberation movements. King, on the other hand, claims that a "progressive" reconciliation with nature will be achieved when women consciously embrace nature and the natural world in the development of their politics. The reconciliation with nature entails everything from a rethinking of motherhood to the hugging of trees, but omits consideration of the issue of abortion. Thus, where Balbus's New Left neo-Hegelianism and King's ecofeminism may be rhetorically significant in terms of the political project of the ecology movement, their abstract pro-nature stance is theoretically unsound and paves the way for the erosion of women's reproductive freedom.

We must move beyond an abstract pro-nature stance as we move beyond the theoretical dependence on Hegel's concept of reconciliation. Rhetoric and neo-Hegelianism must give way to a sustained feminist critical theory that begins from the work of Horkheimer and Adorno on the domination of nature. Such a feminist critical theory would not judge theory solely in terms of its direct application in practice nor use feminism as a mere handmaid of the ecology movement.[18]

NOTES

1. The concept of the dialectical relation between nature and history is sometimes discussed by the authors under consideration as the dialectical relation between nature and culture. Since both concepts are meant to describe the same concern, I have used "nature and history" throughout my discussion to maintain consistency.

2. The concerns of ecofeminism are valid and are not sufficiently addressed in any other form of feminism. Thus, my argument here is not meant to belittle the project set out by Balbus and King but rather to point out the enormity of the theoretical task it presents and the immaturity of the solutions they offer. What emerges from Balbus's eclecticism and King's rhetorical stance is what Adorno calls the Janus-faced argument of contradiction, which presents oppositions and assumes the possibility of a reconciliation but does not analyze contradictions to the point of their own reversal.

3. According to Balbus the domination of nature is a "collective neurosis," originating in the process of our separation from the mother within "mother-monopolized" childcare, which leaves us unable to accept our own death. Thus, the problem of death (Norman O. Brown) rather than objectification (Marx) or sex (Freud) is the focus of his work.

4. Balbus runs into some difficulty here since this theory cannot explain the activism of Native Americans, the Young Lords, Black Panthers, or anyone else who has not been reared according to white-Western child-centered models. In fact, this model doesn't quite explain white middle-class feminist activism to Balbus's own satisfaction (Balbus 1982, 394-95).

5. To say that nature must become "an end in itself" hardly articulates a principle that can ground a feminist politics of abortion on demand. This position, in which the interpretation of the "end" or *telos* of nature is left in limbo, lends aid and comfort to those within the peace, ecology, and antinuclear

movements in the United States who don "the seamless garment" of an abstract pro-life politics that entails an antiabortion stand. For a discussion of the conflict between an abstract pro-nature or abstract pro-life politics and a feminist perspective see Hentoff (1985), Willis (1985) and Pollitt (1985). The same debate appeared in the pages of *The Nonviolent Activist*, a publication put out by the War Resisters League. (See the May-June 1985 and July-August 1985 issues.) According to a report in *off our backs* (August-September 1985, 7), an antiabortion group called Feminists for Life was spawned by this debate.

6. The reclaiming of motherhood is a contentious issue among feminists. Balbus, following Dinnerstein and Chodorow, sees only negative features in human development due to the absence of the father from early childcare. This analysis, however, is quite different from those that see "female-mothering" as the basis for the transformation of society. Feminists like Adrienne Rich, Sara Ruddick, Joanne Ryan, and Caroline Whitbeck find positive features in "mother-raised" children and want to use these features to ground a model of the nondominating relation of self and Other. (See especially Adrienne Rich, *Of Woman Born.*) Even those who agree with Dinnerstein, Chodorow, and Balbus that shared heterosexual parenting is a feminist goal recognize that there are potential dangers. For example, men are not nurturers by training and so may not be able to give the infant the nurturance it requires; men are the source of most familial incest; and men may attempt to divest women of their children in situations in which women have little else.

The emphasis on reclaiming motherhood in feminist theory in the United States often obscures the fact that there are still many unwilling mothers bearing unwanted children and women dying from illegal abortions all over the world.

7. My argument with Balbus first appeared in a review essay of his book entitled "Man-Made Motherhood and Other Sleights of Hand" (*Phenomenology and Pedagogy* 3, no. 3, 1985). The critique offered here is a synopsis of that article.

8. This is not to suggest that the philosophical positions of Horkheimer and Adorno are identical. Despite their collaboration on the *Dialectic of Enlightenment*, they develop different perspectives over time so that liberatory potential is found finally in religion for Horkheimer and in "genuine" philosophy and "autonomous" art for Adorno.

9. Adorno writes: "The need to lend a voice to suffering is a condition of all truth" (Adorno 1973, 17-18); and Horkheimer declares that nature is "a text to be interpreted by philosophy, that if rightly read will unfold a tale of infinite suffering" (Horkheimer, 1974, 126). While Horkheimer and Adorno focus on the memory of suffering, Marcuse focuses on the memory of happiness as redemptive, particularly in *Eros and Civilization*.

10. In a speculative vein, it seems to me that Bookchin's conception of nature maintains a deep affinity with the origins of American nature philosophy as found in Emerson and Thoreau.

11. Interview with Simone de Beauvoir in *Ms.* (August 1983), as cited by

Terry Mehlman, Debbie Swanner, and Midge Quandt, "Obliteration as a Feminist Issue," in *Feminism Lives!* (March 1984). This article is a radical feminist critique of ecofeminism that details the development and consequences of an abstract pro-nature position on the project of women's liberation.

12. While King claims that men raised in our woman-hating culture learn to dominate women for psychological reasons, she never addresses the implications for *women* raised in such a culture. Do we have no psychological problems in terms of our self-identity and our attempts at female solidarity that emerge from this woman-hating culture? I would argue that we do have such problems and that the path to liberation through female solidarity requires an awareness of these difficulties rather than a denial of them.

13. In her reply to Kirkpatrick Sale's assessment of ecofeminism in *The Nation* (December 12, 1987), King implies that she is "pro-choice" (730). My argument here is to be understood not in terms of what she claims about her personal politics but in terms of the analysis she gives, which, in its abstract pro-nature stance, offers no principle for a pro-abortion position.

14. King distinguishes radical rationalist feminists (those who repudiate the connection between women and nature) from radical cultural feminists (those who emphasize this connection and emphasize female difference). For a more historical and comprehensive account of the development of radical feminism from its roots in the New Left to its degeneration into cultural feminism, see Ellen Willis (1984) and Alice Echols (1989).

15. Standpoint theory attempts to articulate an epistemology beginning from the social location of patriarchal domination which allows women to make particular knowledge claims that are not reducible to biological determinism. See Nancy Hartsock (1983) and Alison M. Jaggar (1983, 369-71 and 377-89).

16. In the *Eclipse of Reason* Horkheimer argues that repressed desires generate a resentment, against civilization and against the self, that intensifies the more society dominates nature. Due to the inherent distortion of the instincts by repression (as described by Freud), the revolt of nature against civilization is complicit with, and tends to extend, those very aspects of civilization that maintain domination.

17. Adorno writes: "The feminine character, and the ideal of femininity on which it is modelled, are products of masculine society. The image of undistorted nature arises only in distortion, as its opposite. Where it claims to be humane, masculine society imperiously breeds in woman its own corrective, and shows itself through this limitation implacably the master. The feminine character is a negative imprint of domination. But therefore equally bad. . . . Glorification of the feminine character implies the humiliation of all who bear it" (1974, 95-96).

18. Elsewhere (Mills, 1987) I attempt to develop a feminist critical theory beginning from an analysis of the work of Hegel, Marx, Marcuse, Horkheimer, and Adorno on the relationship between the domination of nature and the domination of women.

REFERENCES

Adorno, Theodor W. 1973. *Negative dialectics*. E. B. Ashton, trans. New York: Seabury Press.

———. 1974. *Minima moralia: Reflections from damaged life*. E. F. N. Jephcott, trans. London: New Left Books.

Balbus, Isaac. 1982. *Marxism and domination: A neo-Hegelian, feminist, psychoanalytic theory of sexual, political, and technological liberation*. Princeton: Princeton University Press.

Bookchin, Murray. 1982. *The ecology of freedom*. Palo Alto: Cheshire Books.

Butler, Judith. 1985. Response to "Women: The one and the many," by Elizabeth V. Spelman. Paper presented to the American Philosophical Association.

Echols, Alice. 1989. *Daring to be bad: Radical feminism in America 1967-1975*. Minneapolis: University of Minnesota Press.

Hartsock, Nancy. 1983. *Money, sex and power*. Boston: Northeastern University Press.

Hegel, G. W. F. 1979. *Hegel's phenomenology of spirit*. A. V. Miller, trans. Oxford: Oxford University Press.

Hentoff, Nat. 1985. How can the left be against life? *Village Voice*. July 16: 18, 20.

Horkheimer, Max. 1974. *Eclipse of reason*. New York: Seabury Press.

Horkheimer, Max, and T. W. Adorno. 1972. *Dialectic of enlightenment*. New York: Herder and Herder.

Jaggar, Alison M. 1983. *Feminist politics and human nature*. Totowa, N.J.: Rowman and Allenheld.

King, Ynestra. 1983. The ecology of feminism and the feminism of ecology. *Harbinger: The Journal of Social Ecology* 1(2): 16-22.

———. 1989. Healing the wounds: Feminism, ecology, and nature/culture dualism. In *Gender/body/knowledge*. Alison M. Jaggar and Susan Bordo, eds. New Brunswick: Rutgers University Press.

Mills, Patricia J. 1987. *Woman, nature, and psyche*. New Haven: Yale University Press.

Morgan, Kathryn Pauly. 1982. Androgyny: A conceptual analysis. *Social Theory and Practice* 8.

Pollitt, Katha. 1985. Hentoff, are you listening? *Mother Jones*. February/March.

Rich, Adrienne. 1979. *Of woman born*. New York: W. W. Norton.

Willis, Ellen. 1984. Radical feminism and feminist radicalism. In *The '60s without apology*. S. Sayres et al., eds. Minneapolis: University of Minnesota Press.

———. 1985. Putting women back into the abortion debate. *Village Voice*. July 16: 15-16, 24.

Ground, Pivot, Motion: Ecofeminist Theory, Dialogics, and Literary Practice

PATRICK D. MURPHY

Cheryll Burgess, in issuing a clarion call for an "ecological literary criticism," observes that "while other social movements, like the civil rights and women's liberation movements of the sixties and seventies, have had a significant impact in shaping literary studies, the environmental movement of the same era has not" (1989, 1). Having gathered momentum throughout the 1980s, the environmental movement, particularly as it is manifested by ecofeminism, will not only make its existence felt in literary studies in the 1990s but has the potential to alter such studies irrevocably. Does this mean, then, that since literary theory and criticism are coming belatedly to ecofeminism, the educational exchange must occur in a single direction? I don't think so. I would like to suggest here that, first, certain areas of literary theory, in particular the dialogic method adumbrated by the Russian theorist Mikhail Bakhtin and its development by feminist critics, can be immensely beneficial to the further development and elaboration of ecofeminist philosophy; and, second, that a more forceful and integrated recognition of the role and place of literature as one element of ecofeminist activism can be gained.

I.

The development of an ecofeminist dialogical method requires significant adaptation of the ideas of Bakhtin, since neither he nor his colleagues ever concerned themselves with ecology or feminism. An adapted dialogics can facilitate a differential unification—rather than a conflation (see Morson and Emerson 1989, 11)—of ecology and feminisms that will maintain the kind of self-consciously antidogmatic development that has been the hallmark of the major strands of feminist thought. At the same time it furthers the correctives to liberal, Marxist, and radical feminisms already under way in ecofeminism (see Warren 1987).

For one thing, Bakhtinian dialogics provides a method for entertaining

Hypatia vol. 6, no. 1 (Spring 1991) © by Patrick D. Murphy debate and consideration of conflicting viewpoints without lapsing into liberal pluralism. Dale Bauer, by distinguishing between pluralism and "multivocality" in *Feminist Dialogics* (1988, xi), persuasively argues that for disagreement to accomplish anything, it requires genuine dialogue that leads to altered understanding rather than a verbal smorgasbord of perspectives. To date, Ellen Rooney in *Seductive Reasoning* (1989) has provided the most devastating critique of pluralism as a popular myth of U.S. politics and foreign policy, as well as an academic form of critical discourse that seeks to recuperate all other critics into a circle of unchanging chitchat. While allowing various "constituencies" to voice their objections, pluralism disavows any need for change other than minor reforms and eschews any theorizing "that would expose the systematic and concrete affiliations that bind critical and political pluralism together as the elements of a heterogeneous yet hegemonic discourse" (33-34). It is also important to note that pluralism has never included everybody: "our cultural discourse is a totality which does not contain everything—did not, for example, contain women, who were decisively not *only* the relative creatures the culture had imagined them to be" (Tarantelli 1986, 180); and continues to dispute whether to include in its purview nature as a subject rather than simply an object of its attention.

Feminists have been utilizing Bakhtin's ideas for some years now, and Bauer makes numerous references to such work. But the critical theory grounding *Feminist Dialogics* develops beyond those other authors who have seen Bakhtin's various dialogic essays as simply source material. Bauer understands Bakhtinian dialogics as a method by which to orchestrate and direct feminist theories of culture and literature. Repeatedly her literary analysis telescopes out from the aesthetic text to larger questions of cultural community and political and ideological power under patriarchy. But that is not surprising, since anyone employing dialogics as a method must find herself constantly shuttling back and forth between text and context, discourse and community, and personal and political (see Díaz-Diocaretz 1989, 136; Zavala, 58). Bauer argues that "what is missing from the dominant mode of Bakhtin scholarship is any interest in gender theory or sexual difference in a materialist-feminist practice" (1988, xiii). Yet what also remains missing from Bauer's analysis is any attention to ecological issues.

Patricia Yaeger has passionately depicted in *Honey-Mad Women* (1988) some of the means by which women writers have employed "emancipatory strategies" within the boundaries of patriarchal norms and imposed exclusion, not only to give voice to the muted but also to challenge the illusion of "norms" that patriarchy persistently generates. It is time that literary critics more systematically begin to search for the "emancipatory strategies" that have been giving voice to ecological narratives and to recover those works that have realized such strategies, while critiquing the rest of the literary canon in terms of just such strategies as they appear or fail to appear in heretofore canonized "major" works.

At the same time, feminist criteria must be brought to bear on the rapidly evolving "canon" of nature writing and environmental literature, which at least in the case of the new *Norton Book of Nature Writing* (1990) is being designed to make nature a province clearly dominated by white male authors. Feminist criteria for canonical debates, including conflicting ones, have been offered by numerous theorists; ecological criteria remain partial and dispersed, with efforts toward relative codification just under way (see Burgess 1989; Campbell 1989; Janik 1976; Kolodny 1975; Meeker 1972; Murphy, "Prolegomenon" and "Sex-Typing"; and Waage 1985).

The influence of Marxism on feminism has led to much attention to dialectical synthesis as a critical praxis. Dialogics, however, can take praxis further because it can encompass Marxist dialectics while at the same time correcting its mechanical progressivism by emphasizing the unity of opposites and their interanimating dynamic tension (see Lenin 1961, 192-28 and 359-63; Mao 1971, 117-25). And it does so without an idealist belief in the immediacy and facility of synthesis and without privileging class contradictions over all others. In both instances, Marxist practice has shown itself utterly insensitive to ecological issues and human/nonhuman relationships. A dialogic method can recognize that the most fundamental relationships are not resolvable through dialectical synthesis: humanity/nature, ignorance/knowledge, male/female, emotion/intellect, conscious/unconscious. Such recognitions are crucial for the development of ecological thought.

Integrated with ecofeminism, dialogics can enable philosophy to move beyond the limitations of the distinctions between things-in-themselves and things-for-us where Marxist theory tends to stop, and to recognize and celebrate the corollary concept of us-as-things-for-others (re: Bakhtin's "I for another," see Morson and Emerson 1989, 23). We need to recognize the existence of the "other" as a self-existent entity, a thing-in-itself (see Jung 1990, 8-9). And let me clarify this term by saying that it has nothing do with Kant's idealist anthropocentrism (see Morson and Emerson 1989, 8; Holquist 1989, 39); rather, "thing" for the purposes of my argument here means any material entity, including humans, animals, and biospheres. At the same time, only by recognizing that humans are not only things-in-themselves and things-for-us but also things-for-others, including the stable evolution of the biosphere, can we begin to understand our appropriate ecological niche and attendant practices.

This is certainly an extremely complex process, and any rush to claim such understanding likely reveals only our own propensity toward reductionism. Such is the case with Dorion Sagan's *Biospheres: Reproducing Planet Earth* (1990). Sagan replicates the imperialist and masculinist ideology of late capitalism when he claims that our ecological purpose is to reproduce "biospheres," which on other planets "would act as a sort of settling propagule to establish an Earthlike environment" (207). He conceives of earth as a white European, which has the right to replicate itself anywhere it chooses. He also assumes that we need not

fundamentally reorganize human interaction with the environment, since technology will provide all necessary solutions (206). Not suprisingly, neither
capitalism nor feminism is listed in the index, and no ecofeminists, or for that
matter any kind of feminists, are referred to in the text.

A dialogical orientation reinforces the ecofeminist recognition of interdependence and the natural necessity of diversity (King 1983b, 119-20; Warren
1987, 7-8). This recognition, then, requires a rethinking of the concepts of
"other" and "otherness," which have been dominated in contemporary critical
theory by psychoanalytic rather than ecological constructs. If the recognition of
"otherness" and the status of "other" is applied only to women and/or the
unconscious, for example, and the corollary notion of "anotherness," being
another for others, is not recognized, then the ecological processes of inter-
animation—the ways in which humans and other entities develop, change, and
learn through mutually influencing each other day to day, age by age—will go
unacknowledged, and notions of female autonomy that have been useful to
women in thinking through the characteristics of their social oppression will end
up complicitous with the traditional American, patriarchal beliefs in autonomy
and individualism. As Barbara Johnson has noted, only a romantic androcentrism can phallaciously raise autonomy over all other relationships: "Clearly,
for Thoreau, pregnancy was not an essential fact of life. Yet for him as well as for
every human being that has yet existed, someone else's pregnancy is the very *first*
fact of life. How might the plot of human subjectivity be reconceived (so to
speak) if pregnancy rather than autonomy is what raises the question of deliber-
ateness?" (1987, 190). Such a question not only interrogates conceptions of
autonomy but also affirms relationship. While the United States has been a
culture that champions individualism as an ideology, it has consistently demonstrated an unwillingness to tolerate individuality whenever such behavior threat-
ens "national security" or "the American way of life" (King, 1983a). An
ecofeminist dialogics would suggest that rather than their trying to imagine
liberatory notions of autonomy, feminist theoreticians would more productively
imagine responsible human behavior through working out the implications of a
theory of *volitional interdependence* among human and nonhuman alike.

Johnson's analysis also privileges nurturing over engendering by implication,
to the degree that these two wholly interrelated phases of parent/offspring
relationship have been separated in Western culture since the time of the
Greeks, with engendering having more status than nurturing. While slaves have
always been thought capable of nurturing, they have never been officially
delegated to engendering the wealthy classes. Johnson's privileging provides a
necessary corrective to the androcentric-based difference between the definitions of "fathering" and "mothering," which in themselves have significant
ecological implications, the former of begetting and unlimited expansion and
the latter of sustaining and cultivating, as Kolodny discusses at some length in
The Lay of the Land (1975).

Finally, Bakhtin's conception of centripetal/centrifugal tension provides a means of countering tendencies toward totalization that can arise within any effort at systemic analysis and critique (1981, 270-75). The centripetal tendency is toward centralizing, homogenizing, and rulebinding; the centrifugal toward decentering, differentiating, and innovating. For Bakhtin, any "totality" is continuously recognized as already a relativized, temporal centripetal entity in need of centrifugal destabilizing. That is to say, a dialogic method can expose the false dichotomy of "center" and "margin" that is utilized by oppositional groups yet in such use codifies the existing power structure's claims to centrality, legitimacy, and authority. There are unequal power relationships and structures that are spun out of such relationships, but if the natural model of mutual interdependence has any validity, then there can be no real "margins" except as ideological constructs. Nor can there be any "centers"; rather, there exist cultural and physical pivots that may or may not resist the inevitability of a next step.

II.

The Bakhtinian dialogical method is becoming widely recognized. But some character traits are less well known and more neglected than others. *Freudianism: A Marxist Critique* (1976), published under Vološinov's name, is the text least related to literature and literary theory per se, but one of crucial importance for Bakhtin's concept of the utterance as the basis for analyzing language-in-practice, *parole*, rather than language-as-system, *langue*. In opposition to what was perceived as Freudian psychoanalysis, *Freudianism* presents dialogical conceptions of the self, the psyche, and the "content of consciousness," which initiate the recognition of the constitution of the individual as a *chronotopic relationship*, i.e., a social/self construct developing within given social, economic, political, historical, and environmental parameters of space and time (Bakhtin 1981, 85). The "other" in its various manifestations, therefore, including *parole*, culture, place, class, race, and gender, participates in the formation of self. The individual occurs as chronotope within the "story" of human interaction with the physical world, but that narrative is only a historical fiction organized by means of a limited perspective through which beginnings, middles, ends, and motivations are substituted for the predominantly non-human, contiguously structured story of the universe that allots us only episodes—the self in and as part of the "other." One can immediately see the connections here with the ecofeminist philosopher Jim Cheney's statement that "narrative is the key then, but it is narrative grounded in geography rather than in a linear, essentialized narrative self" (1989, 126). While Cheney emphasizes local geography in "Postmodern Environmental Ethics," a study of the ways in which narrative can contribute to developing a sensitivity to an ecofeminist bioregional ethics, I think he would agree that such geography participates in a larger, longer story extending beyond this one planet's biosphere.

Just as the "other" participates in the formation of the self, so too does the self as individual-in-the-world participate in the formation of the "other" in its various manifestations. And just as that self enters into language and the use of *parole*, so too does the "other" enter into language and have the potential, as does any entity, to become a "speaking subject," although centripetal structures and cultural forces hinder such a realization. The implications of this "other" as speaking subject need to be conceptualized as including more than humans and as potentially being constituted by a speaker/author who is not the speaking subject but a renderer of the "other" as speaking subject (Bakhtin 1984, 47-57). The pivotal questions here will be the degree to which language is recognized as one type of sign system, the degree to which volition is assumed as a prerequisite for becoming a speaking subject, and the degree to which the other speaking subjects who do not use the *parole* of human beings can "speak" in a sign system that can be understood by humans. Minimally, such considerations tend to take humans beyond the simplistic notion that only they communicate because they understand each other's languages but no other creatures'. It nevertheless leaves problematic the definition of "subject," since in the case of such entities as rocks and rivers humans must rely on imputed notions of their being "interest-carriers" (this remains an intense debate in the pages of *Environmental Ethics*).

Bakhtin emphasizes, from the opening of *Freudianism*, the significance in psychology of the conflicts between inner and outer speech and various levels of inner speech. Communication between the conscious and the unconscious consists of specific utterances that have a speaker and a respondent, a "self" and an other "self," which are not identical but are parts of the same mind (23-24). Even the articulation of the unconscious is a social interrelationship by virtue of its minimal dynamic of being an utterance (79). Thus, the "other" is always implicated in psychical activities and indicates that the "self" itself is not singular or unified but multiple (see Smith 1988, chap.5). But does this have anything to teach us about feminism or ecology?

It is precisely this recognition of nonidentity and the need for inner dialogue, specifically between "masculine" and "feminine" aspects of the psyche, that the ecofeminist sociologist Ariel Kay Salleh sees missing from the propositions of deep ecology, an omission that seriously impairs its subversion of patriarchy's hegemony. As Freud recognized, "the unconscious speaks more than one dialect," i.e., it uses a variety of sign systems, verbal and nonverbal, to communicate (see Bruss 1976, 132-33). To the degree that we are able to articulate verbally the mental activities of our unconscious as well as conscious, these articulations are oriented toward the rest of the world and our position in that world, and they are to some degree, then, part of a "storied residence" (Cheney 1989, 125). I would argue that, like the unconscious, the nonhuman also articulates itself by means of various "dialects," and neither requires volition to do so (see Bakhtin, *Speech Genres* 60-63).

If emotion and instinct arise from historical natural influences on the evolution of the species, then their exertions on our behavior, their entering into consciousness, are a form of the natural world "speaking" to us through signs that our conscious renders verbally. To deny "emotion" as feminine and/or "instinct" as primitive nature is to reserve the role of speaking subject only for the ego and to deny a voice to the "other," which is in reality a part of ourselves. Poet Gary Snyder has called for establishing "a kiva of elders" to represent the nonhuman within democratic institutions:

> The paintings of bison and bears in the caves of southern France were of that order. The animals were speaking through the people and making their point. And when, in the dances of the Pueblo Indians and other people, certain individuals became seized, as it were, by the spirit of the deer, and danced as a deer would dance, or danced the dance of the corn maidens, or impersonated the squash blossom, they were no longer speaking for humanity, they were taking it on themselves to interpret, through their human-ity, what these other life-forms were. (1974, 109)

The point is not to speak for nature but to work to render the signification presented us by nature into a verbal depiction by means of speaking subjects, whether this is through characterization in the arts or through discursive prose. The test for whether such depictions seem accurate renderings of the speaking subjects will be the actions in the world that they call on humans to perform. Unless we believe that the earth is attempting to commit biospheric suicide, we cannot accept arguments based on instrumental reason as a rendering of nature as a speaking subject, nor Ronald Reagan's infamous remarks about trees as polluters, nor Lovelock's assertions that "Gaia" will take care of industrial pollution.

Ursula K. Le Guin has been working on this project in both poetry and fiction for many years. In *Buffalo Gals and Other Animal Presences* (1987), she brings together stories and poems, many of which render the natural world as speaking subject. For example, in "Buffalo Gals, Won't You Come Out Tonight," she does this through a girl's dream vision of the mythical "coyote," who teaches her about the relationship of wild animals in the desert to urbanization. That these stories are part of a project to rethink human/nonhuman and self/other relationships is revealed by Le Guin's remarks about the feminist revisioning of myth in which she is engaged throughout so much of her recent work: "Very often the re-visioning consists in a 'simple' change of point of view. It is possible that the very concept of point-of-view may be changing, may have to change, or to be changed, so that our reality can be narrated" (1987, 75). Snyder argues that we must "incorporate the other people—what Sioux Indians called the creeping people, and the standing people, and the flying people, and the swimming people—into the councils of government. . . . If we don't do it, they will revolt against us. . . . We are beginning to get non-negotiable demands right now from the air, the water, the soil" (1974, 108). It comes as no surprise that such "people" are well-represented in Le Guin's last adult novel, *Always Coming Home* (1985).

Snyder's last remark about "non-negotiable demands" takes us back to a question raised much earlier, whether or not volition is required for a speaking subject, for the existence of signs that can be transmitted by a nonhuman subject and understood and interpreted by humans. When a person cries out in pain, is it volitional? When selenium poisons groundwater, causes animal deformities, and reduces the ability of California farmers to continue to overcultivate, are these signs that we can read? And in reading such signs and integrating them into our texts, are we letting that land speak through us or are we only speaking for it? Nonhuman others can be constituted as speaking subjects, whether or not they are interest-carriers in our understanding of that concept, rather than merely objects of our speaking—although even the latter is preferable to silence—and we need to learn better how to tell such stories.

The analogy I would use to illustrate such learning is that of men adopting feminist theories and practices. Far too often men continue attempting to speak *for* women. It is possible, however, for men to render women as speaking subjects by means of their application of feminist theories, criticism, and scholarship (Heath 1987, 8-9 and 27-28). The feminists who have constituted themselves as speaking subjects have enabled some men to render that voicing. There will certainly always be two voices there, the feminist speaking subject and the rendering male author, just as there will be with the nonhuman speaking subject and the rendering human author, but in neither case does this excuse not waging the struggle for such rendering.

III.

Gayatri Chakravorty Spivak has candidly observed that "one must fill the vision of literary form with its connections to what is being read: history, political economy—the world. And it is not merely a question of disciplinary formation. It is a question also of questioning the separation between the world of action and the world of the disciplines. There is a great deal in the way" (1987, 95). As Adrienne Rich expresses it, "I need to understand how a place on the map is also a place in history, within which as a woman, a Jew, a lesbian, a feminist, I am created and trying to create" (1985, 8; see also Snyder, 1977, 63-64). Literature can certainly help with that understanding, but we need to refine our conception of ecofeminism's relationship to literature.

One approach would be to use ecofeminism as a ground for critiquing all of the literature that one reads. For literary critics in particular, this would mean reevaluating the canon that constitutes the list of major works and texts to be taught, calling for a dialogue between critical evaluations based on humanistic criteria and ones based on de-homocentric criteria. This would require, for instance, reevaluating the poetic tradition of the "pastoral," which tends to be based on an idealization of nature rather than a genuine encounter with it. A brief example here would be that feminist critics have gradually begun pulling Dorothy Wordsworth out of her brother's shadow, looking at her writings and their influence on his poetry. What is needed now is criticism that can evaluate the differences between their writings in terms of ecological criteria, analyzing the implications of Dorothy's willingness to record rather than order nature and to efface the speaker of the text as a dominating, central observer.

Dorothy Wordsworth serves as an example of rescuing from obscurity an author whose writing demonstrates characteristics that could be labeled ecological, if not ecofeminist, because of its attention to nature as subject in its diversity as a thing-in-itself. Willa Cather, on the other hand, serves as an example of an author already famous whose works are being reevaluated in terms of relative merit, as a result of both feminist and ecological criticism. Over the past few years *The Song of the Lark* (1915) has received increasing attention primarily because of its feminist thematics and secondarily because of its ecological implications, which are revealed particularly by means of the protagonist's growth through her relationship with the Nebraska countryside and her aesthetic maturation as a result of immersion in a steep New Mexico ravine. The importance of these aspects of the novel have begun to be analyzed only as a result of changing critical criteria.

With Cather, the critic is not looking for an ecofeminist novel per se but is looking at an author's work in terms of the degrees to which it addresses ecological and feminist issues in positive or negative ways. And while we can certainly talk about feminist rather than protofeminist writing in the Anglo-American tradition as early as the eighteenth century if not earlier, we need to clarify whether such is the case for ecological writing. Is there a difference between "nature" writing and ecological writing? If the Transcendentalists and Romantics are any indication, the answer is certainly yes. Self-conscious ecological writing must be defined as primarily a phenomenon of the late twentieth century, and what precedes it as mostly protoecological. From this perspective, ecologists can more easily explain their utilization of writers such as Charlotte Perkins Gilman, Robinson Jeffers, and John Muir for ecological inspiration without having to attempt to justify every aspect of their visions of nature.

Perhaps one of the first of the current generation of ecofeminist novels is Margaret Atwood's *Surfacing* (1972). A woman in an unhealthy heterosexual relationship, going home with her lover and another couple to search for her missing father and to mourn for her long dead mother, undergoes a metamorphosis. This transformation involves a clearly dialogical process in which the revelations that the woman initially has about the environmental destruction of her childhood Canadian locale are gradually translated into revelations about her oppression as a woman, and the intrinsic and indissoluble connection between these two unbalanced states of being. Near the end of the novel she experiences a rebirth through submersion in the lake, which causes a spiritual regression to a virtual animal state. Through the purification this involves and her decision to become pregnant, she purges the guilt she has felt for years over having an abortion, her complicity in the antiecological, technoindustrial state. At the end, her recognitions of nature's oppression and her own provide her not with a vision of an emancipatory future—Atwood seems always unwilling to offer this—but with an understanding that will sustain her when she returns to the city. The final chapter begins: "This above all, to refuse to be a victim" (222). Then it continues with the protagonist's recognition of relationship with her child, who will be armed with her new understanding of ecological interconnection, which includes human interconnection. At the end, as the protagonist prepares to return to "civilization," she thinks the final words of the novel: "The lake is quiet, the trees surround me, asking and giving nothing" (224).

Atwood has come to be known as a writer of fantastic or speculative rather than realistic prose. And it seems to be the case that the majority of the most daring ecological and feminist novels have been written in some other mode than realism, with almost all of the feminist utopias and dystopias written in the past two decades being predicated upon ecological disaster. While such works frequently do not address how to resolve the ecological crisis, since their focus is on resolving the oppression of women, they almost invariably tie the oppression of women to the degradation of the environment. In Atwood's *The Handmaid's Tale* (1985), the rise of a right-wing theocracy in New England results in part from devastation of the environment. Similarly, in Susy McKee Charnas's *Walk to the End of the World* (1974) and *Motherlines* (1978), a totalitarian patriarchy that attempts to enforce the utter domination of women follows upon the heels of the apocalyptic efforts of a seemingly less malignant patriarchy to dominate nature. In Marge Piercy's *Woman on the Edge of Time* (1976), the future utopian society of Mattapoisett that contrasts with the hell of contemporary North American society oppressing Connie Ramos, the novel's protagonist, is predicated upon ecological balance and equal nurturing of children. In Sally Gearhart's *The Wanderground* (1979), the ecological theme is foregrounded, but the women have abandoned the cities and their men, establishing a completely separate culture and, perhaps, a separate species. These latter two novels, as with Sheri Tepper's more recent *The Gate to Women's Country* (1989), remain highly problematic from an ecofeminist perspective because each is predicated upon some version of biological essentialism, a perception of reality adopted by some who consider themselves ecofeminists but severely criticized by others.

Somewhat different from the preceding utopian and dystopian novels, Kate Wilhelm's *Juniper Time* (1979) is a near-future science fiction in which humanity is beset by two approaching apocalypses of its own making: worldwide drought and food shortages resulting from environmental pollution, and subsequent global tensions making nuclear war imminent. While the plot is complicated by an elaborate hoax to draw the peoples of earth together, the real story is that of

Jean's development into an ecoactivist, who suffers through rape, despair, and then revitalization in the desert among a group of people relearning and adapting the old ways of the Native Americans to the changed environmental conditions. Unlike the previously mentioned novels, *Juniper Time* is primarily ecological and only secondarily feminist, yet it does not seem fortuitous that the hero is female or that she is raped, imprisoned, and oppressed during the course of her experiences. But like the other novels, *Juniper Time* assumes that the building of a new society must be learned through practice, not theories. In this way, the majority of contemporary feminist utopias maintain a dialogical, developmental approach to society building rather than the monological, closed-system approach that dominates much earlier and nonfeminist utopias.

The novel that balances and integrates ecology and feminism more evenly and successfully than any other that I have read is Ursula K. Le Guin's *Always Coming Home* (1985). It combines thematic and formal innovation to the point that it does not conform to the notions popularly associated with the idea of "novel" at all. Rather, it is a novel much more in the Bakhtinian sense of the term, that is, an open, evolving genre predicated upon change rather than stasis, innovation rather than convention. A work of cultural fiction, it provides a main plotted story that could be extracted and treated as a separate narrative. This inner narrative is a feminist bildungsroman detailing the experiences of a girl who chooses between her father's patriarchal culture and her mother's matrifocal one. But around and throughout this narrative-within-a-text Le Guin weaves a series of additional stories, as well as cultural information. She also includes a series of interchapters about herself, allegorically depicted as Pandora the anthropologist, visiting from the past these people of our far-distant future. Suffice it to say that anyone wishing to gain a comprehensive vision of a truly ecofeminist culture must read *Always Coming Home*. But at the same time Le Guin avoids blueprinting, in part by setting the work so far into the future that no immediate steps from here to there are suggested and by showing that the culture depicted remains in a process of development and change, internal debate, and external relationship with other cultures.

Le Guin has developed her ecofeminist themes in poetry as well as in prose. And here she joins company with a host of contemporary women poets. Like many of them, Le Guin's collections contain poems that are feminist but not explicitly ecological, ecological but not specifically feminist, and only very rarely a poem that explicitly combines the two. Yet when one reads an entire volume, such as *Hard Words* (1981) or *Wild Oats and Fireweed* (1988), recognition of the interrelationship of feminism and ecology becomes unavoidable. "At Three Rivers, April 80" (*Hard Words*, 33), for instance, takes a clear stand on nature as a thing-in-itself rather than a thing-for-us:

> A tree that blossoms in the wilderness
> in some April beyond history

> and farther west than all the pioneers
> is in no way less
> though there be none to bless
> and no woman stand in tears
> under the whitening flowers.
>
> Only the tears were ours.

Yet the poem does not stop at making a de-homocentric statement, reminiscent of the last sentence of *Surfacing*. The inclusion of the woman not as neutral observer but as passionate participant in the wonder of spring adds a very subtle feminist dimension in terms of her emotive recognition. On the other hand, poems such as "Danaë 46" (*Hard Words*, 5) critique patriarchy as part of a general revisioning of myth and also establish a series of connections among the women who repeatedly appear throughout the poems in *Hard Words*, including the woman as author, the woman as Native American water carrier, the woman as bearer of emotions (see Murphy, "High and Low" [1989]).

For many male writers, becoming an environmentalist has not necessarily led to reevaluating gender relationships. And it would seem that a number of women writers have submerged the gender question in their development of, or search for, a balanced relationship with the rest of the natural world. Mary Oliver, winner of the 1984 Pulitzer Prize in Poetry, has been recognized as a preeminent nature poet. Is she also a feminist? In the early collection *Twelve Moons* (1979), the answer would seem to be no, or at least not explicitly. *American Primitive* (1983) continues in the same vein. Patricia Yaeger argues, however, that the freedom expressed through identification with the honey bear and with the whales sounding off the coast depicted in several poems indicates a feminist sensibility: "As Oliver's speaker goes honey-mad . . . [t]he tree filled with honey becomes the site of vision and of liberation for the woman writer—a bodily liberation that releases the tree energy, the honey energy into the 'rippling bark' of her poem" (1988, 7). But it is not really until *Dream Work* (1986) that we find an overtly ecofeminist poem, "The River" (20-21). Here sisterhood and human integration in nature, to be understood as "home," are yoked in opposition to "some cold city or other." Yet even so, the ecological awareness remains far more sophisticated than the feminist one, whereas in a poem such as "Resort" by Patricia Hampl (1983) the opposite is the case. For Hampl's protagonist in this long sequential poem structured as a dialogical engagement of self and analyst, nature remains secondary but vital for the process of psychic healing that occurs. Nature becomes crucial as a means for self-understanding. Yet the ecological dimensions of the speaker's understanding in Hampl's poem remain as unsophisticated as the feminist understanding of Oliver's speakers. Both could learn much from each other in terms of integrating ecological and feminist awareness. Yet the poems of Oliver and Hampl can serve as valuable literature for ecofeminism because of the relationships between consciousness and impulse that they represent.

If ecofeminists seek only for a literature that meets equally the criteria of ecological and feminist sophistication, they will be frequently disappointed. If, alternatively, they seek works that to some extent embody both dimensions they will find a vast array of writing that can provide inspiration and evidence of a developing consciousness of the imperatives for cultural change that have given rise to ecofeminism. Similarly, as literary theory and criticism is beginning to incorporate ecological criteria and to address not just feminisms but specifically ecofeminism, ecofeminist philosophy needs to attune itself to and help increase the sophistication of practitioners of such critical work. At the same time, if Bakhtinian dialogics is any indication, there exist aspects of literary theory that can be of benefit in the continued growth of ecofeminist thought and practice. For example, Bakhtinian theory provides valuable critical tools for analyzing the dialogical structure of one of the most well-known ecofeminist texts, Susan Griffin's *Woman and Nature*. Dialogics is helpful in terms of articulating not only its organization but also the variety of double-voicing throughout that gives it so much power and that accounts for the significant tonal shifts as the debate of the text gradually resolves toward the voice of a community of women in nature.

Near the end of his long life Bakhtin wrote that "there is neither a first nor a last word and there are no limits to the dialogic context" (1986, 170). Such a self-consciously maintained context can help keep the ground of ecofeminist theory from solidifying into a dogmatic hardpan. Dialogics reminds ecofeminist practitioners that every position is really a pivot by which to step and dance, to practice and develop, but not to stand or come to rest. Part of this continued motion needs to be greater ecofeminist attention to literature even as literary theory and criticism needs to integrate ecofeminist philosophy into its most basic practices. Many authors today demonstrate a significant awareness of current philosophical trends and efforts at integrating the insights of philosophical and literary theory into their writing. Ecofeminism is clearly becoming a part of that awareness, but so much more needs to be done in both the philosophy and the literature. Literary critics and philosophers alike need to enter into dialogue with ecofeminism in order to continue their own critical praxis and to evaluate the ways in which ecofeminism calls for changes in that praxis, since their work, as the feminist Dale Bauer argues, takes place not only within the classroom but also in "all of the other territories of [their] own lived experience" (1988, xvii).

REFERENCES

Atwood, Margaret. 1972. *Surfacing*. New York: Popular Library. New York: Fawcett Crest, 1987.
———. 1985. *The handmaid's tale*. New York: Fawcett Crest, 1987.

Bakhtin, Mikhail. 1981. *The dialogic imagination: Four essays by M. M. Bakhtin.* Michael Holquist and Caryl Emerson, trans. Michael Holquist, ed. Austin: University of Texas Press.

———. 1984. *Problems of Dostoevsky's poetics.* Caryl Emerson, trans. and ed. Minneapolis: University of Minnesota Press.

———. 1986. *Speech genres and other late essays.* Vern W. McGee, trans. Caryl Emerson and Michael Holquist, eds. Austin: University of Texas Press.

Bauer, Dale M. 1988. *Feminist dialogics: A theory of failed community.* Albany: State University of New York Press.

Bruss, Neal H. 1976. V. N. Vološinov and the structure of language in Freudianism. In *Freudianism: A Marxist critique.* See Vološinov [Bakhtin], 1976.

Burgess, Cheryll. 1989. Toward an ecological literary criticism. Paper presented at the twenty-fourth Western Literature Association meeting, October, Coeur d'Alene, Idaho.

Campbell, Sue Ellen. 1989. The land and language of desire: Where deep ecology and post-structuralism meet. *Western American Literature* 24: 199-211.

Cather, Willa. 1915. *The song of the lark.* Boston: Houghton Mifflin, 1983.

Charnas, Susy McKee. 1974. *Walk to the end of the world.* New York: Ballantine.

———. 1978. *Motherlines.* New York: Berkeley, 1979.

Cheney, Jim. 1989. Postmodern environmental ethics: Ethics as bioregional narrative. *Environmental Ethics* 11: 117-34.

Díaz-Diocaretz, Myriam. 1989. Bakhtin, discourse, and feminist theories. *Critical Studies* 1(2): 121-39.

Finch, Robert, and John Elder, eds. 1990. *The Norton book of nature writing.* New York: Norton.

Gearhart, Sally. 1979. *The wanderground: Stories of the hill women.* Boston: Alyson Publications.

Griffin, Susan. 1978. *Woman and nature: The roaring inside her.* New York: Harper and Row.

Hampl, Patricia. 1983. Resort. In *Resort and other poems.* Boston: Houghton Mifflin.

Heath, Stephen. 1987. Male feminism. In *Men in feminism.* Alice Jardine and Paul Smith, eds. New York: Methuen.

Johnson, Barbara. 1987. *A world of difference.* Baltimore: Johns Hopkins University Press.

Jung, Hwa Yol. 1990. The way of ecopiety: Ethics as if the earth really matters. Paper presented at "The Shadow of Spirit: Contemporary Western Thought and Its Religious Subtexts" conference, July, King's College, Cambridge, England.

King, Ynestra. 1983a. The eco-feminist imperative. In *Reclaim the earth: Women speak out for life on earth.* Léonie Caldecott and Stephanie Leland, eds. London: The Women's Press.

————. 1983b. Toward an ecological feminism and a feminist ecology. In *Machina ex dea: Feminist perspectives on technology*. Joan Rothschild, ed. New York: Pergamon Press.

Kolodny, Annette. 1975. *The lay of the land: Metaphor as experience and history in American life and letters*. Chapel Hill: University of North Carolina Press.

Le Guin, Ursula K. 1981. *Hard words and other poems*. New York: Harper and Row.

————. 1985. *Always coming home*. New York: Bantam, 1986.

————. 1987. *Buffalo gals and other animal presences*. New York: New American Library, 1988.

————. 1988. *Wild oats and fireweed*. New York: Harper and Row.

Lenin, V. I. 1961. *Philosophical notebooks*. Vol. 38 of *Collected works*. 4th ed. Clemens Dutt, trans. Stewart Smith, ed. Moscow: Foreign Languages Publishing House.

Mao Ze-dong (Mao Tse-tung). 1971. On contradiction. In *Selected readings from the works of Mao Tse-tung*. Peking: Foreign Language Press.

Meeker, Joseph W. 1972. *The comedy of survival: Studies in literary ecology*. New York: Scribner's.

Morson, Gary Saul, and Caryl Emerson. 1989. Introduction: Rethinking Bakhtin. In *Rethinking Bakhtin: Extensions and challenges*, 1-60. Morson and Emerson, eds. Evanston, IL: Northwestern University Press.

Murphy, Patrick D. 1988a. Dialectics or dialogics: Method and message in the classroom. *The GRIP report* 8. Proceedings of the sixth annual meeting of the GRIP Project, May 20-22, Carnegie Mellon University. Revised version reprinted in *Literature, nature and other: Ecofeminist critiques*. Albany: State University of New York Press, 1995.

————. 1988b. Sex-typing the planet. *Environmental Ethics* 10: 155-68.

————. 1989. The high and low fantasies of feminist (re)mythopoeia. *Mythlore* 60 (Winter): 1-6.

————. 1991. Prolegomenon for an ecofeminist dialogics. In *Feminism, Bakhtin, and the dialogic voice*. Dale M. Bauer and Susan Jaret McKinstry, eds. Albany: State University of New York Press.

Oliver, Mary. 1979. *Twelve moons*. Boston: Little, Brown.

————. 1983. *American primitive*. Boston: Little, Brown.

————. 1986. *Dream work*. New York: Atlantic Monthly.

Piercy, Marge. 1976. *Woman on the edge of time*. New York: Fawcett Crest, 1977.

Rich, Adrienne. 1985. Notes toward a politics of location. In *Women, feminist identity and society in the 1980s: Selected papers*. Myriam Díaz-Diocaretz and Iris M. Zavala. eds. Philadelphia: John Benjamins.

Rooney, Ellen. 1989. *Seductive reasoning: Pluralism as the problematic of contemporary literary theory*. Ithaca: Cornell University Press.

Sagan, Dorion. 1990. *Biospheres: Reproducing planet earth*. New York: Bantam.

Salleh, Ariel Kay. 1984. Deeper than deep ecology: The eco-feminist connection. *Environmental Ethics* 6: 339-45.

Smith, Paul. 1988. *Discerning the subject*. Minneapolis: University of Minnesota Press.

Snyder, Gary. 1974. *Turtle island*. New York: New Directions.

———. 1977. *The old ways*. San Francisco: City Lights Books.

Spivak, Gayatri Chakravorty. 1987. *In other worlds: Essays in cultural politics*. New York: Methuen.

Tarantelli, Carole B. 1986. And the last walls dissolved: On imagining a story of the survival of difference. In *Women in culture and politics: A century of change*. Judith Friedlander et al., eds. Bloomington: Indiana University Press.

Tepper, Sheri S. 1988. *The gate to women's country*. New York: Bantam, 1989.

Vološinov, V.N. [M.M. Bakhtin]. 1976. *Freudianism: A Marxist critique*. I.R. Titunik, trans. I.R. Titunik and Neal H. Bruss, eds. New York: Academic Press.

———. 1986. *Marxism and the philosophy of language*. Ladislav Matejka and I.R. Titunik, trans. Cambridge: Harvard University Press.

Waage, Frederick O., ed. 1985. *Teaching environmental literature: Materials, methods, resources*. New York: MLA.

Warren, Karen J. 1987. Feminism and ecology: Making connections. *Environmental Ethics* 9: 3-20.

Wilhelm, Kate. 1979. *Juniper time*. New York: Pocket Books, 1980.

Yaeger, Patricia. 1988. *Honey-mad women: Emancipatory strategies in women's writings*. New York: Columbia University Press.

Zavala, Iris M. 1989. Bakhtin and the third: Communication as response. *Critical Studies* 1(2): 43-63.

Ecological Feminism
and Ecosystem Ecology[1]

KAREN J. WARREN and JIM CHENEY

Ecological feminism is a feminism which attempts to unite the demands of the women's movement with those of the ecological movement in order to bring about a world and worldview that are not based on socioeconomic and conceptual structures of domination. Many ecological feminists have claimed that what is needed is a feminism that is ecological and an ecology that is feminist (see King 1983, 1989). They have shown ways in which ecology, understood in its broadest sense as environmentalism, is a feminist issue.[2] What has yet to be shown is that ecology, understood in its narrower sense as "the science of ecology" (or, scientific ecology), also is or might be a feminist issue. Establishing *that* claim involves showing that ecological feminism makes good scientific ecological sense.[3]

In this paper we discuss ten noteworthy similarities between themes in ecological feminism and ecosystem ecology—similarities that show the two are engaged in complementary, mutually supportive projects. Our goal is modest and suggestive. We are *not* arguing for the stronger claims that ecosystem (or, more generally, scientific) ecology must be feminist, that feminists must be ecologists, or that these similarities establish that ecosystem ecology is feminist. To establish these claims, much more would be needed than is provided in this paper.[4] Rather, we are identifying theoretical points of intersection between ecofeminism and ecosystem ecology in the interest of furthering discussion on the nature and direction of future bridge-building between the two.[5]

ECOLOGICAL FEMINISM AND ECOFEMINISM ETHICS

We take ecological feminism to refer "to a sensibility, an intimation, that feminist concerns run parallel to, are bound up with, or, perhaps, are one with concern for a natural world which has been subjected to much the same abuse and ambivalent behavior as have women" (Cheney 1987, 115). Although there are a variety of ecofeminist positions (Warren 1987), the common thread that

Hypatia vol. 6, no. 1 (Spring 1991) © by Karen J. Warren and Jim Cheney runs through ecofeminist scholarship is that the domination of women and the domination of nature are "intimately connected and mutually reinforcing" (King 1989, 18). All ecofeminists endorse the view that an adequate understanding of the nature of the connections between the twin dominations of women and nature requires a feminist theory and practice informed by an ecological perspective and an environmentalism informed by a feminist perspective (Warren 1987, 4-5).

Much of ecofeminist scholarship concerns the ethical nature of human relationships to the nonhuman natural world. Like feminist ethics generally, "ecofeminist ethics" includes a variety of positions. What makes ecofeminist ethics feminist is a twofold commitment to critique male bias in ethics and to develop analyses which are not male-biased (see Jaggar 1990, 23). However, ecofeminist ethics extends feminist ethical critiques of sexism and other social "isms of domination" to include critiques of "naturism," i.e., the unjustified domination of nonhuman animals and nature by humans. As such, ecofeminist ethics critiques not only androcentric but also anthrocentric and naturist bias in ethics. Ecofeminist ethics is grounded in the assumption that the dominations of women and of nature are morally wrong and ought to be eliminated. Like feminist ethics (see Jaggar 1990, 24-5), the practical import of ecofeminist ethics is as a guide to action on issues in the pre-feminist, patriarchal present. This guidance is aimed at assisting persons in resisting sexist, naturist, and interconnected racist, classist, heterosexist practices, and in envisioning and creating morally desirable alternatives. The women-initiated non-violent Chipko movement begun in 1974 in Reni, India, is one such alternative action (see Shiva 1988 and Warren 1988).

One way to image ecofeminist ethics is as a quilt-in-the-making (see Warren 1988, 1990). Like the AIDS Names Project Quilt, ecofeminist ethics is a quilt-in-process, constructed from "patches" contributed by persons located in different socioeconomic, cultural, historical circumstances. Since these patches will reflect the histories of the various quilters, no two patches will be just the same. Nonetheless, the quilts-in-process will each have borders that not only delimit the spatiotemporal dimensions of the quilt, but also put some necessary conditions, "boundary conditions," on what can become part of the quilt. What these boundary conditions do *not* do is delimit the interior of the quilt, what the design or actual pattern of the quilt will be. That design will emerge out of the life experiences, ethical concerns, and specific socioeconomic historical contexts of the quilters (see Warren 1990).

What are some of the boundary conditions of ecofeminist ethics? Just what does, and what does not, belong on the quilt? Since ecofeminism is a critique of interrelated social systems of domination, no "isms of domination" (for example, sexism, racism, classism, heterosexism, naturism) belong on the quilt (Warren 1990). This means that any conceptual framework (or, set of basic beliefs, values, attitudes, and assumptions which grow out of and reflect one's view of oneself and

one's world) which sanctions, justifies, or perpetuates these "isms of domination"— oppressive and patriarchal conceptual frameworks—does not belong on
the quilt. What *does* belong on the quilt are those descriptions and presciptions of
social reality that do not maintain, perpetuate, or attempt to justify social "isms of
domination" and the power-over relationships used to keep them intact. These
will include patches that make visible and challenge local and global forms of
environmental abuse, the disproportional effects of environmental pollution on
women, children, the poor, dislocated indigenous persons, and peoples in so-called
less developed countries; patches that provide present-day alternatives to environmental exploitation; patches that document and celebrate the morally respectful
dimensions of women's experiences with the nonhuman world; and patches that
include the experiences of indigenous people, when those experiences are neither
sexist nor naturist. Taken together, the patches on the quilt provide the ethical
theorist with concrete, pictoral ways of understanding the nature of a morality
which treats both women's moral experiences and human interactions with the
nonhuman natural world respectfully.

Ecosystem Ecology

Many controversies in modern ecosystem ecology about the nature of ecosystems can be understood as arguments between two approaches to the study of
ecosystems: the "population-community" approach and the "process-functional"
approach.[6] The population-community approach focuses on the growth of
populations, the structure and composition of communities of organisms, and
the interactions among individual organisms. It is grounded in Darwinian theory
of natural selection. It "tends to view ecosystems as networks of interacting
populations whereby the biota *are* the ecosystem and abiotic components such as
soil or sediments are external influences" (O'Neill et al. 1986, 8). The population-community approach typically is identified with the work of such ecologists
as Clemens, Lotka, Gauss, and Whittaker.

In contrast, the process-functional approach is based on a quantitative,
mathematical, thermodynamic, biophysical model which emphasizes energy
flows and nutrient cycling. It assumes that the fundamental units of ecosystems
include both organisms and physical components, biotic and abiotic components. The process-functional approach was developed during this century by
such ecologists as Tansley, Lindeman, and Odum.

Although discussions of ecosystems ecology often present "the ecological
perspective" as if there were only one perspective, debates arising from differences between the population-community and process-functional approaches to
ecosystems ecology reveal that there currently is *no single model* of ecosystems.[7]
Furthermore, there is a third alternative way to conceive ecosystems. That
alternative is "hierarchy theory" or what, for important feminist reasons, we
prefer to refer to as "observation set theory."[8] We understand hierarchy theory to

be the most viable attempt to date by scientific ecologists to provide an inclusive theoretical framework for the variety of ecosystem analyses. Ecologists such as O'Neill, DeAngelis, Waide and Allen are among its main advocates (O'Neill et al. 1986).

Central to hierarchy (observation set) theory is the notion of an *observation set*. O'Neill et al. describe an observation set as "a particular way of viewing the natural world. It includes the phenomena of interest, the specific measurements taken, and the techniques used to analyze the data" (1986, 7). Although specific problems always call for particular observation sets, theory making calls for consideration of multiple observation sets:

> Each of these points of view emphasizes different phenomena and quite different measurements. But since neither encompasses all possible observations, neither can be considered to be more fundamental. When studying a specific problem, the scientists must always focus on a single observation set. However, when developing theory, many observation sets must be considered. (O'Neill et al. 1986, 7)

According to hierarchy theory, both an adequate conception of the complexity of ecosystems and meaningful ecosystem comparisons require that one consider multiple observation sets.

Spatiotemporal scale is an important characteristic of an observation set both because it changes as the ecological problem changes and because "ecological principles often do not translate well across these scales" (O'Neill et al. 1986, 20). The meanings of such basic ecological concepts as "stability," "equilibrium," "temporary," "enduring," "local," and "global," are relative to some particular scale. Depending on the spatiotemporal scale used in any given observation set, "ecosystems have been seen as static or dynamic, as steady-state or as fluctuating, as integrated systems or as collections of individuals" (O'Neill et al. 1986, 20). For example, a forest stand can be looked at from an organismic standpoint (e.g., as enduring, stable individual trees or populations of trees) *or* from an energy flow and nutrient cycling standpoint (e.g., as fluxes and flows of carbon and oxygen recycled through photosynthesis). Because the forest stand may accurately be viewed in either way, it is incorrect, in fact impossible, "to designate *the* components of *the* ecosystem"—the designation depends on the spatiotemporal scale and changes as that scale changes (O'Neill et al. 1986, 83).

The basic contribution of hierarchy (observation set) theory is to call attention to the importance of observation sets and spatiotemporal scales to ecosystem ecology. The complexity of natural systems is overlooked or discounted when one focuses on a single observation set. An exclusivist "either-or" approach to describing or studying ecosystems (e.g., an exclusivist population-community or functional-process approach) is thereby viewed as based on a false dichotomy which results in an inadequate, because incomplete, *theory* of ecosystems (O'Neill et al. 209).[9]

SIMILARITIES BETWEEN ECOFEMINISM AND ECOSYSTEMS ECOLOGY

We are now in a position to show some of the similiarities between ecofeminism (particularly ecofeminist ethics) and ecosystem ecology seen through the lens of hierarchy (observation set) theory. These similarities suggest various ways in which ecofeminism and ecosystem ecology inform and support one another.[10]

First, central to hierarchy theory is the view that space-time dependent observation sets provide different vantage points or frameworks from which one makes ecological observations and engages in ecological theory building. It is through the notion of multiple observation sets that the idea of one single model of ecosystems is rejected. In this respect, hierarchy theory rules out any notion of an observation set free or *decontextualized* science: how one views ecosystems will depend on the observation sets one employs.

One is immediately struck by the similarity between the hierarchy theorist's emphasis on observation sets, "windows through which one views the world," and the ecofeminist's emphasis on "ways of thinking," "world-views," and "conceptual frameworks," especially oppressive and patriarchal ones (see Warren 1987, 1990). The notion of a patriarchal and oppressive conceptual framework is as central to ecofeminism and ecofeminist ethics as the notion of an observation set is to hierarchy theory in ecosystem ecology: one could not generate the observations and conclusions of each without them. An attention to observation sets is also an acknowledgment of the importance of the contexts in and through which one observes, measures, and theorizes. One's observation set, like one's conceptual framework, will quite literally shape and affect what one sees; both provide a *context* for theorizing.

There are at least three interrelated reasons why attention to context is of importance to ecofeminist ethics. First, *what* a thing (person, community, population, species, animal, river) is, is in part a function of *where* it is, a function of the relationships in which it stands to other things and to its history, including (where applicable) its evolutionary history. It is this attention to *place* that fuels bioregionalist ecofeminism (see Plant 1990) and the importance many ecofeminists give to narratives, myth, and ritual in the construction of ecofeminist ethics (see Cheney 1987, 1989a; Diamond and Orenstein 1990; Warren 1990). Second, an understanding of context is important in assessing the putatively universal claims of reason and ethical deliberation. Feminist worries about ahistorical and allegedly gender-neutral conceptions of reason and rationality in the Western philosophical tradition provide one way of understanding the importance of context—historical location and gender identity in theory building in the pre-feminist present.[11] Ecofeminist theory building seeks to rid prevailing conceptions of reason, rationality, and morality of whatever male and naturist bias they have.

More than this, however, and this is our third point, an attention to context permits one to stress the idiographic dimension of our ethical journeys through this world and of ethics itself. Holmes Rolston has been a strong advocate for recognizing this aspect of ethical thought in environmental ethics, and this advocacy derives from his understanding that a thing is what it is in part because of where it is. As Rolston puts it:

> An ethics should be rational, but rationality inhabits a historical system. The place that is to be counted morally has a history; the ethics that befits such a place will take on historical form; the ethics will itself have a history. The place to be mapped . . . will have twin foci. One focus will be nomothetic, recurrent; the other will be idiographic, uniquely particular. . . .

The rationality of the ethic, as well as the area to be mapped, will be historical. That is, logic will be mixed with story. The move from *is* to *ought* . . . is transformed into movement along a story line (Rolston 1988, 341-42).

An attention to context does not split off the idiographic as what ethics permits, provided that the universal demands of morality are met. Instead, the ethically idiographic is the very center of each individual's ethical life; it is the place from which we not only test the claims of the "universal" and the "rational," but from which we construct the "universal" claims of "rationality." In this way, the "universal" and the "rational" are always in some manner or other inflected with historicity. The "universal" and "rational" are themselves moments in a story, reflecting some observation set.

The ecological dimension of ethical reflection stems in large part from the fact that ecology is context (or observation set) dependent. We agree with Brennan that:

> what ecology shows is not simply that the context makes a difference to the kind of action we engage in. It shows, rather, that what kinds of things we are, what sort of thing an individual person is, and what sort of options for fulfillment and self-realisation are open, are themselves very much context-dependent. (Brennan 1988, 162)

One way ecofeminist ethics centralizes this context-dependent feature of ethical discourse is by conceiving of ethics as growing out of what Cheney (1987, 144) calls defining relationships, that is, relationships understood as in some sense defining who one is. These relationships include those of moral agents with the nonhuman natural world, including animals.

Second, hierarchy theory provides a methodological means of investigating ecological problems. According to hierarchy theory, the "ontology" that emerges from any particular investigation is relative to the observation set that produces it. This does not make that ontology "subjective" in any pernicious sense; but it does mean that to accept a solution to a particular problem is not thereby to make any ontological commitments in any absolute (i.e., non-observation set dependent) sense. Thus, the methodology of hierarchy theory makes it imperative that the epistemological requirements of particular problems, given in terms of observer-affected observation sets, dictate to ontology (rather than the converse); ecology does not determine that an ecological problem must be pressed into the shape of a preferred ontology. According to hierarchy theory, it would be quixotic to think in terms of striving for an articulation of *the* structure (even *the* hierarchical structure) of an ecosystem.

As a methodological stance, hierarchy theory rejects the view that there is only one way to describe ecological phenomena. Which description is appropriate will depend upon the observation set and on what it is one is attempting to describe, explain, or predict. In this respect, hierarchy theory privileges methodological and epistemological considerations over ontology, the attempt to specify what is "really" in the world. The ontology embedded in both explanation and phenomena being explained is always a function of the appropriate observation set. Any grand attempt to provide one metaphysics of morals seems doomed because misguided: it puts the metaphysical/ontological cart before the epistemological/methodological horse.

Like hierarchy theory, ecofeminism makes no attempt to provide *the* point of view, one single model, an "objective" (i.e., value-neutral, unbiased) point of view—none, that is, beyond the very "boundary conditions" of ecofeminism itself. Ecofeminists criticize up-down, value-hierarchical, value dualistic thinking which they say characterizes Western philosophical thinking about women and nature as being both patriarchal and insular—as if what is observed, prescribed, and theorized is independent of *any* conceptual framework (Gray 1981; Griffin 1978; King 1983b, 1989; Ruether 1975; Warren 1987, 1988, 1990). Ecofeminists acknowledge up front their basic feminist value commitments: the twin dominations of women and nature exist, are wrong, and ought to be eliminated. Ecofeminists see these twin dominations as social problems rooted in very concrete, historical, socioeconomic conditions, as well as in oppressive, patriarchal conceptual frameworks that maintain and sanction these conditions.

As a methodological and epistemological stance, all ecofeminists centralize, in one way or another, the "voices" and experiences of women (and others) with regard to an understanding of the nonhuman natural world. Like hierarchy theory, this is not to say that an ecofeminist "ontology" does not include material objects—real trees, rivers, and animals. It does! But it acknowledges that these objects are in important senses both materially given and socially constructed:

what counts as a tree, river, or animal, how natural "objects" are conceived, described, and treated, must be understood in the context of broader social and institutional practices. Centralizing women's voices is important methodologically and epistemologically to the overall critique and revisioning of the concept of nature and the moral dimensions of human-nature relationships.

Third, hierarchy theory is antireductionist. Population-community based observation sets cannot be reduced to process-functional based observation sets (or vice versa). Consequently, a functional-process understanding of organisms does not render an "object ontology" of discrete organisms (trees, rivers, animals) obsolete, or render organisms mere conduits or configurations of energy, as environmental ethicist J. Baird Callicott has claimed (1986). There *is no* ontologically prior or privileged or fundamental description of nature. Hierarchy theory rules out a view of individual entities (e.g., animals) as ontologically parasitic on something more fundamental (e.g., energy flows or nutrient cycles), a point we return to shortly. If hierarchy theory is correct, then in contemporary scientific ecology, there is no place for a notion of degrees of reality. *Both* individuals and energy flows are real.

Because it is antireductionist, hierarchy theory centralizes diversity; it takes difference or diversity to be a fundamental feature of phenomena, not reducible to talk of the "sameness" of organisms or the "oneness" of energy flows. That would be the case only if one approach had epistemological, metaphysical, or ontological priority over the other. In fact, one of the most interesting features of hierarchy theory is that it privileges the notion of diversity or difference when studying interactions between different subsystems ("holons") of ecosystems, *and* the notion of commonalities among members of the same subsystem. Hierarchy theory is therefore a framework which provides for both an ecology of differences and an ecology of commonalities, depending on the context and observation set.[12]

Ecofeminist ethics is also antireductionist. It is a structurally pluralistic framework that centralizes both diversity or difference (e.g., among women, among people of color, between humans and nonhumans) *and* commonalities (e.g., among women, among people of color, between humans and nonhumans). A nonreductionist ecofeminist stance acknowledges differences between humans and members or elements of nonhuman nature, while nonetheless affirming that humans are animals and members of an ecological community. An ecology of differences and commonalities fits well with an ecofeminist politics and ethics of differences and commonalities.

Fourth, hierarchy theory is an inclusivist theory that offers a framework for mediating between historically opposed approaches to ecosystem ecology, making a central place for the insights of each without inheriting the defects of either when viewed exclusively as the right or correct way to study ecosystems. Hierarchy theory suggests that the future of at least ecosystem ecology may well lie in successfully integrating these two approaches into a model that centralizes the importance of observation sets and locates any particular ecosystem analysis in or relative to a particular observation set.

Similarly, ecofeminist ethics is an inclusivist ethic (see Warren 1990) that offers a framework for mediating between two historically opposed approaches in environmental ethics: deontological rights-, virtues-, or holistic-based ethics and consequentialist-based ethics. Warren has argued that ecofeminism "involves a shift *from* a conception of ethics as primarily a matter of rights, rules, or principles [whether deontological or consequentialist] determined and applied in specific cases to entities viewed as competitors in the contest of moral standing," *to* one which "makes a central places for values . . . that presuppose that our relationships to others are central to our understanding of who we are" (Warren 1990, 143). An ecofeminist ethic may involve a commitment to rights in certain contexts and for certain purposes (for example, in the protection of individual animals against unnecessary pain or suffering); it may use consequentialist considerations in other contexts and for other purposes (for example, when considering behavior toward ecosystems). Like hierarchy theory, ecofeminist ethics is one possible framework for developing such an inclusivist alternative.[13]

As a fifth and related point, hierarchy theory provides a framework for viewing historically opposed approaches as complementary. Dualisms fade into the complexity of multiple vantage points and find complementarity where once there was only oppositionality (e.g., stability or instability, diversity or sameness, energy flow or discrete organism). This rejection of oppositional polarities is accomplished *not* by reducing population-community to process-functional accounts, or vice versa, or by reducing both to a still more basic or primitive ontological framework; it is accomplished by providing a unifying framework for studying and relating to one another various analyses, each with their own epistemology and context-dependent ontology. As a "unified theory," it is a unity which does not erase difference.

The earliest ecofeminist literature was grounded in a rejection of oppositional value dualisms (see Gray 1981; Griffin 1978). Ecofeminist ethics needs to follow suit[14] by emphasizing difference in a way that does not reduce difference to the terms of some (reductionist) privileged discourse.

Sixth, because it centralizes diversity, hierarchy theory complexifies rather than simplifies the variety of ways natural phenomena can be described. It does this by emphasizing the sorts of interrelationships that exist among organisms and the relevance of scalar and other dimensions to the observations made. It rejects exclusivist models of ecosystems (i.e., population-community or process-functional models) that simplify rather than complexify the nature of ecosystems, typically by an imposed naive reductionism that focuses on sameness, similarity, or shared traits. Interrelationships among biotic and abiotic nature that are based on a single, unitary model of ecosystems are viewed as misrepresentations of the variety of relationships in nature.

Similarly, as a context-dependent, inclusivist framework that centralizes difference, ecofeminism complexifies the variety of ways in which ethics is conceived and practiced, in which humans may be in relationship with others (including the nonhuman natural environment), and in which human-nature, women-nature connections may be described. As we have argued elsewhere (Warren 1988, 1990; Cheney 1987, 1989a, 1990), ecofeminist ethics complexifies the moral arena by making a central place for values often lost or overlooked in mainstream ethics (e.g., values of care, love, friendship, diversity, appropriate reciprocity) in the context of human-nonhuman relationships. This includes taking seriously the sort of "indigenous technical knowledge" that women and others who work closely with the land have (see Warren 1988).

Seventh, and perhaps most importantly for ethics, hierarchy theory permits meaningful ecological talk of "individual" and "other" without the caveat that these are nonprimitive notions, ultimately reducible to notions of energy flow and pattern. At the same time, it also permits meaningful talk of "whole-system" behavior in both population-community and process-functional terms, neither of which is reducible to the other. Hierarchy theory thus permits meaningful discussion of discrete (and, in varying degrees and modes, autonomous) individual objects as well as of whole systems. Hierarchy theory shows that "object theory" is not obsolete; it is an acceptable and alternative way to describe organisms—appropriate for some observation sets and not others.

This alternative way of describing ecosystems is accomplished in hierarchy theory in part by an eighth characteristic, one shared by ecofeminism and ecofeminist ethics: it encourages a network or relational view of organisms, whether conceived as "knots in a biospherical web of relationships" or as separate (although not isolated or solitary), discrete individuals, members of species, populations, or communities. In both cases, ecosystems are networks, either networks of interacting individuals, populations, and communities or of interacting energy and nutrient flows and cycles.

This dual acknowledgment of the autonomous existence of individuals (characteristic seven) and the relational existence of individuals in webs of relationships (characteristic eight) fits nicely with those feminist ethics which insist that it is of primary importance to acknowledge and foster individual autonomy (after all, oppressed persons are still trying to have their autonomy recognized) *and* to recognize that people exist in webs of relationships that are to some extent constitutive of who they are. Much work in feminist ethics (often strongly influenced by the work of Gilligan 1982) has emphasized the centrality of relationships in women's ethical thinking. Others (e.g., Friedman 1989 and Young 1986) have critiqued communitarian ideals and stressed the importance for women of autonomy and a politics of difference in a world in which the penchant for defining oneself relationally can easily be turned into sacrifice of the self. Many feminists have been concerned to develop conceptions of self and society that avoid the problems of what Alison Jaggar calls abstract individualism, that is, the position that it is possible to identify a human essence or human nature that exists independently of any particular historical context (Jaggar 1980, 29).

This concern carries over into ecofeminist ethical reflection on nature. An ecofeminist ethic that emphasizes the nature of individuals or "others" as beings-in-relationships permits meaningful ecological discussion of *both* "self" and "other," of "individuals" (populations, communities) and "webs of relationships." For ecofeminists the contexts and relationships that help construct "the self" include ecological contexts and relationships with nonhuman nature. For an ecofeminist one cannot give an adequate account of what it is to be human in terms that do not acknowledge humans as members of ecological communities.

That hierarchy theory provides for meaningful discussion of "self" and "other" suggests one reason ecofeminists are and ought to be suspicious of some of the claims about scientific ecology made by other, allegedly "minority position" environmental ethics. For example, in "The Metaphysical Implications of Ecology," Callicott argues that scientific ecology "undermines the concept of a separable ego and thus renders obsolete any ethics which involves the concepts of 'self' and 'other' as primitive terms" (1986, 301). Callicott's overarching conclusion is that scientific ecology ontologically subordinates matter and living natural objects (e.g., humans, deer, trees) to energy flows, making an "object ontology" inappropriate as an ecological description of the natural environment.

Views such as Callicott's are not borne out by state-of-the-art hierarchy theory in ecosystem ecology. Hierarchy theory shows that even if at some level of inquiry it is plausible to hold that the universe and everything in it are constituted of energy, that everything is a perturbation in an all-encompassing energy field, this does *not* imply that entities revealed through other observation sets (e.g., as individual organisms, populations, or communities) are not "primitive," that they are reducible to the ontology of some other observation set. Hierarchy theory not only permits but demands meaningful ecological discussion of "self" and "other" on the one hand *and* of "whole-system behavior" on the other. Certain ecological observation sets relevant to ethics yield an ontology of autonomous individual organisms interacting with one another. Other observation sets paint a holistic picture of ecosystem function. But there is no a priori or ecological reason (other than a misguided reductionism) to give (ethical or metaphysical) pride of place to the latter.[15]

What *is* crucial is our particular mode of access to the objects of our moral concern. We need to formulate our "ethical ontology" and ethical theory in light of an understanding of our epistemological relationship to the objects of moral concern. In terms of actual practice, we certainly can say things, significant and important things, about individuals without drawing in the rest of the universe. We can gain at least certain kinds of knowledge of individuals without an analysis of the relations that constitute or produce the individual as the individual it is; that is, we can come to know the individual without knowing anything much about the shaping factors.

Ninth, hierarchy theory makes a place for whatever "hard" scientific data scientific ecology produces regarding the natural environment, although it always contextualizes that data relative to a given observation set with specific scalar dimension. It is *always* scientifically relevant to ask about particular observation sets within which and from which the "hard" data are gathered. According to hierarchy theory, all scientific data and questions of ecology come with and have a context; proper scientific theorizing involves making visible the observation sets (contexts) within which one conducts the observations and analyses. Hierarchy theory thereby leaves open the door for saying that whatever ecologists learn about organisms or ecosystems from computer modeling techniques, mathematical or statistical models, or data projections conducted within the closed system of a laboratory may not tell us all there is to know, or even the most relevant information and material we need to know, about terrestrial organisms and ecosystems—i.e., nature outside the laboratory. But we may need to know it, nonetheless, to solve pressing environmental problems.[16]

Ecofeminism welcomes appropriate ecological science and technology. Environmental problems demand scientific and technological responses as part of the solution. These "data" represent a piece of the ecological pie. What ecofeminists insist on is that the perspectives of women and indigenous peoples with regard to the natural environment also be recognized as relevant "data." As a *feminism*, ecofeminism insists that relevant "data" about the historical and interconnected twin exploitations of women (and other oppressed peoples) and nature be included in solutions to environmental problems; as an *ecological* feminism, ecofeminism insists upon the inclusion of appropriate insights and "data" of scientific ecology. What ecological feminism opposes is the practice of one without the other.

Lastly, hierarchy theory invites a reconceiving of ecosystems research and methodolology, objectivity, and knowledge. In its rejection of the view that there is one ahistorical, context-free, neutral observation stance, in its incorporation of multiple observation sets and its refusal to privilege the ontology of one over the ontology of any other, in its acceptance of multiple understandings of ecosystems and the complexity of the relationships that exist within them, hierarchy theory exemplifies, to some extent, what Donna Haraway (1988) has called embodied objectivity. What is obviously absent in hierarchy theory is an ethical and political dimension, however, which is present in Haraway's notion.

Objectivity, as Haraway puts it, is "about particular and specific embodiment and definitely not about the false vision promising transcendence of all limits and responsibility" (Haraway 1988, 582-83). Because all knowledge is "situated knowledge" (Haraway 1988, 581), no knowledge is innocent; all knowledge involves risks and implies responsibility. As Haraway argues:

admitted or not, politics and ethics ground struggles over knowledge projects in the exact, natural, social, and human sciences.
Otherwise, rationality is simply impossible, an optical illusion
projected from nowhere comprehensively. (1988, 587)

The ethical and political dimensions of knowledge and objectivity suggest an
important contribution that ecofeminism can offer hierarchy theory. The "partial knowledges" that emerge from various observation sets do not constitute an
innocent plurality of bodies of knowledge. Both the positions taken (with their
resultant situated knowledges) and the connections made are "power-sensitive"
(Haraway 1988, 589). Situated knowledges are partial knowledges,

not partiality for its own sake but, rather, for the sake of the
connections and unexpected openings situated knowledges make
possible. Situated knowledges are about communities, not about
isolated individuals. The only way to find a larger vision is to be
somewhere in particular. (Haraway 1988, 590)

Since ecofeminism sees theory building, objectivity, and knowledge as historically situated, illuminated, and created, theory is not something static—it is
both "situated" (in Haraway's sense) and "in process," emerging from people's
different experiences and observations and changing over time. It *is* like
quilting.

Are there, then, any ethical implications of ecosystem ecology? It depends.
The ethical implications of ecosystem ecology, like the hierarchy theory that
might be used to support them, only have axiological status within and from the
vantage points of certain observation sets. As ecologist Mark Davis claims of any
ecological model, "any set of ethical implications derived or inspired from the
model must always be regarded as only one of many possible such sets" (Davis
1988, 4).

The contextualist conception of objectivity at work in hierarchy theory is
consistent with the notion of objectivity being developed in some feminist
postmodernist theorizing. The problem faced by postmodern science, as
Haraway puts it, is "how to have *simultaneously* an account of radical historical
contingency for all knowledge claims and knowing subjects . . . *and* a no-
nonsense commitment to faithful accounts of a 'real' world" (Haraway 1988,
579). But just as Haraway would insist upon an ethical and political basis for
objectivity in the sciences, so she would add the idea of the "object" of
knowledge as an active agent in the construction of knowledge. She rightly
points out that feminists have been suspicious of scientific accounts of objectivity that portray the "object" of knowledge as passive and inert. Haraway's
view in response to this passive understanding of the object of scientific inquiry
is as follows:

Situated knowledges require that the object of knowledge be pictured as an actor and agent, not as a screen or a ground or a resource, never finally as slave to the master that closes off the dialectic in his unique agency and his authorship of "objective" knowledge. The point is paradigmatically clear in critical approaches to the social and human sciences. . . . But the same point must apply to the other knowledge projects called sciences. (Haraway 1988, 592-93)

If we understand the objects of scientific inquiry as actors and agents *and* insist upon an ethical and political basis for objectivity, accounts of the world based "on a logic of 'discovery' " give way to "a power-charged social relation of 'conversation.' The world neither speaks itself nor disappears in favor of a master decoder" (Haraway 1988, 593). In this regard, Haraway herself calls attention to the promise of ecofeminism:

Ecofeminists have perhaps been most insistent on some version of the world as active subject. . . . Acknowledging the agency of the world in knowledge makes room for some unsettling possibilities, including a sense of the world's independent sense of humor. . . . There are . . . richly evocative figures to promote feminist visualizations of the world as witty agent. We need not lapse into appeals to a primal mother resisting her translation into resource. The Coyote or Trickster . . . suggests the situation we are in when we give up mastery but keep searching for fidelity, knowing all the while that we will be hoodwinked. . . . We are not in charge of the world. We just live here and try to strike up noninnocent conversations. (Haraway 1988, 593-94)

We agree with Haraway's concluding words: "Perhaps our hopes for accountability, for politics, for ecofeminism, turn on revisioning the world as coding trickster with whom we must learn to converse" (Haraway 1988, 596). The significance of the finding that ecofeminism and ecosystem ecology are involved in complementary, mutually reinforcing projects would then lie in what they can contribute together to our conversation with the world as "coding trickster."

NOTES

1. We gratefully acknowledge the helpful comments received on an earlier draft of this paper from Roxanne Gudeman, Donna Haraway, Sandra Harding, Alison M. Jaggar, Ruthanne Kurth-Schai, Toby McAdams, Michal McCall,

Lindsay Powers, Truman Schwartz, Geoff Sutton, Nancy Tuana, Leslie Vaughan, Anthony Weston, and Cathy Zabinski.

2. See ecofeminist critiques of environmental practices cross-culturally in Caldecott and Leland (1983), Diamond and Orenstein (1990), Merchant (1980), Peterson and Merchant (1986), Plant (1989), Shiva (1988), and Warren (1988).

3. Showing that scientific ecology is a feminist issue is not as easy as one might expect. As scientific ecologists are quick to point out, there is a difference between the ecology movement (or, popular environmentalism) and the science of ecology. Even if the women's movement and the ecology movement are inextricably connected, and even if understanding the connections between the domination of women and the domination of nature is crucial to an adequate feminism, environmentalism, or ethic, still, none of this shows any respects in which the *science* of ecology must be feminist. In this paper, we attempt to put into place some considerations which bear on *that* issue.

4. In helpful comments on an earlier draft of this paper, Sandra Harding pointed out that even if there are striking similarities between ecological feminism and ecosystem ecology, there might be very good reasons for feminists to reject some claims of ecosystem ecology, and vice versa. One such reason would be the inattention to issues of power in ecosystem theory construction and practice. Since an analysis of power is central to feminist critiques of socially constructed "isms of domination," one would need very good reasons for accepting *as feminist* any theory or practice in scientific ecology which did not include an analysis of power and power-over relationships.

5. Our discussion of ecological feminism is limited to emerging themes in ecofeminism and ecofeminist ethics which are not tied to any one feminism. This is because there is not *one* ecological feminism any more than there is *one* feminism; the varieties of ecofeminisms will reflect differing feminist commitments of liberal, Marxist, radical, socialist feminisms as well as feminisms of women of color (nationally and internationally). Similarly, our discussion of scientific ecology is limited to ecosystem ecology, since it is ecosystem analysis that is the focus of much of the current literature in environmental ethics on the ethical or metaphysical implications, if any, of ecology (see Brennan 1988; Callicott 1986; Cheney 1991b; Golley 1987; Rolston 1988, 1989).

6. We express our gratitude to Mark Davis, Department of Biology and Director of Environmental Studies at Macalester College, for the information he provided about the population-community and functional-process approaches to ecosystem ecology and hierarchy theory. Much of that information is presented in his unpublished article "Should Moral Philosophers Be Listening to Ecologists?" (1988).

7. There are also feminist reasons to worry about construing these two approaches as the only approaches to studying ecosystems, reasons having to do both with a general concern about theoretical descriptions of material reality in terms of mutually exclusive polarities. (See, e.g., Gray, 1981.)

8. Insofar as so much feminist, including ecofeminist, theory has focused on a critique of value hierarchical thinking and its function in creating, maintaining, and perpetuating social systems of domination, the name "hierarchy theory" is most unfortunate from a feminist point of view. In her comments on an earlier draft of this paper, Alison Jaggar suggested that the name is "toxic" and could well predispose feminists to be antagonistic toward hierarchy theory from the outset. Since, as will be shown, the notion of an "observation set" is central to hierarchy theory and yet does not connote problematic value hierarchies, we have chosen to refer to hierarchy theory frequently throughout this paper as "hierarchy (observation set) theory." (We do not discuss here that aspect of hierarchy theory which gives it its name, though we do in our forthcoming book *Ecological Feminism*, Westview Press.) If it were not for the established usage of the expression "hierarchy theory" within the scientific ecological community, we would refer to the theory simply as "observation set theory."

9. O'Neill et al. stress that they have exaggerated the differences between the population-community and process-functional approaches and that "few ecologists would hold to either extreme of the spectrum" (1986, 10). The distinction between the two approaches is better viewed on a continuum, with the population-community and process-functional approaches at each end and ecologists "drawn in one direction or the other by the specific problems that interest them" (1986, 10).

10. That the discussion format moves from hierarchy (observation set) theory to ecofeminism is not intended to privilege either perspective. Furthermore, more space is provided below to ecosystem ecology when discussing similarities than to ecofeminism for two main reasons: first, there is a virtual absence in the literature of ecofeminism of any attempt to spell out the details of just how ecological feminism might draw support for its position from, or impart its own insights to, ecological science. To begin to remedy this omission, we deliberately have chosen to focus on ecosystem ecology (rather than on ecological feminism) and *then* show important similarities between the two—similarities that are more detailed and specific about "ecology" than are general appeals to the importance of ecosystems, interconnectedness among life forms, or ecological well-being to the survival of the planet. Second, we have presented elsewhere our views on ecological feminism and ecofeminist ethics (Cheney 1987, 1989a, 1991a; Warren 1987, 1988, 1990) and did not want to duplicate those efforts here.

11. For essays and a literature overview on this issue, see the American Philosophical Association *Newsletter on Feminism and Philosophy* Special Issue on "Reason, Rationality and Gender," edited by Nancy Tuana and Karen J. Warren, vol 88, no. 2 (March 1989).

12. We develop this argument in more detail in our forthcoming book *Ecological Feminism*.

13. Warren has argued that ecofeminist ethics needs to evaluate ethical claims partly in terms of a condition of inclusiveness: *Those claims are morally and*

epistemologically favored (preferred, better, less partial, less biased) which are more inclusive of the perspectives and felt, lived experiences of the most amount of people, particularly including the perspectives and experiences of oppressed persons (Warren 1988, 1990).

14. We say "needs to" because some ecofeminists have been criticized for substituting a value-hierarchical "women are closer to nature than men" ontology and ethics for an unacceptable patriarchal value-hierarchical schema which puts nature and what is female gender-identified together as inferior and opposed to that which is male gender-identified. The criticism is that the very oppositional dualism which prompts the question "Are women closer to nature than men?" is itself the problem. Switching the answer by elevating women and nature (in opposition to men) only perpetuates the problem. (See Griscom 1981; King 1981; Ortner 1974; Warren, 1987.)

15. The implication is clear: just as "it is quite feasible and even reasonable to maintain an individualistic (i.e., Gleasonian) concept of the community and a holistic concept of ecosystem function" (O'Neill et al. 1986, 189), so too it is quite feasible and reasonable to understand the moral community as consisting, in part, of autonomous agents with properties in their own right while at the same time treating that community as in some respects holistic.

16. A popular environmentalist slogan, sometimes endorsed by ecofeminists, is that everything is connected: a tug on any part of the system has an effect on every other part of the system. This image of ecosystems is one that O'Neill et al. take great pains to dispel (86). Critical to the stability of an ecosystem is the relative insulation or *disconnection* of sub-systems ("holons") from one another (with strong interaction within holons and weak interaction between holons). Overconnectedness in a system, where tugs on any part of the system produce effects on all parts of the system, is *unstable* (94). This perspective renders problematic the oft-repeated remark that ecology demonstrates that everything is connected with everything else—the interconnection is only within holons, not between holons.

An adequate ecofeminist ecology, then, must acknowledge that the world, so to speak, "strives" to organize itself into discrete and relatively autonomous holons as a condition of its own stability. This is at least as important a feature of our world as is its connectedness. And, indeed, individuals still come into their own with the same sterling ontological credentials as the energy flow patterns which emerge from process-functional analyses. Everything may be tied to everything else in some sense, but hierarchy (observation set) theory suggests that it is not in any metaphysically reductionist, holistic sense.

REFERENCES

Brennan, Andrew. 1988. *Thinking about nature: An investigation of nature, value and ecology.* Athens, GA: University of Georgia Press.

Caldecott, Léonie, and Stephanie Leland, eds. 1983. *Reclaim the earth: Women speak out for life on earth*. London: The Women's Press.

Callicott, J. Baird. 1986. The metaphysical implications of ecology. *Environmental Ethics* 8: 301-16.

Cheney, Jim. 1987. Eco-feminism and deep ecology. *Environmental Ethics* 9: 115-45.

———. 1989a. Postmodern environmental ethics: Ethics as bioregional narrative. *Environmental Ethics* 11: 117-34.

———. 1989b. The neo-stoicism of radical environmentalism. *Environmental Ethics* 11: 293-325.

———. 1991a. Review of Arne Naess, *Ecology, community and life-style*. *Environmental Ethics* 13(3): 263–73.

———. 1991b. Callicott's "Metaphysics of morals." *Environmental Ethics* 13(4): 311–25.

Davis, Mark. 1988. Should moral philosophers be listening to ecologists? Unpublished manuscript.

Diamond, Irene, and Gloria Feman Orenstein, eds. 1990. *Reweaving the world: The emergence of ecofeminism*. San Francisco: Sierra Club Books.

Friedman, Marilyn. 1989. Feminism and modern friendship: Dislocating the community. *Ethics* 99: 275-90.

Gilligan, Carol. 1982. *In a different voice: Psychological theory and women's development*. Cambridge: Harvard University Press.

Golley, Frank B. 1987. Deep ecology from the perspective of environmental science. *Environmental Ethics* 9(1): 45-55.

Gray, Elizabth Dodson. 1981. *Green paradise lost*. Wellesley, MA: Roundtable Press.

Griffin, Susan. 1978. *Women and nature: The roaring inside her*. San Francisco: Harper and Row.

Griscom, Joan L. 1981. On healing the nature/history split in feminist thought. In *Heresies #13: Feminism and Ecology* 4 (1): 4-9.

Haraway, Donna. 1988. Situated knowledges: The science question in feminism and the privilege of partial perspective. *Feminist Studies* 14: 575-99.

Jaggar, Alison M. 1991. Feminist ethics: Problems, projects, problems. In *Feminist Ethics*. Claudia Card, ed. Lawrence: University Press of Kansas.

King, Ynestra. 1981. Feminism and the revolt of nature. *Heresies #13: Feminism and Ecology* 4(1): 12-16.

———. 1983. Toward an ecological feminism and a feminist ecology. In *Machina ex dea: Feminist perspectives on technology*. Joan Rothschild, ed. New York: Pergamon Press.

———. 1989. The ecology of feminism and the feminism of ecology. In *Healing the wounds: The power of ecological feminism*. Judith Plant, ed. Philadelphia and Santa Cruz: New Society Publishers.

Leopold, Aldo. 1970. *A sand county almanac*. New York: Ballantine Books.

Merchant, Carolyn. 1980. *The death of nature: Women, ecology, and the scientific revolution*. San Francisco: Harper and Row.

Murphy, Patrick D., ed. 1988. Feminism, ecology and the future of the humanities. *Studies in the Humanities* 15(2): 85–89.

O'Neill, R. V., D. L. DeAngelis, J. B. Waide, and T. F. H. Allen. 1986. *A hierarchical concept of ecosystems*. Princeton: Princeton University Press.

Ortner, Sherry B. 1974. Is female to male as nature is to culture? In *Women, culture, and society*. Michelle Rosaldo and Lousie Lamphere, eds. Stanford, CA: Stanford University Press.

Peterson, Abby, and Carolyn Merchant. 1986. Peace with the earth: Women and the environmental movement in Sweden. *Women's Studies International Forum*. 9(5-6): 465-79.

Plant, Judith. 1990. Searching for common ground: Ecofeminism and bioregionalism. In *Reweaving the world: The emergence of ecofeminism*. Irene Diamond and Gloria Feman Orenstein, eds. San Francisco: Sierra Club Books.

Plant, Judith, ed. 1989. *Healing the wounds: The power of ecological feminism*. Philadelphia and Santa Cruz: New Society Publishers.

Rolston, Holmes, III. 1988. *Environmental ethics: Duties to and values in the natural world*. Philadelphia: Temple University Press.

———. 1989. Review of Andrew Brennan, "Thinking about nature: An investigation of nature, value and ecology." *Environmental Ethics* 11: 259-67.

Ruether, Rosemary Radford. 1975. *New woman/new earth: Sexist ideologies and human liberation*. New York: Seabury Press.

Salleh, Ariel Kay. 1984. Deeper than deep ecology: The eco-feminist connection. *Environmental Ethics* 6: 339-45.

Shiva, Vandana. 1988. *Staying alive: Women, ecology, and development*. London: Zed Books.

Warren, Karen J. 1987. Feminism and ecology: Making connections. *Environmental Ethics* 9: 3-21.

———. 1988. Toward an ecofeminist ethic. *Studies in the Humanities* 15 (2): 140-56.

———. 1990. The power and promise of ecological feminism. *Environmental Ethics* 12: 125-46.

Young, Iris. 1986. The ideal of community and the politics of difference. *Social Theory and Practice* 12: 1-26.

Zimmerman, Michael. 1987. Feminism, deep ecology, and environmental ethics. *Environmental Ethics* 9: 21-44.

Notes on Contributors

CAROL J. ADAMS is the author of *The Sexual Politics of Meat: A Feminist-Vegetarian Critical Theory; Neither Man nor Beast: Feminism and the Defense of Animals;* and *Woman-Battering*. She is also the editor of *Ecofeminism and the Sacred*, and is collecting images that depict sexualized animals and animalized women for a book entitled *The Meat Market*.

CAROL H. CANTRELL is Professor of English and Graduate Coordinator at Colorado State University. She has published work on various modernist writers, including Pound and Beckett, and is working on a book about women, language, and nature in selected modernist texts.

JIM CHENEY is Professor of Philosophy at the University of Wisconsin–Waukesha, where he teaches environmental ethics and American Indian philosophies. He has published numerous essays on ecofeminist philosophy and environmental ethics.

CHRIS CUOMO is Assistant Professor of Philosophy and Women's Studies at the University of Cincinnati. She is also a Rockefeller Postdoctoral Fellow in the Department of Science and Technology at Cornell University.

DEANE CURTIN is Professor of Philosophy at Gustavus Adolphus College, where he directs the Community Development in India program. His essays on ecofeminism and environmental ethics have appeared in *Hypatia, Environmental Ethics,* and *Philosophy East and West*. He is co-editor of *Cooking, Eating, Thinking: Transformative Philosophies of Food,* and is working on a book entitled *Ethics and the Margins,* on the ethics of environmental conflicts between the First and Third worlds.

VICTORIA DAVION is Assistant Professor of Philosophy at the University of Georgia. Her research areas include feminist ethics, environmental ethics, and social and political philosophy. She is currently working on a book designed to bring ecological feminist insights to a variety of issues in applied ethics.

ROGER J. H. KING is Assistant Professor of Philosophy at the University of Maine. His articles on environmental ethics have appeared in *Between the Species, Environmental Ethics, Hypatia,* the American Philosophical Association *Newsletter,* and *Feminism and Philosophy*. He is currently working on topics related to an ethics of care for nature, sustainability, bioregionalism, and the tension between wilderness and domestication in environmental ethics.

STEPHANIE LAHAR, Academic Dean at Woodbury College, is a founding member and former chair of the Burlington Conservation Board. Her essays on ecofeminism have appeared in *Hypatia*, *NWSA Journal*, and *Vermont Woman*, and in several books, including *Ecofeminism: Women, Animals, Nature*.

PATRICIA JAGENTOWICZ MILLS is Associate Professor of Political Theory in the Department of Political Science at the University of Massachusetts at Amherst. She is the author of *Woman, Nature, and Psyche* and editor of *Re-Reading the Canon: Feminist Interpretations of Hegel*. Her published articles include work on ecofeminism, women and myth, and the dialectical tradition from Hegel to Adorno; she is working on a project tentatively entitled *Thinking Differently: Meditations for a Feminist Critical Theory*.

PATRICK D. MURPHY, Professor of English at Indiana University of Pennsylvania, is author of *Literature, Nature, Other: Ecofeminist Critiques* and *Understanding Gary Snyder*. He has edited or co-edited seven other books, including *Essentials of the Theory of Fiction* and *Critical Essays on American Modernism*, and is founding editor of the journal *ISLE: Interdisciplinary Studies in Literature and Environment*.

VAL PLUMWOOD is part of a Green women's network in Canberra and author of *Feminism and the Mastery of Nature*.

CATHERINE ROACH is completing a Ph.D. in religion at Harvard University. Her dissertation is entitled "Mother Nature and Human Evil: New Directions in Environmental Theory." She is interested in issues of religion and culture in the modern West, which she explores using psychological and feminist theory.

ROBERT SESSIONS teaches philosophy and humanities at Kirkwood Community College. He is co-editor of *Working in America*, a humanities reader on work. He has published articles on environmental philosophy, education, philosophy of technology, and the philosophy of work.

DEBORAH SLICER is Associate Professor of Philosophy at the University of Montana.

KAREN J. WARREN is Associate Professor of Philosophy and Chair at Macalester College. She has published more than 45 articles on feminism, environmental ethics, critical thinking and ethics, and co-edited five anthologies on ecofeminism. She conducts workshops in philosophy and critical thinking for grades K–12, and has assisted in the development of critical-thinking materials in science education. She is author of *Quilting Feminist Philosophy*.

Index